ANNE FRANK UNBOUND

THE MODERN JEWISH EXPERIENCE

Paula Hyman and Deborah Dash Moore, editors

ANNE FRANK
UNBOUND

MEDIA·IMAGINATION·MEMORY

Edited by

BARBARA KIRSHENBLATT-GIMBLETT
AND JEFFREY SHANDLER

INDIANA UNIVERSITY PRESS   *Bloomington & Indianapolis*

This book is a publication of

Indiana University Press
601 North Morton Street
Bloomington, Indiana
47404-3797 USA

iupress.indiana.edu

Telephone orders 800-842-6796
Fax orders 812-855-7931

♾ The paper used in this publication
meets the minimum requirements of
the American National Standard for
Information Sciences – Permanence
of Paper for Printed Library
Materials, ANSI Z39.48-1992.

Manufactured in the
United States of America

Library of Congress
Cataloging-in-Publication Data

Anne Frank unbound : media,
imagination, memory / edited by
Barbara Kirshenblatt-Gimblett and
Jeffrey Shandler.
    p. cm.
    "This volume of essays was developed
from ... a colloquium convened in
2005 by the Working Group on Jews,
Media, and Religion of the Center
for Religion and Media at New York
University"—Intr.
    Includes bibliographical references
and index.
    ISBN 978-0-253-00661-5 (cloth : alk.
paper) — ISBN 978-0-253-00739-1
(pbk. : alk. paper) — ISBN 978-0-253-
00755-1 (eb) 1. Frank, Anne, 1929–
1945—Congresses. I. Kirshenblatt-
Gimblett, Barbara. II. Shandler,
Jeffrey.
    DS135.N6F73186 2012
    940.53'18092—dc23

                                   2012018657

1 2 3 4 5   17 16 15 14 13 12

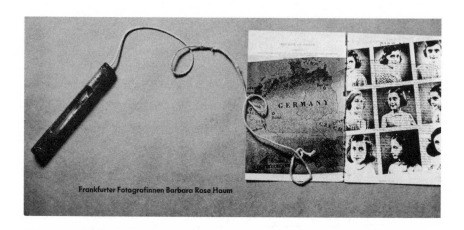

Frankfurter Fotografinnen Barbara Rose Haum

"Expulsion," by Barbara Rose Haum, from the artist's solo exhibition at
the Kommunalen Galerie im Leinwandhaus, Frankfurt am Main, in 1992.
Each image was paired with a text from the Bible. Accompanying this
piece was the following passage: "And he said: when you deliver the
Hebrew women look at the birthstool, if it is a son kill him;
but if it is a daughter, then she shall live." (Exodus 1:16)
Used with permission of Henri Lustiger Thaler

Contents

Acknowledgments

This volume of essays was developed from presentations at Mediating Anne Frank, a colloquium convened in 2005 by the Working Group on Jews, Media, and Religion of the Center for Religion and Media at New York University. We are most grateful to Faye Ginsburg, Angela Zito, and Barbara Abrash of the Center for Religion and Media for their support both of this colloquium and of the working group's many activities during the six years of its existence. During this period, dozens of scholars and artists presented their work on topics ranging from Jewish postcards to televangelist rabbis, Jewish film festivals to virtual worship in Second Life. Members of the working group convened four public colloquia and organized sessions at other scholarly conferences, produced a thematic issue of the journal *Material Religion*, and created a website (http://modiya.nyu.edu) dedicated to teaching and researching this emerging subject of scholarly inquiry.

Anne Frank Unbound exemplifies the working group's commitment to innovative, cross-disciplinary approaches to studying phenomena at the intersection of religion and media, broadly defined. We are indebted to this volume's contributors, both those who participated in the 2005 colloquium and those whose contributions were added subsequently, for their thoughtful work and their patience with the realization of this volume. We likewise thank the other participants in the original colloquium—Barbara Abrash, Michael Beckerman, Jeffrey Feldman, Faye Ginsburg, Judith Goldstein, Barbara Rose Haum, Jenna Weissman Joselit, Mark Kligman, Faye Lederman, and Nicholas Mirzoeff—for sharing their insights.

We are most grateful to Dasha Chapman for her assistance with permissions research and to Matt Jones for his photography. For their generous assistance in the realization of *Anne Frank Unbound,* we thank the Anne Frank Schule Rivierenbuurt, Amsterdam; Marc Aronson; The Concertgebouw, Amsterdam; Jim DeLong and Jon Erickson, The Anne Frank Wall Project, Bret Harte Middle School, San Jose, California; Jonathan Gribetz; Jim Hoberman; Mark Hurvitz; and Dr. Shelly Zer-Zion, The Israeli Center for the Documentation of the Performing Arts, Tel-Aviv University. We are especially grateful to the following artists for their kind permission to reproduce their artwork: Abshalom Jac Lahav, Joe Lewis III, Keith Mayerson, Ellen Rothenberg, and Rachel Schreiber, and to Stuart Schear for kindly arranging funding for the color section of this book. It has been a special pleasure to work with Janet Rabinowitch and Peter Froelich at Indiana University Press.

ANNE FRANK UNBOUND

A wax figure of Anne Frank, in front of photographs of Anne as a child, on its first day of display at Madame Tussauds in Berlin, Germany, December 19, 2008. *Getty Images Photographer: Sean Gallup*

Introduction: Anne Frank,
the Phenomenon

The list is daunting. Dozens of musical compositions, ranging from oratorio to indie rock. A dramatization given hundreds of productions annually. Thousands of YouTube videos. A museum visited by millions. To these, add a growing number of works of fine art, biography, fiction, poetry, and dance, as well as films, radio and television broadcasts, and websites. Plus tributes in the form of commemorative coins, stamps, and other collectibles, memorial sites and organizations around the world, eponymous streets, schools, and institutions, to say nothing of a "day, a week, a rose, a tulip, countless trees, a whole forest, . . . and a village."[1] All inspired by a book that has been translated into scores of languages, published in hundreds of editions, printed in tens of millions of copies, and ranked as one of the most widely read books on the planet.

These wide-ranging engagements with Anne Frank's life and work are a phenomenon of interest in its own right and exceptional in several ways. To begin with, few public figures have inspired connections that are as extensive and as diverse, ranging from veneration to sacrilege. The expression of these connections can be playfully creative or can conform to well-established convention, and they are often deeply personal at the same time that they validate their subject's iconic stature. Among the handful of people who have inspired this extraordinary kind of engagement—Cleopatra, Joan of Arc, Albert Einstein, Elvis Presley—Anne Frank never participated, even indirectly, in her renown. The widespread interest in her rests largely on a single effort—her wartime diary—which no one else had read and few even knew existed during her brief life.

Within a few years of its first publication in 1947, the diary appeared in many editions and translations from the original Dutch, reaching millions of readers. Soon thereafter it won international acclaim for its official dramatization and filming. Widespread engagement with the diary continues, even as the text made available to the public has changed. When it first appeared in 1995, the English-language translation of the diary's *Definitive Edition*, touted as "the first complete and intimate version of the beloved writer's coming-of-age," characterized the text as "a world classic and a timeless testament." The diary's *Revised Critical Edition*, first published in English in 2003, exhorted readers: "Anne Frank *has* lived on—in the minds and hearts of millions of people all over the world."[2] Today, people receiving a copy of the diary learn that they are joining a vast international body of readers of a masterwork and devotees of the author. To read the diary—or to see a play, film, or exhibition about Anne Frank, to discuss her diary in a classroom or hear her name invoked in a poem, song, or religious service—is to encounter and share in this phenomenon.

The Anne Frank phenomenon shows no sign of abating. Tributes to Anne Frank now reach to the heavens (an asteroid was named for her in 1995), she has become a fixture of new social media (a Facebook page was created for her in 2008), and her diary garners ever more prestigious accolades (it was added to the UNESCO Memory of the World Register, along with the Magna Carta and the *Nibelungenlied,* in 2009).[3] As this book went to press, two writers, Shalom Auslander and Nathan Englander, published works of fiction in which Anne Frank figures prominently, as an immortal presence haunting a contemporary American Jewish family's home and an epitomizing test case of personal loyalty, respectively;[4] newspapers report that Anne Frank, among other victims of the Holocaust, was posthumously baptized by a member of the Church of Jesus Christ of Latter Day Saints.[5]

Although the phenomenon centers on Anne and her diary, it extends to others in her family, especially her father, Otto Frank. Recent examples include a book documenting his "hidden life," a published volume of his postwar correspondence with an American teenager, exhibits and publications of his amateur photography, including many pictures that he took of his daughters, and a documentary film about his inspirational meeting with Makoto Otsuka, a minister from Hiroshima.[6] Anne's older sister, Margot, is the subject of YouTube video tributes as well as a musical that imagines the contents of her own diary. Some of the other Jews who hid with the Franks have garnered attention in their own right (for example, a novel about Peter van Pels and a biography of Fritz Pfeffer), as have some of the people who hid them (a television movie based on Miep Gies's memoir, a biography of Victor Kugler).[7] The phenomenon's reach includes Anne Frank's childhood friends (Hanneli Goslar, Berthe Meijer, Jacqueline Van Maarsen), an early sweetheart (Ed Silberberg, né Helmuth "Hello" Silberberg), penpals (Juanita and Betty Wagner of Iowa), and relatives (Anne's cousin Bernd "Buddy" Elias, who serves as head of the Anne Frank-Fonds, and Eva Schloss, who became Anne's posthumous stepsister), all of whom have published memoirs or collaborated on works about their acquaintance with Anne.[8] So powerful is the Anne Frank phenomenon that a book about the wartime experiences of another German Jewish family named Frank, unrelated to Anne, is titled *The Frank Family That Survived;* it describes the family's wartime experiences, including months of hiding in the Netherlands, as traversing "the same route Anne Frank might have taken had she not been betrayed."[9]

This wide-ranging engagement is not simply a response to the topic that first brought Anne's writing to public attention. Other first-person accounts of Jews' enduring Nazi persecution that appeared during the early postwar years—Mary Berg's *Warsaw Ghetto: A Diary,* published in English in 1945, or Sara Veffer's 1960 memoir, *Hidden for a Thousand Days,* about another family's experience hiding in the Netherlands—did not inspire anywhere near as enduring and wide-ranging engagement.[10] Rather, several distinguishing features of Anne Frank's life and work have engendered such an expansive output of responses.

First, there is the distinctive nature of the diary: a text with a complex (and, until the mid-1980s, relatively unknown) history of writing, rewriting, and editing, which involved not only Anne but also her father and others, who encountered the text only after her death. Second, there are the circumstances in which the author, a Jewish adolescent living in Nazi-occupied Amsterdam, created this work: writing first for herself and then for an imagined public, her literary ambitions and her life cut short abruptly and cruelly by the Holocaust. Third is the subject

Poster for *Margot Frank: The Diary of the Other Young Girl*, a musical
performed at William Paterson College in Wayne, New Jersey, in 2008.

of her writing: the Nazi persecution of European Jewry set in motion the circumstances that define the diary's central feature of being written largely while in hiding. However, the diary engages the Holocaust obliquely, from the vantage of someone who was seeking to escape its clutches and was equally preoccupied with the challenges of her own coming of age, intensified by her confinement. Fourth, Anne's reflections on her often fraught relationships with her parents and on her developing sexuality have distinguished her diary as a landmark work in the literature of adolescence, and its reading by millions of teenagers has, in turn, become a rite of passage in its own right. Fifth, the diary's public presence is unusual in nature, as a work that has been, on one hand, extensively promoted and, on the other hand, carefully regulated. Oversight of the diary was maintained by Otto Frank during his lifetime and has also been the task of institutional guardians: the Anne Frank Stichting, established in Amsterdam in 1957, the Anne Frank-Fonds, inaugurated in Basel in 1963, and other official organizations that promote and protect Anne's remembrance. Sixth, from early on, Anne's life and work have been presented to the public—under the aegis of her father as well as by others—as paradigmatic, transcending the particulars of her circumstances.

These features not only distinguish Anne's diary but also have created opportunities that enable the Anne Frank phenomenon to flourish. The diary is an open text, not least because, even as rewritten by Anne, it is an unfinished work, just as her life was cut short by her murder at the age of fifteen. The discrepancy that readers encounter between the diary, written with the author's assumption of a favorable outcome for both her narrative and herself, and the discovery of Anne's death in Bergen-Belsen some seven months after her arrest, as explained in the epilogue to the published diary, creates a disturbing affective disparity as well as a narrative gap. This gap has inspired some readers to seek a way to breach it—whether by tracing the undocumented final months of Anne's life, primarily through the recollections of Holocaust survivors who saw her in various camps where she was held, by recounting her suffering as a tale of morally charged redemption, or by imagining her surviving the war and starting a new life. Attending to the diary's complex history of writing foregrounds the self-conscious nature of its creation, epitomized by one of Anne's most oft-cited diary entries: "I want to go on living even after my death! And therefore I am grateful to God for giving me this gift, this possibility of developing myself and of writing, of expressing all that is in me."[11] This attention has inspired others, some of whom reference this entry, to respond to Anne's life and work in kind with creative endeavors of their own. Some of these efforts forthrightly proclaim their creators' desire to endow Anne with symbolic immortality through their own works.

Responses to the Anne Frank phenomenon have tended to be polar: either uncritically celebratory, claiming the many engagements with Anne's life and work as validating the diary's universal significance, or broadly dismissive of these engagements as inappropriate, distorted, or exploitative assaults on the integrity of the diary and its author. Questioning the singular stature of Anne Frank as *the* representative victim of Nazism and of victimization more generally, literary scholar Alvin Rosenfeld has cautioned, "There is a temptation to readily proclaim, 'We are all Anne Frank.' But, in fact, we are nothing of the sort."[12] Lawrence Langer, another scholar of Holocaust literature, insists that "if Anne Frank could return from among the murdered, she would be appalled at the misuse to which her journal entries had been put," and he faults "those who canonize [Anne] as an archetypal victim" of the Holocaust to be "guilty of a double injustice—to her and to the millions of other victims."[13] Historian Tim Cole has also argued against vaunting Anne Frank as an exemplar—"If there is one lesson that can be drawn from the Holocaust it is precisely that the optimism of Anne Frank was woefully misplaced"—and further suggests that overly upbeat popular representations of her life and work produced in the United States in the 1950s have, if unwittingly, abetted Holocaust deniers, who "dismiss 'Anne Frank'" as a myth.[14] In a similar vein, author Cynthia Ozick has provocatively wondered whether "a more salvational outcome" might have been, instead of the diary being rescued following her arrest, "Anne Frank's diary burned, vanished, lost—saved from a world that made of it all things."[15]

This impulse to restrict or regulate engagement with such a widely read text, though rooted in worthy concerns for historical accuracy and moral rigor, discounts the significance of this engagement by millions of readers. The fact that it takes many different forms, is inconsistent in its sense of purpose, varies considerably in quality of execution, and not infrequently proves to be disturbing for one reason or another does not diminish its value. Rather, what makes the Anne Frank phenomenon compelling is precisely its vast sprawl. Indeed, notwithstanding its global character and use of a wide range of media, from works of fine art to MP3 files, the Anne Frank phenomenon can be considered a kind of folk practice, as it is largely the work of individuals or grassroots communities, inspired by this widely available text to forge their own attachment to Anne's life and work.

The essays in this volume approach the Anne Frank phenomenon as a subject of interest in itself. They do not scrutinize these performances, artworks, and other practices solely in relation to Anne's biography and writing but examine them as cultural enterprises in their own right and on their own terms. Therefore, this volume does not set out to evaluate these works as representations to be measured in terms of their "closeness" to an original life or work or in terms of the "appropriateness" of their engagement with Anne's story. Rather, the interest centers on these acts of engagement in and of themselves, each one situated within an expansive array of possibilities at this confluence of memory and imagination.

Central to this volume's approach to understanding the great diversity of these engagements with Anne Frank is an attention to *mediation*—that is, to what happens when Anne's diary is translated, sung, dramatized, filmed, rendered as a graphic novel or museum exhibition. Mediation does not simply reproduce or transfer its subject; instead, it produces something related to the source but also different—a new work (or practice or experience). Mediations also create new relationships: between the creator of this new work and its subject and audience, as well as between the new work and other works.

Rather than making the disparity between the subject and its mediation an object of criticism, the authors of this volume see in these disparities opportunities for expressive engagement, for adding or changing meaning. Therefore, within this approach the notion of a "faithful" translation or an "authentic" adaptation is a false friend. Every work that engages Anne Frank's diary, from the most painstaking editing and careful translation to the most overtly counterfactual work of fiction or outrageous cartoon, is a mediation that alters its subject and makes an opening for cultural creativity. Regardless of whether the results are celebrated or vilified by others, the task of this volume is not to judge these engagements, but rather to analyze them on their own terms. Moreover, the essays in this volume consider the various engagements with Anne's life and work as mediations through which the diary has been rendered ever more "faithful" to itself, extending rather than contravening its intent.

Mediation is, in fact, key to understanding the text at the center of the Anne Frank phenomenon. Anne's diary has a complex history of missing sections, rewriting, and redaction by more than one person. As Jeffrey Shandler observes in his contribution to this volume, each published edition of the text further reshapes the original dairy. And of course, Anne's original manuscripts are themselves a mediation of her actual experiences over the course of the twenty-six months during which she wrote her entries. Mediation is also key to understanding the cascade of works that engage Anne's diary in relation to one another. The Anne Frank phenomenon is replete with works that remediate other mediations. In her essay in this volume, Leshu Torchin notes that tribute videos to Anne Frank sample and re-edit films and telecasts about Anne that are based on texts (a play, a biography) that are, in turn, adapted from or inspired by the diary. Photographs of Anne, some of them taken by her father and pasted by her into her diary, have adorned the covers of published editions of the diary, found their way into documentary films and, as Daniel Belasco discusses in his essay in this collection, inspired works of visual art about Anne. The Anne Frank House, a site-specific museum that narrates Anne's life and work within the spaces where she hid and wrote the diary, has itself inspired other mediations, ranging from public monuments to comedy routines to commemorative miniatures.

The Anne Frank phenomenon has its own history, a defining feature of which is the ongoing concern over the proprietary rights to the widely familiar diary and the propriety with which it is engaged. The

Miniature porcelain model of the Anne Frank House, in the form of
an alms box (note the coin slot in the rear view), created for the Jewish
Federation of Greater Philadelphia. *Photographer: Matt Jones*

1950s and early 1960s witnessed the diary's first publications in widely
read languages, the presentation of its only authorized dramatization on
stage and screen, the establishment of institutions for safeguarding the
diary and Anne's memory, and the opening of the Anne Frank House,
the diary's official site of remembrance. Thanks in large part to these efforts, Anne Frank's life and work came to be widely known internationally, even as this familiarity was carefully regulated. Most famously, the
writer Meyer Levin's efforts to stage his own dramatization of the diary,
which differs from the authorized stage play by Frances Goodrich and
Albert Hackett, were disallowed by Otto Frank and his counsel. With
greater frequency over the sixty-five years since the diary's first publication, the kinds of responses to Anne's life and work that are explored in
this volume have challenged the diary's regulation by Otto Frank and its
authorized institutional guardians. The first major works that contested
the official framing of the diary's value appeared in the United States

in the 1970s, beginning with Peter Nero's 1970 *The Diary of Anne Frank*. As Judah Cohen observes in his contribution to this volume, Nero's "rock symphony" uses different musical genres to articulate the difference in generational understandings of Anne's life and work. In 1979, Philip Roth's novella *The Ghost Writer,* one of the literary works that Sara Horowitz discusses in her essay in this collection, interrogates Anne's mythic stature in American public culture by provocatively positing that Anne survived the war but realized she was of greater value to the world as a martyr.

The death of Otto Frank in 1980, at the age of ninety-one, marks a watershed in the history of the Anne Frank phenomenon. Beyond the loss of the only member of Anne's immediate family who had survived the Holocaust, her father's death placed the regulation of the diary and the maintenance of an authoritative presentation of its significance completely in the hands of others. Moreover, by 1980, a generation of readers who had discovered the diary in their youth had become adults, and many of their children were now encountering Anne's life and work as an established rite of passage. Reading the diary and performing its dramatization had become fixtures of secondary education in the United States, as Ilana Abramovitch notes in her essay in this volume, especially in relation to the efforts then emerging to teach young people about the Holocaust.

In the ensuing decade, the Anne Frank-Fonds published the *Critical Edition* of the diary (the Dutch edition appeared in 1986, with translations following soon thereafter). This variorum edition made the text's complex history of composition and redaction readily available, both to disprove persistent claims by Holocaust deniers that the diary is a forgery and to provide scholars with the means to examine the creative process behind this widely familiar text. The impact of the *Critical Edition* has been extensive, in ways both anticipated by its creators and doubtless surprising to them. In addition to prompting new scrutiny of Anne Frank's writing by scholars and critics, as discussed by Sally Charnow in her essay in this collection, this new version of the diary motivated a growing number of writers, visual artists, musicians, and filmmakers to offer highly personal responses to Anne Frank's life and work, in some cases foregrounding her Jewishness, femaleness, adolescence, or other aspects of her life that diverge from more established presentations. At the same time, Anne Frank has continued to figure in public presentations as the embodiment of optimism and a universal call for human rights, to mention only a speech by President Ronald Reagan during a controversial visit to West Germany in 1985 and the life-size statue of Anne at the center of a human rights monument erected in Boise, Idaho, in 2002, the latter analyzed by Brigitte Sion in her contribution to this volume.

During the 1990s, the major authorized presentations of Anne's life and work were revamped: the Anne Frank-Fonds issued a new version of the diary for the general reader, known as the *Definitive Edition* (first published in Dutch in 1991), and authorized a revision of the diary's official dramatization (which premiered on Broadway in 1997). In the mid-1990s, the Anne Frank House underwent an extensive renovation that reconfigured visitors' encounter with the building. These changes both reassert the authority of these officially sanctioned works and institutions and respond, if tacitly, to new public attention to the diary's regulation, including news reports of pages of the diary that had been suppressed due to their sensitive content and major studies of Meyer Levin's feud with Otto Frank over the dramatic rights to the diary.

With the passage of time and the passing of the last living links to Anne has come a new sense of urgency to keep her story alive. In 2010 Miep Gies—who, after Otto Frank, was the most widely known living witness to Anne's years in hiding—died at the age of one hundred. That same year saw the demise of the chestnut tree that grew behind the Annex, which had become a powerful emblem of Anne's remembrance, the subject of Barbara Kirshenblatt-Gimblett's contribution to this collection. At the same time that the official keepers of Anne Frank's legacy continue to promote remembering her life and writing in new ways, there has been a proliferation of works that have tested, evaded, or flouted the proprietary rights and expectations of propriety that surround Anne and her diary. These works include, on the one hand, a more liberal licensed use of the diary text (e.g., its citation, with permission of the Anne Frank-Fonds, in *Anne B. Real,* a 2003 feature film about a young female rapper living in East Harlem who is inspired by Anne's diary) and, on the other hand, works that tell Anne's story without quoting directly from the diary, thereby circumventing the issue of securing permissions (e.g., Melissa Müller's 1998 biography of Anne Frank and its 2001 dramatization for television). Highly personal takes on Anne and the diary find their place in blog postings and tribute videos, which, unlike print, film, or broadcasting, resist traditional regulation. Digital media offer ripe opportunities for mashups that copy, rework, and combine texts, images, and sound or video recordings, and that can go viral through social media. Within this culture of open sharing of information and creative work, which has its own social practices and its own ethics, Anne Frank and her diary are truly unbound, and the very ethos ascribed to her life and work is rethought.

The liberal nature of the Internet encourages more expansive approaches to engaging Anne Frank, both playful and earnest. Edward Portnoy's essay in this volume explores recent comedy sketches, plays, and videos, which have variously imagined Anne as a superhero, an Irish barmaid, and a manmade transsexual monster. In the same vein, "Anne Frank's drum kit," a byword for uselessness, is one of several slang expressions that irreverently evoke her name.[16] Earnest engagements with Anne's life and work readily link her name with other figures in the struggle for human rights, from Nelson Mandela to Harriet Tubman, while less well-known individuals are linked to Anne Frank by analogy. She has become not only a paradigm but also something akin to a brand. Thus, just as young Zlata Filipović had been hailed as the "Anne Frank of Sarajevo" when her diary recounting ethnic cleansing operations in the Balkans was published in 1993, the physician Đặng Thùy Trâm was proclaimed the "Anne Frank of Vietnam" after her wartime diary was published in 2005, thirty-five years following her death. Similarly, other women whose writings chronicle the ordeals of political oppression, war, and genocide have earned this title: Hélène Berr is the "Anne Frank of France," Bophana is the "Anne Frank of Cambodia," Hadiya is the "Anne Frank of Iraq," and Nina Lugovskaya is the "Anne Frank of Russia."[17] Books on the experiences of other children during the Holocaust regularly position these stories in relation to Anne's as being by far the best known, doing so both to capitalize on the familiarity of her diary and to inform readers of a wider range of wartime narratives. Thus, the sociologist Diane Wolf titled her study of Jewish Holocaust survivors who had been hidden children in the Netherlands *Beyond Anne Frank,* which, by invoking Anne Frank, juxtaposes these survivors' experiences against her paradigmatic story.[18]

Within its global reach, the Anne Frank phenomenon responds to the particulars of place. The localization of the phenomenon is perhaps most readily evident in the Netherlands. There, telling Anne's story, especially in Amsterdam's Anne Frank House, attends not only to the eight Jews who hid there but also to the Dutch citizens involved in Anne's story, both those who helped hide her and those who participated in her betrayal to the Nazis. Equally complex is the relationship that Germans have had with Anne, as a native of Frankfurt and a victim of the Holocaust. Following her diary's publication and especially its dramatization, Anne emerged in the mid-1950s as a key figure in Germans' coming to terms with the Nazi era, with separate histories for East and West Germany. West Germany published the first book that chronicled Anne's life in its entirety, including her last months following her arrest: Ernst Schnabel's *Anne Frank: Spur eines Kindes: ein Bericht,* in 1958.[19] East Germany produced one of the first works to use Anne Frank's story as the point of entry into the larger narrative of the Nazi era and its legacy in postwar Germany, the 1958 propaganda film *Ein Tagebuch für Anne Frank.*[20] Anne's death in Bergen-Belsen has inspired a very distinct, localized engagement with her life and work, centered on this site of mass murder, as chronicled in the essay in this volume by Henri Lustiger Thaler and Wilfried Wiedemann. Elsewhere, Anne acquires significance as an exemplar of suffering in relation to local struggles, notably, the anti-apartheid movement in South Africa, where political prisoners on Robben Island read Anne's diary as an inspirational work.[21]

The United States has a singular role in the geography of the Anne Frank phenomenon. Though there is scant connection between her story and the United States (Anne briefly corresponded with U.S. pen pals before going into hiding, and her father tried to take his family to the United States in 1938 and again in 1941), mediations of Anne's life and work produced by Americans have reached international audiences. As Edna Nahshon notes in her contribution to this collection, the 1955 Broadway play *The Diary of Anne Frank* quickly became an international

Cover of *Ein Tagebuch für Anne Frank* (A Diary for Anne Frank),
a book published in Berlin in 1959 by Joachim Hellwig and
Günther Deicker, based on their 1958 film of the same name.

success, even as some critics chafed at its Americanness. Indeed, this play is the first major example of an American work about the Holocaust to have a significant impact on the remembrance of this event abroad, including in countries where it took place.

At the heart of the Anne Frank phenomenon is Anne's celebrity status, a development that many critics decry as unjust either to her or to other victims of the Holocaust. Yet celebrity is something about which Anne, like many other teenagers in the modern Western world, dreamed. Contemplating one of the photographs of herself that she pasted into the first notebook of her diary, she wondered whether she might make it to Hollywood.[22] Public attention also appealed to Anne's father, who, before the family went into hiding, had shown a flair for marketing his company Opekta by making promotional films on how to use its products to make homemade preserves (these films are now shown in the Anne Frank House). Otto Frank dedicated his postwar life to promoting awareness of his daughter's life and work, albeit in a restrained and carefully regulated manner. Hence, there has been a very limited licensed materialization of Anne Frank, limited to published editions of her diary, a few authorized books about her life and legacy, and postcards sold in the Anne Frank House bookshop. There are no licensed t-shirts, mugs, or other souvenirs, no official Anne Frank dolls or diary notebooks with red-and-white plaid covers, or other possible commodifications.

Notwithstanding the discomfort that the notion of Anne as a celebrity can provoke (a discomfort worth interrogating in itself), her renown is instrumental to the Anne Frank phenomenon, which relies on widespread familiarity with Anne's name, face, and place in history. Comparing her celebrity to that of others is revealing: like Che Guevera, her portrait has become iconic, if not a fashion statement; like Nelson Mandela, with whom she is analogized in artworks and in installations at the Anne Frank House and the Boise human rights monument, she serves as a metonym, the "face" of a mass phenomenon. Like President John F. Kennedy or Rev. Martin Luther King, Jr., Anne's murder figures powerfully in her renown, prompting speculation as to what she might have accomplished had her life not been cut short so cruelly.

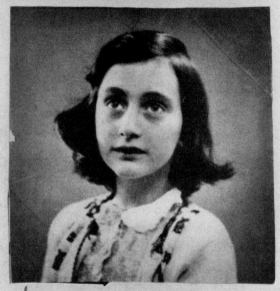

Anne Frank on the cover of *LIFE* magazine, August 18, 1958.
The story focuses on Anne's final months of life, as recounted
in Ernst Schnabel's biography, then about to be published in
English translation as *Anne Frank: A Portrait in Courage.*
Photographer: Matt Jones

And it is by dint of her celebrity that Anne Frank has been widely invoked as a paradigmatic figure—or rather, as a figure for an array of paradigms: as an archetypal Jew, Holocaust victim, human rights champion, girl, adolescent writer, diarist, or feminist voice. At the same time, in none of these paradigms does Anne prove to be a perfect fit. An ongoing concern in Anne Frank remembrance is how to deal with her exceptionalism: she is an atypical victim of Nazi persecution; her sense of Jewishness strikes some observers as limited; her diary is an unusual example of the genre from a formal standpoint and, for some critics, is problematic as Holocaust literature; she has no record of activism, as do the other figures in the pantheon of human rights heroes among whom she is often placed.

This proliferation of paradigms creates provocative contradictions, not all of them intended. The image of Anne wearing a *keffiyeh,* created by the artist known as T., appeared beginning in 2007 as street art in Amsterdam and New York and later circulated on postcards and t-shirts. Does this juxtaposition of two icons—Anne Frank's portrait and the traditional Arab headscarf worn by many people as a sign of solidarity with Palestinians—analogize Jewish victimization during the Holocaust with the contemporary suffering of Palestinians under Israeli occupation? Does this juxtaposition ironize Anne as an archetypal Jew? Does this image present Anne as an exemplar of human rights taking up the Palestinian cause (as some Jews, both in Israel and the diaspora, have done)? Or does this configure Anne, as the eternal rebellious teenager, flouting a Jewish establishment that deems support for Palestinians inimical to Zionism? The image's provocation relies on this clash of icons, made possible by the array of paradigmatic roles into which Anne Frank has been cast.

Disparate as these paradigms are, they are linked by the mode of engaging Anne Frank as a paragon. Practices that associate her with ethical concerns appear early in the history of Anne's renown. For example, the playwrights Goodrich and Hackett established a scholarship in Anne's name shortly after the successful premiere of their dramatization of her diary. Schools, memorials, gardens, and other public institutions have been named after Anne to invoke moral values that her name

now indexes. This association also reflects the wishes of Anne's father, who envisioned the Anne Frank House as not only a site of historical interest tied to the diary but also a center where young people from around the world would convene, in Anne's name, to address human rights concerns.

Frequently, engagements of Anne as a paragon employ the idioms of religious practice, configuring her as something akin to a saint and her diary like a sacred text. Among the most patent examples are musical tributes to Anne in the form of requiems and the practice of symbolically inviting Anne to participate in the Passover seder, an American Jewish ritual innovation examined by Liora Gubkin in her contribution to this volume. The idioms of sanctification also inform official presentations of the diary: issuing a variorum edition that resembles publications of the synoptic gospels, and displaying the original diary notebook like a religious relic in the Anne Frank House, Amsterdam's "Shrine of the Book."[23] Similarly, the chestnut tree that grew behind the Anne Frank House, mentioned occasionally in the diary, has been invested with the power of a relic bearing Anne's aura and through which she continues to have an animated presence in the world. These religious engagements with Anne Frank are not all of a kind. Their character is sometimes distinctly Christian, as when her story is told as a redemptive narrative of martyrdom, and other times particularly Jewish, as when she is conceived as a figure distinguished by a Jewish historical destiny. Practices range from folk religion (e.g., carrying or displaying an image of Anne as a talisman) to civil religion, where Anne Frank stands tall in public monuments or is the centerpiece of educational programs dedicated to universal concerns about tolerance and human rights.

The Anne Frank phenomenon, an object lesson in the workings of contemporary civil religion, shows how practices of sanctification coalesce and how they engender unanticipated consequences. During

Anne Frank wearing a *keffiyeh,* street art by
the artist known as T., Amsterdam, ca. 2007.
Photographer: Jean-Philippe Nevoux
© *Jean-Philippe Nevoux—Fotolia.com*

the decade and a half following the first publication of Anne's diary, a series of undertakings—translations of the text, authorized dramatic adaptations, the establishment of institutions dedicated to memorializing Anne—both consolidated and extended the stature of Anne's life and work as morally paradigmatic. As Anne Frank became famous as an edifying icon, concern over regulating engagement with her life and work increased. In effect, Anne Frank became intellectual property, to be protected not merely for commercial reasons, but even more so for moral reasons. Proprietary and propriety issues converged. Control extended beyond limiting permission to cite or adapt Anne's diary or to reproduce an image of her to ensuring that Anne and the diary would be treated with appropriate respect—as a Holocaust victim, a martyr, a human rights icon—and would continue to offer moral inspiration.

Yet as Anne Frank became more iconic, she also became less specific as an actual young woman, situated in very particular familial, communal, and historical circumstances, and as a symbol. In recent decades, critics have argued that the success of the icon may also be its undoing: overreaching may make the universality of Anne Frank anodyne, while well-intended efforts to protect the symbol's ethical effectiveness by overdetermining affective response may make it kitsch. At the same time, the more reverence accorded to Anne Frank, the greater a target she has become for irreverence.

Irreverent responses are not all of a kind. Holocaust deniers seize the opportunity to challenge the diary's authenticity; comedians exploit this opening to assail the sanctification of Anne Frank as stifling. These profane acts are not directed at Anne herself, but at the keepers of her remembrance. Deniers target Otto Frank as Anne's exploiter, alleging that he fabricated the diary toward his own selfish and dishonest ends. Comedians target the sanctimony of works of Anne Frank remembrance that envelop her life; like some critics, creative writers, and visual artists, they seek, if implicitly, to recover the "real" Anne—the intelligent, creative, ambitious, and often rebellious adolescent author—from beatified representations. These responses, in effect, extrapolate from the diary's intergenerational conflict between a strong-willed teenager and the adult world that seeks to constrain her. Reacting against the authoritative and "proper" use of the diary, they conjure alternative outcomes for Anne,

Anne Frank on a lapel button produced in 2004 by Stay Vocal, which has promoted reused clothing as well as various environmental and human rights issues. This button was one of several made to honor "people from history with strong voices," according to Alex Eaves, the founder of Stay Vocal. *Collection of Mark Hurvitz*

be it rescuing her from Nazi persecution or rescuing her youthful spirit from the heavy-handed moralizing by adults. These responses testify to the power of Anne Frank's original creative efforts and to the Anne Frank phenomenon, which continues to prompt people worldwide to forge their own bond with the diary and its author.

Engaging Anne Frank's life and work has endured beyond the lives of most of the people who knew her; soon it will outlast her cohort of eyewitnesses to World War II. As remembrance of the war passes beyond the last generation of people who experienced it and comes to depend entirely on mediations, Anne will remain one of the best known of its millions of victims, situated amid an array of mediations of unrivaled number and variety. At the same time that her writing, her life—even her name—have been established as fixtures of public culture internationally, people engage Anne Frank within various rubrics: not only as a victim of Nazi persecution, but also as a writer, a young woman, a Jew, an icon of human rights, a celebrity—and, moreover, as the center of a singular phenomenon.

The Anne Frank phenomenon is in large measure a product of the cascade of media, old and new, through which one engages her life and work—remediated, for example, from manuscript to printed book to stage adaptation to film and televised dramatization to digital social media. These works are the subject of "Mediating," the first section of essays in this volume. The essays in "Remembering," the second section of this volume, examine the range and dynamics of practices—the deliberate work of governments, religious organizations, and public institutions as well as impromptu, grassroots efforts—for commemorating this widely familiar figure and imbuing her with symbolic value. The wide-ranging creative engagement with Anne's life and work by visual artists, musicians, and writers is addressed in the third section, "Imagining." Recent efforts by both scholars and humorists to challenge the established understandings of this iconic figure's significance are the subject of the essays in "Contesting," the final section. A concluding essay on the Anne Frank Tree serves as an epilogue to this collection. The history of endowing this tree with a symbolic life of its own, extending to its afterlife since its demise in 2010, both exemplifies the remarkable flourishing of the Anne Frank phenomenon and looks forward to its future course, as new generations encounter Anne's life and work and engage it on their own terms.

I MEDIATING

1

From Diary to Book:
Text, Object, Structure

Jeffrey Shandler

Most of the many mediations of Anne Frank's diary—plays, films, artworks, musical compositions, memorials, lesson plans, even jokes—begin with the book: that is, the published diary. To speak of "the diary" as "the book," though, is to elide the diary's initial, key mediations. Its transformation from the different notebooks and manuscripts that Anne wrote between June 1942 and August 1944 into a published book, which first appeared almost three years after her last entry, entailed extensive editing by more than one hand, including her own. In published form, Anne's diary appeared in a series of languages—first the original Dutch in 1947, then French and German translations in 1950 and English in 1952. These were followed by translations into over thirty more languages within another two decades, including three different Yiddish renderings—published in Bucharest, Buenos Aires, and Tel Aviv—all in 1958.[1] Additional translations continue to appear, such as renderings into Arabic and Farsi in 2008 issued by the Aladdin Online Library, a Paris-based organization combating Holocaust denial in the Muslim world.[2] Some translations attract public attention, hailed for promoting Holocaust awareness and combating anti-Semitism or as a touchstone of human rights. Thus, when the diary appeared in Khmer in 2002, the Dutch ambassador to Cambodia noted that

> Anne Frank's ordeal bears resemblance to the personal history of thousands of Cambodians who have suffered a similar fate at the hands of the Khmer Rouge during the regime of Democratic Kampuchea. . . . I hope that many Cambodians will find something of relevance to their own lives and experience in this book and that it can be a source of comfort. Anne Frank died, as

did 1.7 million Cambodians. But their deaths have led to a strong resolve that the international community should do everything to prevent further crime against humanity.[3]

In the six decades after its initial publication, Anne's diary has appeared in over sixty different languages and sold more than thirty-one million copies, making it one of the world's most widely read books.[4] Moreover, the diary has been printed in hundreds of editions and in diverse formats: abridged versions; anthologized excerpts, some published with Anne's other works; teacher's or student's editions; limited editions for book collectors (including a 1959 oversize publication in French, with a frontispiece by Marc Chagall, and a 1985 two-volume set in English with etchings by Joseph Goldyne);[5] and sound recordings (read in English by Claire Bloom, Julie Harris, and Winona Ryder, among other actresses).[6] The published diary has appeared with different redactions of the original text and with various titles, cover designs, introductions, illustrations, and epilogues. Each publication presents a distinct mediation of Anne's diary.

Even as other mediations of the diary proliferate, the act of reading it in book form remains the foundational (if not always initial) encounter, rooted in an authorized, carefully regulated text and seemingly closest to Anne's own practice of writing. Reading the diary has become a meaningful act in its own right and has been incorporated into other mediations of the diary, including films, fiction, and performance. The book's wide readership has also fostered interest in the original diary's materiality. The object of veneration, suspicion, and scholarly scrutiny, Anne's first diary notebook has become an icon. Its cover or sample pages have been widely reproduced, including in published editions of the diary. Similarly, photographs of Anne and of the building where she hid have appeared in published editions of the diary and hence have become familiar symbols of Anne's life and work. Examining the diary's redaction, publication, and materialization reveals a complex of obscured or easily overlooked mediations between Anne's original writings and her millions of readers, shaping their encounter with her life and work.

Redactions

While Anne Frank's diary might be regarded as exemplary of the genre, it is an unusual and, in some ways, challenging one. The diary went through two major phases of redaction before it was first published, each transforming the text substantially, well beyond the usual editing of a diary for publication. Anne began her diary on or shortly after June 12, 1942, her thirteenth birthday, when she was given the plaid cloth-covered notebook in which she wrote her first entries. Within weeks after starting her diary, Anne and her family went into hiding on July 6, 1942, secreted in abandoned rooms in the rear of 263 Prinsengracht, where Opekta and Pectacon, two businesses run by her father, Otto, had their offices. There, Anne continued her diary; by December 1942 she filled the notebook she had received on her birthday. Miep Gies, an employee of Anne's father and one of the people who helped hide the Franks, gave Anne "an ordinary exercise book" to continue her diary. She also wrote entries in her sister Margot's chemistry exercise book and inserted some later entries (written in 1943 and 1944) in the original diary notebook on pages previously left blank.[7] Anne continued keeping her diary until August 1, 1944, several days before her arrest, along with her parents, sister, and the four other Jews hiding with them, by the Sicherheitsdienst. Gies and a fellow employee retrieved Anne's diaries and other writings soon thereafter, hoping to return them to her after the war. Gies neither read the diary nor showed it to others. "Had I read it," she explained years later, "I would have had to burn the diary because it would have been too dangerous for people about whom Anne had written," referring to those who had helped hide Anne and the other Jews.[8] Ultimately, Gies gave Anne's writings to Otto Frank, the only one of the eight Jews to survive the war, after he learned that Anne was dead.

These manuscripts included two different versions of the diary, each incomplete, works of fiction Anne had written while in hiding, and a notebook of her favorite literary quotations.[9] The diary's first version, written in a series of notebooks, has a gap between December 6, 1942 and December 21, 1943 (apparently, one or more notebooks were lost or destroyed at some point). Anne began the diary's second version in the spring of 1944, after Gerrit Bolkestein, a minister in the Dutch government-in-exile, appealed over Radio Oranje to the Dutch people to keep diaries, letters, and other personal documents as evidence of their resistance to Nazi occupation. By May 20, 1944, Anne noted that she had begun reworking her earlier entries, now writing on loose sheets of paper. In fact, Anne had already transformed some of her entries into literary pieces. About a year after beginning her diary, Anne reworked some entries into short stories and started writing other pieces of fiction. These she kept in a separate notebook, labeled *Verhaaltjesboek* (Book of Tales), which she began on September 2, 1943, continuing to add entries through May 1944.[10]

Anne envisioned the revised diary as a literary project on a larger scale—a book, titled *Het Achterhuis* (literally, "The House Behind," usually rendered in English as the Secret Annex), referring to her hiding place. Anne drafted her revised diary during the final ten weeks of her time in hiding, while continuing to write new entries in notebooks. When she started another notebook for new entries on April 17, 1944, Anne created a title page that suggests she was thinking of both her new entries and the rewritten ones as intended for publication:

> Diary of Anne Frank
> from 17 April 1944 to
> "Secret Annex"
> A'dam C. [i.e., Amsterdam Centrum]
> Partly letters to "Kitty"
> The owner's maxim:
> Schwung muss der Mensch haben! (Zest is what man needs!)[11]

The rewritten diary begins with a prologue, dated June 20, 1942, which provides an overview of her family, ending "and here I come to the present day and to the solemn inauguration of my diary,"[12] followed by an entry for that date. The first entry in the original diary, however, is a brief inscription dated June 12, 1942 (i.e., the day she received the plaid notebook)—"I hope I shall be able to confide in you completely, as I have never been able to do in anyone before, and I hope that you will be a great support and comfort to me"[13]—followed by a more substantial entry dated June 14, 1942. The last entry of the rewritten diary is dated

March 29, 1944, the date on which Anne first wrote about Bolkestein's appeal for documents of wartime resistance.

The differences between the diary's two versions reflect a central shift in agenda between them. Whereas Anne began the first version as, like most diaries, a confessional work, written for her eyes alone, the second version was composed for a public readership as documentation of an experience understood as being of historical importance. The differences between the two versions are apparent in both content and form. Perhaps the diary's best-known feature is its epistolary format. In her revised version (as in the published version), Anne's entries are addressed to an imaginary friend, Kitty, whose identity is explained in the revised diary's opening prologue of June 20, 1942 (and, in the first published version, the entry of that date).[14] This device simplifies the more varied practice found in Anne's original diary, which features entries addressed to a list of imaginary correspondents—all girls—named Conny, Jetty, Emmy, Marianne, as well as Kitty. These are not the names of Anne's actual girlfriends but of characters in *Joop ter Heul,* a popular series of Dutch novels for girls. Choosing these fictional names suggests that, even in her first diary, Anne blurred the line between keeping a diary as a conventional record of daily experiences or thoughts and engaging in a more imaginative, literary exercise. Anne's epistolary entries extend from reportage and introspection to fantasies, especially of companionship and, on occasion, activities (e.g., shopping, ice skating) that she could no longer pursue in hiding.[15]

In her reworked diary, Anne omitted these entries, limiting their range as she simplified the practice of addressing them all to Kitty. Moreover, Anne conceived the revised diary as a different kind of work. In her original diary she wrote on March 29, 1944: "Just imagine how interesting it would be if I were to publish a romance of the 'Secret Annex,' the title alone would be enough to make people think it was a detective story."[16] Indeed, as she reworked the diary, Anne transformed her wideranging entries into a kind of suspense novel *à clef,* featuring continuing characters (with decodable pseudonyms), a running plot interspersed with suspenseful and comic episodes, a narrator offering reflections on the story she is relating, and background information on the larger context in which events inside the Annex take place. Where the original diary's incremental format disrupted Anne's vision of a larger narrative structure, she variously conflated, reordered, expanded, or tightened individual entries. Beyond the usual editing of a diary for publication, which is largely a matter of trimming and annotating, Anne's revisions strove for a publishable work of both historical value and literary merit. Moreover, she implicitly imagined that she would live to complete this work as a validation of surviving Nazi persecution and a celebration of Germany's defeat.

The diary's second phase of redaction, resulting in its first published editions, was initiated after the war by Otto Frank, who selected and compiled material from Anne's various manuscripts in a series of typewritten versions generated between 1945 and 1946. These redactions involved more than one language and editorial hand, and they were prepared for different readers. First, Otto Frank rendered sections of the diary into German, to be shared with his mother (who did not know Dutch); a subsequent typescript was prepared for other family members and close acquaintances. After deciding to pursue publication of the diary, Otto Frank assembled another version of the text in Dutch with the help of Albert Cauvern, a friend who then worked as a radio dramatist. This text integrated material from two incomplete sources—Anne's original and rewritten diaries—into a typescript, presented as a single, integral work. This redaction also incorporated some of Anne's short prose pieces inspired by her life in hiding that were not part of either diary manuscript. Otto Frank also removed some material from the diaries that he deemed either extraneous or offensive to the memories of the others who had hidden in the Annex and then died during the war.[17]

In preparing the text for publication, Otto Frank and Cauvern changed the names of most of the people mentioned in the diary, generally following Anne's notes about pseudonyms to be used in her published version.[18] Thus, the van Pels family, who went into hiding with the Franks, became the Van Daans; the dentist Fritz Pfeffer, who later joined them, became Albert Dussel, and so on. Anne's list of pseudonyms also stipulated changing her own family's last name to Robin, but Otto Frank elected to keep their actual names in the published diary.

Like Anne's own redaction, Otto Frank's posthumous version evolved from a private document (providing family members and acquaintances with a selection of what he considered essential parts of her writing) to a publishable work. He strove to respect Anne's original aspirations for the rewritten diary while responding to new circumstances. In addition to following her vision of a "romance" in diary form about her life in hiding, with the enigmatic title *Het Achterhuis*, Otto Frank regarded the book as a memorial to Anne and the others who had hidden with her and were murdered during the Holocaust. His decision to follow only partially Anne's list of pseudonyms exemplifies this larger, hybridized agenda. Retaining the Franks' actual names directly credited Anne as the diary's author; changing the names of the others, who had died and had no one to speak on their behalf (as Otto apparently did for his wife and daughters), protected them from any disrespect that might arise in Anne's ardent, candid writing and honored her authorial wishes.

This version of the diary—synthesized into a uniform text and considerably shorter than the full inventory of material recovered from the Annex in 1944—was submitted to publishers by acquaintances of Otto Frank, acting on his behalf. The text that was finally issued by the Amsterdam press Uitgeverij Contact in 1947 in an edition of 1,500 copies contained further emendations. Like some of the other presses that had considered the diary and rejected it, Contact requested excisions of passages dealing with Anne's discussion of menstruation and sexuality. With these deletions, which were approved by Otto Frank, the diary first appeared in book form. (Excerpts printed in the summer of 1946 in the intellectual journal *De Nieuwe Stem* mark the first publication of Anne's writing.)[19] Translations of the diary in the ensuing five years into German, French, and English each entailed slightly different redactions. For example, the German edition included passages about Anne's sexuality deleted in the Dutch edition.[20]

This complex history of redaction was not explained in either the diary's first editions or other accounts, such as interviews given by Otto Frank. A 1971 publication by the Anne Frank House does report that "Anne wrote fake names which she intended to use in case of publication [of the diary]. For the time being [i.e., while she was in hiding] the diary was her own secret which she wanted to keep from everyone." The account goes on to explain that, after the war, Otto Frank copied the manuscript for his mother, who had emigrated and was living in Switzerland with relatives. He left out some passages which he felt to be too intimate or which might hurt other people's feelings. The idea of publishing the diary did not enter his mind, but he wanted to show it to a few close friends. He gave one typed copy to a friend, who lent it to Jan Romein, a professor of modern history. Much to Otto Frank's surprise the professor devoted an article to it in a Dutch newspaper, *Het Parool*. His friends now urged Otto Frank to have Anne's diary published as she herself had wished.

This elliptical account of the diary's long path toward publication does not mention that it had been rejected by several publishers before Romein's article appeared on April 3, 1946, hailing the diary as an outstanding example of wartime documentation by a remarkably talented Jewish girl (whose name was not disclosed).[21] The account also offers a limited description of Anne's ambitions to turn her diary into a book and ignores the extent to which the others in hiding with her or who hid them were aware of her diary, if not the specifics of its contents. Rather, this account characterizes the diary as a confessional document of coming of age, a record of "the flowering of a charmingly feminine personality eager to face life with adult courage and mature self-insight."[22] This image of Anne as a model of integrity extends to her father, who redacts the diary with the feelings of others in mind. With regard to both its writing and its redaction, Anne and her diary are characterized as paradigms of awareness and sensitivity.

Publications

The diary received extensive international acclaim after its first publications, prompting more translations and new editions. Consequently, the diary became a more regulated entity. The Anne Frank Stichting was established in 1957 in part to oversee the diary's publication, and the Anne Frank-Fonds, inaugurated in 1963, now controls the rights to Anne's writings. At the same time, variations of the published diary have proliferated, beginning with its title. Few translations maintain the original title, which follows Anne's intention to name her account of life in hiding after the book's setting. Instead, most translations title the work "Diary" and usually include Anne's name in the title, thereby foregrounding the author and the genre, rather than the setting, and conjoining Anne's name with her writing. Moreover, in book form, the diary never stands on its own but is framed by cover art and text and by front and back matter. Each translation and each edition is distinguished by different framing images and texts, which mediate readers' encounter with the published diary itself.

The cover of the first Contact edition of Anne's diary presents an atmospheric, enigmatic image of dark, churning clouds, with a hint of sunlight behind them, over which the title, *Het Achterhuis*, appears in large, bright letters of flowing script. This has proved to be an exceptional cover among the many subsequent editions and is one of the more abstract in its design. While some early editions have very plain covers with no imagery, most published in the 1950s, 1960s, and early 1970s feature a cover image that directly alludes to the book's contents. Some covers include an illustration of a girl, whose features may not resemble Anne's but who appears young and pensive and is sometimes shown to be writing.[23] The dust jacket of the Modern Library edition of *The Diary of a Young Girl* (issued in the United States in 1952) shows a girl with short dark hair viewed from behind, wearing an armband with a yellow, six-pointed star—an unusual indication among early cover designs that the book concerns a Jew (and, more specifically, a Jew living under Nazi occupation). A few covers feature a photograph or illustration of the façade of 263 Prinsengracht, while others reproduce some element of Anne's original diary, either a sample of her handwriting or the first notebook's plaid cover. But since the 1950s the most common feature of covers of the diary is a photograph of Anne, either one of the portraits that she had pasted into her original diary notebook or another picture of her selected from family photographs. The repeated use of these images—the building, the plaid notebook, a photo of Anne—has established an iconography for the diary that has become an extension of Anne's life and work.

Although no text appears on the front cover of the first Dutch edition of *Het Achterhuis* other than the title, the author's name, and the description *Dagboekbrieven 14 Juni 1942–1 Augustus 1944,* some early translations feature promotional phrases on their covers. These include descriptions ("the intimate record of a young girl's thoughts written during two years in hiding from the Gestapo—to whom she was at last be-

Covers of Anne Frank's diary published in the 1950s and early 1960s, translated into English (New York), German (Frankfurt), Spanish (Buenos Aires), and Yiddish (Bucharest).

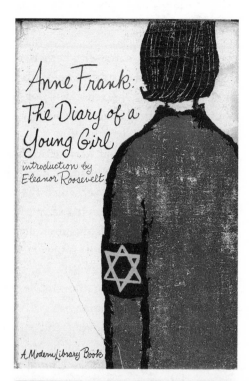

trayed"),[24] promotional copy ("Des pages pleines d'amour et d'angoisse qui ont déjà fait pleurer le monde entier"),[25] snippets from reviews ("'One of the most moving personal documents to come out of World War II'— *Philadelphia Inquirer*"),[26] or excerpts from the diary ("Ich glaube an das Gute in Menschen").[27] Some covers promote not only the book itself but also related mediations. The Yiddish translation published in Tel Aviv in 1958 includes photographs of the Israeli staging in Yiddish of *The Diary of Anne Frank,* the diary's authorized dramatization by Frances Goodrich and Albert Hackett. In conjunction with the diary's 1959 film adaptation, Scholastic Book Services issued a paperback edition of *The Diary of a Young Girl* with a full-cover portrait of actress Millie Perkins as Anne on the cover, which exhorts readers to "see George Stevens's Production" of the "20th Century-Fox Presentation." In 2009, Puffin Books issued a similar tie-in edition of the diary with color photographs of Ellie Kendrick as the star of the BBC's "major new television drama" based on the diary.

As most recent and current editions of the diary feature a cover photograph of Anne, her face is now widely recognized. This extensive familiarity has engendered further reproductions of her image in other media (for example, on commemorative postage stamps and medals) and inspired creative engagements, both literary and visual.[28] Among the range of photographs of Anne to appear on the covers of her published diary, there seems to be a greater tendency for earlier editions to use an image that emphasizes her youthfulness. For example, the first U.S. edition features a portrait of Anne taken by her father in 1939, several years before she began keeping her diary, a photo that she had pasted into her diary entry of October 10, 1942.[29] More recent editions offer a more mature image of Anne, sometimes photographed at a desk or table, looking up from the act of writing. (Of course, all these photographs were taken at some time before she went into hiding.) Although this trend may reflect changes in what images have been available to publishers, it also evinces a shift in how Anne Frank has been presented to the public. Whereas earlier editions tended to show Anne as the "young girl" of the title of the diary's first U.S. edition, thereby heightening a sense of her precociousness, more recent editions are likelier to present Anne as the adolescent writer.

Although Anne anticipated that her published diary required a preface and composed a general introduction in her revised version, published editions of the diary often feature an introduction by someone else, beginning with the first printing of *Het Achterhius*. Introductions to the earliest editions of the diary champion the merits of this work by a then unknown adolescent author. The introductions' authors marvel at Anne's literary talents, as well as her incisiveness and honesty, beyond her young years. And while some acknowledge the diary's value as a record of the war years, which was Anne's original motive for reworking it, these introductions typically stress its significance as transcending a particular experience. At the same time, some introductions situate the reading of Anne's diary for a particular audience defined by the language or country of publication.

Annie Romein-Verschoor, the wife of Jan Romein, wrote the preface to the first edition of *Het Achterhius;* together with her husband, she had tried to help find a publisher for the diary. Romein-Verschoor's preface champions the diary as "a war document, a document of the cruelty and heartbreaking misery of the persecution of the Jews, of human helpfulness and treason, of human adjustment and non-adjustment, of the small joys and the great and small miseries of life in hiding." However, she asserts, "the most important thing about this diary is not the documentation." Rather it is Anne's remarkable self-scrutiny, as she grew "from girl to woman," only to be cut tragically short, like a flower that "bloom[ed] once, richly and superabundantly, only to die soon after."[30] Similarly, Marie Baum, who had been a pioneering social worker in the Weimar Republic, wrote in her introduction to the first German edition of *Das Tagebuch der Anne Frank,* published in 1950, "Poor child! Poor Anne! The blossom, which one would have wished to see flourish and bear fruit, was broken. The beginnings remain, to which one turns one's eyes lovingly and movingly, in these pages." For an early postwar German readership coming to terms with its culpability for the genocide of European Jewry, Baum characterized reading the diary as an act of vicarious suffering and atonement:

> Once again, the unforgivable guilt of Jewish persecution descends upon us as a
> dreadful burden. We tremble with these poor imprisoned people, who, in order
> to escape the clutches of the police, "disappeared" into the hiding place offered

by generous Dutch friends. We breathe with them the trapped air of the Annex
on the Prinsengracht in Amsterdam, which they could never leave; we feel
their daily privations, the gnawing hunger, the distraught nerves. . . ."[31]

The first U.S. edition of *The Diary of a Young Girl* features a brief
introduction by Eleanor Roosevelt, which remained a fixture of U.S.
editions of the diary for decades. Even as she champions Anne's resilience—"the ultimate shining nobility of [the human] spirit"—in the face
of war's "degradation," Roosevelt notes that "Anne wrote and thought
much of the time about things which very sensitive and talented adolescents without the threat of death will write," and so "the diary tells us
much about ourselves. . . . I feel how close we all are to Anne's experience." As the gateway to the first edition of the diary published outside
a country that had been under Nazi control or direct attack during the
war, this introduction ignores issues of concern to West Europeans, such
as the diary's value as a document of wartime experience or warfare's
psychological impact on adolescents. Instead, Roosevelt praises Anne's
spiritual resolve, while ignoring her physical suffering, and emphasizes
her familiarity, while marginalizing her Europeanness and eliding her
Jewishness. Indeed, the introduction hails the book as a "monument"
not only to Anne's "fine spirit" but also "to the spirits of those who have
worked and are working still for peace."[32] Roosevelt's introduction later
became the subject of criticism and some controversy,[33] and it was ultimately dropped with the appearance of U.S. editions of the *Definitive
Edition*. Nevertheless, her words model an enduring American approach
to the diary as accessible and ennobling, with universal moral value.

Whereas the first U.S. edition of Anne's diary distances the text from
the larger circumstances of her persecution, these are foregrounded in
the first Russian translation, published in the Soviet Union in 1960. In
addition to translating Romein-Verschoor's preface to the Dutch edition, *Dnevnik Anny Frank* features an introduction by Ilya Ehrenburg.
This prominent Russian author wrote extensively about World War II
and assembled important early documentation of Nazi atrocities against
European Jewry, the publication of which was largely suppressed under
Stalin in the early postwar years.[34] Ehrenburg's introduction begins
by addressing the diary's phenomenal mediation, noting its "uncom-
mon destiny." A decade after its first publication, it was "translated into

seventeen languages, printed in millions of copies. Plays and films have been made from it, studies have been written about it." Ehrenburg situates Anne's life and work within the Holocaust, asserting that "it is well known that the Hitlerites murdered six million Jews, who were citizens of twenty nations, rich and poor, famous and unknown." The introduction addresses the origins of fascist anti-Semitism and reminds readers of its consequences—after years of public suppression in the Soviet Union of the particular character of Jewish persecution under Nazism—including the ease with which the Holocaust had receded from public attention:

> The moral is clear: in the middle of the twentieth century, it is possible for the murder of old people and children to go unpunished, and [it is possible] to destroy people with poisonous gas and then be silent about it, to wait for a while, so that fifteen years later one can see with satisfaction how young candidates march toward becoming executioners, toward perpetrating the murder of a people.... [Anne Frank's] diary reminds us all to prevent the perpetration of this crime: we cannot allow this to be repeated! Millions of readers know Anne Frank as if they saw her at home. Six million people who were guilty of nothing were destroyed. One pure, young voice lives—as evidence of these violent deaths.[35]

Ehrenburg invokes the international public's widespread familiarity with Anne as strategic for Holocaust remembrance and as the basis for moral exhortation against future genocide. One year after *Dnevnik Anny Frank* appeared, Yevgeny Yevtushenko published his poem "Babi Yar." A landmark of public acknowledgment in the Soviet Union of the Holocaust and Russian anti-Semitism, this poem in effect reverses Ehrenburg's extrapolation outward from Anne Frank's story. "Babi Yar" shifts from the Germans' murder of tens of thousands of Jews in the eponymous ravine in 1941 to a series of images of Jewish life and death, culminating in Anne's romance and arrest while in hiding.

As the diary's readership has expanded over time, so has the scope and format of new editions, especially with regard to providing introductory and contextual material. Some of these additions vaunt the diary's wide acclaim. The first U.S. paperback edition (published by Pocket Books in 1953) opens with excerpts from Roosevelt's introduction and reviews in the *New York Times* and *New York Herald Tribune*, then informs readers that the book "has been read and loved by hundreds of thousands of people all over the world. It is a classic of our time." The copyright page notes that the diary "has been translated into the Dutch [sic], German, French, Norwegian, Danish, Japanese, Hebrew, Swedish and Italian languages" and has "also been published in a British edition." Noting that the diary had been serialized in a dozen U.S. newspapers and a condensed version published in *Commentary* in May-June 1952, the paperback assures readers that it "includes every word contained in the original, high-priced edition." A note on the next page explains the book's original title and the rendering of *Achterhuis* in the translation as "Secret Annexe." Roosevelt's introduction follows, then a page presents the opening inscription from the original diary, reproduced in Anne's handwriting and then translated—"I hope I shall be able to confide in you completely, as I have never been able to do in anyone before, and I hope that you will be a great support and comfort to me." After this epigraph, the first diary entry, dated Sunday, June 14, 1942, appears, in which Anne describes receiving the notebook in which she began to keep the diary.[36] This sequence of prefatory texts positions the reader within a publishing phenomenon of international scope with an array of reading options, as it moves from presenting a mass phenomenon with universal appeal to framing the diary's private, intimate origins.

In his landmark 1952 review for the *New York Times,* author Meyer Levin wrote that "Anne Frank's diary is too tenderly intimate a book to be frozen with the label 'classic.'"[37] Yet editions of the diary soon hailed it as a "classic," implying an established value for the book that is both widespread and enduring.[38] The 1972 "Enriched Classics edition," published by Washington Square Press, vaunts the diary's popularity, while extensive supplementary material testifies to the need to contextualize the diary as well as its reception. This edition opens with a page extolling the book as having been translated "into nearly a score of languages including German," selling "over 5 million copies in its American edition alone," and having an "acclaim" that includes awards for its stage and film adaptations. The same sequence of the note about the term *Achterhuis,* Roosevelt's introduction, and Anne's opening inscription follows, leading to the diary's first entry. The middle of the paperback features a sixty-four-page "Reader's Supplement," which opens with a "Biographical Background" on Anne and a "Historical Background" on the Nazi era.[39] A series of photographs—ranging from the house in Frankfurt where Anne was born to stills from the diary's 1959 film adaptation—follows, each keyed to a particular diary passage. Next is a list of "Literary Allusions and Notes," followed by twenty-two "Critical Excerpts," including selections from prefaces to other translations of the diary, critical assessments, and reviews of the diary and its dramatic adaptation, and concluding with reflections that Israel's prime minister, Golda Meir, wrote in the guest book of the Anne Frank House. Even as this edition brings readers into the diary's extensive community of devotees, some of them prominent, the supplement configures the reading as requiring considerable support material.

With greater distance from the war years, the "Enriched Classics edition" strives to situate the diary within a historical epoch. This entails explaining not only the rise of Nazism and its consequences, but also period ephemera (e.g., Anne's reference to *Rin-Tin-Tin*). Moreover, engaging the diary—though stage and screen adaptations, visits to the Anne Frank House, and reading others' responses to Anne's work—is recognized as a subject of interest in its own right and is imbricated with the reading experience. Although these supplementary materials are extensive and wide-ranging, they may be considered extensions of Anne's own impulses in writing and rewriting her diary. Her revisions took into account the need to contextualize the circumstances of her hiding and incorporated her own reflections on rereading her original entries. The photographs of the film version of the diary might even be regarded as fulfillments of Anne's dreams of celebrity. In her original diary, Anne wrote next to one of the portraits that she pasted into the notebook: "This is a photograph of me as I wish to look all the time. Then I might still have a chance of getting to Hollywood. But at present, I'm afraid, I usually look quite different."[40]

The expansion of supplementary matter in published editions of the diary culminates in *The Diary of Anne Frank: The Critical Edition*, first published in Dutch in 1986 by the Netherlands State Institute for War Documentation. This edition presents the diary as the subject of comprehensive scholarly scrutiny and is meant to enable further study of the diary on an advanced level, especially analysis of its composition and redaction. Rather than championing the diary as a "classic," which intimates a timeless, absolute work of art, the *Critical Edition* foregrounds the diary's complex history of creation, which hitherto had not been fully shared with the public.

Unlike previous published versions, this edition does not offer readers the diary as a redacted synthesis of Anne's different manuscripts, but presents three versions—Anne's first diary, her rewritten diary, and Otto Frank's edited version, published as *Het Achterhuis*—in parallel texts, allowing for ready comparison among them. Striving to present the original manuscripts accurately, the text is coordinated to original page numbers, and reproductions show photographs, drawings, or other insertions or graphic elements of the original manuscript. The text also indicates cross-outs, underscoring, spelling irregularities, and marginal notes, as well as variations in script (cursive vs. printing) and medium (different colors of ink and pencil). The parallel diary texts are preceded by 174 pages of front matter, including: background on Anne's life; an account of her final months following her arrest; the history of the diary's writing and publication; the creation of Goodrich and Hackett's authorized dramatization. The last and longest section of the *Critical Edition*'s prefatory materials recounts "attacks on the authenticity of the diary" with an extensive summary of the diary's examination by the State Forensic Science Laboratory for the Netherlands State Institute for War Documentation, authenticating the original diaries as being written by Anne Frank during the war.

Publishing the diary in this variorum format both validates the diary's authenticity and presents its complex history of composition to the general public, enabling a new kind of reading experience and scholarly examination. As the *Critical Edition* extolled Anne's literary talents—noting that its format enables readers to see "how her thinking and ability to write developed during her two years in hiding"[41]—it also pointed up her father's complicated role in mediating her writing, with consequences for approaching the diary as document and as literature. The editors of the *Critical Edition* note that Otto Frank was committed to publishing what he considered "the essence" of his daughter's "literary bequest . . . in what appeared to him a fit and proper manner." As the diary came to be regarded "as a historical document rather than as a work of literature," his convictions as to how the diary should appear in published form "did not make it easier to ward off attacks on the book."[42] Since the publication of the *Critical Edition,* Otto Frank's posthumous redacting of the diary is perhaps most often discussed as an act of restriction—especially following the discovery of passages omitted from the diary that reveal Anne's awareness of her parents' troubled marriage. At the same time, Otto Frank's redactions might also be understood as continuing his wartime role of safeguarding the diary. While in hiding, he explained in interviews, Anne would give him the diary at night for safekeeping, and he kept it locked in a briefcase by his bed.[43] This information testifies not only to the extraordinary circumstances under which Anne wrote her diary, but also to its singular place in her life in hiding.

In 1991 the Anne Frank-Fonds issued *The Diary of a Young Girl: The Definitive Edition,* providing the general reader with a new version that reckons with the *Critical Edition*'s revelations of the full scope of Anne's writing and its history of revisions. An English-language translation of the *Definitive Edition* appeared in 1995. Billed as the diary's "First Complete and Intimate Version," the *Definitive Edition* offers a new synthesis of Anne's two incomplete versions that is some 30 percent longer than Otto Frank's early postwar redaction. Nevertheless, the *Definitive Edition* asserts its compatibility with the diary's earlier published version. The introduction to this new edition maintains that it "in no way affects the integrity of the old one originally edited by Otto Frank, . . . which brought the diary and its message to millions of people."[44] Indeed, although he had passed away more than a decade earlier, Otto Frank is listed as this edition's co-editor. At the same time, the *Definitive Edition* features new front matter. The (uncredited) foreword chronicles the writing, rewriting, and publishing history of the diary, and it explains the use of pseudonyms for some of the people mentioned in the text, as well as the redaction of the *Definitive Edition* itself. The opening inscription, both in Anne's hand and in English translation, a staple of earlier editions, follows, but there is no other introduction that exhorts the reader to mourn Anne's murder or that celebrates her precocious talents or universal message. Rather, the focus of the prefatory material is on the text itself; Anne's renown and importance are assumed, as is proper affective response to the diary.

Notwithstanding efforts to authenticate the diary as a definitive text with a stable history, public discussion continued to trouble this image. In 1998, reports that five pages of Anne's revised version of her diary had been withheld from previous editions made front-page news. Revealing Anne's candid observations of her parents' unhappy relationship, these pages also evince a complicated understanding of her writing. As she reworked it for a public readership, Anne wrote of the diary on one of these rediscovered pages, "I shall . . . take care that nobody can lay hands on it."[45] Even this complication enriches the diary's value as a text with a layered history of composition, redaction, translation, adaptation, reception, and scrutiny.[46]

In contrast to the varied and sometimes extensive front matter included in the diary's published editions, its epilogue has consistently been relatively terse and blunt. The first edition of *Het Achterhuis* concludes with a brief account, less than one-half page in length. Prepared by Cauvern (though uncredited),[47] the epilogue reports the arrests of the eight Jews hiding in the Annex, as well as two of the people who hid them, on August 4, 1944; the Gestapo's ransacking of the Annex, followed by the retrieval of Anne's diary by Miep Gies and her colleague Elisabeth Voskuijl; Otto Frank's return after the war, the only one of the eight hidden Jews to survive; and Anne's death in March 1945 in Bergen-Belsen. This epilogue appeared in most translations of the diary during the first four decades of its publication history. The *Definitive Edition* concludes with an expanded afterword, running several pages. It also begins with information on the arrests of August 4, 1944, and then details the fates of the seven Jews hidden in the Annex who perished during the war and provides postwar histories of the men and women who helped hide Anne and the others. The afterword ends not with the death of Anne but of Otto Frank in 1980—after "devot[ing] himself to sharing the message of his daughter's diary with people all over the world"—further consolidating his postwar activities centered on the diary with Anne's writing and her motive for doing so.[48]

The epilogue—whether its original form or the revised version in the *Definitive Edition*—marks the diary's abrupt "ending" with Anne's final entry. This ending is, in fact, an interruption of a work-in-progress—not only of a diary, which by its nature is open-ended, but also of a book in the midst of being both written and rewritten, which its author envisioned she would live to see published after the war. Even more striking is the disparity between the inspirational exhortations offered in the introductions to the diary's first published editions and the epilogue's sobering news of Anne's fate, offered without words of uplift or comfort. Leaving readers with unanswered questions about Anne's life, this disparity creates an opening that some mediations of the diary seek to address, whether by filling in what is known about her last seven months of life or by imagining an alternate ending to her story. More generally, the diary's lack of a complete moral or affective resolution has inspired extensive postulating on the significance of Anne's life and work in many works that the diary has inspired.

Materializations

The complex history of the composition of Anne's diary presented in the *Critical Edition* engendered a new level of interest in the original manuscript as a physical object, a subject of attention for decades. Indeed, the original diary is doubtless the most famous example of what literary scholar Bożena Shallcross terms *precarium*—texts handed over or hidden, in the hopes that they will "be returned to their owners upon a positive change of situation"—produced during the Holocaust, notwithstanding the fact that, as Shallcross notes, *precarium* were generated "on an epidemic scale" during the genocide.[49] Pictures of the first notebook in which Anne began writing diary entries, with its plaid cloth cover and metal lock, have appeared in published editions of the diary since the early 1950s; these pictures have also been reproduced more recently in books and on websites about Anne. The original diary has long been displayed in Amsterdam's Anne Frank House, and facsimiles have been exhibited in other venues. Even Anne's *zinnenboek*—her collection of excerpts from works by Goethe, Shakespeare, Wilde, and other writers she read while in hiding, copied into a narrow ledger—was published in a facsimile edition in 2004.[50]

Covers of published editions of the diary sometimes depict the plaid covering of the original diary's first notebook, thereby intimating to readers that opening the book parallels opening Anne's actual diary. Examples date back to the late 1950s, when a Yiddish translation published in Buenos Aires was issued with a plaid cloth cover and clasp that evokes the original notebook.[51] The plaid pattern of the notebook's cover is also reproduced on packaging for audio and video recordings of the diary and its adaptations, becoming, in effect, a form of branding for Anne Frank. While inherently bound to Anne's writing, the diary's iconic value as a material object has a history of its own, which has both enhanced and complicated the diary's mediation.

Consider, for example, the physical appearance of the diary in stage and film adaptations. As Leshu Torchin notes, the appearance of the plaid notebook figures strategically in these dramatizations of the diary as a device that bridges the gap between cinematic storytelling and the diary's first-person narrative.[52] Goodrich and Hackett's stage version does not specify the appearance of Anne's diary; stage directions describe it as a "paperbound" or "pasteboard-bound book."[53] However, the 1959 film version of *The Diary of Anne Frank* uses a careful reproduction of the original diary, including Anne's handwriting in Dutch and the inserted photographs of the actual Anne Frank, rather than pictures of Millie Perkins as Anne. Torchin notes that, although this scene uses a prop with authoritative verisimilitude, the action diverges from the actual history of when and how Miep Gies gave Anne's father her manuscripts. The film, like the stage play, portrays Anne writing entries only in one notebook, which is implicitly the equivalent of the single published volume then familiar to readers. Following the publication of the *Critical Edition,* television dramas about Anne Frank have depicted her writing and rewriting process, including her need for new notebooks to continue her diary. As these telecasts proffer "The Whole Story" of her life (this the subtitle of the 2001 ABC miniseries about Anne), they present the diary's amalgam of notebooks and papers. By the time Wendy Kesselman's authorized revision of *The Diary of Anne Frank* opened on Broadway in 1997, the diary's appearance was an established icon; the script's prop list specifies a "diary in red and white checkered cloth." Moreover, the diary's presence literally looms larger in this revised version of the play. At its conclusion, Otto Frank describes Anne's death, then picks up the diary from the floor, saying "All that remains." The stage directions explain that, as he opens the notebook, "the image of Anne's words fills the stage," before the lights fade to black.[54]

A reproduction of the diary's opening inscription in Anne's handwriting has been a staple of published editions since its first translations in the early 1950s. This inscription gestures to the book's origins as a private document and, like editions with a plaid cover, links reading the published diary with the intimacy of having a look at her actual manuscript. This sample also betokens the diary's authenticity as a historical document, a fact that has entailed a continued need for defense. The published diary's enormous popularity has enhanced the text's evidentiary value far beyond the scope of Anne's chronicle of her wartime experiences. Consequently, Holocaust deniers have regularly attacked the diary's authenticity since the late 1950s. According to historian Deborah Lipstadt, these attacks repeat the same unfounded claims, recycling old misinformation.[55] In response, both the Anne Frank-Fonds and the Dutch government undertook a series of analyses of the original diary to demonstrate that the writing is, in fact, from Anne's hand (based on comparison with known samples of her script) and the materials used were available in the Netherlands during the early 1940s.

Earlier analyses of Anne's handwriting by graphologists extended beyond historical authentication and validated the young author's exceptional character under extraordinary circumstances. Dr. Mina Becker, a graphologist and psychologist, examined the diary in 1960 for a legal proceeding concerning the manuscript's authenticity. Becker not only verified the writing as Anne's but also analyzed her personality as having "reached a maturity which one generally finds only in people of middle age." According to Becker, Anne's handwriting also evinced "a decline in physical health and lack of physical activity and fresh air."[56] In 1967 Dr. Erhard Friess, another graphologist, published his own analysis of Anne's character as reflected in her handwriting, including the following observations:

> The gifted young author has at her disposition a mind that is above average, highly differentiated, lively and empathic. Much can be hoped for from her good habits of mental discipline. Her capacity for good judgment is apparent in her orderliness, clarity, accuracy, multiple relations, marked independence,

thorough objectivity, and spiritedness; however, minor lapses of judgment are
by no means excluded. It is quite unmistakable that her powers of imagination
are far above average; these strike a good balance between a happy fantasy and
compelling logic.[57]

Articulated as though the subject were still alive, these observations
isolate the issue of personality, evinced by handwriting, from the writer's actual life—and death. This analysis implicitly immortalizes Anne's
character, as embodied in her work.

In the early 1980s, the State Forensic Science Laboratory of the
Dutch Ministry of Justice subjected Anne's original notebooks and papers to extensive scrutiny, resulting in a 270-page report authenticating
these as the work of Anne's hand, written with materials available during
the years 1942–1944. An abbreviated version of the report, which appears in the diary's *Critical Edition,* explains that this analysis "has been
based on purely technical considerations. Thus the relationship between
handwriting and personality traits has been ignored. That relationship—
which in the case under investigation might well have been influenced
by the age and the exceptional life situation of the alleged writer of the
diary—falls into the province of graphology or grapho-analysis."[58] In
this report, defending the manuscript's validity entails a separate meth-
odology from appreciating the literary merits or inspirational value of
the text and, by extension, its author. Holocaust deniers' false allegations
are refuted by scrutinizing the diary solely as a material object through
the dispassionate science of forensics.

Attention to Anne's original diary as a physical object extends to
various facsimiles, which are at least as concerned with its materiality as
with its contents, if not sometimes more so. Such is the case for the Anne
Frank Hollow Book Secret Safe, made by Secret Safe Books of Chicago
in 2009. Crafted from an actual published edition of the diary, the hollow
book preserves "the original flyleaf which features [a reproduction of]
Anne's handwriting, to line the interior" and includes a "hidden embedded magnetic closure." Although Anne's text has been excised, her story
nonetheless endows this hollow book with special significance as a secret
cache. The hollow book's creator explains that, "Just as dear Miss Anne
Frank and her family hid behind the thin walls of a place that was in plain
view, you can keep your own valuables safe and secure within the walls

Keychain, made in the United States by Novelkeys, with a pewter miniature of Anne Frank's diary. The back of the book reproduces a citation from the March 6, 1944, entry: "At such moments I don't think about all the misery, but about the beauty that still remains."

of Anne's diary, in plain view."[59] This copy of the diary abounds with metaphors of hiding, a material analogy of the hinged bookcase and the Annex that it concealed.

Miniatures of the diary—both the original plaid notebook and published editions—have been made for doll houses, and a souvenir keychain, sold in the bookstore of the United States Holocaust Memorial Museum in Washington, D.C., in the mid-1990s, takes the form of a small book. The front features Anne's name and portrait; the back reproduces an inspirational citation from the diary. The keychain offers Anne's iconic name, face, and book not merely as a novelty or souvenir of a museum visit, but as a talisman—perhaps meant to be carried on journeys like a St. Christopher's medal or, to use a Jewish example, a copy of *tefilat haderekh* (the prayer for travelers), using not a sacred image or text but the materialization of Anne's life and work as a source of reassurance.

Complementing these miniatures of Anne's diary is a gigantic replication: oversized excerpts from the diary are reproduced, in her handwriting, on the façade of the Montessori School that Anne attended in Amsterdam as a child. Literary scholar Susan Stewart notes that such disproportionately scaled productions establish a "divergent relation between meaning and materiality" and demand attention to "the immediate relation between . . . materiality and the human scale." The miniature book, by contrast, generally invokes an "exaggeration of interiority" and

Anne Frank Schule Rivierenbuurt, the Montessori School in Amsterdam attended by Anne Frank in the 1930s, now bears her name and features a tile façade decorated with an oversized reproduction of Anne's handwriting from her diary. *Courtesy of the Anne Frank Schule Rivierenbuurt, Amsterdam*

the "limited . . . physical scope" of childhood, issues especially resonant with Anne's diary. The gigantic book—in effect, a public monument—constitutes "a fixing of the symbols of public life." The scale endows Anne's diary with the authoritative, didactic power of public art, especially evident "in the function of the inscription; one is expected to read the instructions for perception of the work."[60]

Responding to increased scholarly attention to the original diary, the Anne Frank House, which holds the original manuscripts, commissioned two facsimiles of the various notebooks and loose pages in the late 1990s. Five years in the making, these facsimiles have a powerful symbolic significance beyond their instrumental value for scholarship and preservation. The Anne Frank House characterizes the facsimiles as fulfilling Anne's wish, expressed in her diary on April 5, 1944, "to go on living even after [her] death," explaining: "The extraordinary facsimiles of Anne Frank's diary texts, which have now been brought to life, were created not only with professional expertise but with love as well and they exceed our expectations."

The description of the painstaking process of the facsimiles' fabrication is a remarkable document in itself, testimony to the extraordinary symbolic investment behind the project. For the facsimile of the first diary notebook, vintage postage stamps like those on items pasted into the diary were found and then

> cancelled in the same color ink with a postmark stamp refashioned just for this purpose. In order to recreate the red and white cloth covering of Anne's first diary, the project's weaver counted the threads of the original linen, found the right gauge thread, dyed the sample thread, determined the recurring pattern of the weave and wove a few feet of matching material. The diary's lock, with its small moving part, is strangely tarnished. It therefore took many attempts before the locksmith was able to copy the metal in terms of color and corrosion and until an acceptable replica of the original was created. In this way, everything needed to produce a facsimile of this album—as well as all the elements Anne included in her diary—was copied with painstaking attention.[61]

This savoring of the effort to replicate the physical diaries marks it as a devotional act, undertaken "with love." Moreover, characterizing the facsimiles as bringing the diary "to life" offers them as fulfilling Anne's (and many readers') desire for her to go on living after death through her words. These sentiments intimate that, even though they were conceived as aids to scholarly research, these facsimiles are somehow magical.

In fabricating the facsimiles, special pains were taken to reproduce the photographs of Anne in her diaries. Anne pasted nineteen photos of herself into the diary's first notebook, including its inside front cover, and she wrote captions assessing her appearance in these images. Indeed, the first inscription in the original diary is a comment on her self-styled frontispiece: "Gorgeous photograph isn't it!!!!"[62] Some of these photographs are widely familiar, in part through reproduction on the covers of the diary's published editions. As a consequence, they figure frequently in imaginary engagements with Anne, including other works of literature.

Several authors discuss contemplating Anne Frank's portrait in their own writing, including Chilean poet Marjorie Agosín, who, as a young girl, received a small photograph of Anne from her grandfather. Agosín writes: "There was something in her face, in her aspect, and in her age that reminded me of myself. I imagined her playing with my sisters and reading fragments of her diary to us."[63] Caribbean author Caryl Phillips explained in a 1998 essay that "for the past ten years or so I have worked with a large poster of Anne Frank above my desk. In some strange way she was partly responsible for my beginning to write, and as long as I continue to write her presence is a comforting one."[64] Phillips explained that learning about the Holocaust as a boy in England, where he and his family had emigrated from his native St. Kitts, prompted him to write his first short story, which, like other fiction he has written, links auto-biographical plots with stories of European anti-Semitism.

Even as these photographs inform imagined engagements with Anne, responsive to the intimacy of reading her diary, they pose a distinctive challenge. As they were all taken before she went into hiding, readers must imagine what changes took place in her appearance during those two years, as she went through puberty and grew in size, issues discussed in the diary. In light of Anne's attention to her appearance in photographs, it is not surprising that the desire to imagine her is sometimes realized in photographic form. Especially striking is a digitally altered image that projects what Anne would look like had she survived the Holocaust and lived to celebrate her eightieth birthday in 2009. The photograph was created for the Anne Frank Trust UK, based in London, to mark Anne's birthday and thereby promote awareness of the Holocaust. The Trust also used the image "to encourage British students to consider what kinds of lives they want to lead" by launching "a competition for children to write a letter to their own 80-year-old selves in the future."[65] The Michigan-based firm Phojoe created the image of an eighty-year-old Anne with "forensic compositing" techniques, usually employed to simulate age progression "to help investigators solve crimes. and find missing people."[66] Besides conjuring Anne Frank as living into old age, the composite photograph also implicitly imagines solving the crime of her murder by undoing it, thereby restoring the diary's "missing" author to her public.

A Book with a House / A House with a Story

The diary's first published editions neither reference Anne's inclusion of photographs or drawings in her first notebook nor reproduce them (save the author's portrait, as a frontispiece or on the cover). However, these books do often include another graphic, which does not appear in Anne's manuscripts. Beginning with the first edition of *Het Achterhuis*, many published versions of the diary include a ground plan of the three main floors of 263 Prinsengracht. Appearing in this first edition opposite entries dated June 20 and 21, 1942, the plan occupies a full page. This illustration shows each floor's layout and indicates the role of each room during the period that Anne and the others hid in the rear of the building's upper two stories. Rooms used by Opekta and Pectacon are labeled according to their function (front office, store room, etc.); rooms in the Annex show beds, cabinets, and other furnishings used by the Jews hidden there. The diagram calls special attention to the hinged bookcase linking the hiding place to the business offices; a caption explains: "On the second floor the hinged bookcase connects the landing with the Annex [Achterhuis]."[67] Some editions that do not include the ground plan present one or more photographs of 263 Prinsengracht, especially of the bookcase in both closed and open positions.

In the first Dutch publication, the ground plan appears beside entries dated two weeks before any discussion of Anne and her family going into hiding (first mentioned on July 5, 1942). In subsequent editions, the ground plan usually appears within the entry of July 9, 1942, in which Anne describes the layout of the Annex at length. Anne wrote this account not when the Franks first arrived there but when she revised the diary almost two years later. Although the decision to include the ground plan in the published diary was made posthumously, it extends Anne's authorial impulse to provide readers with a detailed, comprehensive overview of the place in which the ensuing text is set.

Reproducing a ground plan is unusual in a book not about architecture. But seldom has a text been so closely identified with a building as Anne's diary, beginning with its original title, which identifies the book with its setting. Although the ground plan provides a useful reference tool for readers, its presence is not simply instrumental. Rather, the ground plan reinforces the interrelation of text and place for readers by inviting them to envision with architectural specificity the rooms in which the ensuing twenty-five months of diary entries take place. Guided by this diagram, readers can imagine moving about the space where the diary was written and the experiences it chronicles unfolded.

It is not surprising, then, that by the mid-1950s the diary's international success attracted visitors to 263 Prinsengracht. Tours of the unused building were arranged by appointment; these were led at first by Johannes Kleiman, one of Otto Frank's employees who had helped hide the Jews in the Annex. Earlier in the decade the textile company Berghaus bought the block of houses including 263 Prinsengracht, intending to raze the structures and build new offices. This plan was never realized, in part due to efforts to save what came to be known as the Anne Frank House. In 1955 a Dutch newspaper decried the impending demolition of "Anne Frank's Secret Annexe" and argued that it had become an unofficial "monument," noting that "for years now . . . the manuscript of Anne's diary [is] . . . kept here and shown to visitors."[68] The Anne Frank Stichting played a strategic role in raising funds to renovate the building, which Berghaus donated to the foundation for the purposes of creating a cultural center. The Anne Frank House and Museum, which includes both 263 Prinsengracht and an adjoining building, officially opened in 1960 and soon became one of Amsterdam's most frequently visited tourist attractions.[69]

Visitors to the Annex find themselves in a skeletal space, not unlike the ground plan reproduced in the book; the rooms are labeled according to their function during the period of the diary but are largely empty of furniture or other items that would have been used by Anne and the others in hiding. The most striking remnants of Anne's presence in the Annex are the photographs of movie stars and other pictures that she put up on the walls of her room (now behind protective glass) and marks on the wall in Otto and Edith Frank's room, charting their daughters' growth while in hiding. For those who have read the diary, the power of the visit lies in the opportunity to enter the spaces limned in the two-dimensional ground plan, to inhabit briefly the actual space where so much activity familiar from Anne's writing took place, and to fill the empty rooms with details recalled from reading. The visit is therefore an encounter with both Anne's experience in hiding and the visitor's experience of reading the diary.

After passing through the admission area of the Anne Frank House, visitors proceed through 263 Prinsengracht much as Anne did on the day she and her family arrived to go into hiding, walking from the front, ground level of the building up and back to the Annex—moving from the public to the covert and from light into darkness. But then, the Anne Frank House guides readers through a different narration of the events as recounted in the diary. For even though Anne's writing motivates visits to the building now bearing her name, the site imposes its own form onto the telling of her story by dint of its architecture and the protocols of visiting a museum, especially one that is also a historical house, ostensibly taking visitors "back in time."[70] Readers' progress through Anne's diary is defined by time, measured by dated entries, but visitors' movement through the Anne Frank House is defined by space, articulated by proceeding from room to room along a prescribed path. Museum-goers then exit into the adjoining building to continue their visit; readers, by contrast, "enter" the building with Anne on July 6, 1942, and then circulate among its rooms, never "leaving"—except by way of the book's epilogue.

Although the configuration of tours of the Anne Frank House has changed over the years (especially following major renovations in the early 1970s and the mid-1990s), the visit has always framed a walk through the Annex with displays of introductory material—providing context on Anne and her family, the building, and the Nazi era—followed by more displays after visiting the Annex. These displays have offered additional information about the fate of the eight Jews who hid in the building following their arrest, as well as the postwar lives of the people who had hid them. The centerpiece of the exhibition that now follows the tour of the house is Anne's original diary notebook, displayed by itself in a vitrine. Just as published editions of the diary include expanded information about the historical context of Anne's life and work and about the diary's larger significance for a worldwide readership, the Anne Frank House has expanded displays and other productions to enhance the historical and moral significance of encountering the building and the diary as material objects.

In addition to displays relating specifically to Jewish persecution under Nazism, the Anne Frank House has mounted exhibitions on human rights issues unrelated to the Holocaust, following Otto Frank's wish that the institution "should not be a war museum or a shrine, but . . . a place where the post-war generation could seek ways to work for peace."[71] Past exhibitions have examined South Africa's policy of apartheid, the war in Vietnam, right-wing extremism in Europe, and Israel's occupation of Palestinian territories. More recently, the Anne Frank House installed an interactive video presentation, titled "Free2choose: The Limits of Freedom," which addresses a series of contemporary debates on human rights issues, such as the right of Sikh men to wear turbans while serving as policemen in Great Britain, or the challenges that the 2001 U.S. Patriot Act poses to Americans' right to privacy. The Anne Frank House explains that the connection between "fundamental liberties" and Anne's story is "simple: Nazi ideology sought to create a society where all freedoms were controlled. This system was used to plan the assassination of millions of human beings," including Anne. "Fighting for the respect of fundamental liberties and for equality for all people are the major lessons of this era and constitute the basis for all democracies established after the war."[72] Just as published editions of the diary frame Anne's entries with contextual information and moral exhortation, the Anne Frank House frames the time visitors spend in the rooms that are central to the diary with background information on the Nazi era, especially in the Netherlands, and with displays inviting visitors to extend the moral inspiration provided by encountering Anne's hiding place to other, contemporary human rights concerns.

Configuring the museum visit in relation to the diary narrative has prompted different approaches over the years. The renovation of the mid-1990s expanded the restored areas to include the Opekta and Pectacon offices in the building's front half, reflecting the site's value for remembering not only the eight Jews in hiding but also the people who hid them—and, possibly, betrayed them. Before the renovation, the windows of the Annex were uncovered. As literary scholar James Young observed at the time, "light floods into the annex . . . , children lean out of the great windows," whereas during the war, "Anne's only exposure to the outside world . . . was through a small square window in the attic."[73]

Following the renovation, the windows of the Annex were covered with black panels. Simulating the blackout cloths used when Anne wrote her diary there, these panels convey to visitors the cramped, isolated existence of the Jews in hiding.

Another key difference between the building as described in the diary and as experienced by visitors is the bareness of its restored rooms, in keeping with Otto Frank's wishes. A furnished scale model of the Annex was created in 1961 for display inside the museum. In the 1990s, the Anne Frank House created a more elaborate model of the building, as it appeared in the early 1940s, in the form of a CD-ROM, which enables users to take a virtual tour of 263 Prinsengracht that is quite different from a visit to the actual site. For the purposes of the CD-ROM, the restored rooms of the building were dressed with period furniture and artifacts, recreating the environment as inhabited from 1942 to 1944 by the Opekta and Pectacon employees in the building's front half and the Jews in hiding in the Annex. Users can employ the computer's mouse to "move" through the rooms, explore them with a panoptic "gaze," and click on selected items for audio commentary, accompanied by apposite passages from Anne's diary. For example, in the "Frank family room," an open copy of Charles Dickens's *Sketches by Boz* lies on a bed, next to an eyeglass case. The audio narrative explains that Dickens was Otto Frank's favorite author and cites Anne's description, in her entry of August 23, 1943, of her father's reading. Sound effects—creaking stairs, a dripping faucet, church bells—enhance the illusion of walking about the building while its wartime occupants are nearby in other rooms.

The CD-ROM links its virtual tour to a three-dimensional schematic model of the building, which enables users to skip from room to room at will. Subtitled *A House with a Story,* the CD-ROM uses the hyperlinking capabilities of digital technology to imbricate book and building in a complex new configuration. The CD-ROM organizes the narrative not by following either the diary's chronology or the museumgoer's prescribed path, but according to users' idiosyncratic searches of individual rooms and their contents. Everything that users encounter in this virtual tour ultimately leads back to the diary; spaces are labeled according to people it mentions, and objects cue particular entries. Yet even as this virtual tour centers on the diary, the CD-ROM tells a different story—not only of Anne Frank but also of 263 Prinsengracht, providing a timeline of the building that begins before Anne and her family go into hiding and concludes with the establishment of the Anne Frank House itself. As a sign that the CD-ROM's narrative differs from the diary, the disc was sold in the United States along with a paperback copy of the *Definitive Edition*.[74] Further complicating the diary's interrelation with the building, the renovated Anne Frank House now provides computer stations where museum-goers can take the CD-ROM's virtual tour after visiting the actual building.[75] And, before departing, they can purchase a copy of the diary, available in Dutch as well as several translations, in the museum's bookshop.

Under the roof of 263 Prinsengracht, Anne's original diary manuscripts repose amid this complex of mediations. Readers (and potential readers) of published versions of the diary circulate among the building's empty rooms and, as they do so, among the layers of Anne's story—written and rewritten, translated and edited, published and materialized, inhabited and imagined. Even as these layers of mediation are often conflated or elided, they inform the millions of readers' encounters with Anne's life and work. Indeed, readers' discovery of these layers expands the story of Anne's life beyond her short years into another, ongoing narrative about creating, sharing, and engaging with a single life story through a multitude of mediations.

2

Anne Frank from
Page to Stage

Edna Nahshon

Scene: Apartment kitchen, Upper West Side, New York City.

Time: Shortly before Passover, spring 1997.

Characters: the Author of this essay; her Son, a high-school senior, helping in the kitchen.

Author (focused on chopping vegetables, chatting casually): So, what are your friends doing for the holiday?

Son: Well, David is having a seder at home, Avi is going to relatives on Long Island.

Author: And Ruth?

Son: Ruth's family has an invitation for the second seder, but her mom doesn't know how to prepare a seder and she wanted to do "something Jewish," so she bought theater tickets for *Anne Frank.*

Although this conversation—which took place when *The Diary of Anne Frank* enjoyed its first Broadway revival in forty-two years—may seem trivial, it raises key issues about the play. First is the use of theater as a "sacred space" to affirm an ethno-religious identity and moral code. Attending a performance of this play in lieu of a Passover seder may not be a common practice, but the notion that seeing *The Diary of Anne Frank* is an exceptional, morally galvanizing experience has a considerable history, dating back to the play's first production. As literary scholars Peter Brooks and John G. Cawelti have argued, the dramatic and literary form of melodrama, of which *The Diary of Anne Frank* is an example, developed in post-sacred cultures in order to satisfy their need for a secular system of ethics. When replacing the church or synagogue as the forum for contemplating the nature of good and evil, the theater has the power of endowing everyday life with a moral order.[1]

Second is the position of Anne Frank, who by 1997 was a widely familiar iconic figure, in this morally charged experience. Since its premiere in 1955, *The Diary of Anne Frank* has played a prominent role in familiarizing people around the world with Anne's life and work. At the same time, each production of the play has engaged the sensibilities of its audience, situated in a particular location and historical moment. Examining the creation of *The Diary of Anne Frank* in the context of its original Broadway production and its premieres in Germany, the Netherlands, and Israel provides insight into how this play became such an influential mediation of Anne Frank, even as it responded to different performance contexts. This examination also reveals a remarkable history of debates about the play's creation, form, and approach to its subject. Rather than limiting the impact of *The Diary of Anne Frank*, these debates have become part of its significance, further distinguishing it as a cultural phenomenon.

The notion that the theatrical adaptation of Anne Frank's diary was an enterprise of exceptional significance was already in place at the time of its creation. The play's initial productions, first in the United States and later in Europe and Israel, were highly charged events, widely understood as cultural milestones. Critical assessments of the play were frequently more concerned with its moral, historical, or political implications than with aesthetic considerations and particulars of theatrical interpretation. And though over the years a growing number of scholars and critics have found fault with aspects of *The Diary of Anne Frank*, the play endures as a popular dramatic work and is regularly performed by professional as well as amateur and student companies.

As one of the earliest and most widely familiar mediations of Anne Frank's life and work, *The Diary of Anne Frank* is of special interest as a commissioned work written in accordance with the conventions of American commercial theater of the 1950s. These circumstances endowed the script with certain enduring characteristics that are intrinsic to its performance, regardless of language, format, or venue, be it a subsidized public theater or a high school auditorium. As the only authorized dramatic version of Anne's diary, *The Diary of Anne Frank* remains to date the only non-musical stage work that is licensed to cite her writing. In this regard the play is different from the unrestricted abundance of mediations of Anne's life and work in fiction, visual art, and music. While the exclusivity of *The Diary of Anne Frank* has not gone unchallenged, its singular stature as an official stage adaptation informs all other efforts to use live performance as a vehicle for engaging Anne Frank.

The original stage production of *The Diary of Anne Frank* was a watershed event: it marked the first time that the mainstream American theater presented a play whose plot focused on the Holocaust.[2] The play, written by Frances Goodrich and her husband, Albert Hackett, opened on October 5, 1955, at the Cort Theatre and later transferred to another Broadway house, the Ambassador Theatre, where it played until June 22, 1957, closing after a run of 717 performances. As each Broadway theater where *The Diary of Anne Frank* played has a seating capacity of more than one thousand, it is safe to assume that almost three-quarters of a million people saw the original Broadway production. Many more would see the play, though not always with the same cast, when it went on a major national tour, followed by a special tour of the South. *The Diary of Anne Frank* was a critical as well as commercial success, sweeping the 1957 "triple crown" of awards for best play: the Pulitzer Prize, the New York Drama Critics' Circle Award, and the Tony Award.

In the wake of its success in New York, *The Diary of Anne Frank* became an international theater phenomenon. By the early 1960s, the play had been translated into twenty-five languages and published in thirty-four countries.[3] In 1960 and 1961, several years after it had entered the international scene in full force, royalties were still paid from thirteen European countries.[4] Regular international performances of *The Diary of Anne Frank* continued over the years. In the 1980s, Miep Gies, who had helped hide the Frank family during the war, wrote in her memoir: "I am told that every night when the sun goes down, somewhere in the world the curtain is going up on the stage play made from Anne's diary."[5]

During the more than five decades that have passed since the play's premiere, there have been countless productions of *The Diary of Anne Frank* across the United States. In recent years, regional theaters have often presented the play as an educational experience, sometimes producing ancillary materials, such as exhibitions and study guides on the Frank family or the Holocaust, for their audiences.[6] The play has long

Program for the original Broadway production of *The Diary of Anne Frank*,
featuring Susan Strasberg as Anne and Joseph Schildkraut as Otto Frank.

been popular in university theaters and high school drama clubs.[7] In 1958–1959 it ranked tenth among the top twenty plays produced in American colleges and universities.[8] Fifty years later, Dramatists Play Service, which licenses rights to perform *The Diary of Anne Frank*, confirmed its enduring popularity with amateur theater groups, especially high schools, and estimated that during the first decade of the twenty-first century, the play averaged between 150 and 200 productions annually.[9]

"How can this book ever be adapted to a play?"

The great success of *The Diary of Anne Frank* has obscured the challenging task of mediating the diary in dramatic form. When the American author Meyer Levin first proposed a stage adaptation of Anne's diary to her father, Otto Frank's first response was that he "could not see" the diary as a drama.[10] Similarly, the actor Joseph Schildkraut, who originated the role of Otto Frank, recalled that when his wife remarked, after having read Anne's diary, that it would make a great play, he was "flabbergasted" at the suggestion and immediately replied, "How can this book ever be adapted to a play?"[11]

Such responses are not surprising, for, as a genre, diaries defy many of the basic concepts of dramatic literature, especially of the realistic mode that was the staple of American drama in the 1950s. This incongruity of genres is demonstrated by the dearth of dramatized versions of diaries in the Western dramatic corpus. There are several reasons why this is the case: diaries are, by nature, fragmentary and open-ended narratives; as works of personal writing, their perspective is inherently subjective, and the focus is often introspective; instead of following a linear plot, a diary's structure is usually episodic, with a seemingly haphazard appearance of characters and settings.[12] Though much of Anne's diary is uneventful in terms of what is conventionally understood as stageworthy, its dramatization was somewhat facilitated by the circumstances of her hiding, which provided a fixed locale and a limited cast of characters. Moreover, the audience's full and constant awareness of the imminent deaths of Anne and all the other Jews portrayed in the play, except for her father, endows the events unfolding on stage with emotional power, due to the intensifying dynamic of this irony. Thus, *New York Times* theater critic Ben Brantley, who reviewed the 1997 revival of *The Diary of Anne Frank*, likened viewing Anne on stage to "watching a vibrant, exquisite fawn . . . through the lens of a hunter's rifle."[13] This irony is introduced at the very beginning of the play and implicitly linked to its very existence. When Miep Gies attempts to turn over to Otto Frank a bundle of family papers that she rescued and saved after the arrest, he initially tells her to burn all of them. The audience, already familiar with Anne's story, is well aware that these papers include her diary and are not destined for destruction.

Goodrich and Hackett, chosen by Otto Frank and his advisors to render the diary into a theatrically effective script, were successful Hollywood scriptwriters with roots in the professional theater, where they had established careers as actors and playwrights. The couple devoted two years to researching and writing *The Diary of Anne Frank*, going through eight versions before arriving at the final text. The playwrights transformed Anne's diary into a two-act play, each act consisting of five separate scenes, including a prologue and epilogue. The two acts span the period from the moment the Franks and Van Daans went into hiding in the Annex, located at the back of 263 Prinsengracht, Otto Frank's Amsterdam office building, until their discovery and arrest. Each scene is organized around a core event or activity. The scenes alternate between tension and release: a nasty quarrel is followed by harmony and joy, a fearful episode by an idyllic love scene. Linking the scenes are prerecorded voiceovers of passages quoted from the original diary, delivered by the actress playing Anne.

The prologue and epilogue are set in postwar Amsterdam. In the prologue Otto Frank returns to the Annex for the first time since his family's arrest. There, he encounters Miep Gies, who hands him Anne's diary, which Gies had recovered and held in hopes of returning it to Anne. Shaken by the discovery, Otto immediately begins to read his daughter's writing. The eight scenes that follow constitute a flashback, a dramatic rendering of events as described the diary. The sound of Anne's voice reading aloud from her diary entries between scenes serves as a reminder of the act of reading that frames and authenticates the stage action. The epilogue returns to the postwar setting of the prologue, as

Otto Frank finishes reading through the diary. He then tells Gies about what happened after the arrest and the deaths of the other Jews who had hidden in the Annex, bringing the story to its tragic conclusion.

The organization of the play is as follows:

Act 1
    Scene 1: Prologue
    Scene 2: Arrival at the Annex
    Scene 3: Daily life in hiding
    Scene 4: Nightmare
    Scene 5: Hanukkah celebration and break-in
Act 2
    Scene 1: The New Year
    Scene 2: Romance
    Scene 3: Hunger
    Scene 4: Arrest
    Scene 5: Epilogue

In imposing this dramatic structure on the diary, Goodrich and Hackett not only drew very selectively on the text but also elaborated on it and even invented episodes in their entirety. A case in point is the playwrights' expansion of the observance of Hanukkah—mentioned only in passing in the diary on December 7, 1942—into the centerpiece of a scene constructed to provide a strong curtain at the end of act 1. The scene transfers Anne's more elaborate account of celebrating St. Nicholas Day (also in her entry of December 7, 1942) to Hanukkah and also juxtaposes the holiday celebration with a break-in at the offices below the Annex, though in actuality the first of several such break-ins took place several months later.[14] In the face of the threat of the Jews' discovery, which foreshadows the play's penultimate scene, the Hanukkah celebration constitutes a performance of hope and defiance. The scene ends with the singing of a holiday song, led by Anne, which concludes with the declaration, "Together, we'll weather whatever tomorrow may bring."[15]

The script also reveals a reworking of ideas expressed in Anne's diary that reflects the perspectives not only of the playwrights but also of others involved in the play's production. Most striking, at least for many recent critics of *The Diary of Anne Frank*, is the transformation of Anne's musings on the uniqueness of Jewish persecution. On April 11, 1944, she wrote in her diary: "Who has inflicted this upon us? Who has made us Jews different from all other people? Who has allowed us to suffer so terribly up till now?" Anne concludes, "We can never become just Netherlanders, or just English, or representatives of any country for that matter, we will always remain Jews, but we want to, too."[16] In the play, Anne instead offers—moments before the arrest—a statement on the universal nature of suffering: "We're not the only people that've had to suffer. There've always been people that've had to . . . sometimes one race . . . sometimes another."[17] The speech ends with Anne's famous enunciation of hope, which is repeated in voiceover at the end of the epilogue: "I still believe, in spite of everything, that people are really good at heart."[18]

This statement reflects a cluster of larger anxieties shared by the play's producer, Kermit Bloomgarden, and director, Garson Kanin—both of whom were Jews—that the adaptation of Anne's diary would prove to be "too Jewish"—that is, too particularist—and too upsetting for a Broadway theater audience. Kanin insisted on the change in Anne's musings on human suffering after reading the sixth version of the playwrights' script, which included a passage that closely reflected Anne's original diary entry of April 11, 1944. Kanin told Goodrich and Hackett that he regarded this as "an embarrassing piece of special pleading" and explained:

> People have suffered because of being English, French, German, Italian, Ethiopian, Mohammedan, Negro, and so on. I don't know how this can be indicated, but it seems to me of utmost importance. The fact that in this play the symbols of persecution and oppression are Jews is incidental, and Anne, in stating the argument so, reduces her magnificent stature. . . . In other words, in this moment, the play has an opportunity to spread its theme into the infinite.[19]

Taking their cues from Bloomgarden and Kanin, the playwrights explained that in order to gain the audience's identification with the characters' plight they deliberately presented them "not as some strange people, but persons like themselves [the audience], thrown into this horrible situation."[20] Bloomgarden also insisted from the start that the script emphasize Anne's lightheartedness and girlishness. He later recalled telling the playwrights: "I don't want breast-beating or anything of that sort. . . . The only way this play will go will be if it's funny. . . . Whenever anybody's [planning to perform in the play] we always say, 'Get [the audience] laughing. . . . That way, it's possible for them to sit through the show."[21] The playwrights went along with this approach, though apparently not without hesitation. In a letter to her mother, Frances Goodrich revealed her discomfort, remarking, "We are likely to be told we are anti-Semitic, since we have tried to put comedy into the play."[22]

Otto Frank also voiced concerns that the dramatization of his daughter's diary not be either too sectarian or too despairing. The creative team for *The Diary of Anne Frank* venerated Anne's father as the ultimate source of the production's authenticity as well as its moral imprimatur. Moreover, he controlled the dramatic rights to Anne's diary; any work based on it needed not only his blessing but also his legal approval. Goodrich cited in her diary a letter from Otto Frank, in which he rejected one of the earlier versions of the play, noting that the script failed to convey "Anne's wish to work for mankind, to achieve something valuable still after her death, her horror against war and discrimination" and did not show her "moral strength and optimistical [sic] views."[23]

Otto Frank had played a strategic role in preparing the published version of his daughter's diary, including redacting some passages he felt did not respect the memory of those who had died, and he exercised a similar role in the preparation of the dramatization. For example, an early version of the script included Peter van Pels's pronouncement to Anne that if he were to survive the war, he would change his name and deny being a Jew (this was inspired by remarks reported in the diary entry of February 16, 1944). Otto Frank asked that this remark be omitted from the script. He explained that after their arrest he had been sent to a concentration camp with Peter and his father, Hermann. There Frank came to realize that "the boy" had the makings of a "fine, courageous person." Frank cited the fact that, at the end of the war, Peter could have escaped but refused to do so, taking a great risk in order to steal food for his father, an action that led to the young man's death. Frank interpreted Peter's declaration about changing his name and religion as a "natural and very temporary phase" and wrote that the circumstances of his death were so heartbreaking that it was unfair to remember him with such a juvenile remark.[24]

Yet Otto Frank was not always as sensitive to safeguarding the memory of people portrayed in the play and instead yielded to dramaturgical concerns. In particular, he did not veto the episode in act 2, scene 3, in which Mr. and Mrs. Frank catch Hans Van Daan (the pseudonym given in the diary to Hermann van Pels) stealing bread from the household's meager supplies in the middle of the night. In the scene the enraged Franks tell Van Daan that he and his wife must leave the hiding place—a certain death sentence. The crisis is relieved only when Miep enters the Annex and joyfully announces that the Allies' invasion of Normandy has begun. Goodrich and Hackett invented this scene in its entirety, in an effort to create a crisis during the second act, which the production team felt lacked dramatic tension. Nor did Frank object to the unflattering portrayal of the dentist, Dussel, the pseudonym given to Fritz Pfeffer, who, like Hermann van Pels, had died during the war. When Pfeffer's common-law wife, Lotte, complained about his portrayal as a "psychopath" and threatened Otto Frank and the playwrights with a lawsuit for libel, Frank responded that she could not expect "an historical truth" from a work of art and warned her "not to be so childish" as to believe that the playwrights had not consulted a legal authority.[25]

The creative team's concerns about the challenging content of *The Diary of Anne Frank* also reflected the play's origins as a commercial venture. Like other Broadway plays, the production was underwritten by backers who hoped, at the very least, to recoup their investment. Bloomgarden reported in later years that it had been nearly impossible to raise funds for the play's initial production.[26] A production document shows that financial backing came from an unusually large number of investors, many of them Jewish professionals who had no history of show-business investing but may have felt a moral obligation to support the project.[27] Moreover, the advance sale for the play's Broadway run was disappointing, so much so that not long before the scheduled opening in New York, Goodrich noted in her diary: "Bad news. Haven't been able to sell any benefits for N.Y. Both Kermit and Gar[son Kanin] talked their heads off. No good. 'Too serious.' We must count only on what comes in each night at box office."[28] At this point the bread-stealing scene was introduced into act 2 to heighten the drama.

Although Anne's diary had been a popular literary success, a mainstream production of a play about the Holocaust was an untested venture, and its potential appeal caused its creators considerable anxiety. Schildkraut recalled that, when his wife had first suggested the dramatization of Anne's diary, he had responded, "Who the hell would pay six bucks to come and see it? Nazis and Jews—everyone wants to forget about these events. The Jews do not want to be reminded of their terrible suffering under Hitler, and the majority of the Gentiles don't give a damn one way or the other."[29] Kanin reported that, when he discussed his possible involvement in the production in 1954 with his friend Somerset Maugham, the author immediately asked, "Isn't it likely to be a rather harrowing play?"[30] Kanin also related a confrontation with a woman who came up to him during the play's tryout in Philadelphia and complained: "*How dare* you do this to a theater audience? I paid for my ticket, and my husband paid for his ticket, and you bring me into the theater, and you destroy me—*how dare you?*"[31]

Theater critic Walter Kerr, who greatly admired the production, characterized theatergoers' unspoken reluctance to see *The Diary of Anne Frank,* even after it had received glowing reviews, as the dread of an agonizing experience. There had been a similar response, he noted, by the reading public: "When [*The Diary of a Young Girl*] was first published, it was widely admired and, I am given to understand, widely read. Yet I kept running into people who knew its contents 'from the reviews' who professed sincere delight that so touching a document should have been salvaged from the horrors of Belsen, and who had, somehow or other, just missed picking up the book at the lending library." Similar qualms, he wrote, applied to the play, so that "right in the middle of all the admiration" for the theatrical production there was "another little pocket of unconscious resistance. . . . I gather from a few of my friends," he noted, "that they are enormously cheered to hear of its success and that they do mean to get around to seeing it—sooner or later."

Kerr explained this "vaguely suspended enthusiasm" as a response to the disturbing images that the play's subject conjured up for people. Although "everyone is in favor of a sensitive evocation of what Jewish families went through under Hitler—we all deserve to be reminded," at the same time, "everyone is sure he knows what that evocation will

be like. It will be grim, hopeless, heartbreaking: a record of extraordinary nobility in the face of persecution, and a searing experience to sit
through. One imagines a dark play peopled by the wistful shadows of the
condemned." Doing his best to promote a production that he greatly admired, Kerr assured his readers that *The Diary of Anne Frank* was "a radiant play shot through with exuberant humor" and without "a consciously
noble gesture in it."[32] Kanin also championed the play's optimism as both
aesthetically and morally reassuring. In an interview on the eve of the
Broadway premiere, he explained: "This play makes use of the elements
having mainly to do with human courage, faith, hope, brotherhood, love
and self-sacrifice. We discovered as we went deeper and deeper that it
was a play about what Shaw called 'the life force.'" Kanin asserted that
"Anne Frank was certainly killed, but she was never defeated."[33]

"To make every detail credible"

At the same time that the play's creators were concerned with universalizing Anne Frank's story, Kanin took unusual care to give the production
an "authentic" look, regarding it as the creative team's responsibility "to
make every detail credible."[34] In his pursuit of authenticity, Kanin traveled with the playwrights to Amsterdam to visit Otto Frank and other
people involved in hiding his family, to see the Annex for themselves,
and to study the play's historical and cultural context, including local
architecture, dress, and food. Kanin spent an entire night in the Annex,
trying to imagine the experience of its inhabitants. He was also greatly
interested in its aural environment, noting in an interview: "I wanted to
know something about the sounds, which I knew would be different at
wartime than in peacetime. And what you heard in the streets as far as
traffic was concerned. I wanted to know, could you really hear a truck
go by? If someone was talking in the street, or soldiers singing, could
you really have heard them up there?"[35] He secured recordings of Dutch
children's games and street organs, the Westertoren carillon, the tram
that ran to the end of the line a block away, canal sounds, street sounds,
bicycle bells. These recordings were eventually incorporated into the
stage production, not only as verisimilitude but also for their dramatic
value, heightening suspense at particular moments and articulating the

contrast between the clamor of the outside world and the silence inside the Annex. Kanin applied the same acuity to visual elements of the production. While in Amsterdam, he employed a photographer, who spent two days taking pictures of the smallest details of the Annex: door knobs, stairs, sink, stove, windows. These photos were later instrumental in the careful replication of visual details on stage.

Prior to Kanin's involvement in the production of *The Diary of Anne Frank*, designer Howard Bay had prepared a preliminary stage set at the request of the playwrights, who wanted a visual rendition of the space to help them compose the script. However, when Kanin agreed to direct the play, he rejected Bay's design and insisted on developing his own concept of the setting with a designer of his choice. When he first received the script, the director explained, he realized that it called for some fourteen or fifteen separate settings, and he feared that all this scene shifting would interrupt the flow of the performance. Kanin considered using a revolving stage or darkening the lights between scenes, before concluding that these were unsatisfactory solutions.[36] He then requested that Boris Aronson, one of Broadway's most notable designers, be added to the creative team. In lieu of a series of individual sets, Aronson and Kanin decided to put the entire Annex on stage. Aronson's unit set was divided into small rooms that were exposed to the audience at all times, so that the constant visibility of life in the Annex would evoke the lack of privacy endured by the people in hiding. The playing area consisted of three spaces: Anne's room, Peter's room, and the main room, which both served as the Franks' bedroom and was used by all the inhabitants as kitchen, dining room, and living room. (In the actual Annex, the van Pels's bedroom served as this common space.)[37] The decoration of these rooms reflected the individuality of their respective residents and also served to mark the passage of time, as small changes took place between scenes. During blackouts, props and pieces of furniture were shifted, added, or changed in their appearance, having been painted or covered. The Annex, nearly bare at the beginning of the play, was transformed over time into a homey if cramped space, becoming increasingly attractive and livable, even as the people living in it grew shabbier and thinner. In this way, the set became an active participant in the action.

Rendering of Boris Aronson's stage setting for the original Broadway
production of *The Diary of Anne Frank*. *Used with the kind permission of
Marc Aronson. Billy Rose Theatre Division, The New York Public Library
for the Performing Arts, Astor, Lenox and Tilden Foundations*

Aronson's design garnered much praise and was replicated in productions of the play worldwide. His most imaginative contribution was
to surround the Annex with a cyclorama depicting the city of Amsterdam. Based on photographs of Amsterdam that Kanin had brought
back from his visit, the panorama was visible to the audience but not
to the inhabitants of the Annex, thereby emphasizing their isolation
and contrasting the city's architectural splendor with their deprivation.
Although the stage furnishings were a meticulous replication of Kanin's
photographs, sometimes dramatic considerations trumped verisimilitude. For example, the director insisted that the main entrance to the
Annex be a trapdoor, in order to convey to the audience the feeling that
the hiding place was an attic.

Casting posed a different challenge for Kanin, especially the part
of Anne. The actress assuming this role would embody a young woman

Susan Strasberg, who created the role of Anne Frank, examines the
marquee for the opening of *The Diary of Anne Frank* at the Cort Theatre,
New York, 1955. *Billy Rose Theatre Division, The New York Public Library
for the Performing Arts, Astor, Lenox and Tilden Foundations*

whom the many readers of the diary had already conjured in their own
minds. Kanin's search for the actress to play Anne included the Hollywood ingénue Natalie Wood (who was filming the female lead role in
Rebel Without a Cause in the spring of 1955), as well as Eva Rubinstein,
daughter of pianist Artur Rubinstein, before he cast Susan Strasberg in
the role. (Eva Rubinstein, after being tentatively assigned to play Anne,
was eventually assigned the part of Margot Frank.) The slender, diminu-
tive Strasberg, daughter of actress Paula Miller and Lee Strasberg, the
founder of the Actors Studio, was sixteen years old at the time. Although
she had begun performing at an early age, the role of Anne marked her
Broadway debut. Strasberg was widely acclaimed in the role, and it
earned her a nomination for a Tony Award for Best Actress in a Play.

Top billing, however, went to Joseph Schildkraut, who played Otto
Frank. Schildkraut was an established stage and screen actor who had

received an Academy Award for Best Supporting Actor for his portrayal
of Alfred Dreyfus in the 1937 film *The Life of Emile Zola*. Despite fears on
the part of Kanin and Bloomgarden that Schildkraut might indulge in
his tendency toward histrionics, he received rave reviews for his moving
yet restrained portrayal of the Frank family patriarch.

Whereas Strasberg was admired for the "purity" of her "artless"
performance of adolescence—the *New York Times* theater critic Brooks
Atkinson praised her as "flowing, spontaneous, radiant"[38]—Schildkraut
grounded his approach to playing Otto Frank in a social and cultural
context with which he was familiar, as a Jew who was born and began
his career in Europe. Moreover, unlike most of the other actors in *The
Diary of Anne Frank*, he could base his performance on the actual person his character portrays. Over a period of nine months, Schildkraut
conducted an intensive correspondence with Otto Frank, who willingly
collaborated on how he would be portrayed on stage. From him the actor learned how Anne's father extracted a watch from his vest, knotted a
tie, carried a cane, and buttoned a shirt, with Frank providing such tips
as "I have a habit of hooking my thumbs in my lower vest pocket" and
"I have a way of holding a cupped hand over a chessman before moving
it." To these details, Frank added more general observations that offered
glimpses into deeper layers of his character.[39]

Eventually, Schildkraut appeared in the role a total of 1,088 times,
first in New York and later across the United States, and he also portrayed
Otto Frank in the 1959 film version of *The Diary of Anne Frank*. In his
memoir, the actor wrote of his singular attachment to the role, which was
centered not on artistic achievement but on the play's symbolic value:

> I have appeared in plays of greater literary value and in parts not less
> important. And I had won acclaim and praise before. Yet never before have
> I felt such an intimate relationship with a play, never such an identification
> with a part. . . . In her diary Anne Frank actually wrote the epitaph to a whole
> period of the history of Europe, the history of Germany, the tragedy of the
> Jews. That era was marked by the breakdown of the walls of the ghetto and the
> westernization of the Jew. Germany became his promised land. It turned into
> his hell.[40]

Although Schildkraut approached the play in relation to its European context, many in his audience embraced *The Diary of Anne Frank*

as an American work that spoke in some way to the nation's sensibilities and ideals. In this respect, the play is an early landmark of efforts to situate the Holocaust as having particular meaning for the American public, despite the fact that few Americans had any direct involvement in this event. A telling recognition of the play's value for Americans was its receipt of the Pulitzer Prize, which recognizes the best "American play, preferably original in its source and dealing with American life." Although *The Diary of Anne Frank* dramatizes events that did not take place on American soil, the selection committee explained it felt strongly that, in this case, the qualifying clause "preferably" should be ignored: "More than being a brilliant and poignant reminder of the agonies through which the world has recently gone, it is a statement, courageous and immensely human, of the need of all of us in our daily lives to live not merely with death but above it."[41]

Not all observers considered *The Diary of Anne Frank* to be a successfully American work. Writing in *Harper's* magazine in 1958, playwright Arthur Miller reflected on the play's appeal for Broadway audiences. By then the celebrated author of *All My Sons* (1947), *Death of a Salesman* (1949), *The Crucible* (1953), and *A View from the Bridge* (1955), Miller saw the new American drama of the mid-1950s as centered on the tension between young people and their parents, which is also a central concern of *The Diary of Anne Frank*. Yet he noted that a play written from the perspective of a teenager, "even when the adolescent viewpoint is most perfectly announced and movingly dramatized, . . . nevertheless has a nature, an inner dynamic which prevents it from seeing what it cannot see and still be itself." Consequently, he said, *The Diary of Anne Frank* lacks "the over-vision beyond its characters and their problems, which could have illuminated not merely the cruelty of Nazism but something even more terrible," namely "the bestiality in our own hearts." This mattered, he said, so that "we should know how we are brothers not only to the victims but to the Nazis, so that the ultimate terror of our lives should be faced—namely our own sadism, our own ability to obey orders from above, our own fear of standing firm on humane principles against the obscene power of the mass organization."[42]

Critics and scholars have since proposed other possible connections that American audiences might have made in the 1950s between Anne

Frank's story and their own lives. Theater historian Bruce McConachie
suggests that Americans' intense response to the play was also grounded
in their own circumstances during the Cold War, noting that the "smoth-
ering physical and psychological confinement forced on the Frank family
and their boarders by the external evil of Nazism . . . may have been the
closest that many American spectators came to imagining the possible
reality of life in a bomb shelter."[43] Another aspect of the play that may
have appealed to American sensibilities of the 1950s was the portrait
of the Frank family as a close-knit unit, in keeping with the period's
domestic ideal that, historian Elaine Tyler May notes, regarded family
stability as the best bulwark against the dangers of the Cold War. The
play's portrait of Otto Frank as wise, selfless, and doing his utmost to
protect his family from the evils of the outside world while adhering to
moral and intellectual bourgeois values, epitomized the era's ideal image
of a paterfamilias.[44] The play's universalist pronouncement that Jews are
"not the only people that've had to suffer" has been disparaged by some
later critics for obscuring the historical specificity of the Holocaust,
but others note this sentiment's resonance with the politics of the era,
notably the civil rights movement in the United States.[45]

"Jews will be held up as an example"

The Diary of Anne Frank has engendered a distinctive set of responses
among American Jews that extends from the time of the play's creation
to the present. These responses reflect the range and dynamics of American Jews' notions of how to represent and commemorate the Holocaust
as well as their concerns for presenting Jewishness in the American
public sphere generally. As the preceding account of the play's creative
process demonstrates, some of the Jews involved in the original production—including Kanin, Bloomgarden, and Otto Frank—were concerned that Goodrich and Hackett not create a drama that was overly
particularistic in its focus, motivated by ideological as well as practical
reasons.

This concern was no doubt exacerbated by an earlier attempt to
dramatize Anne's diary that proved to have unusually fraught and pro-
tracted consequences. Author Meyer Levin, who had written a glowing

front-page review of *The Diary of a Young Girl* for the *New York Times Book Review* when the diary first appeared in English translation in 1952, soon thereafter secured Otto Frank's permission to adapt the book for the stage. Levin's first effort, a script for a half-hour radio adaptation of the diary, was performed on the NBC religion series *The Eternal Light* on December 14, 1952. However, Frank ultimately rejected Levin's full-length stage version, which several producers had turned down. Frank had his own objections to Levin's dramatization, including a dislike for how he foregrounded Anne's (and other characters') Jewishness, and forbade Levin's version to be produced. Levin responded by mounting a lengthy, costly, and emotionally charged legal and public relations campaign to allow the publication and performance of his script. In the course of these efforts, Levin accused Frank and others, who either advised Anne's father or were involved in creating the play's authorized version, of dishonest dealing, plagiarism, quashing artistic expression, and deliberately suppressing the diary's Jewish aspects.

Levin's feud with Frank resulted in a pyrrhic victory for the author; he was awarded a financial settlement but barred from having his script performed. However, this episode has proved remarkably productive as an enduring subject of interest in its own right. The dispute was the basis for Levin's 1964 novel *The Fanatic* and was also discussed in great detail in his 1973 autobiography, *The Obsession*. Levin's wife, Tereska Torrès, offered her own account of the conflict in her 1974 memoir, *Les maisons hantées de Meyer Levin*.[46] In addition, the feud is the subject of two non-fiction studies, both published in 1997, and has itself been dramatized, as *Compulsion*, by Rinne Groff in 2010.[47]

The story of Levin's conflict with Frank over how to dramatize the diary also figures in some later criticism of the Hackett and Goodrich script, especially from those who take issue with how it deals with Anne's Jewishness. Levin, an ardent Zionist, offered a more forthright presentation of the Franks as Jews and their persecution as uniquely Jewish. For example, in contrast to Anne's speech toward the end of *The Diary of Anne Frank*, in which she relativizes Jewish suffering ("sometimes one race . . . sometimes another"), Levin's script has Anne both assert pride in a unique Jewish history of suffering and claim it as an examplar for others:

PLAYBILL®

THE PUBLIC THEATER

COMPULSION

We will always remain Jews. . . . It is God who made us as we are, and it will be God, too, who will raise us up again. If we bear all this suffering, and if there are still Jews left when it is over, then Jews instead of being doomed will be held up as an example. . . . Who knows, perhaps the whole world will learn, from the good that is in us, and perhaps for that reason the Jews have to suffer now. Right through the ages there have been Jews, through all the ages they have had to suffer, and it has made us strong, too.[48]

Although Hackett and Goodrich's play did have some detractors when it opened (such as Algene Ballif's negative review in *Commentary*),[49] the censure increased beginning in the early 1980s. For example, literary scholar Lawrence Langer's critique of the "Americanization" of the Holocaust in several plays and films cites *The Diary of Anne Frank* as epitomizing a national inability to grapple adequately with the horrors of this subject.[50] A spate of disparaging assessments of the play followed the publication of the *Critical Edition* of the diary in the mid-1980s and, with it, the revelation of the extent to which the book that a generation of readers had embraced was a considerably redacted version of Anne's original writings. Another round of cavils directed at Goodrich and Hackett's script appeared in the wake of the reworked play's Broadway revival. Several critics cite the rejection of Levin's script as a deliberate effort, whether by Otto Frank or his advisors, to suppress the Jewishness of Anne's story, which, these critics felt, did a disservice to her writing and her life.[51] Others faulted the original play for being overly optimistic and sentimental or for portraying Anne as giddy and childish and not as the incisive, precocious writer that she was.[52]

In each case, these critiques reflect their authors' own convictions about the value of Anne's diary in relation to changing notions about Holocaust remembrance, women's literature, or modern Jewish culture. The growing dissatisfaction with the Goodrich and Hackett script also evinces a greater distance from the sensibility of mainstream American public culture during the early postwar years that shaped the play. Ameri-

Program for *Compulsion*, Rinne Groff's
play about author Meyer Levin's obsessive
relationship with Anne Frank's diary,
The Public Theater, New York, 2011.

can Jews were much less prone to assert Jewish difference forthrightly in the public sphere then, as compared to at the end of the century. In the 1950s, the Holocaust had yet to be widely recognized as a moral paradigm for Americans, nor was its narrative established as one in which Jews play a central role as both its subject and its tellers. As historian Hasia Diner has noted, the American Jewish community did commemorate the Holocaust in the 1950s and early '60s, but such practices were, for the most part, internal undertakings.[53] Although later detractors of *The Diary of Anne Frank* denounced its optimism, other efforts to dramatize the Holocaust for American audiences in the early postwar years offered a similarly redemptive response to this recent tragedy.[54] Indeed, it was this approach that brought initially hesitant audiences to see the play on Broadway. It is therefore doubtful that the sort of dramatization of Anne's diary that later critics might imagine as an alternative to *The Diary of Anne Frank* would have achieved the success and global impact that Goodrich and Hackett's script had at that particular historical moment.

"This is more than a show"

Productions of *The Diary of Anne Frank* appeared on stages around the world within less than a year after it opened on Broadway, including in countries that had been at the center of the Holocaust. In the summer of 1956, the *New York Post* reported at least eight upcoming productions in Germany, Austria, Holland, Japan, Brazil, and Scandinavia, as well as near certain plans for a production in London.[55] It soon became apparent that *The Diary of Anne Frank* received special attention by dint of its subject, endowing its production with added significance. This attention concerned not only the performances themselves but also the circumstances of their production and reception.

In some instances, even the absence of a performance of the play was charged with meaning. For example, *The Diary of Anne Frank* soon became entangled in the cultural politics of international diplomacy. In the summer of 1956, the U.S. State Department declined to send the Broadway production to the prestigious Paris International Theatre Festival, against all artistic recommendations, leaving the United States with no representation at the event. According to the *New York Times,* the decision was motivated by the desire to placate French officials, who feared that a play about the persecution of the Jews might jeopardize the cultivation of cordial relations between France and West Germany.[56] The only other major power to forbid a performance of the play at the time was the Soviet Union. The theater of Moscow State University did perform *The Diary of Anne Frank* briefly in 1961, but then it was withdrawn from the repertory. Eventually, the play was presented in 1963 at Moscow's Maly Theatre, where it was performed in Italian by the Compagnia dei Giovani, which was visiting the USSR under a Soviet-Italian cultural agreement. Only after much negotiation had the Soviet Union allowed the Italian troupe to give two performances of the play, which galvanized Moscow's Jews. At the end of the performances, the audience leapt to its feet, weeping, and pelted the stage with flowers.[57]

Especially in countries whose populations had been involved, one way or another, in the Holocaust, productions of *The Diary of Anne Frank* were often regarded as commemorative events. As the commentator for the Amsterdam newspaper *Volkskrant* explained, "what in New York must have been primarily an artistic event had to be in this city, in the first place and above all, a remembrance of very real and very concrete human suffering."[58] In the Netherlands, the recent past haunted the play's production from its inception. After several Dutch companies tried to obtain the rights for the play, they were granted to a repertory company in Arnhem led by Robert de Vries. This theater was selected for this privilege largely because none of its members had collaborated with the Germans during the occupation of the Netherlands, a criterion insisted on by Otto Frank. The company's bona fides were officially and publicly verified by the Netherlands State Institute for War Documentation, which supplied a brief summary of every cast member's wartime activities: de Vries, who played Otto Frank, had been in a concentration camp; Hans Tiemeijer, who played Hans Van Daan, had been sentenced to death; Karl Guttmann, the Austrian-born director of the production, had lost his wife to the Nazis; other members of the company had worked with the Dutch underground.[59]

At first, some Dutch commentators voiced concern that the play would prove too painful for a local audience or were suspicious of the play's American origins. In the independent socialist newspaper *Het*

Parool, which had been a resistance paper during the war, the critic H. A. Gomperts pronounced the play, in advance of seeing the production, as "trash," a work "sailing under a false flag." However, after attending a performance, he changed his opinion and recommended that "anyone whose nerves can stand strong emotions" go see it.[60]

Following runs in Arnhem and Rotterdam, *The Diary of Anne Frank* opened in Amsterdam on November 28, 1956, at the de la Mar Theatre, located a few hundred yards from 263 Prinsengracht. Queen Juliana and Prince Bernhardt attended the premiere, lending it the aura of a state affair, and were visibly affected. Many in the audience had lost family and friends to the Nazis; there were audible sobs in the theater and a strangled cry at the end of the penultimate scene, as the sound of the Germans pounding on the door of the Annex could be heard. After the curtain fell, the audience sat in silence for several minutes. "We cannot divide the play from the reality," observed *De Telegraaf*, a major Dutch daily newspaper. An American journalist covering the event commented, "Such a story defied, for the Dutch, conventional dramatic criticism."[61]

In Germany, performances of *The Diary of Anne Frank* were instrumental in elevating public awareness of Anne Frank's life and work, more so than the initial publication of her diary. When it first appeared in German translation in 1950, *Das Tagebuch der Anne Frank* sold 4,500 copies; in the three months following the opening of the play in 1956, 50,000 copies were sold; by 1960, 700,000 copies had been sold, making it the most popular paperback of the period. The historian Hanno Loewy notes that German readings of the diary were largely shaped "through the filter of the stage play."[62]

In an unusual strategy, the German premiere of *The Diary of Anne Frank* was a nation-wide event. On October 1, 1956, the play opened simultaneously in seven German cities: Aachen, Dresden (the only East German venue), Dusseldorf, Hamburg, Karlsruhe, Konstanz, and West Berlin. The impact of these performances extended well beyond the usual response to a theatrical production. On the day after the premiere, the Reuters news dispatch reported: "Deeply moved theater audiences received the play in shocked silence. When movies actually taken in concentration camps were shown to German audiences just after the end of the war, they were received with derision and disbelief. But the reception given to this play was different. The impact of its portrayal of the horrors of Nazism struck home, as the silence that greeted most of the performances showed."[63]

Paula Miller, whose daughter was then appearing as Anne on Broadway, attended the Berlin premiere. Overwhelmed by the experience, Miller told a reporter covering the event: "In that Berlin theater, something happened for which I was totally unprepared. The play went on. The curtain fell on that final moment of the play. And then there was what I can describe only as deep, dark silence. It seemed to me the people weren't breathing. The entire audience went out of the theater, silently. . . . It brought them back 12 years."[64] The British theater critic Kenneth Tynan described the event: "Last Monday, I survived the most drastic emotional experience the theater has ever given me. It had little to do with art, for the play was not a great one, yet its effect, in Berlin, at that moment of history, transcended anything that art has yet learned to achieve. It invaded the privacy of the whole audience: I tried hard to stay detached, but the general catharsis engulfed me." In concluding, he noted: "All of this, I am well aware, is not drama criticism. In the shadow of an event so desperate and traumatic, criticism would be an irrelevance. I can only record an emotion that I felt, would not have missed, and pray never to feel again."[65]

The Diary of Anne Frank became the greatest dramatic hit of postwar Germany. Within a few months of its premiere, the play was in the repertory of twenty-three municipal theater companies, including six in East Germany, and at least another two dozen theaters scheduled the play for the 1957–1958 season. Tens of thousands of school children attended performances by government cultural education programs, and in Berlin there was a list of seventeen thousand people waiting for tickets to the play. Writing for the *New York Times,* journalist Arthur J. Olsen tried to understand Germans' ecstatic embrace of *The Diary of Anne Frank:* Was it "a sense of public duty? A need to know the full measure of the Nazi terror? A bourgeois urge to follow the crowd to a hit play? To seek justification for that unusual sensitivity to violence which now dominates German public opinion?"

"Thoughtful Germans," Olsen wrote, who privately considered the play "a poor translation of a so-so job of playwriting," were contemplating with utmost seriousness its resounding popularity and its impact, which was unique in the recent history of German theater and unparalleled elsewhere in the world. Olsen interviewed Kuno Epple, the young producer of the Dusseldorf Schauspielhaus who, along with Boleslaw Barlog, director of the Schlossberg Theater in Berlin, was responsible for bringing *The Diary of Anne Frank* to Germany. Epple spoke of the German theater's educational mission, explaining that he and Barlog undertook the play's production "for the sole purpose of contributing to the 'silent discussion' going on inside every decent German on the persecution of the Jews." Epple observed that

> [t]he average man is deeply ashamed. But the natural urge for self-preservation—psychological self-preservation—makes him push this emotion into the outmost corner of his conscience. It was right for the Occupation powers and German politicians to hammer home the facts. But they have done so too much on the look-what-you-did level. This approach causes the accused to recoil. There was a danger that this closing of the mind to too painful reality might result eventually in a myth that it never happened, perhaps a national persecution complex. . . . We watch [*The Diary of Anne Frank*] as an indictment in the most humble, pitiful terms of inhumanity to fellow man. No one accuses us as Germans. We accuse ourselves. This is the case of which Schiller spoke when he said, "The stage becomes the tribunal."

Olsen agreed that the success of *The Diary of Anne Frank* in Germany was that it enabled the audience to come to grips with history personally and did not subject Germans to a direct denunciation. By contrast, he noted, Erich Maria Remarque's play *Die letzte Station* (The Last Station), an accusatory anti-Nazi drama, had proved a critical and financial failure earlier in the season in Berlin. Olsen also quoted the insights of an unnamed American playwright who was then visiting Berlin. Like several other foreigners, the playwright was inclined to interpret Germans' powerful response to *The Diary of Anne Frank* as a cathartic ritual, arguing that people went to performances as "an unconscious act of expiation. . . . To experience vicariously what was done, which the German now repents, is to bring upon himself some of the suffering of the victim. He leaves the theater shocked, sobered, yet cleansed. For the most undeserving victim of Nazi persecution has assured him that, after all, it was an aberration, not a real manifestation, of the German spirit."[66] *The Diary of Anne Frank* went on to be the most frequently performed play in Germany in 1958. During that year it was performed 3,400 times in 122 theaters across the country.

Performances of the play across Europe made it possible to compare artistic choices made in different productions and to note differences in audience responses to the play. Roman Szydlowski, the theater critic of *Trybuna Ludu*, one of Poland's largest newspapers, saw *The Diary of Anne Frank* in Berlin.[67] Comparing the Schlossberg Theater's production with the one directed by Jan Swiderski at Warsaw's Theater of the Home of the Polish Armed Forces, Szydlowski noted that the German director avoided showing Nazis onstage. In the play's penultimate scene, when the Germans come to arrest the Jews hiding in the Annex, the audience only heard sounds approaching from the staircase, per the original Broadway production. In Warsaw, however, this scene was staged with shadows of Nazis bursting into the attic and was filled with the harsh sound of their military boots—it was, Szydlowski wrote, as if Death itself were hounding the trapped victims.

As in the United States and Germany, *The Diary of Anne Frank* was a landmark of Holocaust theater in Israel. Although the diary had received considerable attention when it was published in Hebrew in 1953, Israeli theater had yet to mount a successful production that addressed the Holocaust forthrightly.[68] At the time, Israeli playwrights focused on dramatizing the Zionist enterprise and on issues pertaining to forming a new political and social order. On those rare occasions when these playwrights did evoke the Holocaust, they did so to articulate the difference between the *sabra* (the native-born Israeli Jew) and the European Jewish refugee. Playwrights depicted the former as a model of self-reliance and the latter as the exemplary victim, in dramas such as Nathan Shacham's *New Accounting* (1954) and Leah Goldberg's *Lady of the Castle* (1955).[69]

Thus, *The Diary of Anne Frank,* which opened at Tel Aviv's Habima Theater on January 22, 1957, was the first play of note to be staged in Israel about the Holocaust. Habima's interest in producing the play was no doubt sparked by its international success. Shimon Finkel, who played the role of Otto Frank, wrote that, before embarking on the production, Habima was experiencing an artistic and financial crisis, and it was widely felt that only this play could bring audiences back to the theater.[70] In fact, Habima had already commissioned a Hebrew translation of the script but could not secure the rights to stage the play at first, because of restrictions imposed by the U.S. court where Meyer Levin was suing the creators of the original Broadway production. The theater proceeded with planning for the production, keeping its preparations confidential, until performance rights were obtained.

In a letter to Habima, the president of Israel, Yitzhak Ben-Zvi, confirmed his plans to see the play and mentioned its international success as an important reason for producing it in Israel: "It has come to my attention that the play based on the diary is now shown in many lands, including Germany.... If the play proves to be of such great value overseas, it is only natural that it should have particular value for the Israeli public, which has absorbed during this period 900,000 refugees, most of them victims of the Nazi Holocaust." The letter was reproduced in the playbill, endowing the production with the approbation of the state.[71]

The production opened with all the trappings of a national event. Local dignitaries attending the premiere included Moshe Dayan, chief of staff of the Israeli Defense Force; Pinchas Labon, secretary general of the Histadrut, Israel's powerful organization of trade unions; and Pierre Gilbert, the dean of the Israeli diplomatic corps, along with many of its members. A congratulatory letter from the president of Israel was read aloud, and its text was immediately telegraphed to Otto Frank in Switzerland. The telegram also announced that the theater would plant a forest named after Anne Frank in the hills of Jerusalem and invited her father to attend the planting ceremony.

In an unusual move, the opening of Habima's production of *The Diary of Anne Frank* was marked by another official event, held in Jerusalem a week later. Attending the event were the president, cabinet members, diplomatic representatives, the staff of the Dutch diplomatic mission, the wife of the chief rabbi of Israel, as well as Hanneli Pick-Goslar, a childhood friend of Anne's (who is mentioned in the diary as "Lies"), who then lived in Jerusalem.[72] Reciprocal gestures recognizing the play's moral significance were sent to and from Israel. A cable sent by Otto Frank thanking the president and the theater company was read aloud, as was a message from Goodrich and Hackett, announcing that their royalties from the Israeli production would be used to set up

Program for Habima's production of *Ana Frank,*
Tel Aviv, 1957. *The Israeli Center for the Documentation
of the Performing Arts, Tel-Aviv University*

an Anne Frank fund for young Israeli writers. The mayor and aldermen of Amsterdam also sent their warm wishes and thanks for the flowers that Habima had sent to be laid at the Resistance Monument for Amsterdam dockworkers at a ceremony that included the chief rabbi of the Netherlands, church leaders, and members of the Dutch cast of *The Diary of Anne Frank*. After seeing the play at Habima in April 1957, David Ben-Gurion, Israel's prime minister, wrote: "The show is gruesome and shocking, because the great horror is hiding behind the walls.... I think that it has an educational merit, but I doubt whether I'd have the inner fortitude to see it for a second time."[73]

In Israel, as in the Netherlands and Germany, attending a performance of *The Diary of Anne Frank* came to be regarded as an experience that transcended an ordinary evening in the theater. Israeli critics repeatedly characterized the performance as something akin to a ritual. Baruch Karu, the literary editor of the daily *Haboker*, wrote: "The audience, who is familiar with Anne Frank's diary from the book ... received the play as religious rite, a sacrament, a prayer, and a requiem. It was theater in the Greek sense, a personification of fate, this time Jewish, not universal fate."[74] *Davar*, the labor newspaper, chided members of the audience who clapped their hands at the play's conclusion, considering this a boorish act of sacrilege. Chaim Gamzu, the dean of Israel's theater critics, was unusually emotional in the piece he wrote for *Haaretz* immediately after the opening, in which he noted that it was impossible and pointless to discuss the production in professional critical terms. "This is more than a show. It is the unveiling of a monument, the lighting of a memorial candle for the dead."[75]

Both Habima and the Israeli press vaunted the authenticity of this production of *The Diary of Anne Frank*, because it was directed by Israel Becker, a Holocaust survivor. Becker had performed in Yiddish theater in prewar Poland and during the war in the Soviet Union. He directed and starred in the 1948 film *Lang iz der veg* (Long Is the Road), a landmark portrait of Holocaust survivors in Germany. After coming to Palestine and fighting in Israel's 1948 War of Independence, Becker joined Habima as an actor and director. Becker made two telling changes to the script of *The Diary of Anne Frank* that reflect his sense of what was truer both to the actuality of the Jews hiding in the Annex and to the sensibility of the Israeli audience. Instead of the song used during the final scene of act 1 in the Broadway production, he had the cast sing the traditional Hanukkah song "Ma'oz Tsur" (Rock of Ages). Becker also changed the play's last line—Otto's response to Anne, heard in voiceover saying, "I still believe that people are really good at heart"—from "She puts me to shame" to "I don't know, I don't know," with the actor shaking his head doubtfully.

Critics were unanimous in their praise for Ada Tal and Shimon Finkel, who played Anne and Otto Frank, respectively, but were less impressed by the rest of the cast. Moreover, most critics considered the Goodrich and Hackett dramatization sentimental and programmatic in its structure, and some felt that the play's sensibility was too American and not quite suitable for a Jewish audience.[76] Nevertheless, Israeli audiences flocked to see *The Diary of Anne Frank.* When it reached its one-hundredth performance, Habima noted that a hundred thousand people had already seen the play—a highly unusual occurrence in a country with a total population of slightly more than one-and-a-half million people.

Habima's production of *The Diary of Anne Frank* eventually ran a total of 179 performances. Seeing this success as a watershed in Israeli public culture, critic Asher Nahor denounced the Israeli theater and cultural establishment for having thus far avoided the "dangerous" topic of the Holocaust. Nahor criticized Israel's various public acts of Holocaust commemoration as superficial, arguing that they "are all imbued with a feeling of fulfilling one's obligation, of quieting one's conscience. A genuine feeling of sorrow is missing. . . . The success of the production of *The Diary on Anne Frank* can signal the beginning of our liberation from this estrangement. Multitudes have come to see the show not in order to enjoy it aesthetically, but out of the desire to pay a debt that weighs on their conscience."[77]

The Diary of Anne Frank served as catalyst for Habima to commission another play about a young female victim of the Nazis: Hannah Szenes. A poet and ardent Zionist, Szenes moved from her native Hungary to Palestine, joined a kibbutz, and then volunteered to return to Hungary to help rescue Jews from Nazi persecution, only to be captured and executed. These two plays linked Anne Frank and Hannah Szenes in

Israeli public discourse. On one hand, Szenes was sometimes described as Anne Frank's "older sister"; on the other hand, Anne Frank served as the paradigm for commemorating Szenes through theater. When Habima initially conducted a competition for a play about Szenes, the theater required that the play's format be "diary based, . . . like the play based on Anne Frank's diary."[78] Aharon Megged, the author of the play, admitted that he had originally suggested to Habima that they entrust the dramatization to Goodrich and Hackett.[79]

Although *The Diary of Anne Frank* has enjoyed regular productions in regional and amateur theaters in the United States, it did not return to Broadway until more than forty years had passed since its debut. In an unusual step, a new version of the authorized script by Goodrich and Hackett was commissioned for this revival. This version, prepared by the playwright Wendy Kesselman, opened at the Music Box Theatre on December 4, 1997, and ran for 221 performances, closing on June 14, 1998. Directed by James Lapine, the cast included Natalie Portman as Anne, George Hearn as Otto Frank, and Linda Lavin as Petronella Van Daan.

The decision to rework the script may have been prompted by mounting criticism of the original play's redemptive and universalist message. In addition, the revival presented Anne Frank to a very different audience from that of the mid-1950s. Factors that shaped the original production—Cold War politics, idealizing a normative family life, American Jewish concerns of appearing too particularist in mainstream culture—no longer informed public discussion as they once did. By 1997, Anne's diary was required reading in many American schools. Moreover, she had become one of the most widely recognized figures associated with the Holocaust, now a prominent landmark in the moral landscape of the United States. In his review of the Broadway revival of *The Diary of Anne Frank*, Ben Brantley noted that, unlike the 1955 production, this one "never relaxes its awareness of the hostile world beyond the attic." Similarly, the audience for the revival knew what to expect from the play emotionally, even if its script had been considerably reworked. "This version," Brantley wrote, "is undeniably moving, with snuffles and sobs from the audience beginning well before the first act is over."[80]

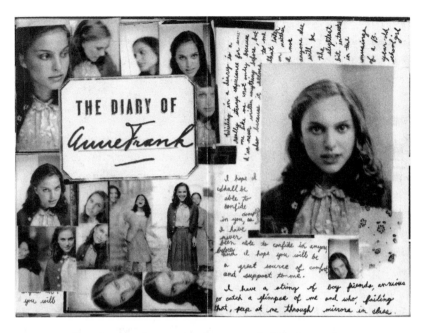

Promotional brochure for the 1997 Broadway revival of *The Diary of Anne Frank,* starring Natalie Portman. The brochure text begins: "For over half a century, one young girl has captured the world's heart. Be there this fall when her remarkable story comes to life on Broadway." *Collection of J. Hoberman*

The impulse to present an alternative to the one authorized dramatization of Anne's diary has a longer and more diverse history. Interest in performing Meyer Levin's script, despite the ban against doing so, dates back at least to 1966, when the newly formed theater company of the Israeli Defense Force produced his version, performed by young soldiers who had practically no professional acting experience. As soon as the information about the production reached New York, legal measures were taken, forcing the show to close. In 2007, a reading of Levin's script was presented by the City Repertory Theatre, an Off-Off-Broadway company; among the cast, in the role of Hans Van Daan, was Steve Press, who had played Peter Van Daan in the original Broadway run of the Goodrich and Hackett play. The Museum of Jewish Heritage in New York presented a staged reading of Levin's half-hour dramatization for radio in 2009.[81] Several musical adaptations of Anne Frank's story have been essayed over the years, including in the United States, France, and Russia. Some of these are unauthorized treatments that evaded legal censure by not quoting directly from the diary.

Other plays written since the 1990s recall Anne's life before going into hiding (James Still's *And Then They Came For Me: Remembering the World of Anne Frank*), conjure encounters with Anne through time travel (Cherie Bennett's *Anne Frank and Me*), or imagine her in conversation with another human rights martyr (Janet Langhart Cohen's *Anne and Emmett*, a fictional exchange between Anne Frank and Emmett Till). Anne's story has been dramatized for children (Bernard Kops's *Dreams of Anne Frank*) and enacted through puppetry (Bobby Box's *Anne Frank: Within and Without*, created at the Center for Puppetry Arts in Atlanta); the diary has inspired a drag parody (Ilya Sapiro's *The Diary of Anne Frankenstein*), and a musical about Anne's sister (Lori Mooney and Diana Rissetto's *Margot Frank: The Diary of the Other Young Girl*).[82] As efforts to engage Anne's life and work through live performance continue to proliferate, they extend a theatrical discourse that is not only rooted in the diary but is also haunted by its seminal, official dramatization and its rich, unusual history.

3

Anne Frank's
Moving Images

Leshu Torchin

I have a vivid memory of watching the 1980 television adaptation of the Frances Goodrich and Albert Hackett play *The Diary of Anne Frank*, especially my response to Melissa Gilbert, who played the role of Anne. Gilbert was then best known for portraying Laura Ingalls Wilder on the television series *Little House on the Prairie* (NBC, 1974–1983). Her Anne did not resemble the one I had imagined in my own prior reading of the diary. I didn't care for the dramatic adaptation—I found the characterization of Anne too childish—and I suspect that the casting of Gilbert buoyed my annoyance, because I associated her primarily with what I perceived to be another unsatisfying interpretation of a beloved memoir: Wilder's *Little House* series, rendered sentimental and borderline histrionic in the adaptation. This was not the stoic, complex, and vivid portrait of American pioneers that had proven so compelling in the original books.

Casting Gilbert as Anne demonstrates how media works inform one another, here adding layers of meaning that are extrinsic to the original work in question. To use a concept drawn from Chris Rojek's work in tourist studies, Gilbert "drags" Wilder and her distinctly American memoir into a European narrative.[1] This casting decision reinforces the Americanness of the telecast, rooted in the English-language adaptation of Anne's diary for the Broadway stage. Gilbert's performance as Anne exacerbated my dissatisfaction with the Hackett and Goodrich script. Yet for some other viewers—and for those who produced the 1980 telecast—Gilbert's presence may have added value to the production precisely by enhancing its presentation of Anne Frank's story as comparable

Melissa Gilbert as Anne
in the 1980 American
telecast of the play *The
Diary of Anne Frank*.

to that of an American heroine. What is at issue here is not a question of
what constitutes fidelity to the source text, its stage adaptation, or even
the target audience. Rather, my recollection of this telecast points to the
importance of considering the specific ways that the media of moving
images contribute to public understandings of Anne and her diary. This
issue concerns not only a sizable body of work—dozens of films and
television programs, as well as countless online videos, all produced
internationally over the past half-century in an array of genres. The issue
also entails audiences, sometimes quite large, including both those who
are also among the diary's many readers and those who have no other
acquaintance with Anne's life and work.

The challenges of remediating Anne's life and work that are specific
to the media of moving images arise as the private encounter of reading a
text—especially such an intensely personal work as a diary—becomes a

communal experience. Anne's diary, written in epistolary mode, directly invites the individual reader into her confidence. Shifting to a medium that is both collaborative and public disrupts this intimate, confessional relationship. There is no longer a fixed authorial "I," and the "you" to whom the work is addressed is no longer Kitty (or the individual reader) but has become an audience, generalized and plural.

These media works further complicate encounters with the diary by presenting it as a work of Holocaust testimony—typically understood as a first-person narration of experience with morally transformative properties—and its author as a witness to the Holocaust. Anne herself understood her diary's testimonial value by reworking what was originally a private journal into a document of wartime experience meant for publication. Film and television adaptations of the diary elaborate on Anne's redaction of the text by structuring the encounter with Anne and her writing to facilitate a number of transformations: to teach about the Holocaust as the culmination of European anti-Semitism; to create a community of support for universal human rights, inspired by the Holocaust as a paradigmatic event; or to motivate young people to creative personal expression, among others.

Mediating Anne's diary as testimony through film and television both maintains the text's communicative intention and challenges its testimonial authority by shifting from a first-person narrative, in the form of a written text, to images and performances. These media works employ various strategies in an effort to close the "veracity gap," a term that media scholar John Durham Peters employs to characterize the "trustworthiness of perception" of both the human and the mechanical eyewitness that is the camera.[2] Films and television broadcasts about Anne Frank wrestle with the "veracity gap" at two levels: first, this issue arises when these media works address the challenge of providing Anne's authorial voice when adapting the diary text for the screen. Second, this issue arises when these adaptations strive to present both the diary and, by extension, the films and telecasts themselves as Holocaust testimony, which entails providing evidence of events not reported in the diary or witnessed by the author at the time of its writing. Thus, even as these films and telecasts seek to produce an encounter with Anne's testimony by remediating the diary, they also demonstrate the text's testimonial limits. In doing so, these moving image mediations assert their own testimonial value, both by bearing witness to the significance of Anne and her diary and by guiding viewers toward the expected encounter with her testimony.

Adaptations

The most widely familiar adaptation of Anne's diary remains its authorized dramatization, Goodrich and Hackett's *The Diary of Anne Frank*, produced on the Broadway stage in 1955 and then filmed, under George Stevens's direction, in 1959. However, this is neither the first nor the last screen adaptation of the diary. Others include translations of the Goodrich and Hackett script produced in Yugoslavia (*Dnevnik Ane Frank*, 1959), the Netherlands (*Dagboek van Anne Frank*, 1962), East Germany (*Das Tagebuch der Anne Frank*, TV, 1982), and Spain (*El diari d'Anna Frank*, 1996). There are additional adaptations of the diary, both authorized (*The Diary of Anne Frank*, England, 2009), and unauthorized (the anime *Anne No Nikki*, Japan, 1995, and its French version, *Le Journal d'Anne Frank*, 1999; the 2001 ABC-TV miniseries *Anne Frank: The Whole Story*), as well as unrealized projects. Among these is a much-publicized version to be penned by American playwright David Mamet; as of this writing, the future of this production is uncertain.[3] This uncertainty may be linked to the comic response that news of this adaptation elicited, with various websites posting their own versions of Mamet's Anne, usually deadpan and edgy and always foul-mouthed.[4] This response speaks to the investment many hold in the idea of an original text (which, in this case, may be not only the diary, but also the most prevalent adaptation) and the talent appropriate for its mediation.

Although Anne's diary was written and first published in Dutch, English has played a leading role in its dramatic adaptation for both stage and screen: its first screen adaptation was for American television, the authoritative film version and model for most subsequent screen versions was made in Hollywood, and several of the most recent adaptations have been in English as well. Therefore, English-language adaptations of the diary warrant special attention both in their own right and as influences on other mediations.

Before the authorized Goodrich and Hackett dramatization, there were others. On November 16, 1952, NBC television's ecumenical religion series *Frontiers of Faith* aired the first American dramatization of the diary: *Anne Frank: The Diary of a Young Girl*, adapted by Morton Wishengrad and produced by the Jewish Theological Seminary (JTS).[5] This thirty-minute teleplay, appearing only a few months after the U.S. publication of the diary, introduces narrative and thematic features that continue to appear in subsequent adaptations. Wishengrad's script presents different aspects of the diary's author: the pubescent Anne, who quarrels with her mother and entertains a romance with Peter; the writer Anne, who narrates key components of her life in hiding and articulates her aspirations for the future; and the hopeful and faithful Anne, who expresses her feelings about humanity, religion, and God. These plotlines and characterizations relate the story of Anne and her diary as a series of conflicts and reconciliations that validates the importance of religion for peaceful resolution and coexistence, in keeping with the larger agenda of *Frontiers of Faith*.

The play begins shortly after the liberation, with Otto Frank and Miep Gies returning to the ransacked Annex, which, Miep assures him, has remained untouched since the day of the arrest. She kneels and, from the debris, pulls out a single book—the diary—which she delivers to Otto. This exchange condenses discrete historical events: Miep had, in fact, found the diary, which actually comprised several notebooks and a sheaf of papers, shortly after the Franks were arrested. She kept the diary in anticipation of Anne's return and gave it to her father only after he learned of Anne's death. The sequence in Wishengrad's script tacitly assures the legitimacy of Otto Frank's stewardship over the diary, including its subsequent publications and adaptations. Moreover, this enactment of the diary's discovery demonstrates that its untouched voice, once abandoned, has been preserved and is now ready to speak. Such a gesture obscures any attention to the diary's mediation, whether Otto Frank's redaction or Wishengrad's adaptation, and suggests instead a seamless portal to a moment in history.

As Otto proceeds to read aloud from the diary, Anne's disembodied voice joins in. Father and daughter read in unison, a gesture that forges the connections between past and present, writer and reader, and child and parent. Their conjoined voices underscore Otto Frank's authority over the diary's publication; then, Anne's voice becomes the only one reading, as Otto's image fades out. This reading precipitates a flashback, which outlines the wartime persecution of Jews and introduces the diary's other characters, thereby realizing the text's function as historical testimony. The stage directions specify the next scene as "the landing outside the secret cupboard," where Miep fumbles in the dark before offering a coded knock.[6] The choice of the "secret cupboard" as the first site of the past reinforces this notion of reading (and the performance of reading) as portal. After the knocks and the opening of the door, the Annex and Anne become visible. The plot proceeds swiftly through a series of episodes that demonstrate the adaptation's own testimonial function. Anne fights with her mother, who calls her "headstrong and conceited"; this is a hostile and frustrated Anne, who cannot bring herself to love her mother as much as she does her father. When Anne confesses as much, her father shakes his head and an object lesson follows: "Outside . . . there's a world full of hate. Human beings are taking other human beings and loading them into cattle cars. At least here let there be no hate and no enmity and no misunderstanding."[7] His statement ushers in details of the Holocaust taking place outside the world of the Annex, while providing a new understanding for the tension between Anne and her mother. The drama is not only about the expected friction between a mother and her daughter but also a morality play about the need for humans to overcome their differences and get along. Soon viewers see that Anne has absorbed this lesson. "Things are better between Mummy and me," she writes, and continues, "The sun is shining, the sky is a deep blue."[8] As with Otto's lesson, the inside and the outside are intimately connected. What Anne learns or expresses inside has bearing outside, and, implicitly, what happened in the past is relevant in the present.

These connections are reinforced in Anne's scenes with Peter, as she tutors him first in French and then in faith. She explains to him how she cheers herself: "I . . . look out the window and remind myself that the world is full of beauty. This way I can find myself again, and God."[9] When Peter expresses his own bitterness and frustration with the God who has created "this unhappiness and suffering" for Jews, she responds by acknowledging that others suffer as well, Christians and Jews together, and that what remains is to "wait calmly for its end."[10] Anne's lesson conforms to her father's earlier instruction, echoing his observation that Anne and her mother were split by a lack of mutual understanding. Beyond its general humanitarian value, this endorsement of greater tolerance and unity exemplifies JTS's approach to promoting Jewish integration into the American mainstream in other ecumenical broadcasts that it produced during the early postwar period. Wishengrad's dialogue posits a Jewish identity that is "loyal and well-integrated" and suggests that any moments of historical particularity were "incidental to the fundamental universalism of Judaism."[11] This portrayal of Jewishness contrasts with Anne's assertion of an essentialized Jewish difference, articulated in national terms, in her diary entry of April 11, 1944: "Here we can never become just Netherlanders, or just English, or any nation for that matter, we will always remain Jews, we must remain Jews." Instead, on American ecumenical television in the 1950s, Anne speaks more generally of the uplifting power of faith: "People who have religion should be glad, for not everyone has the gift of believing in heavenly things," Anne is heard reading in voiceover as she is shown writing in her diary. "It isn't the fear of God, but the upholding of one's own honor and conscience," she continues, as the wails of sirens and the explosions of bombs grow louder.

The escalating sounds of war outside only distract Anne momentarily; the script indicates that she looks up before taking to the floor to continue writing. At this point, her most often-cited words are voiced (and penned): "I still believe that people are really good at heart. I simply can't build up my hopes on a foundation of confusion and death." Although Wishengrad's Anne also expresses her fear of the "approaching distant thunder," per the original diary entry of July 15, 1944, she concludes by voicing the belief that "it will all come right." Here, Anne's commitment to writing and her expression of hopefulness merge, recalling an earlier moment in the script that links her writing with her faith and hope. Before telling Peter that Jews and Christians must wait together for this time to pass, she states, "[I]f God gives me the gift of expressing all that is in me, I won't be insignificant." This earlier sequence augurs the teleplay's conclusion. After the narrator reports Anne's fate, the screen shows the image of a candelabrum (perhaps a menorah, though this is not specified in the script), as Anne is heard in voiceover: "Will I ever become a journalist or a writer? Oh, I hope so very much. I want to go on living after my death. And therefore I am grateful to God for giving me this gift, this possibility of developing myself and of writing, of expressing all that is in me."[12] The placement of this narration after the announcement of her death suggests that Anne does live on through the diary, which has superseded both the confusion and the death that she mentions in the now-famous passage. The diary is the ultimate witness—and yet is also an impossible one. According to the script, the cover of the diary appears "out of" the candelabrum, rising until "it fills the entire screen." With this sequence, the diary and its adaptation for television are presented as testimony of a historical event that here serves a distinctly American ecumenical mission: to bring Christians and Jews together in peaceful union.

George Stevens's 1959 feature film version of Goodrich and Hackett's play *The Diary of Anne Frank* offers audiences a similarly hopeful Anne. Running almost three hours, the film provides an extended look at the lives of the eight Jews hiding in the Annex. Like Wishengrad's television adaptation, the screenplay (also by Goodrich and Hackett) pays particular attention to Anne's friction with adults, her love of writing, and her romance with Peter (Richard Beymer). The film's Anne also observes in one of her speeches, albeit briefly, that the conflict in the world will also pass, much like her disagreements with her mother. Still other similarities to the 1952 telecast evince a common approach to introducing the diary as a work of testimony in cinematic terms. The film opens with Otto's postwar return to the Annex, and his reading of the diary (in its distinctive plaid cover) launches the flashback to 1942, as the voices of father and daughter merge. Here, too, the postwar Annex appears in a state of disarray, intimating that the diary has remained untouched, a documentation of the past preserved for revelation—what literary scholar Cathy Caruth characterizes, in her study of trauma, as "a voice crying from the wound."[13] By reading the diary, Otto (Joseph Schildkraut) liberates Anne's voice from its hiding places—the diary as well as the Annex—and presents it to the public.

As the film locates Anne's testimony in both the diary and the Annex, it secures Otto's legitimacy as the bearer of her legacy. In the opening scene, he is seen arriving at the building on Prinsengracht, traveling on the back of an open truck with other people who are presumably returning from wartime displacement. Among them is a man wearing a striped prisoner's uniform, implying that Otto has also returned directly from a concentration camp. Unlike the Wishengrad version, Otto enters the Annex alone in the film; only later do Miep and Kraler (a composite character created by Hackett and Goodrich)[14] join him, having noticed Otto's arrival. At the end of the film, which returns to the postwar attic, Otto informs them of the fates of each of the other Jews who had been hidden in the Annex. As he speaks, Otto is positioned in the center of the frame and appears to look directly into the camera, providing a testimonial encounter that implicitly exhorts the audience to take moral responsibility for this history. His awe—or rather, as he states, his "shame"—in the face of Anne's hopeful expression in her diary privileges her testimony as offering a lesson for all, even her father.

Millie Perkins, a twenty-year-old model making her acting debut, plays Anne. Her portrayal is very much that of a teenager in the postwar American mold, whose vivacious expressions of frustration annoy the stodgier adults. Anne doesn't care to be "dignified," she tells her mother, after being chastised for stealing Peter's shoes; she wants to have fun. Perkins's pouting and prancing, which highlight Anne's irrepressible spirit, aspire to the gamine qualities of Audrey Hepburn, who reportedly turned down the role despite the personal request of Otto Frank that she play the part.[15] Perkins's petulant, coy performance is consistent with the screenplay's avoidance of the diary's many precociously insightful, sometimes cutting, observations of the adult world, as well as Anne's considerable discussion throughout the diary of her developing sexuality. Instead, the film presents Anne's romance with Peter as very chaste; the squabbling between them echoes the fussing before reconciliation of Hollywood screwball comedies.

The film's tempering of the more provocative elements of Anne's thoughts and behavior, as revealed in her writing, renders her more an innocent child than a developing, occasionally moody adolescent, a

AT 20TH CENTURY-FOX, GEORGE STEVENS HAS COMPLETED

the diary of anne frank

IN WHICH A GIRL WHO HAS NEVER APPEARED ON THE SCREEN
IS ALREADY WORLD FAMOUS

strategy that serves the film's depiction of Anne as a universal symbol of hope. Unlike Wishengrad's adaptation, scripted for a program produced by a Jewish religious movement, the film diminishes Jewish specificity in order to provide a more universal Anne in both identity and message. The film's Anne does not discuss the particularity of Jewish suffering, as do many of the actual diary entries, nor does she express pleasure at the assassination attempt on Hitler, as the actual Anne did in her diary entry of July 21, 1944, in which she wishes that "the impeccable Germans" would "kill each other off." Instead, she responds to Peter's anger over their situation as persecuted Jews by reminding him that "We are not the only people who have had to suffer. Everyone has to suffer, sometimes one race and sometimes another."

Stevens's film was highly praised for its universal message, including by some Jewish observers. John Stone, the director of the Jewish Film Advisory Committee, declared, "this screenplay is even better than the stage play. You have given the story a more 'universal' meaning and appeal."[16] This universal Anne was open to metaphor for audiences anywhere. As other scholars of the film have remarked, American audiences could relate her generalized moral insights to injustices closer to home, including McCarthyism and racial discrimination throughout the United States, especially Jim Crow laws of the South.[17]

Indeed, the film's conclusion implies a distinctly Christian understanding of redemptive suffering. At the close of her observation of cycles of human suffering throughout history, Anne states, "I still believe that people are good at heart." Although these words appear in the diary entry of July 15, 1944, the script shortens Anne's thoughtful struggle in this entry with the challenges that suffering poses to faith and hopefulness. Moreover, the film follows Anne's speech about suffering and goodness with a double climax: the arrest of the Jews hiding in the Annex and a kiss between Anne and Peter. This structure imposes onto Anne's life a Christian trajectory of martyrdom, the proclamation of faith followed

A 20th Century-Fox promotion for the 1959 film version of *The Diary of Anne Frank,* featuring model Millie Perkins in her screen debut as Anne.

by bodily suffering. As the eight Jews stand in the Annex, awaiting their arrest, Anne's demeanor suggests a willingness to die for her cause. She does not weep or hide, but stands still, solemn, and upright.

Otto then echoes Anne's hopeful message, telling the other occupants of the Annex, "For two years we have lived in fear, but now we can live in hope." This sentiment is puzzling, at the very least, given that viewers know it to be so at odds with what awaits these Jews, but it reaffirms Otto as the legitimate heir to his daughter's testimonial, and therefore moral, legacy. Anne is heard in voiceover, reading what is an impossible diary entry: a narration of the arrest, followed by a request to the diary's reader (and, by extension, to the film's viewer) to preserve the diary, because, "I hope—." The film's version of the diary ends with these words, presenting not an Anne robbed of the ability to live the rest of her life in peace (as readers of the published version of the diary learn in an epilogue) but an Anne who provides audiences an open-ended expression of optimism. During these final words, an image of Anne awaiting her fate appears on screen, superimposed on the open diary, suggesting that this message moves from Anne to the diary and then to all who read it. Indeed, as Otto completes both the diary and his grim narration of Anne's fate, he nonetheless can still promise, "From now on, we'll live in hope." This message is extended beyond the characters in the Annex to the audience, as the camera pans out the window to show a sky filled with birds and clouds, emblematic of the uplift that Anne's words have inspired.

This film's uplifting conclusion differs from the ending originally envisioned by Stevens, who, as a member of the U.S. Army Signal Corps during World War II, had filmed the liberation of Dachau concentration camp and helped prepare Nazi atrocity footage for presentation as evidence at the first Nuremberg trial. Stevens had wanted to end *The Diary of Anne Frank* by showing Anne's fate following her arrest and screened a version of the film at a cinema in San Francisco that concluded with Anne "in a concentration camp uniform swaying in a numb miasmic fog."[18] The audience (or perhaps the studio) responded poorly to this ending, which "was deemed too tough in audience impact and against 20th [Century–]Fox's desire to have the film considered 'hopeful' despite all."[19] In later years, the on-screen depiction of Anne's fate in

Bergen-Belsen would come to be seen as key to a more complete mediation of Anne as witness to the Holocaust.

Other than translations of the authorized dramatic adaptation of the
diary, no others appear on film or television until almost forty years after
the Stevens film. These more recent screen adaptations not only reflect
the diary's continued popularity among an international readership but
also respond to new developments in its public presence. The publication of the *Critical Edition* of the diary in 1986 in Dutch, followed by an
English-language version in 1989, presented readers with the full text of
Anne's diaries and their redaction both by her while in hiding and by
her father after the war. A new English-language *Definitive Edition* of the
diary, much expanded from the early redactions of the 1950s, appeared
in 1995. In addition to prompting new understandings of Anne's life and
writing, these new editions of the diary fueled criticisms of its authorized
dramatic adaptation. Subsequent adaptations have either engaged this
expanded diary text directly or, when denied permission to do so, approached the story of Anne's life obliquely, without citing her writing.

Such was the case with the 2001 ABC-TV miniseries *Anne Frank:
The Whole Story,* based on Melissa Müller's unauthorized 1998 biography
of Anne.[20] The miniseries courted controversy on more than one count.
First, it presented Anne's fate after the diary is abandoned. This decision
rectified the muting of the Holocaust of the earlier adaptations, challenging how they used "I still believe, in spite of everything, that people are
really good at heart," twisted into an expression of banal, hopeful optimism from a child martyr (a usage that author Cynthia Ozick argues, in
a 1997 essay for *The New Yorker,* gives off "a perfume of bitter mockery").[21]
Second, the miniseries is based on a provocative source. Bernd Elias,
chairman of the Anne Frank-Fonds in Basel, Switzerland, and cousin of
Anne, had disavowed the Müller biography for incorporating passages
from the diary in which Anne reflected on the unhappiness of her parents' marriage—passages that had been excised in the initial publication
of the diary. The foundation refused to grant the producers of the miniseries permission to cite directly from Anne's diary; like Müller's book, the
script could only dramatize her life without recourse to her writing. Elias
raised his objections regarding the planned miniseries, on the grounds
of copyright infringement, with Steven Spielberg, then on board to be

アンネはあなたにちょっと似ている。

its executive producer, and Michael Eisner, then CEO of Disney, which owns ABC. As a result of Elias's objections, Spielberg withdrew from the project.[22] The entire affair speaks to the complexity of the question that Ozick posed in the title of her essay: "Who Owns Anne Frank?"

The 1999 animated film *Le Journal d'Anne Frank*, the French version of the Japanese *Anne No Nikki* of 1995,[23] challenges the task of addressing the "veracity gap" not only by a lack of citations from the diary, but also by dint of being an animated film. In the West, at least, this genre is often associated with comic and fantastical cartoons. However, this medium also enables the reenactment of events described in Anne's diary with a level of control over detail that live-action film cannot rival. Instead of quoting passages from the diary, which would require permission from the Anne Frank-Fonds, the film portrays them, following the diary as if it were a script. *Le Journal d'Anne Frank* begins not with the postwar discovery of the diary but, much as the diary does, early on the morning of Anne's thirteenth birthday, when she is given the diary as a gift. She lies in bed, wriggling about before she bursts out from under the covers and runs to a window, where a cat brushes up against her legs. The detail is striking in its correspondence to the diary entry of June 14, 1942, per the *Definitive Edition*, in which Anne chronicles the day. She recalls waking at 6:00 AM but needing to stay in bed until 6:45 AM, after which she could not wait any longer. She went to the dining room where "Moortje (the cat) welcomed me by rubbing against my legs."[24] In this opening, which links Anne's introduction to her diary with the audience's introduction both to her and to her writing, the diary is implicitly present, even prior to its presentation to Anne as a gift.

Like the adaptations of the 1950s, *Le Journal* characterizes Anne as righteous, if giddily girlish, and it uses voiceover to simulate Anne's writing her diary entries. And similar to the Stevens film, the animation treats the diary as a testimonial document to be entrusted to a future reader. Upon the arrest, Anne prepares her bag. She pulls the diary— again, a plaid notebook—from the bag to place on her desk. "Goodbye,

Poster for *Anne No Nikki*, a 1995 Japanese anime adaptation of Anne's diary. *Photographer: Matt Jones*

Kitty," she says, "Don't forget me. Someone will protect you." Her hopeful farewell suggests the diary is a "message in a bottle," a metaphor that sociologist Fuyuki Kurasawa uses to characterize the practices and risks of testimony.[25] The message is provided explicitly in a voiceover that follows the arrest. As in the Stevens film, it takes the form of an impossible final diary entry, delivered over a meticulously recreated Amsterdam cityscape that is eerily empty of people: "Dear Kitty, You are my friend, and I know you understood my message of freedom, humanity, compassion for all children, women, and men, no matter their race, religion or belief. Help me to make this world a better place."[26] After these words, text appears on the screen to inform viewers of Anne's fate. In its conclusion, *Le Journal* conforms to the earlier, authorized adaptations by offering Anne's testimony, followed by her martyrdom, as a universalized moral exhortation. The medium of animation facilitates the universalizing of Anne's life and work by allowing for dubbing the dialogue in different languages (here, Japanese and French) and, potentially, for changes in the script. Animation roots the story's specificity in the visual, with its carefully detailed depiction of wartime Amsterdam.

The 2009 BBC-TV miniseries, *The Diary of Anne Frank*, directed by Jon Jones and written by Deborah Moggach, revisits the project of adapting the diary for the screen by using the full text that had been made available in the 1980s. In an interview, Moggach explains that the miniseries offers a more honest and nuanced portrait of Anne than seen heretofore, as it is the "first adaptation to have permission to use Anne's own words and also to have had full access to passages of the diaries previously excised by the family."[27] The BBC's adaptation is thus positioned as not only truer to the diary but also a corrective to earlier renderings. Although attempting to cover some of the same aspects of Anne that caused *The Whole Story* to be denied permission to cite from the diary, this miniseries affords a picture of a more historically specific Anne with the benefit of her own words.

Opening with the Frank family's walking in the rain to go into hiding in the Annex, before flashing back to the day Anne (Ellie Kendrick) received her diary, the miniseries distinguishes its approach to its source text from the outset. This strategy emulates devices that Anne used in her own reworking of the diary for publication to establish a novelistic

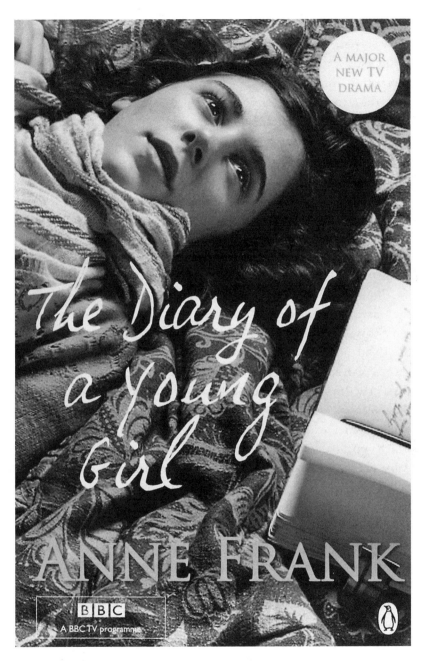

A MAJOR
NEW TV
DRAMA

*The Diary of
a Young
Girl*

ANNE FRANK

BBC
A BBC TV programme

Cover of the Penguin paperback edition of *The Diary of a
Young Girl*, promoting the 2009 BBC miniseries *The Diary
of Anne Frank*, starring Ellie Kendrick as Anne.

narrative sequence for her readers within the rubric of chronological diary entries, by providing background information about her life, her family's history, and the broader context of Amsterdam under German occupation. Aired in thirty-minute installments over the course of five days, the structure of the miniseries suggests the diary format of periodic entries that provide a chronicle of daily life. Indeed, the miniseries portrays Anne's everyday existence in this otherwise extraordinary circumstance. The opening installment shows scenes of the tedium of a life in hiding, narrated by Anne in voiceover. These scenes include the family sitting quietly at the table, waiting for lunchtime and the opportunity to move and speak, as well as the challenges and personal habits of bath time. Distasteful moments, too, receive attention, such as a scene that reenacts Anne's account, in her diary entry of March 25, 1943, of her father using a long stick to tackle a clogged toilet.

The miniseries establishes its portrayal of Anne as an adolescent with the first voiceover delivery of a diary entry, in which Anne reflects on her sense of isolation within a life of popularity. Over the images of her thirteenth birthday party, she asks how a girl with "thirty people I can call friends" can be "alone in the world," echoing the diary entry of June 20, 1942, in which she explains the value of her diary as a friend. Presenting the adolescent Anne also entails, in Moggach's words, revealing a "sexual young woman whose hormones are all over the place." This comment, which appeared in an article in *The Sunday Times* titled "BBC Unveils Anne Frank the Sexual Teenager," demonstrates that the juxtaposition of this new portrait of Anne against more established ones was integral to the conception of the miniseries as well as to its public reception.[28]

The miniseries pays considerable attention to Anne's sexuality, incorporating material from the diary not included in previous adaptations and introducing the subject into more familiar episodes. In a conversation with Margot (Felicity Jones), Anne announces the "whitish smear" she finds on her panties, which surely means that her period will come soon, a piece of dialogue drawn from the entry dated October 20, 1942.[29] Like earlier adaptations, the miniseries chronicles Anne's evolving romance with Peter (Geoff Breton), including their occasional make-out sessions. The fervor of their relationship is tempered by also presenting both Anne's early exasperation with Peter and her later waning interest in him. This dynamic follows the progression of Anne's feelings as chronicled in the diary. It begins with her dismissive characterization of Peter as "a clot" (a word choice that identifies this as a British portrait of Anne), referencing the August 21, 1942, entry: "I still don't like Peter any better, he's so boring he flops lazily on his bed half the time, does a bit of carpentry and then goes back for another snooze. What a fool!"[30] And after the height of their romance, the miniseries' Anne begins to doubt the relationship, echoing Anne's growing awareness, voiced in the diary, that "he could not be a friend for my understanding" (July 15, 1944).[31]

The miniseries' more complex portrait of Anne includes her more petulant side and dramatizes some of the more unpleasant confrontations between Anne and Margot, Edith (Tamsin Greig), and even Otto (Iain Glen). In one scene, Anne brazenly ignores her mother, walking past her to dote on her father. As she does so, a voiceover diary entry discusses the conflicted relationship with her mother and expresses the impulse "to slap her across the face."

Moggach characterizes the inclusion of such scenes as part of a corrective move away from images of Anne as "sanctified," the "child martyr and symbol of Jewish suffering."[32] Producing a distinct counter-portrait to the previous sanctioned adaptations, Moggach's Anne is significantly less hopeful than earlier portrayals—or rather, the miniseries presents Anne's efforts to maintain hope within moments of despair. Moggach includes Anne's popular and often decontextualized statement, "I still believe, in spite of everything, that people are truly good at heart." But whereas previous adaptations offer this sentence on its own or as a chipper palliative for Peter's angst, in the miniseries Anne's most famous words are embedded within a more extended citation of the original diary entry of July 15, 1944, wherein Anne articulates her doubts, fears, and amazement that she hasn't abandoned ideals in a "world being slowly transformed into a wilderness."

Even as the BBC miniseries complicates the traditionally simplified sentiment associated with Anne's expression of hope and moves away from portraying Anne as a child martyr, the plot retains traces of a Christian testimonial. The scene in which Anne writes her diary entry of July 15, 1944, is followed immediately by an extended, emotionally terrifying depiction of the arrest. Unlike Stevens's version, which avoids showing the encounter between the eight Jews in hiding and the arresting officers, the miniseries affords Anne no chance to narrate the experience and express her hope. Instead, she is seen crying, hiding, and holding fast to her parents. As officers ransack the Annex in search of valuable goods, they take Anne's bag, spilling its contents to make room for their loot. In the process, Anne's diary—here comprising the plaid notebook, along with an additional journal and sheaf of papers, representing the full scope of her diary in its original and reworked versions—is thrown to the floor. The gesture provides a powerful, if tacit counter-argument to earlier portraits of Anne. Here we have not only a physical suggestion of the entire diary but also a presentation of a young girl fiercely attempting to retain faith in humanity despite evidence to the contrary.

Yet even as the miniseries provides this more human vision of Anne, it occasionally upholds the sainted child martyr. Indeed, I argue that the desire for a more complex, fully human portrayal of Anne, as offered in this miniseries, is part of this devotion to her, as it is gives her increased relevance in a contemporary world that finds earlier portrayals of her too facile. Moggach also clings to the notion that Anne's life and work convey a broader message of hope and redemption. Like Wishengrad, she links this message to the power of Anne as a writer, declaring the diary to be "a real testimony to the power of imagination and writing—how that sets you free, whatever your circumstances."[33]

Closing the "Veracity Gap": Mechanisms of Truth

Part of testimony's strength relies on the power of a first-person narration of suffering. Therefore, dramatic adaptations of Anne's diary face the challenge posed by the "veracity gap" to maintain the authority of Anne's voice as a witness to history in a genre that involves multiple voices. Film and television adaptations employ a range of strategies to secure this witnessing presence that, as communications scholar Paul Frosh observes about television documentaries, "anchors the discursive authority of the film as a source of testimony about an event which is removed from the audience in space and time."[34] As these adaptations strive to preserve Anne's witnessing presence, they seek to legitimize their mediation of her testimony by extending its scope.

One key strategy to assuring Anne's witnessing presence in these films and telecasts is their use of the diary as a material object. Not only does the plaid notebook appear in all these dramas, but it is also regularly positioned as the point of entry to the on-screen presentation of its (ostensible) contents. The diary figures in some of these adaptations even before the drama proper begins. For example, the video of *Le Journal d'Anne Frank* arrives in a box designed to look somewhat like the diary, with a ribbon tie to be undone by the viewer. This physical portal to this adaptation of the diary anticipates the film's narrative, which opens on the day Anne receives the diary. The film proper maintains the diary's presence, sometimes implicitly; for example, the kitchen table in the Annex also bears a similar red-checked covering, a visual reminder of the diary's cover. The BBC television miniseries juxtaposes opening credits with photographs of Anne and the original scrawl of her diary entries. These images move outward, suggesting that one is plunging deeper into this world of words, a vortex that eventually delivers the viewer to the televisual adaptation. Just before this transition, the last of the opening credits appears alongside a photograph not of Anne, but of the actress Ellie Kendrick as Anne. Kendrick is posed like a photograph of Anne sitting at a desk, in the act of writing, familiar to many for its appearance on the cover or as the frontispiece of published editions of the diary.

In Stevens's film, by contrast, Otto opens the notebook to reveal the distinctive scrawl of Anne's handwritten entries (in Dutch) and, more notably, a photograph of the actual Anne Frank, as opposed to a picture of actress Millie Perkins. This photograph and the diary notebook, which carefully replicates the appearance of the original, signify Anne's presence and thereby authenticate the film, reducing the "veracity gap" inherent in the diary's translation and dramatic adaptation. At the same time, the presence of the "actual" Anne still relies on mediation in the form of a photograph; similarly, the single notebook offers a condensed representation of Anne's multiple diaries—and, of course, even the diary entries themselves, by their very nature, constitute a mediation of Anne's experience.

The 1988 docudrama *The Attic: The Hiding of Anne Frank*, based on Miep Gies's memoir *Anne Frank Remembered: The Woman Who Helped to Hide the Frank Family* (1987), honors Gies as a righteous gentile, who

Pages from the souvenir program for the premiere of George Stevens's 1959 film
of *The Diary of Anne Frank*. Made to resemble Anne's original diary notebook,
these pages feature the screenwriters Frances Goodrich and Albert Hackett
and the composer Alfred Newman. *Photographer: Matt Jones*

risked her own safety to protect not only the eight Jews in the Annex but
also Anne's diary. In one scene, Miep (Mary Steenburgen) and Anne
(Lisa Jacobs) have a conversation about diaries. Lamenting the loss of
her own diary, Miep comments that she would have liked to have it,
in order to know what sort of girl she had been. This remark implicitly validates Anne's diary (which here is also represented by the iconic
plaid notebook) as a portal to her wartime experiences, a role it serves in
docudramas and documentaries as well as dramatic adaptations. At one
point in their conversation, Anne asks Miep for more paper, as she has almost filled the diary she received for her birthday, and she expresses her
dismay with Miep for having thrown away her own diary. "You should
have kept it for always," she chastises, before continuing, "I'm keeping
mine for always." Miep is subsequently shown honoring both of Anne's
wishes: in addition to bringing papers and notebooks to Anne, Miep
rescues the diary after the arrest, preserving it first for Anne and then
for the world, extending her wish that the diary be kept "for always." *The
Attic* defers to the diary's primacy as conduit to the historical actuality.
Although Gies's memoirs serve as the basis of the docudrama, it refers to

the characters by the pseudonyms given to them in published versions of the diary: the van Pelses remain the Van Daans, and Fritz Pfeffer is known as Albert Dussel. Seeking to go beyond Anne's writing in order to know her better, the film still relies on Anne's own mediation of her life.

Two documentaries distributed through the Anne Frank House— "Dear Kitty": Remembering Anne Frank (1999) and The Short Life of Anne Frank (2002)—engage this complex negotiation of historical referentiality and mediated testimony. As these two films look beyond the diary, they, too, rely upon it as the authoritative conduit to Anne's life and work. The menu on the DVD for both films is telling: it displays an image of the diary, its strap undone, poised to allow the viewer to enter each chapter of Anne's life in hiding and the larger context of the war. The Short Life of Anne Frank begins with a close-up of the diary's plaid cover. Before the image dissolves into a close-up of a written entry, a girl's voice is heard: "Will I ever be able write something great? I hope so. . . . Writing allows me to record things." With that statement, Jeremy Irons takes over as narrator, recounting Anne's life, as the viewer sees Frank family photographs and actuality footage from the period, including depictions of political rallies in Germany, Jewish persecution, and the liberation of concentration camps. Prompted by Anne's reference to her writing as a record, the film establishes the diary as the point of entry not only to her life but also to a broader history of the Nazi era and World War II, using actuality footage that documents events outside Anne's diary and her own ability to witness. For example, liberation footage shows an event that Anne did not live to see.

In Dear Kitty the same tensions are enhanced. The documentary features recollections of Anne and the others in hiding by Miep Gies, as she walks through the rooms in the Annex. A female voiceover reading passages from the diary, illustrated by photographs and actuality footage, punctuates Miep's recollections. One of these passages refers to stories of Germans gassing prisoners, which Anne had heard about while in hiding; the delivery of this passage is accompanied by footage of a concentration camp. However, while Anne was haunted by radio reports of the camps, filmed reports were beyond her point of reference (especially given that newsreels with footage of concentration camps were not shown to the public until the very end of the war in Europe).

The footage of the camp is the record of another witness—most likely, a member of the Allied military forces. Although the use of such images may call attention to the limits of the diary as a point of entry to a larger narrative of the war, the intent is clearly to elide these limits and extend the diary's scope, thereby securing Anne's role as a Holocaust witness.

The Anne Frank House, which authorizes the films, uses them to bolster the significance of Anne, her diary, and the site of the Annex, now a museum. *Dear Kitty* establishes the museum as a site of testimony by presenting Gies's recollections as she walks through its rooms. Each space prompts a new remembrance, in particular the bookcase that hid the door to the Annex. It is not surprising that this artifact should be so resonant, as it provides a physical manifestation of the diary's secret world as well as its revelation. Like the plaid notebook, the bookcase appears in all the dramatic adaptations of the diary. In Stevens's version, the bookcase is present at the time of the Franks' arrival at their hiding place and is linked with the diary both aurally (Anne's voiceover chronicles the family's arrival) and visually (soon thereafter, she is seen receiving the gift of the diary). As with the diary notebook, the physical reproduction of the bookcase is accurate, but its appearance at this point in the narrative is not. Anne's diary reports on August 21, 1942 that the bookcase was added weeks after the Franks' arrival; she writes of this addition that "now our Secret Annexe has truly become secret." All adaptations of the diary wrestle with the challenge of an efficient dramatic exposition; this particular conflation of events unites the diary and the Annex, thereby producing two icons—the plaid notebook and the bookshelf—to serve as twin portals to Anne Frank.

In other films, the bookcase is used, like the diary, not to move further into Anne's private world but to move outward from Anne and facilitate access to the world beyond the limits of her experience. The documentary "Who Killed Anne Frank?," aired on the CBS television series *The Twentieth Century* in 1964, investigates the Nazi engineers of the Jewish genocide, using not only Anne Frank but also the Annex as its starting point. Journalist Daniel Schorr launches the quest for Anne's murderer by opening the bookcase, a gesture that authorizes the Anne Frank House and, implicitly, the diary as points of entry to the Holocaust as a whole.

The relationship between the diary and its mediations—dramatic adaptations, documentaries, the museum—is recursive; even as they extend the witnessing potential of Anne's diary, the mediations rely on its authority. Conversely, as the diary continues to provide the point of entry to Anne's life, it is only by going beyond the scope of the diary through these mediations that her life is thoroughly represented and its significance appreciated. The 1995 documentary *Anne Frank Remembered*, directed by Jon Blair, relies on diary passages (read aloud by an adult actress, Glenn Close) to establish authority but extends the role of witnessing to individuals who had known Anne before she went into hiding, such as Hanneli Goslar, a childhood friend, and Werner Pfeffer, Fritz Pfeffer's son. Werner Pfeffer is never mentioned in the diary, and his existence is denied in the Stevens film, in which Anne describes Albert Dussel as having no children.[35]

The most touted moment in *Anne Frank Remembered* is a rare glimpse of Anne, lasting all of seven seconds, excerpted from a home movie of a wedding filmed in front of the Franks' home in Merwedeplein in 1941. Like all other photographed images of her, this footage shows Anne before she went into hiding. She is caught unawares by a camera casually surveying the crowd. Leaning out of a window of the Franks' apartment, she watches the bride and groom below. The amateur footage, with its loose, hand-held style, provides its own cinematic marks of authenticity, familiar to audiences from watching their own home movies or documentaries that deploy an observational, "fly-on-the-wall" style. The promotion of the documentary's "discovery" of this footage confers a revelatory ethos that enhances the truth. In fact, this footage had appeared previously in the 1967 documentary "The Legacy of Anne Frank," an episode of the ecumenical television series *The Eternal Light*. Whereas *Anne Frank Remembered* presents the home movie footage toward the end of the documentary, thereby positioning it as the climactic revelation of a mediation of Anne having an unrivaled liveness, "The Legacy of Anne Frank" incorporates the footage in its chronological narrative of Anne's life, as a last glimpse of her before she went into hiding. The status of this snippet of footage is elevated considerably between these two documentaries, as it moves from being one among an array of visual resources to offering a privileged glimpse—indeed, an apotheosis—of

Anne. At the same time, an irony underpins this wondrous experience of seeing images not of an actress playing Anne but of the actual Anne in motion—she is, for once, entirely voiceless, as the footage is silent. This seven-second clip ostensibly brings the viewer closer to Anne's life, but in doing so it leaves behind her intimate expression, her testimony.[36]

The ABC miniseries *Anne Frank: The Whole Story*, having been denied permission to cite directly from the diary, found other ways to establish its authority and bring the viewer into intimate contact with Anne (Hannah Taylor-Gordon) and the diary. Early in the miniseries, Anne sees the plaid notebook in a shop window and gazes lovingly at it, declaring her desire for a diary. The structure of the shot establishes the bond between Anne and the diary as a physical object. Although the shop window keeps the two apart, it reflects a ghostly image of Anne superimposed over the notebook and then, in a reverse shot, provides a reflection of the notebook beside Anne.

Though never quoted in the miniseries, the diary is not silent, thanks to dramatizations of Anne's life prior to hiding and detailed reenactments of events mentioned in the diary. For instance, the depiction of Anne's thirteenth birthday party in *The Whole Story* includes Otto (Ben Kingsley) looping film through a projector. The film starts to play and an Alsatian dog appears on the screen, suggesting that this is the Rin-Tin-Tin film mentioned in Anne's diary entry of June 15, 1942, which describes the party. Another sequence dramatizes a sleepover between Anne and her friend Jacque van Maarsen, in which Anne asks if she might feel her friend's breasts—a clear reference to the diary entry of January 6, 1944, wherein Anne reflects on her body's changes. Even as this reenactment introduces a more pubescent and less innocent Anne than portrayed in earlier, authorized adaptations, it assures the miniseries' link to the diary.

The ABC miniseries makes use of other mediations of Anne and her diary, including images familiar from photographs, documentaries, and other adaptations. In addition to the plaid notebook and the bookcase guarding the entrance to the Annex is a sequence at the seaside, where the Frank family sits at the beach with friends, including Fritz Pfeffer and his girlfriend, Charlotte. Anne runs out of the water and wraps herself in a striped dressing gown, simulating a photograph taken in June 1939 of the Frank family at the beach.[37] *Le Journal d'Anne Frank*, which also does not quote directly from the diary, similarly replicates Frank family photographs, seen positioned throughout their home on walls, tables, and the mantelpiece. These family photographs, which have been published in some editions of the diary and in other books about Anne, provide an ontological proximity to her that makes them logical mechanisms for closing the "veracity gap."

At the same time, *The Whole Story* appears to rely just as much on prior adaptations of the diary, which have familiarized a wide audience with an imaginary engagement with the events of Anne's life, especially in hiding. The poster for the ABC miniseries depicts a pensive Anne staring out a window, her chin resting on her hand, recalling a similar gesture of Millie Perkins as Anne in an advertisement for the 1959 adaptation. Although this pose also invokes photos of the actual Anne in a dreamy state, the placement of the actress by the attic window is an image familiar only from earlier dramatizations of the diary. A dialogue between adaptations emerges, in which they rely on each other as authoritative reference points. Similarly, both the Stevens film and the ABC miniseries provide vivid shots of a sky filled with soaring birds as emblems of Anne's inspirational worldview. Through this ongoing dialogue of references, these moving image mediations establish their own conventions for representing and authorizing Anne's testimony.

The Whole Story also interrogates the limits of the diary as testimony by placing the symbolic, hopeful Anne in a dialogue with the historical Anne, particularly in its rendering of her brutal life after her arrest. Her suffering is agonizing in its own right, and its impact is heightened by portraying the "wilderness" against which Anne struggled internally in the well-known diary passage of July 15, 1944. In doing so, the miniseries tests the burden of meaning that Anne has come to bear. Anne is seen receiving work in a munitions factory in the detention camp at Westerbork, where she attempts to inspire those around her, as well as herself, by asserting the feeling of hope one can take from hard work. The scene presents Anne's hopefulness in a context that calls such an inspirational message into question. As the film progresses, Anne loses those who are close to her, beginning with the separation from her father, and then from her mother, Mrs. van Pels, and finally, her sister. She watches fellow prisoners steal shoes and socks in their desperate bids for survival. In a stunning contrast to the image of Anne as the pensive and idealistic diarist, she is shown in Bergen-Belsen kicking a woman who attempts to steal some food that Anne has secured, in a frantic response to her horrific situation. Anne's loss of hope is painful to watch, in part because it demonstrates that in the *univers concentrationnaire* even the hopefulness epitomized by Anne Frank could be destroyed. As *The Whole Story* attempts to liberate Anne from sentimentality and beatification, its enactment of this brutal passion play demonstrates her vulnerability and extends her role as a witness to the Holocaust far beyond the scope of the diary.

Testimonial Presentation and Intention

Some films and telecasts extend the diary's testimonial function beyond the cause of Holocaust memory and into the struggle for social justice in contemporary scenarios. For example, the ABC ecumenical television series *Directions* aired an episode in 1972 titled "The Heritage of Anne Frank," in which teenagers from United States, Scotland, Japan, and the Netherlands gathered in the attic of the Anne Frank House to discuss the war in Vietnam and apartheid. Taking up issues that lie well beyond the scope of the diary at the site of its writing, these young people, who are approximately the same age as Anne was when she wrote her diary, attempt to identify these concerns with the "message" so often ascribed to her work. In a telling statement, an American girl fuses Anne and the physical site of encounter with her testimonial authority by describing the Anne Frank House as a "plea," before continuing, "She's trying to say, let's not have this happen again."

This telecast stages something similar to a common classroom practice of adults giving Anne's diary to adolescents to read, with the expectation that this encounter will promote greater moral insight. This classroom encounter with Anne's life and work as a moral catalyst is staged in a number of films and telecasts, wherein the diary serves to inspire youth in both moral and creative arenas. In the 2003 feature film *Anne B. Real*, the subject of this transformative encounter is Cynthia Gimenez (Janice Richardson), a Dominican high school student living in the New York neighborhood of Spanish Harlem, who aspires to be a writer and rapper. She lives in a tiny apartment with her immigrant mother and grandmother; Cynthia's sister is an unwed mother and her brother is a drug-dealer. The cramped quarters, as well as her experience of daily chaos and violence, ready Cynthia for identification with Anne Frank. In a flashback sequence, viewers learn that Cynthia's late father had given her *The Diary of a Young Girl* as a source of comfort and a guide to life after the murder of one of her friends. Cynthia finds inspiration from the diary and purchases her own plaid journal, in which she records her thoughts, feelings, and rhymes. The diaries—both Anne's and her own—give Cynthia the strength to stand up for herself when she learns that her brother has been selling her rhymes to a professional rapper, who has recorded them and presented them as his own. At the film's climax, Cynthia rises above these difficult circumstances to take the stage as the artist "Anne B. Real" and claim her creative voice. This use of Anne's diary as a catalyst for self-realization met with the approval of the Anne Frank-Fonds, which permitted the makers of *Anne B. Real* to quote directly from the diary.

Freedom Writers, a 2007 feature film based on the actual story of high school teacher Erin Gruwell (Hilary Swank), places the diary at the center of the creative and moral transformation of a group of adolescents—a class of Los Angeles high school students, many of them members of rival gangs, who are surrounded by violence, racism, and the tumultuous aftermath of the Rodney King riots of 1992. Anne's diary is only one of several reading assignments given to the class (another book they read is a memoir of a former gang leader), but it plays a weighty role in the film's narrative. *The Diary of a Young Girl* is the first book the students are seen reading; a montage sequence shows them in various locations—on a bus, in a park, at home—engrossed in the text. Each shot is accompanied by a different diary passage, read by the students in voiceover. This strategy both links Anne with the students, as their voices recite her words, and presents the students as a class, sharing in the same activity. This sequence also demonstrates the diary's paradigmatic value for these young people. Lines from the diary, such as "Who would be interested in my thoughts?" and "Here [in the diary] I can be myself," implicitly express the students' own sense of isolation and helplessness. Living in something akin to a war zone, they also share Anne's fear of violence. The diary's list of anti-Jewish laws, which are also read aloud in this sequence, may educate them about a historical period, but it also resonates with the racism they experience in their daily lives.

The story of Eva (April L. Hernandez), one of the students, highlights the transformative properties of their encounter with Anne's diary. Initially resistant to classroom activities, Eva also struggles with a powerful moral dilemma: as a witness to a murder, she has been asked to commit perjury in order to protect a gang member from her neighborhood, but doing so would condemn an innocent man to prison. Anne's diary both distracts and inspires the recalcitrant Eva. Her excitement is conveyed through questions to the teacher, such as "Why doesn't Anne smoke Hitler?" Gruwell responds that this is not a Hollywood action film; the answer to Eva's questions, of course, is to keep reading. And after reading the passage in which Anne characterizes the world as a wilderness, Eva is seen running into the classroom in tears, distraught upon learning of Anne's capture. "If she dies, what about me?" asks Eva, whose very question (including its use of the present tense) collapses the distance of geography and history, forging a potent, if naïve, identification with Anne.

Eva's fellow student Marcus (Jason Finn) provides the answer. "To me, she's not dead at all," he states, while taking note of all his friends who've been killed. "How many [of them] have you read a book about? Have you seen them on TV or in a newspaper? That's why this story's dope. . . . Anne Frank understands our situation. My situation." He voices his own identification with Anne, also expressed in the present tense, while declaring that it is her mediation that maintains her existence and her ability to speak for their contemporary situation. As the film continues, the diary's capacity to stimulate insight is repeatedly proven. Marcus is moved to research his new hero, Miep Gies, and soon involves the class in a mission to invite her to their Long Beach classroom. Gruwell sends the invitation to Gies, in care of the Anne Frank-Fonds (which also granted permission to cite from the diary in this film), along with the students' own testimonies about their lives and their feelings about the diary. As Gruwell prepares the students' materials, an advertisement for the documentary *Anne Frank Remembered* is visible beneath the stack of papers on her desk. Only the portrait of Anne peers out, but her countenance serves as an imprimatur of moral authority and insight.

Miep Gies (Pat Carroll) appears in *Freedom Writers* as a central figure in mediating Anne Frank. Gies extends Anne's testimony not only by having saved the diary or through her recollections of the Frank family, but also with her capacity to inspire others in her own right. During her visit to the class, Gies recounts the Franks' arrest on August 4, 1944. Then, when Marcus calls her a hero, she demurs and instead turns the discussion to the present. Having read the letters the class wrote to her, she tells them they are "heroes" every day. They each have the capacity, she exhorts them, to "turn a small light on in a dark room." With this inspirational message, Gies performs her role as an extension of the diary's authority of witnessing. In addition to having protected the diary, which has since inspired countless readers, Gies herself inspires others by placing the power of transformation and expression within their reach. After Gies's visit, Eva decides to tell the truth at the trial, risking her safety but ensuring justice. In addition to moral inspiration, the students' creativity abounds; they decide to collect and publish their own diaries, a result of their classroom assignment, "like Anne Frank." Notably, it is not simply the private expression that prompts comparison but the act of public exhortation. Their texts are called the "Freedom Writer" diaries, a title that links Anne Frank's inspiration to the American civil rights movement, ensuring her continued relevance in the postwar United States by offering broader messages of creativity and tolerance.

(Ir)reverent Anne: Comic Mediations

The inspiring messages that educators seek to impart to students through the reading of Anne's diary are not always received as planned. The pilot episode of the ABC drama series *My So-Called Life* (1994) opens in an American high-school classroom, where students are discussing the diary with their teacher. She asks Angela (Claire Danes), the protagonist of the series, how she would describe Anne Frank. "Lucky," Angela responds. The teacher replies with confusion and outrage, asking how Anne, who had perished in a concentration camp, could be construed as "lucky." Angela grudgingly explains, "I don't know. Because she was trapped in an attic for three years with this guy she really liked?" This interaction, which inaugurates the series' scrutiny of the trials of being an American teenage girl in the 1990s, suggests the limited possibilities for "appropriate" responses to questions that well-intentioned adults pose to young people about the value of Anne Frank's life as a moral paradigm, which had by then become a fixture of American adolescent education. This scene also points up the possibility that identifying with Anne, considered foundational to the text's ability to offer moral inspiration, might lead to a "misreading" of her diary. Angela's reading is, in fact, a genuine projection; she yearns for her classmate Jordan Catalano and so overlooks, among other things, Anne's doubts about Peter that framed the diary's potent expressions of longing for him. Indeed, why should Angela do otherwise? The adaptations and interpretations of the diary that were then available to the American public rarely did so; instead, they generally emphasized the romantic narrative and fused it to a reading of the diary as a message of hope.

"Misreading" the diary's established significance as a hallmark of moral inspiration, broadly defined, figures in some of the comic mediations of Anne Frank appearing on television situation comedies and variety shows since the final decades of the twentieth century. Seemingly irreverent, these works implicitly define the "correct" response to Anne's life and work by offering comically negative examples, while also critiquing what the creators of these comic works regard as mere platitudes about the diary as its misuse. These comic works do not disrupt the testimonial encounter or challenge the role of Anne as witness. On the contrary, they demonstrate how mediating Anne Frank becomes a limit case for good taste, whose threshold of propriety is found and crossed with each comic salvo.

Consider, for example, a sketch from the HBO comedy series *Mr. Show* (1995–1998) aired in 1997 and set in the Anne Frank House.[38] A satire of the MTV reality show *Road Rules* follows Chut and Dilly, two American university students, on a reality program called "Culture Hunt," which requires its participants to find six beanbags hidden in major landmarks throughout Europe. As they search the Annex, it soon becomes clear that they are not there to learn about Anne Frank but to "find that beanbag and go straight to the hash bar." However, the space proves almost too powerful for them. Periodically, they consider Anne and her life, marveling at the details of her daily life in hiding, such as the inability to use the toilet during office hours or even the challenge of an adolescence experienced in such close, inescapable quarters with her family. But despite the strength of history or of this historic setting, Chut and Dilly's preoccupation with trivialities trumps these moments of reverence. "Thanksgiving from hell," one of them describes the prospect of going into hiding with one's family. The other conflates the historical moment at hand with his failure to comprehend it by stating, "At least they didn't have my landlord; he's a total Nazi." When they find the beanbag, the boys abandon all reflection and shout with delight, "We found it, we found it!"—a phrase with disturbing resonance in this site. The sketch ends with a freeze frame of the scene as a holiday snapshot, as a voiceover remarks, "Well, that was our trip to that place." Chut and Dilly prove to be comic lost causes, failing to be properly transformed by their encounter with what is widely regarded as something akin to a sacred space—unlike, say, the junkie Fontaine in a sketch from Whoopi Goldberg's one-woman show *Whoopi Goldberg: Direct from Broadway*, which was televised on HBO in 1985. During a visit to the Annex, this character, lost in the fog of dope, is pulled into a moment of sober reverence and awe. This response suggests the proper outcome of the testimonial encounter, even as that encounter itself is mediated by place and is not necessarily a result of actually reading the diary and engaging with Anne's own words.

Other comic broadcasts interrogate this sacred treatment of Anne's life and work, often using parody to point up the banality of overly earnest treatments. Among mock trailers for imaginary adaptations of the diary is one that aired on the first episode of *Monkey Dust* (BBC3, 2003–2005) a British animated comedy program.[39] A spoof of Hollywood's treatment of European history, the trailer presents an adaptation of *The Diary of a Young Girl* that willfully bears no resemblance to either the original text or its adaptations and is rife with errors (for example the American-accented voiceover describes the setting as "the tiny continent of Europe" and mispronounces "Reich" as "Reesh"). Anne hides in an "Amsterdam Holland attic" with a "tiny band of defiant Jews," who are shown wearing bright green clothes and dancing jigs in a pub, a ludicrous mishmash of Jews with Irish stereotypes. Anne appears as a busty barmaid with a cross around her neck who boasts, "We Jews enjoy the craic [a good time] as much as anyone." Instead of Peter, Anne's boyfriend is an American soldier named Johnny. Anne is captured and comes face to face with Hitler, who comments that this girl "has caused such trouble for the British Reich." The animated sketch articulates multiple annoyances that British viewers have with Hollywood: its promotion of American heroism and portrayal of the British as villains, as well as a general lack of knowledge of European history and a willingness to transform history to suit American ideology. As sacrilegious as these comic portrayals of Anne Frank may seem, they suggest their protective and reverent impulse toward her by placing her at the center of their mockery. Indeed, while the creators of these irreverent portrayals of Anne may seem at first to have failed to learn anything from her life, they offer object lessons on the limitations of facile mediations.

The Vlogs of Anne Frank: Tribute Videos

Anne Frank tribute videos posted on YouTube might also seem at first to flout "proper" response to the diary's testimonial value. However, they are in keeping with the history of creative engagement with Anne's life and work, as well as with Anne's own inventive approach to keeping her diary, which included revising it for an anticipated postwar readership. Earlier, Anne wrote diary entries in the form of letters to imaginary girlfriends, whom she named after characters in Cissij van Marxveldt's *Joop ter Heul* series, inventing a bond with imaginary figures and incorporating them into her own creative idiom. At the same time, she also drew on the available idiom of the series, which was epistolary in format, with the main character first writing letters before eventually keeping a diary. Is it surprising, then, that readers of her diary might do something similar with mediations of Anne? Just as students have been handed the diary with the expectation that they, too, will become inspired to write, young people now encounter the moving image mediations of Anne Frank and are inspired to produce media works of their own. Media scholars Jay Bolter and Richard Grusin observe that the borrowing

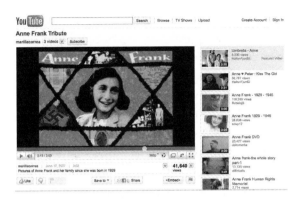

Screen capture of a 2007 Anne Frank tribute video on YouTube.

and refashioning inherent in remediation are forms of homage.[40] Or, perhaps a better word for this devotional and creative engagement is "fandom." These videos are much like "vids," the term applied to fan-made videos that pair source material with musical selections to explore characters and romantic pairings or celebrate texts. Similar to this fan phenomenon, these Anne Frank videos are user-generated works that mix a host of media samples—including diary excerpts, Frank family photographs, actuality footage, as well as dramatic adaptations—and set them to music. And like the fan vids, this practice allows the "vidders" (as they are known) to celebrate Anne and her diary and to explore various romantic pairings involving her.[41] Yet these videos, drawing on source material based in history, also engage in memorial practices and the promotion of Holocaust awareness more generally. These videos integrate fan practice with the established valuation of the diary as a work of witnessing. In addition to incorporating samples from prior mediations of Anne Frank, they build upon them by extending the dialogue of references among different adaptations. In this regard these fan videos are a logical outcome of earlier mediations, combining devotional response with historical awareness and creative practice—in particular, a creative practice in an adolescent idiom. Like Anne Frank, vidders build on their favorite books and films to express their beliefs and feelings about the world.

The producers of these videos are mostly teenage girls located throughout the world, including (but not limited to) Australia, Brazil, Canada, Denmark, Italy, Peru, South Korea, Spain, Sweden, the United

Kingdom, and the United States. The range of hits that these videos receive varies significantly, from as few as 1,400 to over 300,000. Remarkably, the transnational community drawn together by an affinity for Anne Frank posts very few negative comments underneath these videos. When the occasional "troll" writes something unpleasant, the comment is either removed or is simply lost amid a flood of appreciations. Typically, comments on these videos echo established memorial sentiments, writing "R.I.P." for Anne, the 1.5 million children, or the 6 million Jews who were victims of the Holocaust. Others profess their love for Anne or how her diary inspired them, or they offer condemnations of war and other forms of violence. Occasionally commenters exchange information, recommending films or describing other atrocities of World War II, such as the massacre of Poles in Katyn.

There are three genres of videos, each with their own subsets. The first type is a photo-tribute or commemoration. Like the commemorative videos Malin Walhberg describes in her work on YouTube commemoration, these are slideshows set to music.[42] They combine Frank family photographs with vintage images of Hitler, concentration camps, their prisoners, and Jews wearing yellow stars, followed by pictures of sites of Anne Frank remembrance: the monument to Anne and Margot Frank at Bergen-Belsen, the diary's plaid notebook, the Anne Frank House, and the statue of Anne in Amsterdam's Westerkerk Square. Typically, classical music, or popular music in a classical idiom, accompanies these montages, underscoring the gravitas of their mission of placing Anne in the historical context of the Holocaust. (More than one of these videos uses the theme from *Schindler's List*, composed by John Williams.) Mournful pop songs, such as the instrumental version of "My Heart Will Go On," the theme from James Cameron's 1997 film *Titanic*, is also a common choice, most likely for its evocation of historical tragedy, tragic lovers, as well as its resonance with Anne's wish to "live on even after my death." This and other quotations from the diary, especially "I still believe, in spite of everything, that people are good at heart," appear in these videos as intertitles or superimposed on images. The frequent quoting of Anne's desire to live beyond her death both reinforces the memorial nature of these videos and celebrates the broader power of creativity.[43]

Whereas most tribute videos have simple sound tracks, "Anne Frank 'Speaks' + Holocaust Documentary," posted by Ubuntubird of Tonga in 2007, is unusual in that it includes diary passages in a girl's voiceover instead of relying solely on visual text.[44] In common with the other Anne Frank photo tributes, this video brings together personal and political history. Ubuntubird conflates the diary's list of anti-Jewish decrees with its account of Margot Frank's call-up notice, thereby invoking the diary's historical value as a means of securing the value of the video itself. "Anne Frank 'Speaks,'" like some of the other videos, also incorporates "Give," one of several short prose pieces Anne wrote while in hiding. (In 1943, she copied these works into a separate book, entitled *Stories and Events from the Annex*.)[45] In this essay, Anne questions the humanity in the treatment of beggars; in the video, this text becomes a comment on the Holocaust. "It's terrible, really terrible, that people treat each other this way," Anne laments, as images of starving children and prisoners in concentration camps appear. She continues musing about the lack of essential difference between the beggar and the person with money, as the video presents images of the Anne Frank House, thereby evoking the site's commitment to promoting universal human rights and linking Anne with a general message of justice and tolerance. The narration of "Give" ends in mid-essay, with the words "Everyone is born equal," as an image of the monument to the Frank sisters at Bergen-Belsen appears, rooting the notion of Anne as a humanitarian within the context of anti-Semitic violence and the Holocaust. The introduction of Anne's lesser-known work suggests that at least some of these videos are dedicated to calling attention to her authorial voice. At the same time, some of these tribute videos rely on images drawn from adaptations. For example, although Mariliacorrea's 2007 video "Anne Frank Tribute" is described as "Pictures of Anne Frank and her family since she was born in 1929," it includes stills from *Anne no Nikki*.[46] Mediations across the continuum of indexicality, from photograph to animation, come together in this picture tribute, as they do in other videos that favor incorporating stills from adaptations and miniseries.

A second type of tribute video builds on this blending of mediations by remixing clips from other films about Anne Frank. The favorite source film for these videos appears to be *Anne Frank: The Whole Story*, most likely because it extends the diary's limited scope of witnessing the Holocaust. These videos frequently rely on the same shots from *The Whole Story* that follow Anne's life after her arrest: Anne's head being shaved, Anne cradling Margot and looking up at the sky, and Anne huddled by an electrified barbwire fence. Pop music, both sober and upbeat, accompanies these assemblages. HallonFjun92 of Sweden, the creator of numerous popular Anne Frank tribute videos, uses the Gary Jules song "Mad World" in her video, titled "Mad World—Anne."[47] (This song is used in a number of YouTube videos that call attention to humanitarian crises, both historical and contemporary, notably the genocide in Darfur.) In the Anne Frank tribute video "My Heart Will Go On—Anne," posted in 2007, HallonFjun92 promises to present "the whole Anne Frank story in one video." As the title suggests, it is set to theme song of *Titanic*, sung by Celine Dion.[48] This video begins with glimpses of a young Anne among her classmates, followed by an overhead shot of leaflets tumbling down over her while walking in the street. Anne is heard saying, in voiceover, "I've decided something. After the war I'm going to live," which articulates the link between the *Titanic* song and HallonFjun92's commitment to endowing Anne and her diary with immortality. The video continues to follow the course of the miniseries—Anne's life in hiding, her romance with Peter, and her death in Bergen-Belsen—before concluding with these texts: "R.I.P. Anne Frank and all of them who died in the Holocaust" and "We'll never forget." HallonFjun92's heart does indeed go on, extending her private adoration of Anne, the diary, and their mediations into the public realm of YouTube. As suggested in earlier mediations of Anne's life and work, her creative capacity confers immortality and greater presence in the world not only upon Anne herself but also upon others inspired by her. It falls upon them to maintain the intended messages of remembrance, creativity, and hope delivered in Anne's name.

A third type of Anne Frank tribute video also remixes film clips but does so in order to expand or focus on particular favorite elements of her story, such as the romance with Peter or the often neglected Margot, who enjoys a small number of fans.[49] The prolific HallonFjun92 regularly edits clips of *The Whole Story* into narratives of furtive glances, kisses, and turmoil between Anne and Peter. At times, HallonFjun92 explores the potential of an alternative point of view, such as Peter's longing for Anne, which is depicted in the 2007 video "Anne ♥ Peter: Kiss The Girl," set to the song "Kiss the Girl" recorded by *High School Musical* star Ashley Tisdale.[50] The video provides numerous images of Anne, many of her turning and smiling, whether cheerfully at a birthday party or wistfully as she stands by the attic window. These many close-ups rely, in turn, on the extensive restaging of photographic portraits of Anne in *The Whole Story*, while also presenting her as a figure worthy of adoration (or at least a kiss). Cut in between these images of Hannah Taylor-Gordon as Anne are shots of Nick Audsley as Peter looking, implicitly, at her; some of the edits are retained from the original miniseries, but others are the vidder's own invention. The repetition of Peter's gaze and its object of attention corresponds to HallonFjun92's description of the narrative: "Peter keep[s] hearing this voice in his head that he should kiss the girl, Anne. . . . That's the story lol. [sic]" Ultimately, Peter gets his wish, as the video closes with Peter and Anne kissing in the attic, freezing them in a pose of everlasting love.[51] HallonFjun92 comments on the video: "Anne and Peter would probably still be in love if they survived the Holocaust . . . so sad! [sic]"

The video's insistence upon romance beyond the limits of what is described in the diary resembles the interventions of fan vidders and writers of fan fiction generally, in which readers rework familiar texts as expressions of their own imaginative engagement with beloved characters in these texts, exploring other potential plots and narrative directions. Like fan fiction, these videos provide Anne Frank vidders with an opportunity to express their love of Anne Frank by reanimating her and making her seem closer, as they participate in what media scholar Henry Jenkins characterizes as a like-minded community of affinity—in this case, a community of Anne Frank devotees.[52] Vidders enact their sense of empowerment in relation to a text that is often used to encourage their own inspiration and sense of self. Occasionally, this involves departing from the canonical Anne Frank story to create a decidedly fictional version of Anne's life. For example, a 2007 video by YouTube user AnnelieseMarieFrank (i.e., Anne's full name) called "What Hurts Most" re-edits *The Whole Story* to narrate a romance between Anne Frank and Fritz Pfeffer.[53] Comments posted in response to this video engage the creative process of exploring the possibilities of Anne's romantic life beyond Peter. Some commenters appreciate the video's unusual imagination of Anne's romantic life, while others ask why AnnelieseMarie-Frank didn't focus on the young man named Hello, a romantic interest of Anne's prior to her life in hiding, who appears in the ABC miniseries. Other videos offer alternative endings to Anne's life in an effort to provide some measure of happiness for Anne and fan alike. HallonFjun92's 2007 video "Somebody Help Me: Anne" envisions a happier outcome for Anne by combining footage from *The Whole Story* and another film, *The Fine Art of Love: Mine Ha-Ha*. This 2005 feature, directed by John Irvin, stars Hannah Taylor-Gordon in a story of lesbian longings in a girls' school. HallonFjun92's use of *The Fine Art of Love* is likely due to the presence of the same actress in both this film and *The Whole Story*, as shots of longing and devotion centered on Taylor-Gordon provide material for the video's adoring depiction of Anne, which is described as follows: "Anne Frank survived the war. She lost her memory and moved to Italy to start a new life in a public school. Slowly she gets her memories back, all of her memories from the camps. In the end she gets her happy memories back too:)."[54] The comments on "Somebody Help Me" are positive, most responders expressing wishes that Anne had survived. One exception, Joyann1, writes, "if she had survived[,] her diary wouldn't have been so famous"—a debatable point, given Anne's ambitions. At the same time, this comment speaks to the problematic nature of this adulation, for it is not the actual Anne but the multiple mediations of her life that foster the love and adulation.

There is precedent for the discussion engendered by this video. Philip Roth's 1979 novella *The Ghost Writer*, which was adapted for the PBS drama series *American Playhouse* in 1984, also entertains an alternate history for Anne Frank. Roth's protagonist (and literary alter ego), the budding writer Nathan Zuckerman (Mark Linn-Baker), fantasizes that Amy Bellette (Paulette Smit)—a college student he meets in the late 1950s at the New England home of an older writer, E. I. Lonoff (Sam Wanamaker)—is, in fact, Anne Frank, who has survived the war incognito. She cannot reveal her true identity, however; having read the diary and seen the stage adaptation, she has become aware of her own sanctified status: the world needs her to have suffered and died. At the same time, Zuckerman imagines marrying Amy/Anne, believing that doing so would protect him from accusations of Jewish self-hatred, in response to unflattering portraits of American Jewish life in his own fiction. In the face of these attacks, Anne Frank would be the "ultimate trophy wife."[55]

Through this fantasy, Roth considers the implications of fetishizing Anne, who in the early postwar years had already become so burdened with meanings that extended beyond the actual girl that they threatened to leave her behind. Much like the creators of Anne Frank tribute videos, Roth is drawn to earlier mediations of Anne's life (the published diary and the Broadway play), but instead of iterating and elaborating their devotion to her, he interrogates, among other issues, their reliance on her death in order to maintain the value of Anne and her testimony.

* * *

In order to manage the shift from written text to moving image, the films, television programs, and videos that mediate Anne Frank's life and work draw on a range of authorizing mechanisms to ensure the continued presence of both the witness and her testimony. While the diary is prominent among these devices, it is remarkable how many other mechanisms these media works entail. Anne's authority is derived not only from her authorship but also from her position as a witness to the Holocaust, a position expressed less through the diary than through media works that place her testimony alongside the camera as witness to the Holocaust. Moreover, as time passes and images of Anne's life proliferate, these mediations themselves supply the authorizing mechanisms, providing icons (photographs of Anne, the Anne Frank House) and conventions of representation (Anne's authorial voice through voiceover, the door to the Annex as portal to Anne's life and work) that secure their own legitimacy. To continue the work of mediating testimony, films and television programs provide instruction on the expected response of moral and creative transformation and thereby also set tacit limits regulating proper engagement with Anne Frank. Even the comic engagements with Anne, despite their attempts at edginess, rely on a recognition of Anne's iconic status. Notwithstanding the extent and variety of Anne Frank tribute videos, they share a common impulse to engage the diary as transformative testimony. Like the earlier films and telecasts that they revisit and rework, these videos position Anne as witness and reinforce established expectations that encounters with her are inspirational. Following the lessons learned from earlier mediations, the creators of these videos have identified with Anne, idolized her, and become creative artists themselves through their engagements with her—or more precisely, with the many mediations of her life, from her diary to the latest film.

II REMEMBERING

4

Hauntings of Anne Frank:
Sitings in Germany

Henri Lustiger Thaler and Wilfried Wiedemann

In stark contrast to the extensive attention paid to Anne Frank's life since the first publications of her diary, especially the years she spent in hiding in Amsterdam, the story of her death in the Bergen-Belsen concentration camp, which took place at some time in March 1945, was long neglected. There is an inherent disparity between her life and her death as encountered in the diary. For readers who come to the diary already knowing her fate, the text foreshadows her eventual capture and death with every turn of the page—and yet, these events are extrinsic to the diary itself, as its final entry is dated several days before Anne's arrest. The unknowing reader learns about Anne's final months in an epilogue that appears at the end of published versions of the diary. The diary reveals to the public in great detail the story of Anne's life in hiding, as well as this singular young woman's private thoughts, in her own voice. But Anne's death at Bergen-Belsen, even as it is a widely known fact, was for many years enveloped in silence and obscurity. Until 1999, no memorial had been erected to commemorate her imprisonment and death at the camp, where the location of her remains is unmarked. Nevertheless, the site of Anne's death is key to understanding the impact of her life and work in the Federal Republic of Germany throughout the postwar years, where her remembrance exemplifies Germany's postwar grappling with the crimes of National Socialism.[1]

Little is known of how Anne and Margot Frank spent their final months at Bergen-Belsen. They were sent there as slave laborers, part of a group of three thousand young Jewish women from Auschwitz-Birkenau, in early 1945. Sightings of the sisters appear in the memoirs of friends and acquaintances from Amsterdam who had also been interned at the camp.[2] They offer fragmented and episodic accounts of the sisters' last days, as thousands of inmates were dying of hunger and typhus. Trapped in an evil, unforgiving environment beyond her control or expression, Anne appears as a shadowy presence in these accounts, in stark contrast to the pages of her diary, which brim with her inner life and self-understanding. Like the more than fifty thousand prisoners who lost their lives in Bergen-Belsen, her remains repose somewhere in one of many mass graves. Moving from Anne's life to her death thus entails a shift from the singular to the anonymous. Whereas her life in hiding in Amsterdam, so richly documented in her widely read writing, is commemorated in a museum on the very site where she and seven other Jews lived in secret, her death brings one to the abyss, in a field of mass graves. And it is there that Anne Frank became a spectral figure, who has returned repeatedly to haunt Germany's problematic memory of the Holocaust.

Anne Frank's afterlife in Germany is inexorably linked to both the emergence of postwar democratic culture and the acceptance of responsibility for the Holocaust. Indeed, Anne became a subject of public attention in West Germany—following the publication of the diary in German translation in 1950 and the popular reception of its dramatization, first performed there in 1956—well before the Holocaust was conceptualized as a separate historical entity and established as a subject of institutional commemoration. At a time when many Germans had suppressed remembrance of the persecution of European Jews under National Socialism—and, moreover, often claimed to be its first victims—their attention to Anne Frank as a victim of Nazism was quite singular. Within a cultural context of silence on the genocide of European Jewry, Anne Frank's powerful symbolic presence enabled some Germans, especially youth, to address the crimes of their elders. In these intergenerational encounters, young Germans struggled to develop approaches to remembering the Holocaust in the early postwar years, doing so in tandem with their commitment to the advancement and protection of democratic culture in their country.

By the early 1960s, the symbolic value of Anne's life and work had become a fixture of West Germany's official reckoning with the crimes of Nazism. In 1963, State Attorney General Fritz Bauer, who led the pros-

ecution of the Frankfurt Auschwitz Trials, invoked her memory in a
lecture entitled "Living Past":

> Anne's destiny brings into question the meaning of the sacrifice for which she
> became a symbol. She represents those who were persecuted, the unlucky ones
> wherever they lived or live, whatever their suffering was or is, wherever they
> died or die, because the state carries out unjust acts or tolerates them. It is about
> the relationship of people and their institutions to an evil and demeaning state.[3]

In conjunction with the inauguration of this historic war crimes trial,
Bauer's remarks situate Anne Frank's fate not only within the history of
Germany's then-recent past but also in relation to crimes that were still
taking place wherever sovereign states continue to commit "unjust acts."

The following are profiles of four sitings of Anne Frank in Germany,
centered on the place where she died: first, the Flowers for Anne Frank
movement, which took place in the late 1950s; second, the role that Anne
Frank played during the much-publicized visit of President Ronald Reagan to Bitburg and Bergen-Belsen in 1985; third, a series of local debates
that took place in the wake of Reagan's visit over the public commemoration of Anne Frank in towns located near the former concentration
camp; fourth, the contemporary commemorative practice by visitors,
especially children, of leaving objects at the monument to Margot and
Anne Frank that now stands on the grounds of the Bergen-Belsen Memorial. Taken together, these four moments track the dynamics of Anne's
strategic role in Holocaust memory in Germany, from the early postwar
years to the present, in which the site of her death, not her life or writing,
is the point of entry.

* * *

Bergen-Belsen has a complex postwar history of its own as a locus
of remembering—and forgetting—the Nazi era, beginning shortly after
Germany's surrender to the Allies. The British Army, which liberated
Bergen-Belsen on April 15, 1945, began to bring the murderers of Anne
Frank and her fellow inmates to justice by convening war crimes trials
shortly after the end of the war. Even though these trials resulted in
prison or death sentences for some defendants, most of the more than
five hundred SS staff members at Bergen-Belsen were never brought

to justice by either British or, later, German courts. In 1949, when the Western Allies transferred all responsibility for investigating and prosecuting Nazi crimes to the Federal Republic of Germany, this newly established government regarded these judicial proceedings as essentially completed. West Germany placed a greater emphasis on amnesty for former Nazis and their integration back into German society. As a result, members of the old elite—including corporate executives, professors, civil servants, and judges who had openly supported Hitler and his regime—quickly recovered their earlier positions. During this period, which lasted into the early 1960s, Nazi crimes were routinely ignored, minimized, or flatly denied.

At the same time, many Germans regarded the victims of Nazism within a hierarchy that reflected more general attitudes toward war crimes. Germans saw themselves as the first victims of Hitler's policies. In addition to mourning the loss of many thousands during the war, they suffered the postwar expulsions of German civilians from the Eastern territories. In a survey of Germans conducted during the U.S. occupation in 1952, the first in their hierarchy of victims were the widows of soldiers; the victims of Allied bombings came in second place, then the people displaced from the Eastern provinces, then the widows of resistance fighters, and in fifth and last place, the Jews.[4]

Against this tendency to suppress crimes of the Nazi past—or to recall them only selectively—a minority of Germans initiated a campaign for justice, calling for judicial and historical investigations of German crimes against humanity that would result in compensation for their victims. This democratic counter-movement attracted support from political organizations as well as individuals, including those who had either emigrated as political opponents of Nazi rule or had survived internment in concentration camps. Despite having no resources except for the power of their public statements, the supporters of this counter-movement called attention both to the crimes of the Nazi era and their perpetrators and to abuses of the new German Federal Republic's constitutional protections of human rights and the rule of law.

At the same time that this counter-movement took shape, so did German public awareness of Anne Frank's life and work, which eventually became implicated in politically charged acts of recalling Nazi war

crimes. Although the first publication of Anne's diary in German translation did not attract much attention, performances of its dramatization by
Frances Hackett and Albert Goodrich had a major impact on the West
German public. After the debut of *The Diary of Anne Frank* on Broadway
in 1955, the play was performed in German, beginning in the fall of 1956,
on more than twenty stages in cities throughout West Germany. The
production was the biggest theatrical success of that year—in Hamburg alone, more than forty thousand people saw the play—and sales
of the book skyrocketed as a result. By May 1957, over 400,000 copies
of the German edition had been published. Although heretofore most
Germans had resisted the Allies' exhortations to address Nazi war
crimes, Anne's diary and its dramatization engendered a spontaneous
public debate on the Nazi era. This, in turn, had an impact on public
attention to Bergen-Belsen, which many Germans now knew to be the
site of Anne Frank's demise.[5]

Flowers for Anne Frank

The actual sites of Nazi war crimes in West Germany, including Bergen-
Belsen, had been largely neglected since the end of the war. Shortly after
the liberation of Bergen-Belsen, British forces set fire to all the prisoners'
barracks to prevent the spread of contagious diseases. The remaining
structures included a crematorium, fences around the camp, watchtow-
ers, and a few barracks that had escaped destruction. All these structures
were subsequently razed in order to clear the area for the creation of a
vast cemetery. In the absence of buildings or other traces of the original
camp, the site became something of a blank slate for memorial practices.
Dominating the grounds is a series of mass graves marked with stones
inscribed with the number of dead (ranging between eight hundred and
five thousand) interred within each heather-covered mound. Polish prisoners put up a large wooden cross immediately following the camp's
liberation (a replica now stands in its place). In the spring of 1946 a Jewish
memorial was unveiled, and a memorial to Soviet prisoners of war interned at Bergen-Belsen was erected. The following year, the camp's most
prominent monument—a thirty-meter-high stone obelisk and wall of
inscriptions, located at the edge of the mass graves—was initiated by

order of British occupation forces. Responsibility for the site was handed over to the state government of Lower Saxony in 1952. Although the site was officially named the Bergen-Belsen Memorial (Gedenkstätte), it provided no information for visitors about the crimes that had been perpetrated there. By the mid-1950s, newspaper reports described the site as neglected and undignified.[6]

Public awareness of Anne Frank, largely as a result of the dramatization of her diary, prompted about two thousand people, most of them students, to travel from Hamburg to Bergen-Belsen to pay homage to her memory at the place where she perished. On Sunday, March 17, 1957, they traveled some sixty miles south to the camp grounds in buses, private cars, and even on bicycles. The young people included both entire school classes and groups from religious youth organizations. Also traveling to the camp were young workers, members of trade unions based in Hamburg, who assembled under the umbrella of the German Trade Union Congress. The site had particular meaning for them, because during the Nazi period many trade unionists had been persecuted and murdered. Most participants were dressed in black, and all carried flowers for Anne Frank. Upon arrival at Bergen-Belsen, they gathered at the obelisk. A young Christian priest recited the Lord's Prayer and a young Jewish man read the Kaddish, a prayer recited in memory of the dead. Then the visitors walked to the mass graves. As there was no way to know where Anne Frank was buried, the visitors silently placed flowers on every mass grave. With this gesture, remembering Anne Frank was linked to remembering all who died at Bergen-Belsen.

This event began spontaneously, when one young student had traveled from Hamburg to Bergen-Belsen to visit Anne Frank's grave in 1957 and was disappointed that he could find neither her grave nor any flowers at the camp. He resolved to bring a wreath with some of his fellow students on the next anniversary of Anne's death. When a newspaper report mentioned this project to honor Anne Frank, hundreds of young people responded, eager to participate. A teacher who had accompanied her fourteen-year-old students to Bergen-Belsen explained to a reporter from Zürich's *Die Weltwoche* magazine, "My class learned about Anne Frank through a school play, and they begged me to take them to her grave at once. For weeks they barely talked about anything else."[7]

A German woman places flowers at a mass grave containing 1,000
victims of Nazi persecution at the memorial site of the Bergen-Belsen
concentration camp, March 1957. © *Bettmann/CORBIS*

Most of those who visited the site of Anne Frank's death in 1957
were under twenty-four years of age; the oldest among them had lived
through the Nazi period as youngsters. Unlike their elders, they had
no need to evade the responsibility of having perpetrated or tolerated
Nazi war crimes. They were the first generation of Germans to be in a
position to confront the Nazi past independent of a personal sense of

culpability. They knew that their elders had not come to terms with the specter of National Socialism and had avoided confronting the truth of what had occurred in Bergen-Belsen. These young Germans explained to a journalist covering their visit to the camp that "our parents and even our teachers evade our questions when we ask if they had ever known about what was going on and why they did nothing against it. But we really want to know."[8]

Press coverage played a strategic role in establishing the Flowers for Anne Frank movement as a watershed in Germany's public engagement with the Nazi past. Visits by German youth to Bergen-Belsen received attention outside Germany as well. *Aufbau,* a German-language Jewish newspaper published in the United States, explained that "every TV and radio station and the world press reported from the site," and noted that Dutch, Norwegians, Italians, Poles, Russians, Jews, and Germans had lost their lives at Bergen-Belsen. *Aufbau* quoted Erich Lüth, director of the state press office in Hamburg, who had addressed the young people at Bergen-Belsen on March 17, 1957, urging them not to repeat their parents' mistakes: "Be braver than we, your elders, were. Always protect the innocent when they are persecuted. We came here to free the dead from their loneliness. This is our way to help our people free themselves from their past."[9] Lüth thus invoked remembrance of Anne Frank as a bridge that linked the democratic counter-movement's campaign against Germans' suppression of the memory of the Nazi era to the need to remember all the other people whom the Nazis had murdered and other war crimes of the Third Reich.

The Flowers for Anne Frank movement was soon organized by the Society for Christian-Jewish Cooperation (SCJC), one of several groups associated with the democratic counter-movement. SCJC advocated for the investigation and punishment of all crimes perpetrated by Germans during the Third Reich, arguing that "peace without truth . . . can only lead to another catastrophe."[10] The group undertook actions against the anti-Semitism that was still prevalent in Germany by guarding Jewish cemeteries against vandalism and organizing rallies that called attention to Nazi crimes. Anne Frank's diary was central to the moral agenda of the SCJC and played a key role in legitimizing its ongoing work. For example, the SCJC capitalized on the excitement of young people eager

NY TYSK UNGDOM PÅ MARSCH

"German Youth on the March." This cartoon, showing young Germans bringing flowers to Anne Frank's grave at Bergen-Belsen, appeared in the *Stockholm Tidningen,* a liberal social democratic newspaper, on March 19, 1957.

to travel to Bergen-Belsen by including a trip to the site in their program for Brotherhood Week, observed annually in March.

The following year, another trip from Hamburg to Bergen-Belsen was organized to honor Anne Frank's memory on the anniversary of her death. Coordinated by the newly founded Anne Frank Youth Council of the SCJC of Hamburg, the 1958 trip involved several thousand young people. The widespread positive response in the press during the previous year inspired youth organizations from many other cities to take part. To prepare for the trip to Bergen-Belsen, these organizations were given as recommended reading an essay by Rudolf Küstermeier, a political prisoner who had survived Bergen-Belsen.[11] In this text he suggests that the trip to the former concentration camp is meant not only as a symbolic gesture of respect but also as a way to understand the scope and context of Nazi crimes. Other youth groups visited Bergen-Belsen during 1958, and seminars to train educators in preparation for trips to the camp were held in Hamburg, supported by UNESCO's Section for Teacher Education.

On May 29, 1959, Jewish organizations based in Hamburg called once more for a trip to Bergen-Belsen. They announced that 4,000 young people from Lower Saxony and another 1,300 from Berlin would take part, indicating a significant surge in the number of participants. The 1959 appeal did not mention Anne Frank's presence at the camp. Rather, situating the trip in response to recent anti-Semitic incidents in Germany, the appeal promoted "the ideals" of "freedom and human dignity."[12] Anne Frank's diary had apparently served its purpose—showing "the German public another side of the war in daily life and persuad[ing] them to recognize the suffering inflicted by the nation upon innocent people"—and so it was no longer necessary to invoke the diary or its author.[13]

Protests against the neglected condition of Bergen-Belsen voiced by groups visiting the memorial site soon yielded results. Reporting on maintenance work done at the cemetery, the union publication *Welt der Arbeit* proclaimed, "Dignity has been restored to Bergen-Belsen."[14] Under increasing pressure to act, local authorities also expanded the Bergen-Belsen Memorial by exhibiting historical documents and providing other information to visitors. In 1960, the government of the State of Lower Saxony commissioned a research paper on the history of the camp, resulting in the publication of the very first monograph on a concentration camp, *Bergen-Belsen: Geschichte des "Aufenthaltslagers" 1943–1945* in 1962.[15] This book became the basis for a new exhibition at the camp, which opened in 1966. For the first time since its liberation, visitors to Bergen-Belsen could learn *in situ* about its history and the people murdered there. The exhibition included a short biography of Anne Frank, which was displayed beside short biographies of four men who had been deported to the camp as resistance fighters and whose remains were also buried in its mass graves. Together with the 1961 war crimes trial of Adolf Eichmann in Jerusalem and the Frankfurt Auschwitz trials, the establishment of Bergen-Belsen as a well-maintained and well-documented site of remembering Nazi crimes marks the inauguration of Germany's public "coming to terms with the past." This undertaking continued for another twenty years, until it was well established that the genocide of European Jews had been the great crime of the Nazi regime.[16]

Anne Frank appeared in German public culture at this crucial moment, defined by the moral imperatives of a new generation. Initially, the diary and its dramatization presented Anne's story to Germans as a tragedy with universal implications. This reading soon gave way to using Anne's story as a vehicle for articulating a generational divide that centered on exposing a postwar culture of ignoring Nazi war crimes. Anne's life and work enabled young Germans, both as individuals and as members of larger movements, to take up the challenge of confronting the past. By embracing the words of hope articulated in Anne's diary, this young generation of activists distanced themselves publicly from the crimes of their elders. No longer understood as a narrative of Anne's dashed hopes, her diary and the story of her death at Bergen-Belsen now voiced the hopes of German youth as a bridge to a more hopeful future.

Ronald Reagan, Bitburg, and Bergen-Belsen

In contrast to the grassroots origins of the Flowers for Anne Frank movement, the next major landmark of Holocaust remembrance at Bergen-Belsen in which Anne Frank figured as a spectral presence occurred on May 5, 1985, when West German chancellor Helmut Kohl and U.S. president Ronald Reagan paid an official visit to the camp. In the previous year, Kohl and French president François Mitterand attended a ceremony of reconciliation in Verdun at the graves of soldiers who had died during World War I. As this initiative was widely praised in West Germany, Reagan and Kohl decided to mark the fortieth anniversary of the end of World War II with a similar German-U.S. reconciliation ceremony. German officials suggested, and then insisted, that the event be held at the Kolmeshöhe military cemetery near the town of Bitburg, which was the site of a U.S. military base. In this cemetery, soldiers who had fought in the Wehrmacht were interred next to members of the SS, a fact that provoked considerable international protest, especially from citizens of Israel and the United States.[17] While the planned visit to Bitburg elicited some criticism in West Germany as well, news reports of the time indicate that many people agreed with the plan.[18] Kohl's description of the SS buried in Bitburg as victims of the Nazis was in keeping with the legend that West Germany had cultivated over the preceding decades, which maintained that ultimately all Germans had been victims of National Socialism.

Protests by U.S. veterans of World War II and members of the American Jewish community convinced Reagan to request that the ceremony also include a visit to a memorial to civilian victims of National Socialism. At Kohl's suggestion, Reagan decided to precede the visit to the Bitburg cemetery with a ceremony honoring the victims of Nazi crimes at Bergen-Belsen, located more than three hundred miles northeast of the cemetery. There, Reagan acknowledged the German people's strength and willingness "to confront and condemn the acts of a hated regime of the past." Toward the end of this speech, Reagan invoked Anne Frank:

> Three weeks before she was taken prisoner, the young Anne wrote these words: "It's really a wonder that I haven't dropped all my ideals because they seem so absurd and impossible to carry out. Yet I keep them because in spite of everything I still believe that people are good at heart." . . . Somewhere here lies Anne Frank. Everywhere here are memories—pulling us, touching us, making us understand that they can never be erased. Such memories take us where God intended His children to go—toward learning, toward healing, and, above all, toward redemption.[19]

Many commentators described Reagan's recourse to Anne Frank's memory as awkward. At the time, critics argued that these were especially inappropriate words to quote from the diary while standing at the edge of the mass graves at Bergen-Belsen, where Anne and so many others had been murdered. Reagan—or, more likely, his speechwriters—had doubtless selected this quote for the benefit of the American public, in order to offer them a familiar image of the Holocaust as a situation where hope endures despite everything. And he surely had in mind the German people, represented by Kohl, who had been waiting for many years for reconciliation and forgiveness.

In the ceremony held later that day at Bitburg, Reagan tried to placate the concerns of Holocaust survivors, who criticized him for having acceded to Kohl's choice to include a stop at the concentration camp in his state visit, by declaring in his speech at Bitburg that "reconciliation leads to forgetting." But Reagan also had his hosts in mind when he said, "The war against one man's totalitarian dictatorship was not like other wars. The evil war of Nazism turned all values upside down. Nevertheless, we can mourn the German war dead today as human beings crushed by a vicious ideology."[20] With his choice of words, Reagan endorsed the official West German political view of the Nazi era. Anne Frank was implicated in this process of reconciliation and forgiveness when Reagan cited her diary in an effort to move beyond recalling the crimes of the Nazi period and renew an alliance between nations fighting together in the Cold War, unburdened by their opposition in another war of the recent past.

Reagan summoned the popular image of Anne Frank's exuberant humanism, long attributed to her diary and stressed in its dramatization, in order to offer retrospective absolution to German society. This invocation of Anne Frank's memory at Bergen-Belsen is the exact opposite of that made by the democratic counter-movements at the same location a generation earlier. Ostensibly addressing future relations between West Germany and the United States, Reagan was, in fact, interfering with the difficult process of remembering and taking moral account of the Nazi past. His remarks implicitly sought to dispel the power of remembering Anne Frank to haunt Germans; instead, she would assuage them with the thought that, if all people are "good at heart," then the treacherous ideology of Nazism cannot speak for the ordinary German. In Reagan's speech, excerpts from Anne Frank's diary became words of forgiveness offered by proxy to the German people and gladly accepted.

Inscription through Naming

Reagan's visit to Germany had a significant impact on efforts to renovate Bergen-Belsen. At the time, the original 1966 exhibition was still on display in the memorial hall (Dokumentenhaus) of Bergen-Belsen. Unchanged for twenty years, the exhibition bore no trace of the latest research on the site, indicating an institutional laxity with regard to scholarship and its ongoing role in Holocaust commemoration. In 1985, a citizens' initiative named Arbeitsgemeinschaft Bergen-Belsen (Study

Group Bergen-Belsen) advocated updating the exhibition in light of then current research and establishing an educational center at the camp-grounds for visitors. This group also recommended that the memorial recognize the approximately twenty thousand Soviet prisoners of war who had been murdered in Bergen-Belsen. These changes might well have remained unrealized even longer, were it not for the international interest in Bergen-Belsen at the time of Reagan's visit. The parliament of the State of Lower Saxony added this item to its deliberations in April 1985—three weeks before the American president's arrival—and the proposed changes to the exhibition were approved unanimously.

Then, three days after Reagan's visit, a public controversy about honoring the memory of Anne Frank erupted in Bergen, a town of eighteen thousand people, located less than four miles from the concentration camp grounds. The Social Democrat (SPD) members of the town council introduced a motion to change the name of the street leading from the town to the former concentration camp site from Belsen Street to Anne Frank Street. The SPD noted that they had "long voiced the concern to keep Anne Frank's memory alive by naming a place after her" without success and argued, in an effort to enhance their case, that "this time the American president has mentioned Anne Frank and quoted from her diary in his speech at Bergen-Belsen."[21]

The publisher of Bergen's newspaper, the *Stadt-Anzeiger*, who was also a town council member, objected to the proposal to rename the street after Anne Frank and distributed leaflets to every household in town in an effort to rally right-wing opposition to the plan. On July 27, 1985, he presented a counter-proposal at the town council meeting: a "peace monument" that, in his words, would ensure that "the names of the fallen or missing soldiers, women who assisted the defense forces, Red Cross workers, victims of Allied air-strikes and the forced relocation campaign, . . . would be remembered forever."[22] The conflict between these two proposed memorials exposed the faultlines that had developed in Germany over the course of the postwar period and continued to determine the discourse of remembrance. Efforts to honor the memory of those persecuted by the Nazi regime were routinely countered by people who argued that millions of Germans had been victims of the Nazis as well as of the military offensives and policies of the Allied Forces.

During Bergen's debate over honoring the memory of Anne Frank, local exponents of the right-wing position did not hesitate to refer to the model that Reagan had provided in his speeches at Bitburg and Bergen-Belsen. A letter to the editor in the *Stadt-Anzeiger* on July 3, 1985, proclaimed: "If misdeeds were perpetrated, it is those who perpetrated them who should be blamed, not the entire German people, because they were never asked if they agreed. And certainly the American president was aware of this when he said that the German people should not be plagued by feelings of guilt."[23]

Opposition to the initiatives to memorialize Anne Frank triggered strong reactions in both the German and the international press. This response encouraged the local representatives of democratic movements to build a coalition in support of the SPD proposal. The SPD members of the Bergen town council also decided to expand its proposal, in case renaming the street did not pass, and adopted the suggestion of the Christian community to name a local public school for students eleven to thirteen years old after Anne Frank. In the end, the proposal to rename Bergen Street was voted down, but a majority of the council did approve renaming the school. The statement of the council's decision read: "This homage to Anne Frank is intended to honor all people—but more specifically the children—who lost their lives in concentration camps. . . . The naming of a school after Anne Frank should point to the duty of our young people to stand up for the safeguarding of human rights and to denounce or prevent injustice and unprovoked violence."[24] In February 1986, the school was officially renamed in an hour-long ceremony, in which local and regional authorities took part, as well as the president of the Federation of Jewish Communities in Lower Saxony.

In the following years, the Anne Frank School developed programs to teach its students about Anne Frank's life, her diary, and the circumstances that brought her to Bergen-Belsen. The school organized visits with people who had known her, including Miep Gies, who had helped to hide Anne and her family, as well as her cousin Buddy Elias and childhood friend Hanneli Goslar. Teachers also made it a point to broaden their students' awareness of those who were persecuted by the Nazis besides Anne Frank. To that end, the school invited concentration camp survivors to speak to students and taught them about the experiences of child victims of Nazi persecution. Students of the Anne Frank School participated in many events at Bergen-Belsen, reciting poems, reading from eyewitness accounts, and performing songs. Every year, groups of students visited the grounds to help maintain the mass graves. Often, these activities were undertaken at the children's initiative. It is telling that the school only undertook these and related activities after it was officially named after Anne Frank. Teachers at the school also noted a shift in attitude that took place in Bergen after the renaming, including parents' positive response to their children's activities in relation to the Bergen-Belsen Memorial. The act of naming the school after Anne Frank in effect catalyzed pedagogical and memorial projects concerning the Nazi era that had previously not been part of the school's activities.[25] Activities organized around the memory of Anne Frank and other victims of Bergen-Belsen continue there to the present.

At the same time, another local institution underwent a similar change of name: the Christlicher Verein Junger Menschen (CVJM, the equivalent to the Young Men's/Young Women's Christian Association) in Oldau. Located seven miles from Bergen-Belsen, the CVJM had been known, since it opened in 1955, as a well-run educational and after-school facility. At first, its programming had only occasionally touched on the history of National Socialism and its consequences. Yet in the spring of 1985, leading members of the CVJM began to campaign for the long-overdue restoration of the Bergen-Belsen Memorial. When the state parliament of Lower Saxony decided to renovate the site, the CVJM chose to focus on the study of what it termed "working out the Nazi past—learning from history." The CVJM leadership described its agenda as follows:

> We want to keep alive the memory of what happened here during the Third Reich. Our geographical proximity determines our emphasis on Bergen-Belsen. . . . We want to end the anonymity of Bergen-Belsen; we want to uncover something about the lives of specific people. Anne Frank is a natural subject for us to focus on as the starting point of a seminar. By describing her life and following her on her journey, we initiate a process of identification that is especially powerful for young women. For this reason, we make a point of describing Anne Frank as only one example.[26]

With the encouragement of the Anne Frank-Fonds in Basel, the CVJM in Oldau was named the Anne Frank House in 1992. The Anne

Frank House has since served as a center for youth activities related to Bergen-Belsen. In 2005 it expanded its program by opening a new building that houses seminar rooms, a library, and a dormitory, all open to young people from around the world.

Divisions that had riven German society since the fall of the Nazi regime reemerged in the debates surrounding both successful and failed attempts to rename places after Anne Frank. On one side was the generation that had shaped public opinion during the Nazi era and continued to uphold the early postwar policy for contending with the recent past by dismissing, denying, and suppressing it. On the other side stood the democratic counter-movement, made up of church-sponsored youth organizations, trade unions, as well as Lutheran and Roman Catholic clergy, journalists, and scientists. Uniting around memorial efforts at Bergen-Belsen, they promoted an openly judicial and historical approach to Nazi crimes.

The ideological ground shifted with the aging of the older generation, whose ideological successors had become a political minority, and the coming of age of the new generation. Thus, on June 27, 2007, representatives of the small community of Loheide, where the Bergen-Belsen Memorial is located, decided unanimously to name the spot where the memorial buildings are located Anne-Frank-Platz (Anne Frank Square), both to honor Anne Frank's memory at the site of her death and to express support for the larger political and cultural goals of the memorial site. The site's authorities agreed to this proposal.

By then, the ideological battles over remembering the Nazi era had been played out and largely won by the democratic movement. Having established the genocide of European Jews as the paradigmatic crime in the history of humanity, their goal has become to ensure that current and future generations focus on the history and consequences of genocide.

Gifts for Anne Frank

Over the years, the Anne Frank-Fonds had been following the course of these developments to honor the memory of Anne Frank in and around Bergen-Belsen, including discussions of erecting a memorial stone in her name on the grounds of the former concentration camp. The foundation

Stone marking the Bergen-Belsen Memorial's Anne Frank Square,
which was named in 2007. *Photographer: Henri Lustiger Thaler*

long shared Otto Frank's concern that a monument to Anne at Bergen-
Belsen might be attacked or desecrated. Despite the continued presence
of right-wing supporters in the region, concerns about such an attack
subsided as democratic values in Germany were strengthened. In light
of this development, the Anne Frank-Fonds decided in 1999 to place a
monument to Margot and Anne Frank on a field in Bergen-Belsen, near
the mass graves. Similar individual memorial stones, dedicated to the
memory of individuals who died at Bergen-Belsen, are randomly placed
near the mass graves. These monuments, usually erected by family members, disrupt the cold anonymity of the site.

The monument to Margot and Anne Frank has since become a place
where visitors to Bergen-Belsen leave gifts, as it is the one location at this
site of mass destruction where visitors can make a personal gesture to a
well-known individual victim of Nazi persecution. As in the Flowers for
Anne Frank movement of the late 1950s, her iconic stature again elicits a
memorial response. People leave jewelry, notes, words etched on worn

The monument to Margot and Anne Frank, erected at Bergen-Belsen in 1999. Though it resembles a tombstone, the monument does not mark the sisters' grave, as the location of their burial is unknown. The Hebrew inscription reads, "The light of the Lord is the soul of man" (Proverbs 20:27). *Photographer: Henri Lustiger Thaler*

stones, stuffed animals, miniature flags, and medals, among other items. While the practice of leaving objects at the monument to Margot and Anne Frank recalls the thousands of flowers left by democratic counter-movements at the mass graves at Bergen-Belsen in the 1950s, these recent practices are highly individualized rather than collective and underscore a widening of the memorial culture that Anne continues to inspire. Moreover, these individualized responses arise from a mediated relationship to Anne Frank of long standing, now taking place within the commemorative institution of Bergen-Belsen as a site of destruction, wedded to the memorial narrative of her brutal death, rather than to the diary and the palliative political and cultural uses made of it in the past.

Although individual objects left at the memorial to Margot and Anne Frank may appear at first to be quite ordinary, they gain power through the cumulative effect of repeated acts of spontaneous and individualized gifting. These gifts gain resonance in the barren but ideologically charged memorial space of Bergen-Belsen by materializing individual relationships to Anne Frank, quite apart from her stature in history and politics. Most of the items at the monument are left by children, who encounter Anne as a fellow child. By placing commonplace objects that are most often related to childhood at the memorial stone, visitors in effect restore to Anne the childhood taken from her by persecution and her early death. In this practice, the dense memorial narrative of Anne Frank allows young visitors to become what the philosopher Avishai Margalit has called "a moral witness," able to give personal voice to a broader ethical community's reaction to the evil that took place at the site.[27]

In contrast to the mass murder recalled at the site, the messages left at the memorial by young visitors are empathetic in their framing of remembering Anne Frank as a personal and yet shared encounter. In one letter, a young writer thanks Anne for her courage and imagines how wonderful it would be if she were alive to celebrate her seventy-fifth birthday. A stone left at the site is inscribed with the wish that the writer and Anne Frank will meet in heaven. These objects materialize visions of a future society in which Anne Frank, an innocent child victim of the most heinous crime against humanity, figures as the iconic opposite of evil. The objects left by children at the monument to Margot and Anne Frank are gathered by the staff of the memorial at the end of each week and placed in the archive of the museum at Bergen-Belsen. These individual, ephemeral gifting practices by young people exemplify a shift in the performance of Holocaust remembrance, articulating the generational impact on memory and commemoration as well as the dynamic relationship of individualized memory to institutionalized collective memory.[28]

Legal and memorial practices address justice in different ways. The Tuol Sleng Genocide Museum memorialized the Khmer Rouge Reign of Terror atrocities more than thirty years before the first criminal, Comrade Duch, was finally brought to trial in 2007.[29] In contrast, the Bergen-Belsen trials preceded memorial practices by several decades. Although the trials, which were held in 1945, were consistent with the political and cultural standards of the time in Germany, judicial justice did not in itself secure the memory of injustice or the obligation to remember.[30] It was only decades later, when Anne Frank came to haunt German memory from the heather-covered fields and mass graves of Bergen-Belsen, that the ethical potential of memory to render a different kind of justice was realized.[31] Remembered from her unmarked grave, not from the Annex in Amsterdam, the transit camp at Westerbork, or even Auschwitz-Birkenau, the "German" Anne Frank demonstrates the potential of an appeal for justice as truth—and not in the service of a state—thereby extending to Bergen-Belsen, as a site of mass murder, the ethical potential of memory.

Six of the many objects that visitors to Bergen-Belsen
have left at the monument to Margot and Anne Frank.
The Bergen-Belsen Memorial staff collects and archives
these items. *Photographer: Henri Lustiger Thaler*

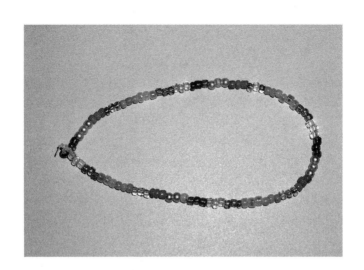

5

Teaching Anne Frank
in the United States

Ilana Abramovitch

Millions of readers around the world have encountered Anne Frank's diary in the classroom, perhaps more than in any other setting.[1] The diary was first published as a text for all readers, not especially for young people or for students, but within a few years of its first appearance in print, teachers began to assign it to their classes. By 1960, this grassroots interest by individual educators led to the adoption of *The Diary of a Young Girl* as required reading in school systems throughout the United States. It remains a fixture of American pedagogy: according to a 1996 survey cited on the Anne Frank Museum website, 50 percent of American high school students had read Anne Frank's diary as a classroom assignment.[2]

Teaching Anne's diary mediates the encounter with her life and work in distinctive ways. As with any other text, when the diary enters the classroom, it is situated within particular disciplines, courses, lesson plans, and assignments. The book has long been taught in the United States in courses on world literature and modern history, sometimes in courses that focus on World War II or the Holocaust. Teachers have long recognized the diary's potential to raise with students a wide range of topics, not necessarily related to the Holocaust. By the early 1970s, one educator listed twenty such topics, ranging from "the way of history and historical personalities" to "thoughts for the future," "understanding our parents" to "race relations," and "self expression" to "sex education and the relationships between boys and girls."[3] Accordingly, Anne Frank's life and work appear in less traditional curricula, including courses in genocide studies, peace studies, and conflict resolution, as well as character education programs, especially those concerned with combating prejudice and promoting ethics, with names such as "Teaching Tolerance," "Respect for Differences," "The Importance of Democracy," and "The Importance of Individual Responsibility." More recently, the diary is sometimes taught in primary schools and in a broadening range of interdisciplinary settings, such as classes that integrate dance or art with English language and literature, and has even appeared in health education. This array of approaches to teaching the diary evinces the great value invested in it as a text that engages young people.

At the same time, the diary does not stand on its own as a pedagogical tool. Each of the many possibilities for teaching about Anne Frank frames her life and work in relation to some larger subject—modern literature, Holocaust history, human rights, character development, creative writing—that informs how students approach the diary. Uniting all these possibilities is an expectation that from reading the diary students will make a connection to a larger body of knowledge or set of insights.

Moreover, educators are concerned that students' connections will not automatically follow from simply reading the diary. Even as the diary is valued as a conduit to greater insights, teachers acknowledge that the text itself requires mediation. This concern has been addressed both in materials especially created for that purpose—such as teacher guides, educational exhibitions, online student activities—and through works not originally intended for the classroom that teachers have repurposed for this setting. Salient among the latter is the official dramatization of the diary by Frances Goodrich and Albert Hackett. Their play, *The Diary of Anne Frank,* has long been one of the most popular works staged by American high school drama groups, and it is also often used in the classroom, alongside or even instead of the diary.[4]

Although Anne Frank pedagogy emerged as a grassroots phenomenon, an extensive body of material for teachers has been produced on this subject by official, authoritative sources, including organizations specifically devoted to Anne's life and work as well as institutions dedicated to larger subjects, such as Holocaust education or teaching tolerance. The ongoing relationship between these institutions and individual schools and teachers, who continue to develop their own approaches to teaching the diary, is emblematic of a larger dynamic between those seeking to regulate engagements with Anne Frank and independent, personal initiatives.

Institutions

In response to the popular reception of his daughter's diary, Otto Frank helped found two institutions that remain central authorities on Anne's life and work to this day: first, the Anne Frank House, a museum based in the Amsterdam building that originally housed the Franks' hiding place, which opened its doors to the public in 1960; second, the Anne Frank-Fonds, which was established in Basel in 1963 to "promote charitable work and to play a social and cultural role in the spirit of Anne Frank" by contributing "to better understanding between different religions, to serve the cause of peace between people and to encourage international contacts between the young."[5] In its original conception, the Anne Frank House not only provided the public with the opportunity to visit the Annex but also was home to the International Youth Center, in which "the post-war generation could seek ways to work for peace" by discussing "problems of discrimination, democracy, cross-cultural communication, religion, and international cooperation."[6] At the time of their founding, these institutions' missions reflected Otto Frank's understanding of the larger significance of his daughter's life and writing. Moreover, they conformed to the universalist political culture of Cold War-era liberalism in the West.

Over the past half-century, both organizations have produced widely respected educational materials, offered teacher training, and initiated international youth projects, all centered on Anne and her diary, while also serving as watchdogs for racism and genocide worldwide. In addition, these organizations cooperate with other Anne Frank centers, established more recently in Germany, Austria, the United Kingdom, and the United States, which also produce "a variety of educational programs, including exhibitions, workshops, and special events" that offer a similar approach to Anne's life and work.[7] These organizations serve as nodes for the broad dissemination of educational resources in a variety of media. For example, the Anne Frank Center USA sponsored the

Anne Frank House's traveling exhibition, "Anne Frank in the World," which was visited by more than 5.8 million people in 550 sites in 23 countries between 1985 and 1995.[8] A more recent traveling exhibition produced by the Anne Frank House, "Anne Frank: A History for Today," is displayed more than 150 times a year.[9] This exhibition's themes— "Discrimination is cruel and irrational," "Ordinary people discriminate against others," "Discrimination is a matter of personal choice," and "Stereotypes persist"—while rooted in the story of Anne's experience of persecution under Nazism, conform to Otto Frank's foundational vision of his daughter's story as a point of entry to addressing universal lessons in human rights. Although the Center provided supplementary educational materials for these exhibitions, individual U.S. states and school boards produced resources of their own. The Utah State Office of Education, for example, created an elaborate online "Teacher Workbook," containing lesson plans on Anne Frank and the Holocaust for all grades from third through twelfth, accompanied by timelines, readings, and overviews.[10]

In 2010 Maureen McNeil, the director of education at the Anne Frank Center USA, characterized its work as "practicing freedom," using Anne as an "enduring model." The Center creates educational programs and exhibitions "to teach literacy, tolerance, character-building, culture, emotional intelligence and resilience. At the heart of every program is reading Anne's Diary and Diary writing." The broad reach of the Center's activities show how "Anne Frank's simple volume continues to open doors around the world to the lessons of hope that were learned so well during her 26 months hiding from the Nazis." Just as learning about Anne Frank's story entails connecting the past with present and local concerns, so reading the diary involves linking the pursuit of social justice with personal development. A program that the Center runs in the Bronx, for example, addresses bullying through the "Art of Self Discovery," with a local community advisory committee to help solve problems "that range from racism to teacher parking." The Center educates adults as well as children. Among programs for adults is its Prison Diary Project, inspired by the notion that "Anne thought no matter how bad our situation in life, it is our responsibility to develop our character."[11]

Disciplinary and Methodological Challenges

The educational materials produced by these official organizations dedicated to Anne Frank straddle distinct pedagogical goals and, with them, different methodologies. These institutions pay considerable attention to documenting the historical context of Anne's life, using her story as a point of entry to the larger narratives of the Nazi era and the Holocaust. At the same time, these institutions position Anne as an exemplar of transcendent courage and personal expression, quite apart from the particulars of history. Thus, individual passages of the diary are frequently cited as sources of inspiration, not unlike the citing of passages from canonical literary works or even the Bible.

The tension among these pedagogical goals and the approaches to realizing them exemplifies larger challenges faced in Holocaust education, in which teaching about Anne Frank has long played a significant role. Holocaust education emerged in American public schools during the late 1970s, coinciding with the growing movement to teach history through a "social studies" approach organized around students' interests, concerns, and problems.[12] This approach contrasts with more traditional methods of teaching history that emphasize chronology, causation, and the particulars of each historical period. Instead, the social studies approach calls students' attention more to historical parallels between the past and the present, often drawing lessons from comparison with today's world. Similarly, the Anne Frank organizations' approach to teaching about her life and work has prioritized establishing students' affective connection to Anne Frank, responding to her tragic fate and building on her idealism, rather than emphasizing traditional history lessons.

Each approach has its champions and detractors. Historians of the Holocaust, such as Lucy Dawidowicz, have voiced concerns about approaches to the subject that, for example, teach students about prejudice generically, rather than examining the specifics of racial anti-Semitism implemented by the Nazi regime that culminated in the Holocaust.[13] Conversely, champions of the social studies approach fault traditional methods of teaching history as failing to engage students affectively and to help them relate historical lessons to the present, especially with regard to informing students' moral awareness. Teaching Anne Frank's life and work figures in these larger debates, including the argument some scholars make that using her diary to teach about the Holocaust is misleading, because, as literary scholar Lawrence Langer writes, Anne's diary does not offer "a view of the apocalypse"—that is, the full enormity of genocide.[14]

Different pedagogical concerns surround the teaching of Anne's diary in courses on literature and language arts. There, the diary has long been a classroom staple, though students are often assigned only excerpts of the diary, sometimes reprinted in an anthology, or the dramatic adaptation by Goodrich and Hackett, instead of reading the diary in its entirety.[15] In the United States students typically study Anne's life and work in the eighth grade—that is, when they are about the same age that Anne was when she began keeping her diary. This proximity in age informs the way the diary is often taught in language arts and literature classes as a narrative resonant with the emotional lives of many students: descriptions of feeling hemmed in, having a crush on someone, being angry at a parent, frustration with a sibling, and dreams of future glory. Teachers report that girls often connect more directly with the diary's female narrator, whereas boys often relate more to Anne's relationship with her parents or her accounts of the war.[16]

At the same time, teaching the diary in these settings entails some discussion of the historical context in which it was written. This task can prove challenging both because of the disturbing nature of the Holocaust and because of the diary's problematic relation to the larger story of Anne's life as well as the war. It is especially difficult because language arts teachers often have no special training in how to teach about the Holocaust. One master teacher, Elaine Culbertson, describes this as a common pedagogical problem:

> The abrupt ending of the book with the sudden departure of the family signaled the end of any real explanation; some [teachers] would say things like "then the Nazis came to get them," or "it seems that they were informed upon and they were taken away." That was usually enough to satisfy students who were more intrigued with Anne's teen troubles than they were with her reason for being in the attic in the first place.[17]

Less problematic for the language arts and literature classroom is the opportunity to study the diary as a literary work, focusing on Anne's

talent and growth as a writer. Teaching the diary in the context of language and literature pedagogy can reveal to students Anne's growth as
a young writer during her years in hiding, as her self-knowledge and
language grew more complex and her observations became more mature
and incisive. Literary approaches to the diary have been addressed in a
recent exhibition at the United States Holocaust Memorial Museum,
"Anne Frank, the Writer—An Unfinished Story," on the "Edsitement"
website of the National Endowment for the Humanities (NEH), and in
books about the diary, including Francine Prose's *Anne Frank: The Book,
The Life, The Afterlife*.[18]

Attention to the diary's literary quality enables students to consider
the text from a variety of analytic approaches. For instance, one of the activities the NEH website suggests for teaching the diary is to ask students
to compare Anne's "Ode to My Fountain Pen: In Memoriam" (which appears in the diary entry of November 11, 1943)[19] with Pablo Neruda's odes
to everyday objects, such as his "Ode to Salt," thereby asking students
to consider Anne's work in relation to an accomplished author from a
completely different background. This approach can extend to teaching
the dramatization of the diary. For example, a Maryland middle school's
writing assignment on *The Diary of Anne Frank* emphasizes attention to
the formal elements of the drama more than its content. Students are
asked to analyze the playwrights' approach to issues of time, to describe
how dialogue and stage directions work together to create characters and
plot, as well as to consider how elements of plot, especially climax and
resolution, play an important role in this drama.[20]

Prose, among others, is critical of teachers who teach about Anne
Frank with the Goodrich and Hackett play, arguing that "the drama has
been effectively pre-censored and pre-vetted for an acceptable balance
of upsetting and uplifting," unlike the unpredictability of Anne's diary.[21]
But some teachers, including Holocaust master educators, are advocates
for using the play as a point of entry to teaching this subject. One such
teacher, Ellen Bisping of Minnesota, responds to arguments against doing so as follows:

> While I am aware that Anne Frank's experiences were not typical, and that
> teaching Anne Frank is not teaching the Holocaust, still I found reading the
> play (original version) with my eighth graders the best way to introduce a

4-week unit on the Holocaust. It piqued their interest and sensitivities by focusing on one individual (instead of statistics and generalities) who was much like them and with whom they could relate. Reading the play in class, with students reading the roles aloud, was a participatory experience which led to spontaneous questions, discussions, and interactions that are not possible when students read to themselves. Through the use of discussions, targeted lectures, projects, research, speakers, video, additional Holocaust books and materials (including those from the Anne Frank House), and classroom activities, significant historical background was disseminated.[22]

The ongoing debate of how to teach this text, which has proved to be as pedagogically challenging as it is widely read, has emerged as a topic in its own right, generating several studies on the teaching of Anne Frank. In one such study, English teacher Scott Christian describes a web-based literary project undertaken in 1993, called "The Anne Frank Conference," in which middle school students from Alaska to Mississippi were asked to write to one another in an online forum about Anne Frank's diary, using this platform to extend their exchanges on the diary to discussions on a wide range of shared interests. Through this collaborative effort of teachers and students, new kinds of writing emerged in an "online dialogue about growing up, human nature, literature, life, and more."[23] In this project, the study of Anne as a writer served as the model and motivation for students' exploring an evolving sense of themselves through writing of their own.

In their study of teaching Anne Frank's diary in eight-grade English classes, education scholars Karen Spector and Stephanie Jones report that pupils often are motivated to study more about Holocaust history by first learning about the diary and empathizing with Anne Frank. Many educators agree that learning about the Holocaust through personal stories is the best way for students to begin to make a connection to this difficult period of history, which cannot be easily assimilated through statistics and other data that are deemed both overwhelming and dry. Spector and Jones note that some teachers and students avoid information about Anne that reveals the painful events after the Annex inhabitants' arrest by the Nazis. Having bonded with Anne as a result of reading the diary, some students resist hearing of her brutal treatment, suffering, and death. In one class that Spector and Jones observed, students were asked to write about Anne's feelings after her arrest. One student in the class wrote: "Knowing Anne, she was happy in the concentration camps. She didn't have to be quiet anymore; she could frolic outside. She could be in nature. She loved nature. I think this was a welcome relief for her."[24] Aside from reflecting the student's gross misunderstanding of the nature of Anne's fate, such a response raises provocative questions for educators: does empathizing with Anne, as encountered in the diary, make it difficult, if not impossible, for some students to come to terms with the details of her arrest, imprisonment, and death? Might this response reflect the impact of the last scene of *The Diary of Anne Frank,* in which Otto Frank tells Miep Gies that Anne was happy at the concentration camp, happy to be outside in the fresh air?[25]

Each classroom in which the diary is taught surrounds it with a complex of expectations and, often, surprises. The common goal of promoting a connection with Anne—whether her diary is read in courses on history, literature, writing, or ethics—is challenged by the very different circumstances of her life when compared to the students' lives, their shared experience of adolescence notwithstanding. When Elaine Culbertson was a high school English teacher in Philadelphia in the 1970s, her inner city students did not feel great compassion for Anne, because she had her family with her, as well as some food to eat and a cute boy to flirt with. The students experienced their own lives and those of people around them as more stressful and dangerous.[26]

Simulations

Uniting the desires to establish students' empathic connection with Anne, on one hand, and to have them comprehend the remote and profoundly disturbing history in which she lived and died, on the other hand, is a shared anxiety about doing a disservice to the remembrance of Anne and other victims of Nazi persecution through educational approaches that are deemed trivializing. Samuel Totten, co-author of the U.S. Holocaust Memorial Museum's influential "Guidelines for Teaching about the Holocaust," issued in 1993, has complained about the widespread use of Holocaust learning activities that are "set at the lowest levels of the cognitive domain."[27] These guidelines strive to help teachers determine what constitutes accurate and respectful approaches to teaching the Holocaust and to avoid superficial or offensive treatments.

Among the most provocative of pedagogical methods for teaching about Anne Frank is the use of "experiential learning" techniques, including role-playing or simulation exercises, to facilitate an affective connection with the subject through an intense experience that is understood as superseding the dispassionate quality of a pedagogy centered on intellectual engagement. These techniques have special appeal for educators who feel that the Holocaust's lessons can be learned only through an emotionally charged encounter with its anguish.

Experiential learning techniques rely on creating an immersive environment, in which learning is engaged through an embodied performance. This pedagogy is indebted to techniques derived from theater's realization of the imaginary through emotionally charged action. When used to teach about historical epochs, experiential learning exercises typically provide students with scenarios—including information about the period, the actions, characters, possibilities, and limitations of the setting—which they then act out.

Advocates of experiential learning exercises for teaching history argue that past societies whose ethical values differed greatly from our own—U.S. slave-owning communities and Nazi Germany are often mentioned as examples—reinforced the normalcy of values now held to be morally repugnant through a sociocultural system of practices. Teaching these societies' challenging value systems is "all about the rules of the game," claims historian Patrick Rael of Bowdoin College. "If a simulation is constructed properly, it can allow the student to experience the kind of choices that historical actors had to make."[28]

Simulation exercises used to teach about Anne Frank entail a broad spectrum of approaches: some are physically or emotionally arduous exercises, meant to reinforce historical lessons about deprivation, obedience, and brutality, such as confining students for fifty minutes in a crowded classroom "cattle car," during which they must remain silent.[29] Other exercises focus on simulating Anne Frank's experience of hiding. In one example, students are instructed to live for two hours at home "as Anne did," without wearing shoes, turning on lights, and abstaining from "talking, eating, use of running water, watching TV, walking, or anything that makes excessive noise, such as flushing the toilet."[30] Students are instructed to record their thoughts, reactions, and activities in their own diaries. One school's exercise of simulating life in the Annex in the form of a "school sleepover" attracted the bemused attention of local media:

> Eighth graders at Florida's Bethany Christian School, which promises "academic excellence in a Christ-centered environment," traded their iPods and cell phones for potatoes, bread, and carrots in an attempt to turn their classroom into Anne Frank's attic for a strangely ascetic sleepover over the weekend, according to a report in the *South Florida Sun-Sentinel*.[31]

According to online comments on the newspaper's article, eighteen hours in the schoolroom "Annex" convinced some students that they understood better how Anne Frank felt in hiding. The disparity between the particulars of the simulations and Anne's actual experience—not only the duration of a few hours vs. more than two years, but also an exercise whose end is known vs. the unresolved ordeal that Anne and the other Jews with her faced throughout their time in the Annex—call into question the ability of these exercises to foster a meaningful empathy with Anne's ordeal. At the same time, these classroom exercises resemble other venerable practices, notably religious simulations of suffering—such as evoking the ordeal of slavery with ritual foods during a Passover seder, or walking the Stations of the Cross to recall the martyrdom of Jesus—which are deliberately much less arduous than the actual experience being invoked and are intended, in part, to inspire reverence for exemplary figures' greater suffering.

In contrast to simulations that center on embodied experiences are those that focus on writing. In these exercises, students are asked to imagine being in particular situations similar to Anne's and then to write their own diary entries in response to having read hers. A curriculum website hosted by North Carolina State University, for example, provides a fifteen-unit lesson plan that links studying Anne's life with student journal writing.[32] After familiarizing themselves with background on Anne Frank and the Holocaust, students are to begin writing their own guided journal entries. The assignment for the second journal entry begins: "Pretend you had one hour to prepare to go into hiding. You can

NEVER return to your home. You cannot carry a suitcase." Students are then asked to describe the few items they would take with them and how they would disguise them en route. Further journal requirements have students, like Anne in act 1, scene 4, of *The Diary of Anne Frank*, describe the first thing they would like to do after many months in hiding and explain why. Even as these exercises address details of Anne's wartime ordeals, they invite students to emulate her efforts of self-expression through writing, as opposed to emulating her suffering through physically or emotionally uncomfortable simulations. With their attention on honing writing skills, they may stop short of asking students to contemplate Anne's fate, after she was no longer able to write in her diary.

Most authorities on Holocaust education disapprove of simulation exercises, including the U.S. Holocaust Memorial Museum, the Jewish Anti-Defamation League, Facing History and Ourselves, and Teaching Tolerance, a project of the Southern Poverty Law Center. Critics claim that these exercises "can reinforce negative views of the victims,"[33] that students "often forget the purpose of the lesson,"[34] or that "the unfortunate message [of these lessons] is, 'Now you know what it feels like to be ... a Holocaust survivor.'"[35] Holocaust survivors and scholars question the possibility of trying to simulate accurately "what it was like to live on a daily basis with fear, hunger, disease, unfathomable loss, and the unrelenting threat of abject brutality and death."[36] Among the defenders of simulation as potentially effective pedagogy is Simone Schweber, who bases her argument on an empirical study of the work of one successful and thoughtful teacher. Despite her own initial skepticism, Schweber discovered that the simulation "spelled out the possibility for students to deliberate very powerful moral dilemmas with a sense of real consequences."[37]

Expanding—and Limiting—Anne Frank Pedagogy

The impulse to expand the teaching of Anne Frank to a greater range of disciplines and subjects and to implement this teaching through a proliferation of pedagogical methods extends in other directions as well. One recent development is the creation of books and activities about Anne

Frank addressed to younger students who are considered too young to read the diary. Biographies of Anne written for young readers, some of them in the form of picture books, focus on acquainting children with some aspects of her life story, especially her turn to writing while in hiding. Some of these books are volumes in series that situate Anne among a roster of other "world figures," "modern heroes," or accomplished girls and women, thereby providing a rubric within which young people begin to situate Anne's accomplishments.[38] While none of these books are authorized biographies, the Anne Frank House elected to publish a graphic biography of Anne Frank in 2010, as part of its ongoing mission to bring Anne's story "to as large an audience as possible," including through "this innovative and accessible manner."[39]

Pedagogical activities about Anne Frank for younger students are more wide-ranging in their focus, reflecting a trend in Holocaust education more generally. Although Holocaust educational institutions generally recommend not teaching this subject before the fifth grade, there are some that offer other "age-appropriate" activities for younger students. Often these activities focus not on the historical particulars of the Holocaust but on values related to the teaching of this subject, such as countering bullying and prejudice. For example, the Utah Education Network offers an online Anne Frank Unit that includes lesson plans for the third grade in health education, building on Anne's diary entries about food:

> "We have been through a good many 'food cycles'... periods in which one has nothing else to eat but one particular dish or kind of vegetable. We had nothing but endive for a long time, day in, day out, endive with sand, endive without sand, stew with endive ... then it was spinach and after that followed kohlrabi...."—Anne Frank (April 3, 1944)[40]

A similar pedagogical concept informs a lesson plan in this unit on movement and isometric exercises:

> "I have a craze for dancing and ballet... and practice dance steps every evening diligently. My stiff limbs are well on the way to becoming supple again like they used to be. One terrific exercise is to sit on the floor, hold a heel in each hand, and then lift both legs up in the air. I have to have a cushion under me, otherwise my poor little behind has a rough time."—Anne Frank (January 12, 1944)[41]

Here, lessons about nutrition and exercise that are universally applicable are given a focused significance by relating them to the circumstances of an important person in history. Conversely, this attention on diet and physical health, usually not a focus of readers of the diary, highlights what were, in fact, ongoing concerns of the Jews hiding in the Annex and their protectors. In addition to taking an expansive approach to thinking about Anne's life, these lessons prompt innovative ways for students to imagine her experience in hiding. In the latter exercise, teachers are instructed to lead their students in exercises that Anne could have quietly done in the Annex. The lesson plan also suggests that students may want to compose tunes for their workout: "If Anne had a personal stereo and access to batteries as she might today, her dancing and ballet practice could have had undetectable music accompaniment."[42] These activities situate Anne as an imaginary member of the class, in need of the students' attention.

The Internet not only enables the wide circulation of curricular models and resources; it also facilitates the expansive engagement of student readers of Anne's diary with one another. Exemplary of how students of Anne Frank's diary are availing themselves of the Internet is the Anne Frank Wall project, initiated in 2002 by Jim DeLong, a language arts teacher based in San Jose, California. DeLong's eighth-grade students had read the diary, seen a documentary about Anne Frank, and listened to speakers knowledgeable about her life. Yet DeLong wanted "students to feel that we can have an impact beyond the limits of our lives, in ways we never anticipate or know. . . how the human spirit can rise above suffering and adversity."[43] DeLong's students began taking photographs of friends and family members living in other cities or countries, all prominently holding a copy of Anne Frank's diary. The photos were displayed in the classroom, their number growing so large that they encircled the entire classroom. As the project continued to expand, it shifted to displaying the images on the Internet, where its website won the prestigious Internet Innovators Award sponsored by National Semiconductor. The online "wall" projects a virtual community comprised of individual readers of the diary, in multiple languages from over forty countries around the world. The project links its aspiration to promote an embrace of Anne Frank on a global scale with the

desire to assert her immortality. On the website, DeLong explains that
the project is intended to

> have the students discover how alive [Anne's] spirit is today throughout the
> world. . . . Anne Frank wrote in her diary "I want to go on living, even after
> my death." In a single glance, this wall shows both the power of her teenage
> writing and the triumph of the human spirit over adversity. By capturing her
> experiences in writing, Anne Frank realized her wish to "go on living" even
> after her death from typhus three weeks before the Allies liberated the Bergen-
> Belsen concentration camp. Today, her diary is published in over 60 languages
> and read by millions around the world.[44]

Even as many educators seek to expand awareness of Anne Frank
and extend possibilities for learning from her writings, there are others
who have elected to exclude the diary from classrooms. Given how wide
is the embrace of Anne's diary as a pedagogical touchstone, decisions
not to teach it seem to demand a rationale. Indeed, veteran Holocaust
educator Elaine Culbertson published an essay entitled, "The Diary of
Anne Frank: Why I Don't Teach It."[45] As materials for teaching about
the Holocaust have proliferated, some educators have students read only
selected passages from the diary, while other teachers have abandoned it
altogether, feeling that there are better materials for teaching about the
main events of the Holocaust. Among this array of materials, Anne's diary suffers by comparison as an atypical account and peripheral to the
genocide. To situate Anne's diary in this context, some teachers have students also read excerpts from other diaries kept by children during the
war, which document a range of experiences, including ghettos, camps,
and living under false identities.[46]

In other American classrooms, Anne's diary has been removed from
curricula not because of what it lacks but because of what it contains.
In 1982, the diary was challenged in Wise County, Virginia, by parents
who complained that the book was offensive, due to its sexual content.[47]
Religious and politically conservative educators continue to ban the
diary from classrooms, especially since the *Definitive Edition* was published in English in 1995. Some Orthodox Jewish schools no longer assign Anne's diary, because they can no longer obtain the first edition of
the diary, from which passages related to Anne's sexual awakening had
been redacted. Teachers in these schools consider these passages, which

Photographs from the Anne Frank Wall: Taehoon Ahn at the Spanish Steps in Rome, and Dave Torrano in St. Petersburg, Russia. In 2006, both of these eighth-grade students "released" the copies of *The Diary of a Young Girl* that they are shown holding through bookcrossing.com, a website that promotes social networking through shared books. *Courtesy of Jim DeLong and Jon Erickson, The Anne Frank Wall Project, Bret Harte Middle School, San Jose, California*

do appear in the *Definitive Edition,* as inappropriate for their students. In addition, teachers in these schools consider more recently published personal narratives of the Holocaust written by religiously observant Jews, whose accounts discuss religion more centrally than does Anne's diary, to be more fitting for their classes.

In 2010, parents in Culpeper County, Virginia, who were concerned about the sexual content of Anne's writing led the local public school board to decide to remove from the *Definitive Edition* of the diary certain passages "that might be inappropriate for classroom discussion." Bobbi Johnson, the superintendent of Culpeper County schools, explained that the "essence of the story, the struggle of a young girl faced with horrible atrocities, is not lost by editing the few pages that speak to adolescent discovery of intimate feelings. While these pages could be the basis of a relevant discussion, they do not reflect the purpose of studying the book at the middle-school level."[48] After this decision attracted considerable attention beyond Culpeper County, local officials decided that the diary would continue to be taught but possibly at a higher grade level. "This is not intended to censor or limit," Johnson explained, in response to protests against the board's decision.[49] In fact, the school board had deliberated over some of the same questions of what belonged in the published version of Anne's diary that had concerned both Anne, when she revised her diary during her final months in hiding, and her father and others who prepared it for posthumous publication. Some of the sections that had alarmed parents in Culpeper County were ones that Anne herself had decided not to include in her rewritten diary and were restored to the published text only a half-century after her death.

As teaching about Anne Frank in the United States has become a subject of discussion in its own right, Americans attend to its international reception as a barometer of the values they have invested in the diary in other locales. Failures to appreciate Anne Frank as a human rights touchstone are read as signposts of a larger moral failure. For example, in 2004 CBS News reported that "North Korea is using her diary, not to teach how Anne suffered at the hands of the German Nazis, but to warn the students how they could suffer at the hands of those they call 'American Nazis.'" In this report, Dutch journalist Miriam Bartelsman explains that "in North Korea, the diary is being used to promote war," and while students may sympathize with Anne, they do not respect her, because "she didn't win. She was not a hero." In the words of one North Korean youngster: "For world peace, America will have to be destroyed. Only then will Anne's dream of peace come true."[50]

Anne Frank's diary has a singular place in American education. Adopted by teachers within a few years of its publication in English translation, it soon became the first widely taught text about a victim of the Holocaust. *The Diary of a Young Girl* also became the most widely read diary in American schools and the most widely read work written by an adolescent girl. The diary has attracted an expanding application to areas of study and has inspired diverse methodologies for its teaching. Even as teachers continue to champion the diary as a key text for young adults, and as it continues to inspire legions of new readers, its pedagogy is a site of contention—between educational authorities and individual teachers, among competing claims on the pedagogical value of Anne's diary, between advocates for the diary and those who wish to see it removed from classrooms, and ultimately between teachers' various investments in the diary and the responses of their students.

Central to teaching about Anne Frank in the United States, from the start, is an inherent distance—cultural as well as geographic and, increasingly, temporal—between the circumstances of her life and death and the American classroom. The challenge of mediating that distance is addressed every time a student is assigned to read *The Diary of a Young Girl*. Sam Wineburg, a professor of education, advocates an approach to teaching about the past that develops "our ability to navigate the jagged landscape of history, to traverse the terrain that lies between the poles of familiarity with and distance from the past." Though looking for the familiar may be the most accessible approach to teaching history, it runs the risk of ignoring "vast regions of the past that either contradict our current needs or fail to align easily with them."[51] The many efforts to teach Anne Frank's diary demonstrate the value—as well as the challenge—of affirming this tension between the familiar and the distant.

6

Anne Frank as Icon, from Human Rights to Holocaust Denial

Brigitte Sion

Anne Frank was one of *Time* magazine's twenty "heroes and icons of the 20th century," along with such honorees as Albert Einstein and Princess Diana.[1] Unlike these other figures, Anne gained this status posthumously, through the publication of her diary and its later mediations. Translated into dozens of languages, the diary has become a canonical text of Holocaust writing—often the first, and sometimes the only, introduction to this subject for many readers, especially the young. However, the diary is an incomplete account of Anne's victimization by the Nazis. Her entries end before her arrest by the Gestapo and deportation to the Westerbork transit camp, then to Auschwitz, and finally to Bergen-Belsen, where she was a slave laborer before dying from typhus in March 1945. Anne's diary is therefore considered what the historian Tony Kushner terms a Holocaust text "without tears, without bloodshed, without . . . the mass production of death."[2] The incomplete nature of the diary and its publication years after Anne's murder have enabled wide-ranging interpretations of the meaning of her life story. Even as the extensive popularity of the diary has transformed Anne into an iconic figure, her symbolic value has been far from uniform.

Indeed, in a remarkable paradox, Anne Frank has come to play a central role in the discourses of both human rights advocates and neo-Nazis, whose ranks include Holocaust deniers, each engaging Anne's iconic status in order to bolster arguments supporting their respective missions. These polarized appropriations of Anne Frank converge in what may seem to be an improbable site: the Anne Frank Human Rights Memorial in Boise, Idaho, which opened to the public in August 2002. The Idaho Human Rights Education Center, which oversees the memorial, itself admits, "Anne Frank and downtown Boise may seem like an unlikely pairing."[3] There, representations of Anne's life in hiding and hopeful quotations from her diary articulate the memorial's universal message of tolerance. At the same time, the memorial strives to absolve Idaho of its reputation as safe haven for neo-Nazi groups. When the white supremacist movement Aryan Nation settled in Idaho in the 1980s, its presence stirred controversy both locally and beyond. Although the group left the state in the early 2000s, the association of neo-Nazis and Idaho has endured. When plans to build the Anne Frank monument were announced in 2000, Reuters reported that "mainstream Idaho is drafting a heroine of anti-Nazi literature to help put things right."[4]

This agenda positions the Boise memorial at the intersection of two opposing movements, each of which finds value in turning to Anne Frank. Human rights advocates, in Boise and elsewhere, champion her diary as an eloquent expression of a universalized faith in humankind even in the face of adversity. This vision is in keeping with how Otto Frank, who oversaw the redaction and publication of his daughter's diary, positioned the significance of Anne's life and work, a vision that has been sustained by the Anne Frank Stichting, initiated in 1957, and the Anne Frank-Fonds, established in 1963. These institutions have overseen the publication of the diary, the opening of the Anne Frank House in Amsterdam, and the creation of an array of educational programs, exhibitions, and publications. As the literary scholar James Young has observed, under the aegis of the Anne Frank-Fonds, "Anne's father set a clear precedent for the widest possible application of Anne's beliefs against discrimination and racism of all kinds."[5] Holocaust deniers, however, have long claimed that Anne's diary is a forgery, invented by Otto Frank in a crass scheme to make money. Neo-Nazi and white supremacist groups often embrace the claims of Holocaust deniers, who challenge the authenticity of Anne Frank's diary under the guise of scientific inquiry to legitimize their claims. This tactic is part of a larger strategy that brings some Holocaust deniers and neo-Nazi groups together in common cause. By questioning the actuality of the Holocaust, deniers seek to shift the moral onus away from the champions of Nazism and onto Jews. Consequently, Anne Frank has served as a redemptive figure in efforts to restore the tainted reputations not only of human rights advocates in Boise but also of those seeking to prove that the Holocaust is a hoax.

Idaho's Anne Frank Human Rights Memorial opened to the public in August 2002, seven years after three Boise women—Leslie Drake, the Reverend Nancy Taylor, and Lisa Uhlmann—were inspired by the traveling exhibit "Anne Frank in the World," which was developed by the Anne Frank House in Amsterdam, to create a permanent tribute to Anne in their city. They raised $1.5 million, mostly from supporters in Idaho, and found a location for the memorial along the Boise River greenbelt, in the heart of the city's downtown. Designed by Kurt Karst, an Idaho Falls architect, the memorial is an outdoor monument and educational center that entails a complex of elements, including

> two reflective ponds and three small waterfalls symbolizing universal faith, renewal, cleansing, and essence of life. A butterfly garden, bookcase, and stairway sit right on the greenbelt. This features a cityscape wall that gives a remarkable likeness to Amsterdam in the 1940s and the setting of the warehouse and Annex. The bookcase is life-size and is positioned in front of the staircase leading up to the Annex, to allow visitors to mimic the footsteps of Anne Frank when she left the world behind for 2½ years. The Annex is built in size proportionally to the space that Anne Frank's family would have had while living in hiding. Sawcuts on the cement ground show the size of the two-level hiding place that housed eight persons. On one side of the Annex stands the life-sized bronze cast of Anne Frank.[6]

This memorial is characterized by its hyperlocal nature, from funding to design to educational agenda. At the same time, it embraces the universal and imports charismatic figures from far away to reinforce this purpose. The memorial park is punctuated by sixty quotations, etched on stone tablets placed throughout the site. These texts are selected both from Anne Frank's diary and from the words of an international array of renowned human rights leaders, including Mahatma Gandhi, Martin Luther King, Jr., and Nelson Mandela, as well as anonymous victims of discrimination in South Africa and in the United States. Anne Frank is the author of eleven of these quotations and the only figure represented by a statue. She is positioned as the centerpiece of the site, and yet its creators explain that it

View of the Anne Frank Human Rights Memorial,
Boise, Idaho. *Photographer: Brigitte Sion*

is not simply a static space to reflect on [Anne's] short life or even the horrors
of the Holocaust. It was instead designed to actively engage us to think, to talk
with one another, and to respond to the human rights issues we face in our
community, our country and our world. Both the triumphs and tragedies of
the human story are on display, but in every quote and every idea, we see the
profound power of a single voice or bold action to overcome great odds and
alter the course of history.[7]

The memorial's architecture seeks to provide visitors an affective
engagement with Anne Frank through embodied encounters with its
replica of wartime Amsterdam and the Annex. However, the memorial
is in many ways the opposite of Anne Frank's actual living conditions
while in hiding. Instead of the confined space that once housed her and
seven other Jews, the memorial is an outdoor structure, limited only by

the sky. Instead of showing Anne hiding in dim light, the five-hundred-pound statue of Anne depicts her standing on a chair as she looks out a large windowsill, which opens onto the outside world. And instead of elbowing their way up a narrow staircase behind the hinged bookcase, as they would do at the Anne Frank House, visitors to the Boise memorial can wander about without physical constraints after they enter a two-dimensional replica of the Annex floor plan in the form of sawcuts on the ground and freestanding walls.

The Boise memorial neither offers a kinetic experience of Anne's life in hiding nor generates a feeling of discomfort and oppression, as do other structures that engage Holocaust remembrance, such as the United States Holocaust Memorial Museum in Washington, D.C., or the Jewish Museum in Berlin.[8] In memorializing Anne Frank, the Boise memorial does not, in fact, do so primarily to recall the Holocaust. Rather, she serves as the point of entry to other concerns of the Idaho Human Rights Education Center, which are closer to contemporary local issues, including "equality for lesbian, gay, bisexual and transgender (LGBT) Idahoans" and "justice for immigrant families."[9] Nothing in the Boise memorial's mission statement, its official literature, or at the site itself directly identifies Anne Frank as a Jewish victim of the Holocaust or explains the reason for her hiding, let alone for her arrest, deportation, and death in a Nazi concentration camp. The spatial configuration of the memorial contributes to this de-historicized presentation of Anne's life and work by situating her within a larger landscape of famous combatants for peace and tolerance and among other icons of hope in the face of suffering, such as Rosa Parks and Mother Teresa, as well as less well-known or anonymous Native American, Rwandan, and Bosnian figures, whose inspirational words are etched on the Memorial Wall. These include words of Rwandan teacher Rose Kayitesi—"We are trying to teach them to trust the world again, but it is very difficult"—and of a class of Bosnian fifth-graders: "War is here, but we await peace." Most quotes are displayed on this 180-foot-long marble wall that identifies their authors but provides little additional context.

The statue of Anne Frank at the center of the Anne Frank Human Rights Memorial. *Photographer: Brigitte Sion*

At the center of this pantheon, Anne exemplifies a universalized optimism through the quotations from her diary displayed in the memorial park. In particular, the well-known sentence, "I still believe, in spite of everything, that people are truly good at heart," excerpted from her diary entry of July 15, 1944, epitomizes the memorial's transformation of Anne Frank from a Jewish Holocaust victim to a universal symbol of hope and tolerance. This citation, which is displayed in larger print on its own wall, cuts short the full diary entry, just as the diary ends before Anne's arrest and tragic demise. In fact, the next sentences in this entry are pessimistic in tone: "I simply can't build up my hopes on a foundation consisting of confusion, misery, and death. I see the world gradually being turned into a wilderness, I hear the ever approaching thunder, which will destroy us too, I can feel the suffering of millions."[10] This anguish is followed by yet another expression of optimism, reflecting Anne's mixed emotions and ambivalent perspective on her condition. A distinctive quality of Anne Frank's diary is its dynamic and often conflicting expressions: of hope and despair, over the ongoing struggle with her inner feelings, about her life in hiding, as well as concerning the larger political situation (or the limited information about it that reaches her in the Annex). In the Boise memorial the diary is reduced to brief quotations that stand alone, like epigrams or mottos. This presentation not only removes these sentiments from their place within the diary's unfolding, introspective discourse but also strips Anne's words of all ambivalence. Instead, they voice an unwaveringly positive advocacy of universal human rights. Together with the much larger number of quotations etched in stone throughout the memorial, which were taken from other figures and their respective contexts of struggle, the monument creates a generic space of reconciliation, from which the particulars of the Holocaust, or of any other tragedy, have been excluded.

Universalizing Anne Frank, whether in the Boise memorial or in other presentations of her life and work, encourages members of the public to empathize with her, irrespective of their own experience. As cultural studies scholar Alison Landsberg notes, "whereas sympathy relies on an essentialism of identification, empathy recognizes the alterity of identification. Empathy, then, pertains to the lack of identity with victims but a way of both feeling for and feeling different from the subject of inquiry."[11] The Boise memorial strives to enable empathizing with Anne Frank by creating a space that both fosters identification with her and articulates a distance from the object of identification, with many contradictions that prevent one from identifying with Anne fully. For example, the relaxed posture of the statue, the outdoor location, and the univocal narrative of hope are at odds with a nearby plaque, which explains that Anne died at the age of fifteen from "starvation, exposure, brutality, and disease."

Thus, even though the Boise memorial centers on Anne Frank, the identification with her that it offers visitors is limited. The replica of the Annex is an incomplete simulation of this place and of its occupation by Anne and the other Jews who hid there; the quotations from her diary on display do not represent the full complexity of her writing or tell the whole story of her life. Consequently, the possibilities for empathizing with Anne Frank are also limited to identifying with her faith in human-ity and hope for a better future, as opposed to acknowledging her tragic fate as a Jewish victim of the Holocaust. This structuring of empathy for Anne reflects assumptions that the monument's creators have made on behalf of its audience. As folklorist Amy Shuman notes, "empathy presumes the ability to understand another's life story; its opposite, the inability to empathize, is reserved for situations that the normal person cannot imagine (including, notably, unspeakable evils and insanity). In other words, empathy describes the sphere of the normal and allows us to imagine what any normal person would do."[12] The Boise monument implicitly situates Jews' experience of Nazi persecution as being beyond its visitors' conceiving.

As the Boise memorial delimits its audience's potential to empathize with Anne Frank, the site imbues her life with new meaning by situating her within a different rubric—a pantheon of humanitarian heroes—which is centered on proffering redemption. In this respect, the memo-rial follows the model for presenting the significance of Anne Frank's life offered decades earlier in its official dramatization, which was first staged in 1955 and then filmed in 1959. Film historian Judith Doneson observes that the cinematic version of Frances Goodrich and Albert Hackett's *The Diary of Anne Frank* affirms the "Christian belief in the universal tenet 'love thy neighbor,' [which] forms the basis of the relationship between

Christians and Jews and assumes the majority Christians will act in good faith on behalf of the minority Jews when these are in trouble."[13] The Boise memorial offers a similar redemptive message, as have the Paper Clips project, based in Whitwell, Tennessee, Yom Hashoah commemorations staged in Nebraska, and other Holocaust remembrance practices in America's heartland. Situated far from large centers of the nation's Jewish population, these efforts all demonstrate, according to historian Alan Steinweis, "the extent to which the Holocaust has been absorbed into the American consciousness as a paradigmatic evil."[14] In the Boise memorial, Anne is the paradigm of goodness in the face of evil, her virtue reflected in the diverse voices of other champions of human rights surrounding her.

The mission of Boise's Anne Frank memorial has not gone unchallenged. Since its unveiling in 2002, it has been vandalized twice: in March 2007, it was plastered with stickers bearing swastikas and the name of the neo-Nazi group Combat 18; two months later, the statue of Anne was knocked over and damaged. However, both the Idaho Human Rights Education Center and local police stopped short of calling these incidents "hate-related" or "anti-Semitic." Rather, they expressed the hope that the perpetrators "will revisit the memorial and learn why it's here."[15] In effect, these officials configured the crime as not only an attack on the memorial but also an argument for its necessity. By downplaying the significance of racism in these attacks and promoting the memorial's redemptive mission, advocates elided both the tragedy of Anne's death as a victim of anti-Semitism and Idaho's tarnished reputation as a haven for hate groups. As Doneson notes of the film *The Diary of Anne Frank*, here too "Anne's words give man the opportunity to continue living without guilt because she still believes in him. Her belief becomes a form of forgiveness."[16]

Boise's Anne Frank memorial exemplifies an American approach to Holocaust remembrance as civil religion, which, Jewish studies scholar Jeffrey Shandler notes, "emphasizes affect over intellect, the generic over the specific, the redemptive over the disturbing, and the integration of competing or dissenting ideologies into a consensual commitment to the importance of belief at its most abstract."[17] Yet even as it avoids the specific, complex nature of Anne Frank's life and death, in keeping with this approach to Holocaust remembrance, the Boise memorial cannot escape becoming itself a site of ambiguity and conflict, rooted in a particular historical and cultural configuration of its own.

Whereas the Boise memorial offers Anne Frank as a positive and universal symbol of human rights activism by eliding her Jewish identity, Holocaust deniers have reduced her status to that of an ordinary teenager, by paying heightened and distorted attention to her Jewishness. Holocaust deniers consider the Holocaust a fraud invented by Jews in order to obtain financial and political gains, such as German reparation payments and the creation of the State of Israel. Early in the public history of Anne's diary, Holocaust deniers grasped the significance of this book's extensive influence on the public. Historian Deborah Lipstadt notes, "The diary's popularity and impact, particularly on the young, make discrediting it as important a goal for the deniers as their attack on the gas chambers. By instilling doubts in the minds of young people about this powerful book, they hope also to instill doubts about the Holocaust itself."[18]

Holocaust deniers in Europe and the United States have seized upon the challenges posed by remediating Anne's diary as an opportunity to make claims that it is a forgery. The fraught efforts to create a stage adaptation of the diary in the 1950s provided grist for the deniers' mills. In 1952, Otto Frank engaged the author Meyer Levin to turn the book into a play. After Levin wrote a script that was turned down by various Broadway producers, Anne's father cancelled his agreement with Levin and commissioned two well-known screenwriters, Frances Goodrich and Albert Hackett, to adapt the diary for the stage, and their version went on to become an international success. Levin sued Otto Frank and the producer of *The Diary of Anne Frank*; the lawsuit was eventually settled out of court, and Levin received financial compensation. Holocaust deniers made their first attacks on the diary's authenticity at the same time as this public disagreement between Frank and Levin.[19] The deniers accused Levin of having authored the diary and conspiring with Frank to promote this fraud for profit. As the play became an international success, the attacks on the diary's authenticity spread as well. In 1958, a group of protesters denied the existence of Anne Frank at a performance of *The Diary of Anne Frank* in Vienna; similar protests took place in other European capitals.

Since the 1970s, Holocaust deniers' attacks on what they term derisively the "religion of the 'Holocaust'" have included denouncing the cult of "Saint Anne (Frank)."[20] These ironic references to religion imply that criticizing the Holocaust is taboo, tantamount to sacrilege. At the same time, deniers' use of religious language is in itself an acknowledgment of Anne's iconic status for both Holocaust remembrance and Holocaust denial. The deniers manifest their skepticism about the Holocaust in a hypercritical approach to scrutinizing its factuality that mimics genuine academic research (with abundant quotations, footnotes, and bibliographic references) presented by "distinguished faculty" in the form of "conference proceedings" and scholarly "journals" with austere layouts. Despite their legitimate appearance, these undertakings lack actual scholarly rigor; for example, citations in denier publications are routinely truncated, edited, taken out of context, or doctored in various ways. Attacks on the authenticity of Anne Frank's diary exemplify the pseudo-scholarship of Holocaust deniers.

A case in point is a lengthy essay, titled "Is *The Diary of Anne Frank* Genuine?" published in 1978 by one of the most active Holocaust deniers, the French professor of literature Robert Faurisson. In this essay, which appeared in the *Journal for Historical Review,* a revisionist periodical with a restricted circulation, the author attempted to expose the diary as a hoax. Faurisson was not the first to question the diary's authenticity, but he claimed to use serious methods of "critical enquiry" in his exposé. Faurisson was one of the first deniers to present his claims to the general public, publishing op-ed essays in the prestigious French daily *Le Monde* and using his academic credentials to legitimize his claims. He attacked the diary first by positioning it as a document that purports to prove the existence of the Holocaust—which, of course, it does not—and then by questioning both the materiality of the diary and some of its contents. He accused Otto Frank of authoring "a literary fraud" and concluded, "The Diary was a 'cock and bull story,' a novel, a lie."[21] In a follow-up article published in the same journal in 2000, Faurisson offered additional—and unverified—information about Otto Frank, claiming that, as a banker in Frankfurt, Anne's father was "implicated in various shady dealings" and had to flee Germany in 1933 for this reason, rather than to escape Nazi persecution. Furthermore, Faurisson alleged that Otto Frank managed to continue to make money in the Netherlands "thanks to various subterfuges" that continued during the war, even "during his time in hospital at Auschwitz," intimating that Anne's father collaborated with the Nazi regime through "Aryan" business associates. Finally, Faurisson suggested that this alleged "financial swindling" constitutes a precedent for Otto Frank's "literary swindle"—the fabrication of Anne's diary.[22]

Faurisson made his case against Anne's diary by invoking shopworn anti-Semitic stereotypes: dishonesty, insatiable greed, a conspiratorial nature, and a disregard for the law. These calumnies are directed not at Anne, but at her father, who survived the war and, with the publication of the diary, represented and shaped Anne's public legacy. Faurisson characterized Anne as a victim not of Nazi persecution but rather of her father's archetypal Jewish deceit and greed. Moreover, Faurisson reduced Anne to an ordinary teenager who did not write anything and who, like many other casualties of World War II, simply died of typhus. Faurisson concluded that Otto Frank fabricated the diary in order to amass a fortune, exemplifying how the Holocaust is a sham that Jews exploit to enrich themselves financially and politically. Following Otto Frank's death in 1980, Faurisson extended his attack to the Anne Frank-Fonds, which continues to oversee the public remembrance of Anne's life and work. Faurisson denounced the foundation as "profiteers who have exploited [Anne's] memory for so long" and who "wage ruthless wars over the corpse of Anne Frank and the remains of her late father."[23]

In contrast to the Boise memorial, which disassociates Anne from the specific context of her hiding and death in order to made her into a universal icon of human rights advocacy, Faurisson located Anne and her diary in a thoroughly—and thoroughly disparaged—Jewish context. At the same time, though, Holocaust deniers such as Faurisson resemble human rights activists in their use of Anne Frank as an instrument of redemption that advances their own agenda. Faurisson's attack on Anne Frank's diary serves the larger political agenda of Holocaust deniers: to exonerate and rehabilitate Nazism and to hold Jews responsible for

World War II, for milking Europe through reparations, and for continuing to plot schemes to control the world.

After learning of Faurisson's accusation that the diary was a forgery, Otto Frank agreed to meet with Faurisson and to submit the original diary notebooks to forensic examination. Like other Holocaust deniers before him, Faurisson alleged that the materials used to write the original diary manuscript dated to the postwar era, proving that it could not have been written by Anne. Tests conducted in 1980 by the Netherlands Forensic Institute confirmed that the diary is authentic—the ink, glue, cloth cover, and writing implements dated from the early 1940s and not from the 1950s, as Faurisson and other deniers claimed.[24] This scientific assurance of the diary's authenticity has not deterred Holocaust deniers from continuing to call it a forgery, however, or from extrapolating their theories of the diary's fabrication to the Holocaust at large.

Other deniers' attempts to discredit Anne Frank's stature follow a similar pattern: they attack the authenticity of the diary and hold it up as the most profitable example of Jews' enriching themselves through the Holocaust myth. When the British Holocaust denier David Irving sued American historian Deborah Lipstadt for libel in 1998, based on what she had written about him in her 1993 book *Denying the Holocaust*, a number of court hours were spent discussing Anne Frank's diary, recirculating Faurisson's claims and the forensic counter-expertise.[25] In late 2009, the American denier Bradley Smith, the eighty-year-old founder of the California-based Committee for Open Debate on the Holocaust, a denier organization, uploaded weekly videos on YouTube, called "Coffee with Bradley Smith," in which he addressed well-known "Holocaust myths" such as Anne Frank's diary and the Anne Frank House.[26] As these Holocaust deniers repeatedly assail the diary, they reiterate old calumnies. Their assertions—remediated in journal articles, courtroom testimony, online videos, advertisements run in college newspapers, and other forums—do not advance the argument that Anne Frank's diary is a forgery or respond to demonstrations of its authenticity. Rather, they provide Holocaust deniers with ongoing opportunities to instill doubt in the minds of a wide and, especially, a young audience that "believes in 'the Anne Frank diaries,'"[27] which they read while growing up. The logic of this strategy is not lost on scholars and jurists working to combat anti-

Semitism. "If Jews somehow magically conspired to create what the deniers call a 'Holohoax,' then wouldn't the seminal piece of Holocaust-era literature have to be fake?" asks the attorney Kenneth Stern, an expert on hate crimes. "The claim that [Anne Frank's] diary is a fraud is both a natural outgrowth of the denier's own anti-Semitism, and a part of the effort to promote the old anti-Semitic canard of the 'Jewish conspiracy,' Jews having demon-like power to make the world believe a lie."[28] By arguing that Anne's diary is a fabrication, Holocaust deniers also seek political redemption for the Third Reich, exonerating the Nazi regime of all wrongdoing by attempting to shift the criminal onus onto Jews as war profiteers, which, the deniers contend, continues in the form of the books, plays, and movies that Jews fabricate about the Holocaust.

Both of these discourses in which Anne Frank figures as an instrument of redemption—the discourse of human rights activists and that of Holocaust deniers—reflect what Amy Shuman characterizes as "the appropriation of others' stories," which "depends on stories traveling beyond their owners, beyond the personal, and beyond the claim to experience."[29] Even as these two discourses center on Anne's diary, they shift away from this personal record of her thoughts and experiences in opposite directions, and they do so not only ideologically, but also strategically. Whereas the human rights discourse, exemplified by the Boise monument, offers an overly generalized, elevated Anne Frank, removed from the circumstances of the Nazi persecution of Europe's Jews, in an effort to configure Anne as universally inspiring, the discourse of Holocaust deniers is overly minute in its focus on the particulars of the diary, in an effort to reduce Anne Frank to an ordinary teenager, bereft of her considerable literary talent, deserving of anonymity.

As an icon, Anne is the object of two very different kinds of visibility in the cases at hand: in Boise, she is at the center of a physical monument in an open public space; in the hands of Holocaust deniers, she is the target of intangible attacks from hidden forces, largely based in print and cyberspace. Whether the gaze looks upward or downward at Anne Frank, and whether it aggrandizes or minimizes her, it contributes to the expansion of meaning that she has accrued as a symbol, meanings located at an ever-increasing remove from the confidential, first-person account she originally wrote in her diary. And yet the attention to Anne from such completely polarized perspectives also confirms the iconic status of her diary—even when some attempt to discredit it as a fraud.

Purged of personal issues, fragmented into stand-alone quotations, decontextualized from history, emptied of all ambiguity, its material components separated from its content, the diary has, through multiple mediations, moved far beyond Otto Frank's universalist wishes, as well as Anne Frank's dreams of becoming a famous writer. The greatest challenge for readers of the diary today may not be defending Anne's life and work from attack; rather, it may be engaging her individual history and personal vision free of the redemptive values with which she has been burdened by others.

7

Anne Frank, a Guest
at the Seder

Liora Gubkin

Anne Frank never mentions the Jewish holiday of Passover in her diary. There is no evidence in the diary that Anne ever attended a seder, the ritual meal traditionally held in Jewish homes on the first and second nights of Passover. Yet, every year when Jews recount the story of their freedom and redemption from slavery in ancient Egypt, Anne is a "guest" at many a seder through her presence in several American Passover haggadahs. Her appearance speaks not only to her familiarity and popularity, but also to the extent to which her writing has been readily adapted. The best-known words of Anne Frank—"I still believe that people are really good at heart," part of a diary entry written on July 15, 1944—foster creative engagements with diverse understandings of slavery and freedom and their implications for American Jews wrestling with the legacy of the Holocaust.

Passover is one of the most popular holidays for American Jews, and the haggadah, the text used to conduct the seder, is the most widely published Jewish text in the United States.[1] Thousands of versions of the haggadah have been created over the centuries.[2] Today, one can purchase or download a haggadah for a wide array of interests, including haggadahs with traditional commentary, a haggadah for Jews and Buddhists, a haggadah for a thirty-minute seder (the traditional ritual can last several hours), and haggadahs for activists committed to a variety of political causes. These politically engaged haggadahs follow the models of self-published haggadahs by left-wing activists in the 1960s and '70s and, before those, haggadahs issued by secular Yiddishists and Zionists beginning in the 1930s. The traditional haggadah exhorts seder participants to reflect upon the personal nature of oppression and its relevance in the present by encouraging an imaginative ritual performance of identification with the oppressed and by issuing a call to end all subjugation. While innovative haggadahs typically follow the basic structure of the traditional text, they may complement ritual instructions, biblical passages, and early rabbinic commentaries with selections from modern and contemporary texts, including Anne Frank's *Diary of a Young Girl,* that span the dimensions of time and place. Many innovative haggadahs published in the United States during the last forty years use these additional texts to deliberately link the ancient Israelite journey from slavery to freedom with such contemporary social and political issues as the threat of nuclear war, the Israeli-Palestinian conflict, vegetarianism, feminism, the oppression of Soviet Jewry, and the Holocaust.

This approach to personalizing Jewish religious practice by connecting it to current concerns is consistent with a major trend in contemporary American religious life generally. In the post–World War II era, many Americans expect religious practice to be personally meaningful. Rather than simply accepting the religious beliefs of their forebears, Americans today are more likely to approach religion as an individualized quest for spiritual meaning and thus feel entitled to adapt their religious rituals accordingly.[3] Because the Passover seder is a domestic practice, most often celebrated with family and friends in the home, it is especially prone to personalization. The haggadah presents a script replete with lines to recite and actions to perform. Ritual actions, such as washing hands, breaking matzah, and drinking wine, provide a rich sensory experience for participants and facilitate their identification with the ancient Israelites celebrating freedom after surviving the harsh conditions of slavery. Accordingly, participants recite personal declarations such as "We were Pharaoh's slaves in Egypt" and "It is because of that which the Lord did for me when I came forth from Egypt." Identification is not only a matter of connecting the distant past and the present. Rather, the haggadah informs participants that slavery and redemption recur "in every generation."

Mid-twentieth-century European Jews readily connected their situation with the plight of the ancient Israelites, naming Hitler as the Pharaoh of their day. Haggadahs that interpret the Nazi persecution of

European Jewry as parallel to the ancient Israelites' experience as slaves in Egypt were created during World War II, and seders held by Holocaust survivors in Displaced Persons camps immediately after the war further developed this connection.[4] American Jews also articulated the parallel between the ancient story of Passover and the Holocaust in new versions of the haggadah, beginning with an oblique reference to the persecution of European Jews in the dedication to *The Haggadah of Passover for Members of the Armed Forces of the United States,* issued in 1943. There, the Committee on Army and Navy Religious Activities notes, "The Passover Festival of Freedom has never been observed more poignantly than today, when we are struggling to preserve freedom for man."[5] The start of the Warsaw Ghetto Uprising during Passover 1943 further prompted commemorations of the Holocaust during the holiday.[6] Beginning in 1952, the "Seder Ritual of Remembrance," a three-paragraph text "for the six million Jews who perished at the hands of the Nazis and for the heroes of the ghetto uprisings," was distributed broadly in the United States by the American Jewish Congress. Over several decades, this moving memorial text was likely read by thousands of Jews at both public commemorations and private Passover seder meals.[7]

Commemorating the Holocaust during Passover gradually became an established practice during the early postwar years. In a 1960 article on contemporary American celebrations of Passover, folklorist Beatrice Weinreich noted: "Ever since the murder of six million Jews in World [War] II, a need has been felt by many Jews to amend the various Haggadoth [sic] to include a passage about this catastrophe, thus giving Passover an additional memorial function." Weinreich correctly predicted that Holocaust commemoration would become a permanent feature in many American haggadahs, including those produced by mainstream religious movements as well as alternative groups.[8] The presence of the Holocaust in haggadahs has not abated with the passage of time, reflecting both the continued widespread observance of the holiday and the expanding importance of Holocaust remembrance for Jews.[9]

As a result of this enduring practice, Anne Frank often joins the guests at the Passover seder as they evoke memory of the Holocaust decades after her death in 1945. Several American haggadahs published since the mid-1970s ask seder participants to engage with Anne Frank's most famous statement: "In spite of everything, I still believe people are really good at heart."[10] Jews have integrated Holocaust remembrance into their observance of Passover in a variety of ways, reflecting differences in their understandings of the Holocaust, Passover, and Jewish culture generally. Thus, even when the same line from Anne Frank's diary appears in several innovative haggadahs, it can take on different meanings, depending on where it is recited within the haggadah narrative, what other texts and images appear in conjunction with Anne's declaration, and what ritual activities or interpretative cues are given to seder participants at that point. While not an exhaustive survey, the following four examples of haggadahs that incorporate Anne Frank into the ritual text demonstrate the wide range of possibilities for wrestling with the legacy of the Holocaust through these famous words. Examining them together reveals that mediations of Anne Frank in American haggadahs use the rubric of this ancient religious ritual to encourage acts of imagination. These acts promote personal, emotional identification with the Holocaust as it recedes into the past, through the forever-young Anne Frank, and with the ancient past of the Israelite exodus from Egypt, made present through the Passover ritual. In addition, these mediations of Anne Frank affirm particular ideological and theological commitments expressed in each haggadah.

A Passover Haggadah

The first haggadah that integrated the Holocaust into the Passover celebration published by the leadership of a mainstream American Jewish denomination is *A Passover Haggadah,* issued in 1974 by the Reform movement, currently the largest of the four major Jewish religious movements in the United States.[11] A. Stanley Dreyfus, a member of the liturgy committee of the Reform movement's Central Conference of American Rabbis, which created *A Passover Haggadah,* reflected twenty years later on this impetus for change, noting that "the enormity of the Holocaust on the one hand, and on the other, the establishment of the State of Israel brought a reawakening of faith and commitment and, for Reform Jewry, mandated a complete revision of its liturgy."[12] Whereas the Holocaust called into question the unbridled optimism of earlier liturgical texts, the founding of Israel in 1948 marked the end of a strong anti-Zionist strain in American Reform Judaism. The aspirations of the twenty men of the liturgy committee, listed on the opening page of *A Passover Haggadah*, are eloquently presented in the preface by Herbert Bronstein, the haggadah's editor. In order to create a ritual text that could inspire both a "regeneration of values" and a "living experience of redemption," the committee studied the ancient sources of the hagga-dah and attempted to allow "the genius of the original" text to speak to contemporary Jews by drawing on "archetypal" rather than current ref-erences and relying on symbol and metaphor to bring forth the potential multiplicity of meanings embedded in the Passover celebration. And yet, current texts and contexts are also present. After stating several times that the committee eschewed didactic explanations and contemporary references that would mar the "elemental structure" of the haggadah, Bronstein explains, "the tragedy and exaltation of our historic existence have already provided a place for [the Holocaust and State of Israel] within the Seder."[13] The liturgy instantiates the strong need articulated by Bronstein and Dreyfus to situate both the Holocaust and the State of Israel as organic components of the Passover narrative and not simply as contemporary additions to the story.

Nevertheless, when *A Passover Haggadah* offers texts that reference the Holocaust or other current concerns, they are designated as optional, supplementary readings. As participants work through the seder, the haggadah includes instructions indicating where these readings might be integrated into the ritual or where to continue if one chooses to skip them. The excerpt from Anne Frank's diary is the best known of several Holocaust readings presented in *A Passover Haggadah* and includes the diary's most famous sentence:

> That's the difficulty in these times: ideals, dreams, and cherished hopes rise within us, only to meet the horrible truth and be shattered. It's really a wonder that I haven't dropped all my ideals, because they seem so absurd and impos-sible to carry out. Yet I keep them because in spite of everything I still believe that people are really good at heart. I simply can't build up my hopes on a foundation consisting of confusion, misery, and death. I see the world grad-ually being turned into a wilderness. I hear the ever-approaching thunder, which will destroy us too. I can feel the sufferings of millions and yet, if I look up into the heavens, I think that it will all come right, that this cruelty too will

end, and that peace and tranquility will return again. In the meantime, I must uphold my ideals, for perhaps the time will come when I shall be able to carry them out.[14]

By the 1970s, these words were widely recognized in American culture as a powerful expression of human goodness from a young girl who never gave up hope despite the horror that surrounded her. The placement of the diary excerpt in the haggadah, however, prompts the possibility of several alternative readings of Anne's words, drawing on the rich interpretative opportunities provided by both the traditional seder ritual and other contemporary writings to complicate the conventional reading of Anne Frank's most famous words. This strategy responds to the challenges that the Holocaust posed to the liberal theology of Reform Judaism, with its optimistic view of human nature and confidence in human progress.

Consider the context in which the optional reading from Anne Frank's diary appears within the traditional structure of this haggadah, as the ritual moves from recalling shame, degradation, and slavery to offering praise and promises of redemption.[15] In *A Passover Haggadah*, the diary passage appears rather early in this trajectory, as part of a set of readings about the Holocaust titled "For More Than One Enemy Has Risen Against Us," to illustrate a modern instance of degradation. Immediately preceding this set of optional readings, seder participants are asked to lift their glasses of wine and, following the traditional ritual, recite: "For more than one enemy has risen against us to destroy us. In every generation, in every age, some rise up to plot our annihilation. But a Divine Power sustains and delivers us."[16] In keeping with traditional practice, participants place their cups of wine back onto the table without drinking. Generally, wine symbolizes joy, and drinking wine during the seder signifies God's saving power.[17] Here, however, the wine is not tasted, even though the text recited for this ritual concludes with affirmation of God's redeeming powers. This ritual, with its disjunction between words and action, prepares participants for the possibility of reading Anne Frank's most familiar words in a new light.

The excerpt from Anne Frank's diary follows immediately after this traditional ritual, as the first reading in "For More Than One Enemy Has Risen Against Us." No additional information is provided about the

excerpt or its author; the haggadah assumes its users are already familiar with Anne Frank and her diary. After this set of optional readings,
the haggadah resumes the traditional seder ritual, with the recitation of
the Ten Plagues that were visited upon the Egyptians after Pharaoh's
initial refusal to free the Israelite slaves. These readings thus disrupt, if
momentarily, the haggadah's trajectory from affirming a "Divine Power"
that "sustains and delivers" to demonstrating God's saving power, by
recalling the persecution of Jews in the modern era.

The juxtaposition of the diary excerpt with the other optional texts
in this section suggests additional possible readings of Anne's words.
Immediately following the diary excerpt is a translation of the Hebrew
poet Abraham Shlonsky's "A Vow," which offers a strong counterpoint
to the idealism and optimism expressed in Anne's words. Shlonsky, who
wrote several poems about the horror and devastation faced by European
Jewry, begins this poem by placing the reader in proximity to witnesses
to the Holocaust:

> In the presence of eyes
> which witnessed the slaughter,
> which saw the oppression
> the heart could not bear. . . .

Shlonsky's poetry reflects an encounter with the aftermath of the Holocaust, which Anne Frank's diary cannot offer. In the middle of the poem,
Shlonsky begins to voice a series of oaths: "I have taken an oath: To remember it all, / to remember, not once to forget!" The poem concludes
with more oaths, avowing a commitment to learn from these difficult
memories and put these lessons into action:

> An oath: Not in vain passed over the night of the terror.
> An oath: No morning shall see me at flesh-pots again.
> An oath: Lest from this we learned nothing.

These oaths pose a stark contrast to an idealistic future as configured in
the conventional reading of Anne Frank's diary familiar to many Americans. Whereas Frank's words appear without introduction, the poem "A
Vow" is followed with attribution and explanation: "Abraham Shlonsky,
'A Vow,' translated by Herbert Bronstein. The original poem may be seen
in the Yad Va-Shem Holocaust Memorial in Jerusalem and is recited at

many S'darim [the Hebrew plural of *seder*], as a regular practice, in the land of Israel."[18] This explanation both identifies the poem as an example of Israel's distinct culture of Holocaust remembrance and positions the poem as something for American Jews to consider incorporating into their own practices.

In this section of *A Passover Haggadah,* Anne Frank's celebration of life also resides uneasily next to an imposing, full-page drawing of the Angel of Death by the haggadah's illustrator, the American Jewish artist Leonard Baskin. Against a background the color of blood orange, the angel sports winged arms jutting out from his muscular body, drawn in somber tones of green, blue, and gray. This dramatic illustration may be intended to lead the participant back to the seder proper and the recitation of the Ten Plagues, in which the Angel of Death appears in the final plague as the slayer of the Egyptian first born. The illustration's placement may also serve as a commentary on the Holocaust texts by Frank and Shlonsky, whether as an avenging angel who destroys those who rise up against the people of Israel "in every generation" or, conversely, as the persecutor who "rises up" in each generation.

Two more readings for this optional section follow Baskin's illustration. Next is "1959, Russia," an excerpt from the Soviet Yiddish poet Samuel Halkin's "Poem—1959," which expresses longing for freedom "from barbed-wire fences and the lightless prisons."[19] Incorporated into the selection of Holocaust-specific texts without any editorial commentary, the image of "barbed wire fences" links the persecution of Soviet Jews, a pressing concern for American Jewry in the 1970s, to the Holocaust and further complicates the reading of the words of Anne Frank. The concluding reflection was written specifically for *A Passover Haggadah* by the American Jewish poet Anthony Hecht. A member of the U.S. Army's 97th Infantry Division who participated in the liberation of the Nazi concentration camp in Flossenburg, Hecht won the 1968 Pulitzer Prize for Poetry for his collection *The Hard Hours,* which includes his famous Holocaust-related poem "More Light! More Light!" In his contribution to *A Passover Haggadah,* Hecht says that the words "in every generation" are likely to evoke memory of victims of the Holocaust: "To remember them on this evening as ones who once shared in this service, is right. Yet we must guard against letting our bitterness at their extermination deflect our hearts from, or diminish our gratitude for, the gift of deliverance that we celebrate tonight." Hecht concludes by directly addressing seder participants as "part of the remnant that survived," which both collapses participants' distance from the Holocaust and brings with this association additional obligations. Participants, Hecht writes, "are entitled only to ask, 'Are we among the Saving Remnant? Are we fit for that?' and on this evening, in that hope, to purify our hearts."[20]

Hecht's contribution to *A Passover Haggadah* exemplifies its creators' complex understanding of Anne Frank and the implications of including her famously optimistic words in the Passover seder and inserting them into the ritual trajectory from degradation to redemption. For Hecht, both the destruction of the Holocaust and the "complete and miraculous" deliverance of Israelite slaves from Egypt are, essentially, beyond comprehension. Seder participants are left with the call to question and to hope. Taken in its entirety, the set of optional readings capitalizes upon the charged ritual action of raising the cup of wine and not drinking from it as an innovative way to relate modern events to this ancient celebration. The ambivalence of this ritual corresponds to the complexities of Holocaust remembrance evoked by the readings in "For More Than One Enemy Has Risen Against Us." Beginning with the diary excerpt, the series of readings and their placement in the seder invites readers to look beyond simple optimistic readings of Anne Frank's famous words and understand them in relation to the challenge of maintaining confidence in human progress in the wake of the Holocaust.

The Dancing with Miriam Haggadah

Anne Frank appears with only a single line of text in this 1995 haggadah, compiled for a women's seder, where her voice joins a chorus of women protesting their oppression and celebrating their journey toward freedom. Since the first women's seder, which was held in New York in 1975, these rituals have become increasingly common in the United States, as have special haggadahs that emphasize the contributions of women during the Exodus, the silencing of women throughout Jewish history, or the status of Jewish women today. These rituals and texts reflect the impact of feminism on Jewish communal and religious life over the past forty-five years. One such seder was first held on the fourth day of Passover in 1994, when 198 women gathered to celebrate the holiday in Palo Alto, California. Now an annual event, this celebration inspired the creation of *The Dancing with Miriam Haggadah: A Jewish Women's Celebration of Passover.* In their preface to its third edition, editors Elaine Moise and Rebecca Schwartz advocate for a women's seder as an opportunity to integrate women's voices and experiences into Judaism. Anne Frank appears in *The Dancing with Miriam Haggadah* as part of an effort to bring together "voices of Jewish women throughout our history and pre-history who have carried forward the life and spirit of Judaism."[21]

Throughout *The Dancing with Miriam Haggadah,* the traditional elements of the seder are revised to make women full participants in this central story of Jewish peoplehood. Consider, for example, this haggadah's reworking of the Four Questions, a text recited early in the traditional seder, in which the youngest child asks about the different ritual foods and actions that make the seder night "different from all other nights." *The Dancing with Miriam Haggadah* poses one question—"Why is this night different from all other seder nights?"—and gives four answers that foreground this haggadah's feminist goals: hearing "the voices of our mothers," celebrating "the heroic deeds of our sisters," criticizing oppression, and rejoicing in "our empowerment as Jewish women."[22] This seder invokes the presence of twenty-four women by reading aloud their words during the course of the ritual. The majority of these virtual guests are women mentioned in the Bible; among those women from the modern era who join the celebration, along with poet Emma Lazarus and radical activist Emma Goldman, is Anne Frank.

The Dancing with Miriam Haggadah quotes Anne Frank in the section that immediately follows the feminist rendition of the Four Questions. In this section, Moise and Schwartz recast the masculine grammar of the traditional Hebrew text *'Avadim hayinu* ("We were slaves") in the feminine, as *'Avdut hayinu,* which they translate as "We have been enslaved." The use of the present perfect in the English translation implies that enslavement, for women at least, continues into the present. The traditional text for this section of the seder is reworked as a poem in free verse, opening with references to biblical enslavement—not the Israelite slaves in Egypt, but Jepthah's and Lot's daughters, who were "sacrificed" on the altars of war and hate, respectively. Throughout this haggadah, women who are silent in the Bible are given voices at the seder. For example, Lot's daughters exhort the seder participants: "Our father would have cast us out into the street for the sake of strangers; only the intervention of angels saved us from a brutal assault. To all women whose bodies, experience and opinions have been devalued and discounted: we are with you." The bond of sisterhood forged from shared oppression is extended from these silenced biblical women to their contemporary counterparts. The second stanza of "We have been enslaved," like the traditional Hebrew text that it reworks, moves from the past to the present—"We have been excluded from tradition / Denied our own voice"—as it recounts a "struggle for liberation," within which there is also joy and celebration: "But yet, like Sarah, we laugh. / Like Miriam, we dance."[23]

The poem concludes, "*B'avdut hayinu*—we have been enslaved. / Tonight, together, we vow: / Never Again." Here, the vow "Never Again" refers explicitly to the enslavement of women, but it also invokes the Holocaust, as this phrase has become a common watchword of Holocaust memory. As remembrance of oppression jumps from the biblical past to the Holocaust, Anne's words appear, representing all "those women whose lives were directly altered by the Holocaust; those who perished and those who survived to bear witness."[24] Together, participants read a single line from the diary: "In spite of everything, I still believe that people are really good at heart."

Unlike the direct appeal from Lot's daughters or the communion with Biblical matriarchs Sarah and Miriam, Anne's voice—which is cited from her written work, rather than imagined through creative engagement with biblical texts—remains distinct from the women participating in the seder. They are not invited to identify with her, even as they read aloud the words from her diary. Thus, after reading Anne's assertion that people are "good at heart," seder participants respond with a less certain statement of hope: "May her words prove to be true." This section of *The Dancing with Miriam Haggadah* concludes with a full affirmation of freedom, recited by all the women present: "*We have been enslaved, / Now we are daughters of freedom.*" In contrast to this solidarity among Jewish women through the ages, Anne's words of faith in humankind remain hers alone ("I still believe"); rather than simply affirming her faith, the women at the seder express a more cautious optimism.

A Different Night

Anne serves forthrightly as a beacon of hope in *A Different Night: The Family Participation Haggadah*, published in 1997 by the Shalom Hartman Institute, a center dedicated to enriching Jewish life through the study of Jewish texts. Editors Noam Zion and David Dishon describe the haggadah as a "project in Jewish family education," explaining their approach in a brief foreword.[25] First, the editors remind readers that the word "rabbi" means "teacher" and that the traditional haggadah, which was created by rabbis, teaches Jewish families about the holiday of freedom. Second, Zion and Dishon explain their desire to create an "inclusive and pluralistic" haggadah. This agenda is supported by the six testimonials printed on the last page of *A Different Night*, written by rabbis identified with the Reform, Conservative, Orthodox, and Reconstructionist movements, as well as a professor and a psychotherapist. Finally, the editors emphasize that Passover belongs to each individual Jew and that, as one's needs and understandings change, so should the seder.[26] Hence, *A Different Night* presents an especially wide range of readings, images, and interactive activities, including the words of Anne Frank.

Like the Reform movement's *A Passover Haggadah*, *A Different Night* includes an extended excerpt from Anne Frank's diary entry of July 15, 1944. However, Dishon and Zion title the excerpt differently and situate it elsewhere within the traditional sequence of the seder, thereby creating other possibilities for interpreting Frank's words. Whereas *A Passover Haggadah* includes the diary excerpt among a group of readings dealing with Jewish persecution, *A Different Night* titles the reading "Anne Frank: I Still Believe." This title recalls the Hebrew song "Ani Maamin" (often translated as "I Still Believe"), which has long been performed at Holocaust remembrance ceremonies in the United States. Hasia Diner notes the song's prevalence in postwar American Jewish songbooks of the late 1940s and 1950s as well as its performance as part of late twentieth-century Holocaust commemorations that "employ some of the very same rituals that Warsaw Ghetto memorial meetings of the late 1940s and 1950s relied on."[27] "Ani Maamin," which includes words by the medieval rabbi Maimonides affirming the coming of the Messiah, is reputed to have been sung by Jewish resistance fighters in ghettos as well as by Jews about to be killed in gas chambers.[28]

Underscoring this cue to read Anne Frank's words as an affirmation of hope, the diary excerpt appears in the penultimate section of the seder, which includes the ritual of the "Cup of Elijah." The harbinger of redemption in Jewish tradition, the biblical prophet Elijah makes a dramatic symbolic entrance during the Passover seder. In many homes, a cup of wine for Elijah is set in the middle of the table before the seder begins and remains there throughout the ritual. As the seder moves toward concluding blessings and songs of praise, attention shifts from the table to the front door of the home. A participant, often a child, opens the door to welcome Elijah's arrival. Elijah symbolizes freedom, not only from past slavery or present oppression, but also for the future, culminating in his announcing the advent of the messianic age. Instructions for the welcoming of Elijah in *A Different Night* direct the readers' attention the ritual's relation to the future: "Now the seder focuses on the hope for future redemption symbolized by Elijah the Prophet, bearer of good news." Whereas, in ancient Egypt, the doors were shut tight, the haggadah explains, at a contemporary seder "doors are opened wide in expectation," because this night also marks "the dawn of hope." The instructions conclude: "It is, as the Torah calls it, a Night of Watching in expectation of great changes for the better."[29]

Situating Anne Frank's words in relation to the ritual of welcoming Elijah suggests that her diary looks to the future with hope. However, the other texts presented in *A Different Night* alongside the diary excerpt temper these expectations. Under the title "Filling the Cup of Redemption Ourselves," the haggadah provides alternate instructions for filling Elijah's cup. Following a nineteenth-century Hasidic custom, each person at the seder table is asked to pour wine from his or her own cup into Elijah's cup. Zion and Dishon explain, "This symbolizes the need for everyone to make their own personal contribution to awaken the divine forces of redemption." *A Different Night* also offers a "menu of meanings" that explain the ritual of welcoming Elijah. The menu's first two items, "Trust in Divine Security" and "Expectation of Redemption," speak to the affirmation of faith and anticipation of joy when the door is opened for Elijah.[30] The third possible meaning for this ritual, however, is not felicitous, nor does it look forward to divine redemption but back in time to a period of Jewish persecution. Recalling medieval accusations of blood libel, when Christians accused Jews of murdering Christian children and using their blood to make matzah, Zion and Dishon offer this interpretation of opening the door: "The Jews wanted to see who might be eavesdropping and spreading malicious—in fact, deadly—rumors about the seder."[31] Within this context, considering the significance of Anne Frank's diary is tied to interpretations of the ritual of welcoming Elijah that range from hope directed toward the future to fears associated with the Jewish past.

A *Different Night* marks the transition from the third cup of wine drunk at the seder to the ritual of welcoming Elijah with an illustration by Marc Chagall, titled "Opening the Door for Elijah." The black and white image depicts a winged Elijah, holding a cup of wine. He floats above the open door of a house. A young woman peers out the door, looking as if she might float through the air to meet Elijah. Behind her sits another woman, who is engrossed in reading a book. Chagall's drawing marks a transition from commemorating with wine God's saving acts of the past to the hope for future redemption, signified by Elijah. This image also suggests several possibilities for understanding the excerpt from Anne Frank's diary, in keeping with the editors' goal of eliciting multiple interpretations in discussions among seder participants. Because Chagall's art appears to the right of the diary excerpt, the young woman at the door appears to be looking at Anne Frank's words, while the title of the illustration implicitly links them to Elijah's promise of redemption.

Or perhaps the young woman might be understood as Anne Frank herself. Her hands appear to break through the wall that confines her, and she gazes longingly out above the skyline, where trees, houses, and the sky appear in the distance. For those who are familiar with the diary, the image evokes Anne's longings to emerge from hiding, as described in the diary entry of December 24, 1943:

When someone comes in from outside, with the wind in their clothes and the cold on their faces, then I could bury my head under the blankets to stop myself thinking, 'When will we be granted the privilege of smelling fresh air?' And because I must not bury my head in the blankets, but the reverse—I must keep my head high and be brave, the thoughts will come, not once, but oh, countless times. Believe me, if you have been shut up for a year and a half, it can get too much for you some days. . . . Cycling, dancing, whistling, looking out into the world, feeling young, to know that I am free—that's what I long for.[32]

As Chagall's drawing is dated 1946—that is, one year before the first publication of Anne Frank's diary—this reading of the image entails an act of imagination, made possible both by the editors' juxtaposition of the diary excerpt with the image and by a reader's prior familiarity with Anne's life and work. As *A Different Night* situates participants reading the diary excerpt within a seder ritual that expresses "hope for future re-demption," the haggadah encourages a range of possible readings of the passage among seder participants, in keeping with the haggadah's larger agenda of promoting a pluralistic approach to Jewish family education.

Love and Justice in Times of War Haggadah

The *Love and Justice in Times of War Haggadah,* published on the Internet in 2003, locates Passover's hope for redemption most clearly in human hands and in the present. This haggadah is the work of Dara Silverman and Micah Bazant, self-described queer, "white, Ashkenazi middle-class folks and long-time activists/organizers." They envision their readers as potential friends who will "help build loving, justice-seeking communi-ties of Jews and allies who will gather around the table and eat, work as agitators for everyone's liberation, rock our traditions with our love and be our truly freaky selves."[33] To bring this vision closer to reality, Silver-man and Bazant strove to create a haggadah that was accessible, inclu-sive, and spiritually meaningful. Both authors acquired their knowledge of Jewish sources as adults. Accordingly, the *Love and Justice in Times of War Haggadah* is brimming with explanatory notes, beginning with instructions on how to use the haggadah, a survey of the variety of Jew-ish cultures, a discussion of the dominance of Ashkenazi traditions in American Jewish practice, a list of words and concepts to describe God, and a caveat about gendered language. Almost every section includes explanations crafted to simultaneously entertain and educate seder participants. The authors' commitment to inclusivity extends far beyond reaching out to Jews from disparate cultural and ethnic backgrounds or with varying degrees of Jewish literacy. Allies from beyond the Jewish community are also included, both at the seder table and in the haggadah. For Silverman and Bazant, a spiritually meaningful haggadah is also political. The authors decry the then-current involvement of the United States in "yet another war on poor folks of color" and acknowledge their own struggle as American Jews to protest the "horror of what is done in our name" to Palestinians. Silverman and Bazant offer their online haggadah as a resource for "cultural, spiritual and personal healing" that will help progressive Jews to gather together at a seder and relate their activism to Jewish traditions.[34]

Anne Frank appears in the *Love and Justice in Times of War Haggadah* in a section titled "The Four Adults," which complements a feature of the traditional haggadah, the Four Children. These children—one wise, one wicked, one simple, and one unable to ask—are paradigmatic of the individuals who attend any given seder, each one prompting a different approach to explaining the significance of the ritual. (In the spirit of this haggadah's celebration of the alternative, the Four Children become "The 'Other' Children": the Tranny, the Revolutionary, the Gentile, and the Eco-feminist Crusty Punk Rock Vegan Hypochondriac.) Silverman and Bazant precede their four "Other" Children with "The Four Adults," in order "to remind us that as adults we have a lot to learn from youth."[35] Each of the Four Adults is identified with an emotion, expressing feelings that potentially impede commitments to social justice, and each adult's question is answered by citations from one or more people offering reassuring guidance. For example, the Angry Adult says, "violent and oppressive things are happening to me, the people I love and people I don't even know. Why can't we make the people in power hurt the way we are all hurting?" The activist Cambodian Buddhist monk Maha Ghosananda responds with Buddhist teachings about ignorance and loving-kindness.

The excerpt from Anne Frank's diary appears in response to the Compassionate Adult, who asks, "How can I struggle for justice with an open heart? How can we live in a way that builds the world we want to live in without losing hope?" Here, the *Love and Justice in Times of War Haggadah* presents the same excerpt from the diary entry of July 15, 1944, that was reprinted in *A Passover Haggadah* and *A Different Night*. This passage is followed by a citation from Rabbi Abraham Joshua Heschel, who fled Europe in 1939 and lost most of his family in the Holocaust. After settling in the United States, he became well known for his activism during the civil rights era. In the passage by Heschel included in this haggadah, he affirms that "Just to be is a blessing." Silverman and Bazant preface Frank's and Heschel's responses to the Compassionate Adult with the comment, "This is the question that we answer with our lives." It is a statement filled with irony, perhaps unintended, for Anne Frank did not have the opportunity to answer with her life—except, unwillingly, by losing it—in contrast with the others who respond to the Four Adults: Ghosananda, who led peace marches throughout the Cambodian countryside in the 1990s; Marianne Williamson, a Unity Church minister who founded the Peace Alliance and Project Angel Food, a program that delivers food to people with AIDS; the Rev. Dr. Martin Luther King, Jr.; and Rabbi Heschel. Anne Frank's diary, however, has a life apart from the life of its author and has taken on a significance it might never have had if she had not succumbed to typhus in Bergen-Belsen.

By including this citation from Anne Frank's diary, the *Love and Justice in Times of War Haggadah* not only repeats a choice made for innovative haggadahs over the preceding three decades; it also follows a suggestion of the diary's symbolic value as presented to its readers in English from the time of its first publication. In her preface to *The Diary of a Young Girl*, Eleanor Roosevelt championed the book as a testament to "the degradation of the human spirit" that is a casualty of war as well as to the "ultimate shining nobility of that spirit." Roosevelt, a key supporter of the Universal Declaration of Human Rights, considered the diary a monument not only to Anne's spirit but also "to the spirits of those who have worked and are working for peace."[36] Generations of readers who have read Roosevelt's stirring introduction have, accordingly, linked Anne's writing with the words of religious leaders whose spirituality infused their commitments to social justice activism.

Anne Frank at the Seder

Some readers of Anne's diary might find her lack of any reference to Passover, and the limited discussion of Judaism in general, surprising. In fact, the only Jewish holiday that Anne mentions in the diary is Hanukkah, and she writes much more about Easter and St. Nicholas Day. It is worth remembering that the Franks were not traditionally observant Jews; moreover, Anne's diary reflects the Nazis' persecution of Jews as a race, not a religion. Nevertheless, both religious and secular concepts of Jewishness informed Anne's sense of herself as a victim of anti-Semitism. Her diary entry of April 11, 1944—written during Passover of that year— includes reflections about God, suffering, redemption, and the place that Jews and Judaism should occupy on the world stage. Anne wrote this, the longest entry in her published diary, following a break-in at the warehouse beneath her hiding place. She begins the entry by describing the normal routine of the previous days and parenthetically refers to the previous Friday afternoon as Good Friday. Immediately following a detailed summary of the break-in, Anne begins her reflections on the event by attributing her family's safety to the assertion that "God truly protected us," and she asks God to "go on saving us!"[37]

Although it never mentions Passover, this passage is resonant with the holiday's commemoration of persecution and salvation "in every generation." As Anne describes the impact of the break-in on their daily routine, limiting their freedom even further, she offers a more expansive discussion of their circumstances: "We've been pointedly reminded that we are in hiding, that we are Jews in chains, chained to one spot, without any rights, but with a thousand duties." Anne asserts that says they must do "what is within our power and trust in God" and await the day when they will be "people again, and not just Jews," after which she explains what it means for her to be a Jew:

> Who has inflicted this on us? Who has made us Jews different from all other people? Who has allowed us to suffer so terribly up till now? It is God that has made us as we are, but it will be God, too, who will raise us up again. If we bear all this suffering and if there are still Jews left, when it is over, then Jews, instead of being doomed, will be held up as an example. Who knows, it might even be our religion from which the world and all peoples learn good, and

for that reason and that reason only do we have to suffer now. We can never become just Netherlanders, or just English, or representatives of any country for that matter, we will always remain Jews, but we want to, too.[38]

For the reader aware of the coincidence of this entry with Passover, the holiday's significance resonates with the text's rich engagement with themes such as chosenness, suffering, and freedom. Nevertheless, it is the beloved and familiar text from July 15, 1944, and its broader discussion of human goodness that creators of innovative haggadahs select time and again in order to allow seder participants to feel at home with Anne Frank's reflections.

The fact that Passover is never mentioned in Anne's diary has enabled participants in these seders to link Anne's aspirations with their own within the rubric of the seder by including her as a virtual guest at the ritual meal. A traditional seder opens with an invitation to the stranger in one's midst; all who are hungry are invited to come and eat. These haggadahs invite Anne to the seder—but not as a stranger. In fact, it is her presumed familiarity that makes her such a welcome and frequently invited guest. These haggadahs assume that most of their readers know who Anne Frank is and already know the famous line from her diary that they all cite. This familiarity facilitates acts of imagination and of identification, which resonate with the project of imagination and identification that is at the heart of the Passover celebration. At the seder, Jews are asked to imagine themselves as ancient Israelites and to identify with their experiences of slavery and redemption. When Anne Frank appears as a guest at the seder, participants do not imagine themselves as her or as some other victim of the Holocaust; rather, each haggadah imagines Anne's presence—whether as a Jewish woman in solidarity with other Jewish women, a spiritual leader and social justice activist, a representative of oppression in every generation who still aspires to act for the good, or, like traditional seder participants for generations, a Jew awaiting the messianic age with hope and expectation—and encourages participants to identify her ideals as their own.

III IMAGINING

8

Literary Afterlives of
Anne Frank

Sara R. Horowitz

As a book in which the act of writing figures so centrally and self-consciously, Anne Frank's widely read diary has, not surprisingly, engendered an especially rich array of literary responses. These include the literary efforts of inspired teenagers as well as poems and prose fiction by accomplished adult authors and extend to other works—exhibitions, films—in which Frank's writing and the act of reading it become subjects of interest in themselves. As she is known as a chronicler and a symbol of something beyond her own life and historical moment, the literary figuring of Anne Frank and her diary gives a sense of the ways in which her life and writing have been engaged and given meaning. Her diary provides a model for later journaling under oppressive regimes or difficult economic, social, and personal circumstances. The matters that Frank mulls as she waits out the war—issues of divine and human nature, meaningfulness, identity, sexuality—as well as the unknowingness of the diary, and the imponderability of her fate—take on new dimensions in the hands of later novelists and filmmakers. Reaching across time and continents and in a range of languages, the reimagined Anne is understood as speaking not only to such things as anti-Semitism, human nature, and good and evil, but also to contemporary Jewish identity, fascism, sexuality, psychic pain, abuse, and resistance.

More than the subject of her own reflections, Frank and her diary become literary figures, interpellated into the narrative imaginings of others. In different languages and across a variety of cultural contexts, Anne Frank's life, death, thoughts, even her very writerliness, trigger associations with other historical events or cultural moments. Inscribed back onto her diary, the experiences, anxieties, and values of later readers create a verbal (and sometimes visual) montage of meanings spanning nationalities and decades. Prompted by particular passages in the diary; the context of its composition; the intelligence, sensitivity, and tragic fate of its author; or the diary's subsequent cultural stature, these works envision alternate futures for Anne or her companions, imagine her as a listening presence, or hear her voice as a commentary on their own life and times. By means of intersections and variances with the events narrated in the diary, stories of encountering the historical Anne Frank are backshadowed by the brutal death that awaits her, unknown to the girl who writes and edits, but already known to her reader. The literary narratives about Anne embody the same dramatic irony, recapitulating an imagined past encounter with the always already doomed girl in a story arc that is both innocent and knowing. Anne's appearance as a character, object, referent, or addressee in a range of literary genres gives the murdered writer a complex of afterlives tied to her literariness: as authorial role model, as publishing brand, as imagined companion or lover, as literary icon to be reckoned with. These literary works mediate sets of later cultural meanings ascribed to the wartime diarist, sometimes reproducing and sometimes critiquing them. They prompt questions about our relationship with the past and about assumptions and desires readers bring to the act of reading, both regarding the Holocaust and more broadly.

The Writer on Display

In her history as a public figure, Anne Frank has received more attention as a writer in recent years. A notable case in point is an exhibition titled "Anne Frank, the Writer: An Unfinished Story," mounted at the United States Holocaust Memorial Museum in 2003. Marking the tenth anniversary of the museum's opening, the exhibition focused on Frank's life as well as her talent and creativity not simply as a chronicler but as a writer. While the items on display also addressed her fiction and essays, the iconic diary, on loan from its repository in Amsterdam, anchored the exhibition. The exhibition sought to embed the diary in the actual life of a Jewish girl by displaying photographs selected from Otto Frank's scrapbook showing her from infancy to adolescence. The photographs placed her in normal, everyday settings—at home, on the street, in parks, with family members, with other children—that were at shocking odds with the situation she documented in her diary and the events that overtook her and took her life after the diary abruptly ends. The 1941 photograph selected for both the exhibition poster and the exhibition's entry panel emphasizes her writerliness. In it, a mature-looking Anne gazes out contemplatively; in one hand a pen hovers above the notebook on which her other hand rests. Her serious expression suggests the precocious talent that is already doomed by the time the viewer apprehends it.

By museum estimates, the exhibition drew approximately 750,000 visitors.[1] Many responded to the exhibition about Anne, the writer, in kind, by signing a guest book, leaving a plethora of comments about the girl, her diary, her fiction, and her fate; some directed their remarks to Anne Frank herself.[2] In stark, transparent, and sometimes dramatic terms, the amalgamation of comments encapsulates how the figure of Anne Frank has been interpreted, transformed, or made to signify in the almost three-quarters of a century after her murder.

Visitors' comments overwhelmingly identify Anne Frank with the Holocaust in its entirety. Frank did not merely endure hardships and finally die as a result of Nazi brutality; she, one of millions, stands—or stands in—for the Holocaust as a whole. To read the diary, then, even to gaze upon it, is to know the Holocaust, to encounter it intimately and personally, even though many scholars object to seeing Anne Frank this way. Lawrence Langer, for example, views Anne Frank's story as a soft version of the Nazi genocide, one that allows an easy identification with the girl who has not yet encountered the concentration camp universe and whose expressions of optimism leave one feeling good about humankind and the world generally. According to Langer, the diary "helps us to transcend what we have not yet encountered, nonetheless leaving behind a film of conviction that we have."[3] The United States Holocaust Memorial Museum strove to address this issue by placing the diary within the wider framework of the Holocaust. Wall text noted that "[f]or many, especially younger readers, Anne's diary is their first encounter with the history of Nazi Germany's attempt to murder all the Jews of Europe during World War II." Nonetheless, visitors seem to confirm Langer's worst fears when they note in the guest book, "Now I know what the Holocaust was about."

In their comments, visitors—many of whom have read the diary—identify themselves with the voice of the diary. They feel that they not only read history or about Frank's life, but rather that they plunged directly into her lived experience and experienced it with her. The level of detail in Frank's account and the intimacy of the diary genre contribute to this impression. Although Frank edited her more spontaneous, private diary for publication, and Otto Frank further edited the manuscript after the war, it is a testament to her talent as a writer that the published text has been read as an unfiltered and uncensored outpouring of a young girl's heart. Francine Prose has demonstrated that this effect is due less to the circumstances of writing and more to Anne Frank's artfulness, her attention to telling detail, her recreation of dialogue, and the structuring of narrative episodes.[4] One might say that the redacted diary feels more "real" and immediate than the original. Frank's double position—contemporaneous writer and retrospective editor—combines the feel of a diary with the pointed structure of a memoir. The exhibition reinforces, even mimics, the intimacy between Frank's diary and her readers (and museum visitors) with the wall text's repeated references to her as "Anne" rather than "Frank."

What so disturbs critics such as Langer, and so moves many museum visitors, is Frank's work's ability to generate inspirational meanings. One visitor, like many others, says of her diary that it is, "after the [B]ible, the most life-altering text as it inspires us to be better than our nature." Frank and her writing become witnesses, not merely in the historian's sense of testifying to past events, but in the sacral sense of testifying to God's enduring presence. One reads in the guest book that Frank was "touched by God"; that she, and other victims of Nazi atrocity, are "examples of God's unconditional love, hope, joy, peace and good will"; that she is "a blessing from our God" and "can see far into the future." Frank's account serves as evidence that "God still reigns," "God gives strength," and tenders "the fruit of the spirit"; that the diary is "a true miracle from the pen of a child." Transposed into a secular register, the diary becomes witness to the triumph of the "human spirit," which "lives on" and is "reinforced." To her role as witness, Frank's youth adds a Christological emblem of unsullied innocence, undeserved suffering, and precocious, spontaneous truth-telling. Her "insight," "wisdom," and "profundity" are all the more extraordinary in someone so young.

On many pages of the guest book, the physical diary emerges as something of a sacred relic, capable of effecting redemption. Its very presence purifies and saves a corrupted world. One visitor writes that, if "everyone in the world" could see Frank's diary, "we would see more peace," and another writes that "it would be a better world." Others comment on the diary's "inspiration to be a better person," or Frank's horrific fate as "loss with a residue of great gain." Reading the diary or even viewing the original notebook is transformative. In the guest book, visitors enjoined imagined others to "remember" Anne Frank and "her suffering." By "experiencing" Anne's life and sharing in her suffering, they suggest, one may be ennobled.

Indeed, visitors attach a range of moral lessons to the author's reflective capacities and her death. Whether secular, religious, ethnic, national, or political, these messages suggest that visitors see themselves reflected in Anne Frank's life and work, which "teach" them what they knew all along. Some focus on the need to oppose hatred and racism, asserting that "We are all equal in God's eyes" or that "We must never hate." Some hear an imperative to intervene when others are victimized, stating, for example, "May we always remember to assist others who are in danger or in any need." Some call for a remedy for socioeconomic inequities, committing to aid the "weak and innocent ones who suffer at the hands of evil men, greedy for power and wealth," in Frank's time and now, or to giving "love, respect and goodness to the rich and poor alike."

While many express gratitude for their own more fortunate circumstances, with renewed appreciation for a "free country," others ominously observe ongoing events as evidence that we have not fully learned the diary's lessons. Jewish visitors to the exhibition—commenting in a range of languages, but predominantly English and Hebrew—see Anne and her story as recounting not a universal but a specifically Jewish experience. They identify with her less as a generic victim or tragic diarist than as a fellow Jew who lived and died under Nazi anti-Semitism, the lowest point of Jewish diasporal experience. Frank's diary, through which her voice outlives her, comes to stand for Jewish survival, inspiring the

Hebrew motto *"Am Yisrael hai"*—the Jewish people lives. Comments in several languages identify their writers as descendants of Holocaust survivors. A number of commenters express pride in their Jewishness and commitment to Jewish identity.

Although most comments respond to Frank as victim of the Holocaust, several express a deep and powerful connection to her simply as a writer. Adult visitors recollect having read Frank's diary as children, noting her uncanny presence in their lives, "like I grew up with Anne." One comment, in adult handwriting, notes, "I am a writer, too, but more important I am a child in pain." Others aver, "I trust my diaries as you trusted yours," "Makes you want to write about your life." These visitors identify strongly with Frank as a kindred spirit, sharing her impulse to write and, sometimes, to endure pain through writing. In a more adolescent hand, one entry reads, "me and anne are also alot [sic] alike. We both *LOVE* to write." Such comments suggest that what some visitors found most compelling about "Anne Frank, the Writer" was the discipline to journal daily, to examine one's life and surroundings, and to commit to honesty, rather than the triumph over evil or the poignancy of dying young. Taken together, the comments in the guest book suggest that a visit to this Anne Frank exhibition was a form of pilgrimage, whether secular or religious, collective or personal, to the shrine of the diary.

Unwanted Encounters

Beyond the compass of her diary and other writing, Anne Frank has a growing literary presence in fiction, poems, and film that utilize the figure of the girl or the diary as character, icon, and frame of reference. As one reviewer of a novel centered on Frank noted, "Anne Frank attracts writers."[5] A cluster of works anchor themselves in the story of the historical Anne Frank. Developing historical or imaginary characters whose lives intersected with the now celebrated diarist, these works reimagine aspects of her life, her capture, or her death from different perspectives, opening up space for other possibilities. In two very different novels, the diary's ubiquitous presence projects the present of the narrative into the wartime past and the events of the past into the postwar future. Both novels reimagine Anne Frank's story, intervening in historical memory by unfolding scenarios in which other things occur or secrets are revealed. Richard Lourie's 2007 *Joop: A Novel of Anne Frank* engages questions of moral responsibility and evasion through the retrospective account of an aging Dutch man whose narrative reveals the identity of the unknown person who betrayed the location of the Annex, sending all of its inhabitants to concentration camps, most going to their death. Ellen Feldman's 2005 *The Boy Who Loved Anne Frank: A Novel* focuses on postwar Jewish American identity in the wake of the traumatic past, through the figure of Frank's companion in hiding, Peter van Pels. Feldman's novel rests on the notion that, although presumed dead, van Pels survived the Holocaust and lived out an American life under an assumed name. In differing degrees, both *Joop* and *The Boy Who Loved Anne Frank* narrate a wartime past and a postwar existence destabilized by the diary's ubiquitous presence.

Joop is narrated by its eponymous protagonist, a Dutch man whose recollection of his wartime adolescence in Nazi-occupied Amsterdam comprises most of the novel. Recounted more than half a century later by the aging man, his story of wartime suffering, struggle, and betrayal is framed by an extended scene between the elderly Joop and his younger brother, Willem. The two brothers have been separated since shortly after the war, when their parents divorced, and only recently met when Willem embarked upon a "roots" trip and looked up his estranged brother. While the older Joop had remained with his ailing father in Amsterdam, the younger boy had moved with his mother to California. Willem is portrayed as thoroughly Americanized—nicely dressed and successful, with a brood of children and grandchildren back in the United States eager to hear about his trip. Joop, by contrast, has lived alone and in modest circumstances all of his life. Bitter and angry, he relates a remembered wartime that begins with their family's difficult circumstances and an increasingly stressful family dynamic and culminates in the betrayal of the inhabitants of the Annex.

In the old man's recollection, his younger self emerges as a boy starving for his parents' affection and approval. His father grows increasingly angry and brutal as wartime conditions push the family into the poverty shared by many of their countrymen. Prematurely propelled into a freedom that characterizes other wartime accounts of adolescents, and into the equally common role reversal that made children responsible for their parents' welfare, Joop first finds work in a food warehouse and eventually runs special, illegal food deliveries, taking advantage of the opportunity to steal provisions for his family. Finally, under pressure to provide luxury items for his mother and nutrition for his ailing father, Joop learns that a high bounty can be earned by betraying the location of Jews hiding from Nazi roundups. A set of circumstances leads Joop to a warehouse at 263 Prinsengracht where, behind a hinged bookcase, the Franks and their associates are hidden. During a nocturnal visit to the warehouse to verify the presence of Jewish refugees, Joop catches a glimpse of a white robe emerging from a secret doorway behind the bookcase, pulled back by a whisper calling, "Anne!"[6] Joop reveals the secret of the bookcase and the doorway to the German authorities. Haunted years later by feelings of guilt but unwilling to look squarely at his behavior, Joop weaves a story that implicates his brother, then a toddler, exposing the latent and overt anti-Semitism of his family and their fellow Dutch.

Joop's ambivalence about his past actions drives the narrative. As he recounts it to his brother many years later, the diary's prominence and its young author's fame bring his repressed feelings to the surface. A televised documentary about Anne Frank, the others with whom she hid in the Annex, and their unknown betrayer gives Joop's anonymous Jews names and faces, throwing off the delicate psychological balance he had maintained since the war. More troubling to his conscience, they were not simply any Jews, but Jews who had gained posthumous celebrity. "No one gave a shit about their victims. But mine has to leave a book that half the world's read. I've got the worst goddamn luck in the world." Understanding in retrospect the implications of his adolescent deed, Joop admits to neither guilt nor regret; he characterizes his feelings about the diary as "Angry. Unlucky."[7] As the embittered man weaves his wartime tale, he spreads blame in many directions. Most notably, he points to the pervasive anti-Semitism of the 1940s, both overt and beneath the surface, which constructed an ethos that made Joop's behavior acceptable. Joop's maternal uncle joined the Dutch National Socialist Party, enabling him to amply supply Joop's family with food and luxuries during a period of growing scarcity. Although Joop's father disapproved of the party, he accepted the sustenance that his brother-in-law provided. While not advocating the genocide of the Jews, Joop's father expresses his prejudices to his son. He observes that Jews "think they're smarter than anybody else, smarter than dumb Dutchmen," and that while Jews are not necessarily bad, "it'd just be better if they weren't around." When pillaging the abandoned home of deported Jews, he tells Joop that he discerns "Jew smells," a reference to the *Foetor Judaicus,* or Jewish stench, a longstanding trope of European Christendom associated with the Jewish rejection of Jesus.[8]

The father's offhand remarks about Jews exemplify comments by others as well. These comments capture prevailing cultural attitudes that made trading in Jewish refugees acceptable, if shadowy. Moreover, while Joop's father shows disdain for his brother-in-law's Nazi sympathies, Joop's mother is proud of her brother and his uniform and is eager to accept the material pleasures that his privileged status brings her way. Dutch society, though suffering under the weight of German occupation and fearful of the consequences of resistance, is revealed duplicating German society under National Socialism rather than offering a different, ethically superior model. Fear of repercussions suppresses resistance to genocidal action, while crushing poverty and opportunities for profit create an atmosphere not so much of lawlessness but of dismissal of the ethical claim of law, making both petty crime and human trade palatable. This generalized exposure of the German and Dutch wartime ethos forms the backdrop against which Joop's actions take place. Anti-Semitism is not particular, but systemic; Joop's betrayal of the Franks and their cohorts involves a chain of people. Joop's confessional narrative blankets Holland of the early 1940s with a diffuse sense of culpability for the betrayal that pricks at his conscience.

But Joop focuses blame most intensely at two targets: Willem and Anne Frank herself. Beginning his account to Willem of the betrayal of Frank and her cohorts, he accuses the person he holds responsible: "You."[9] In Joop's account, Willem figures as a root cause of the household dynamics that leave Joop so desperate to win his parents' attention and approval. Born in the early 1940s, Willem is one of a set of twins who occupy their mother's full attention, to young Joop's distress. The other twin dies in a diphtheria epidemic introduced into the home by Joop, who hovers near death himself. Mistaking their grief for anger, Joop is convinced that his parents blame him for the baby's death, seeing in him his brother's "murderer." Thus, even during the war's early years, Joop portrays himself as a perpetrator of sorts and as already struggling with a kind of survivor's guilt—in this instance, dissociated from actual culpability. He characterizes himself as "the carrier of the disease, the one who infected his brother and survived himself."[10] In effect, Joop is always already guilty, regardless of his choices, so that he has little to lose in selling the location of hidden Jews.

At the same time, the narrative links the twin boys with the doomed Jews. Like the figuring of Jews in the European imagination, Joop believes that the twins have special powers, which are deployed against him. Because the twins are attracted by the yellow stars that mark the targets of the Nazi genocide, Joop amuses them by attaching gold stars to their clothing when he babysits, so that in public a Jewish couple mistakes them for Jewish children. This becomes Joop's first link to people he can identify as Jews; he provides them delivery services for a fee while stealing from their parcels. Willem provides Joop not only a connection with the exploitable, but also a motivation for doing so. When Joop explores the warehouse on Prinsengracht to confirm the presence of a Jew's hideout, he is frightened by vermin. About to flee, he imagines Willem's face before him, as though reprimanding, "You killed my brother, now save our father."[11] Joop also blames Willem for profiting from the exploitation and betrayal of Jews, but without getting his own hands dirty. Unlike Joop, Willem is not left to suffer the repercussions of yielding to the privileges and pressures of a wartime childhood. He has no personal history of exploitation and betrayal—in fact, no wartime memories at all. His mother's immigration to the New World spared him the privations of the postwar European economy, especially as exacerbated by an incapacitated father needing constant care and support. Joop repeatedly refers to his older brother's Americanness, calling him "my lucky American brother, who has so few bad memories that he had to come all the way to Holland to get some."[12]

On his part, Willem wishes to repudiate his brother's wartime memories. Although Willem's grandchildren are eager to connect with stories of their ancestral past, Joop's narrative of war profiteering and trafficking in Jews leads the Americanized brother to decide to bury the past—to report back that he could not locate his older brother or that he found him suffering from dementia. Joop threatens to bring his past to Willem's American family and foist upon their sunny California locale the shadowy past that Willem does not wish to carry back. The belated encounter between the two estranged brothers and their responses to the moral demands of the past emblemizes certain European and American responses to the Holocaust. The European wishes to spread culpability around widely, coloring the narrativized past in shades of gray, so that in the end no one can be held responsible, flattening the moral dimensions of the past. The American wishes to keep the darkness of the past at a distance, casting his own cultural innocence against a corrupted Europe. Like Joop's account, the European version of the past is dark and knowing, filled with details of deadly circumstance and the moral ambiguities and compromises that were insinuated into everyday life. Neither the war against the Germans nor the war against the Jews was encountered as an external force of evil, but rather as an intimate pull that reaches inside one's innermost circles and one's innermost self. The American version of the past, like Willem's, is a story of dimly recollected roots, a combination of nostalgia and innocence that distances one from the pressures of the past, while setting good and evil in stark relief.

Most vehemently, Joop blames Anne Frank for his suffering, first by claiming a victimization equal to hers and then, turning the tables, by construing himself as her victim. Obsessed with her diary, he speaks to its author constantly, noting their shared wartime adolescence. "My life is nearly over and I've never really lived. I died about the same age you did, Anne." He compares his detested diet of tulip bulbs during the war's worst hours with what he considers the better fare at the Prinsengracht hideout, faulting Frank for complaining about the monotony of beans. He casts her as a "spoiled" and "snobby little rich girl," contrasting her class privilege with his own lower social status.[13] Ultimately, he recasts the past as a showdown between the two of them, a zero-sum game in which either his family or hers survives. Joop's ailing father requires the nutritious food that the Jews' bounty can buy; Anne's family needs simply to be left alone, their secret hideaway undisclosed to those who will come for them. In retrospect, Joop imagines the moral dilemma as Anne's rather than his, giving her the power to elect her family's safety or Joop's family's welfare. He asks his imagined Anne, "If you love life, if you love your family, if you want to save me from the sin of betraying you, nod your head. And you do nod, Anne; in my little movie, you do nod."[14] Thus Joop situates himself and Anne as equals: the same age, similar deprivations, and morally equivalent in a struggle to survive that his account casts as justifiably selfish and beyond moral judgment. Moreover, Joop's assertion of his victimization against Anne's recapitulates a European narrative of the war years that utilizes the oppression under Nazism to deny a concurrent victimization of Jews. One is reminded of Sarah Kofman's assertion, following the philosopher Maurice Blanchot, of the impossibility of an ethical account about the Holocaust in its aftermath: "no story [*récit*] is possible, if by a story [*récit*] one means: to tell a story [*une histoire*] of events which makes sense."[15] *Joop* is part of a line of postwar fictional works, including Albert Camus's *The Fall,* that utilize the form of the récit—a first-person, narrative monologue—to construct an account of guilt that is at once a confession and a denial.

Joop's obsession with Frank's diary and his insistence on flinging responsibility in all directions suggests an unacknowledged and unmastered past, a denied guilt whose suppression exacts a toll. Perhaps anticipating a debate about the author's (or the publisher's) own moral integrity in relation to the issues raised in the novel, the publisher includes at the back of the volume a set of study questions, one of which raises the possibility that the author has exploited the memory of the historical Anne Frank and the fame of her diary in order to garner his own commercial success: "Does the book exploit the memory and image of Anne Frank, or is it a sincere attempt to understand what motivates people during wartime?"[16] The question suggests that Frank might be extraneous to the novel, that a long-ago betrayal of anonymous victims would elicit the same torturous struggle. If so, the novel's insistence on Frank's centrality to Joop's troubled conscience may be seen as a commodification of Anne Frank and a diminution of the significance of the millions of other victims. Simultaneously, the novel prompts doubts about the trustworthiness of the account. At several points, Joop suggests that he might not be an altogether reliable narrator but has invented a story designed to elicit certain responses in his long-lost Americanized brother. The centrality of Anne Frank and her diary, then, suggests both an unwanted fantasy—a return of the repressed triggered by Frank's ubiquity—and a narrative built around a sacralized, celebrated figure of the Holocaust whom even a distanced Californian may be certain to recognize.

The unanswerable questions prompted by the diary and the fate of inhabitants of the Annex open up a space of literary imagination and moral speculation. During the war, Anne raised questions that would occupy later writers: about human nature, religious meaning, ethics, and writing itself. Anne uses her imaginative powers to get by on a day-to-day basis—not only picturing freedom and the war's end but also imaginatively transubstantiating her unpalatable food to something delectable. Repeatedly, she and her companions imagine for themselves futures that never come to pass, except in the pages of later novels. Readers of the diary encounter Anne's life through her own voice and identify with her strong desire to survive, to live past the end of the war (and of the diary) to embrace the freedom that hovers promisingly just beyond reach. Notwithstanding our knowledge about the staggering number of Jewish deaths in the Nazi genocide, we come to our reading with a desire for a happy ending, for affirmation of a value-laden universe. As Rachel Brenner has observed, the "posthumous, hagiographic treatments" of Anne Frank's diary signal a "postwar tendency to mitigate the horror" by imagining that "justice has been done."[17] In imagining a betrayer evading justice but brought to account by the presence of the diary— the endurance of its author's voice in the world after her death—*Joop* emerges from and speaks to the desires that drive readers and shape reading practices. The girl dies but remains present in the world; the speculation in the diary about human goodness—which comes to characterize Anne Frank's diary in the popular imagination—is affirmed by the sterility and anguish of her betrayer.

Similarly, Feldman's *The Boy Who Loved Anne Frank* builds on a "what-if" scenario that takes off from the desire for a happy ending—a readerly desire that mimics Anne's own intense wishes even as it ignores her history. Imagining, against history, a life plucked from the ashes, Feldman's novel begins with the premise that instead of dying in Mauthausen on May 5, 1945, Peter van Pels (referred to by the pseudonym Peter Van Daan in the diary) survived the war, immigrating to the United

States in the late 1940s. As in *Joop,* an unwanted encounter with Anne
Frank's diary years after the war impels the protagonist of Feldman's
novel to confront suppressed memories and powerful feelings of guilt,
pain, and denial. For the narrators of both novels, Anne Frank is not only
an icon of Holocaust representation but also a figure in their own past,
whose versions and interpretations of events they do not wholly endorse.
Picking up from Frank's February 16, 1944, diary entry, in which she
reports Peter's assertion that after the war he would live as a Christian
rather than acknowledge his Jewishness, Feldman imagines him living
out his adult life under an assumed name as a non-Jewish war refugee
from the Netherlands. In spite of himself, Peter is drawn to Jews. He mar-
ries a Jewish American woman (despite her family's objections), establishes a business with a Jewish partner (who finds that a gentile partner
opens doors), and secretly visits a synagogue where no one knows him.
Early in the novel Peter loses his voice for no obvious reason. He briefly
consults with a Jewish émigré psychiatrist, who questions him about his
war experiences. Barely able to whisper, Peter relates selected details of a
childhood in Amsterdam—scarcity, parents who perished—but not his
Jewish origins. He fantasizes that the psychiatrist imagines his family as
Dutch anti-Semites, possibly Nazi collaborators. The psychiatrist proposes administering truth serum to uncover the traumatic cause of Peter's muteness. Nervously looking around the room, Peter notices Anne
Frank's diary. He suddenly recollects that his wife had been reading the
diary when he lost his voice and finds he can speak again.

Although Peter does not wish to read Frank's diary, he cannot avoid
it. He sees it everywhere, hears people discussing both the book and
the theatrical adaptation. As he is exposed to Frank's narrative of their
shared life in hiding, he takes issue with her version of events—in particular, her portrayal of his parents. The popularity of her diary has publicly
immortalized a distorted and unsympathetic image of them. Peter's inner dispute with Anne Frank's account triggers unwanted memories and
offers a different perspective on life in the Annex and its inhabitants. He
continues the narrative past the diary's abrupt ending, which signals the
author's death soon thereafter. Because sharing his pained and outraged
feelings would reveal his secret, he tells no one, but the injury festers. Not
fully cognizant of his own behavior patterns, through his wife's remarks

he (along with the reader) is made aware that he has repeated episodes of intense and irrational anger.

Peter's ambivalent relation to the past is depicted in his conflict about the number tattooed on his forearm, the bodily manifestation of experiences about which he will not speak and critically connected to the question of who he is. "There were no numbers just like mine. That was the point. The numbers were the only individuality they had left us. One after another we stepped up to the table, Mr. Frank, Dr. Pfeffer, my father, I, and presented our arms, as directed. . . . We were only numbered, that day, consecutive numbers. Mine differed from my father's by only one digit. My indelible legacy." Peter consults a doctor, who repeatedly promises to "erase the past," noting that he has removed not only such numbers but also SS tattoos.[18] But Peter balks at the notion that one's deeds can be blotted out, whitewashed, equalizing victim and victimizer. Moreover, to erase the number would be to erase the self, to erase the trace of the past shared with the other men in the Amsterdam hideout. For Peter the number on his forearm becomes a double sign, even if its meaning is cryptic: of trauma and of Jewishness. It is the correlative of circumcision, the mark of the covenant that links generations to one another and to their history, defining who one is. After the birth of his son, Peter reflects, "Just as I had been numbered as my father was, the same number, off by only one digit, so I had been cut as my father was, the same cut of Abraham, the same sign of the covenant."[19]

Two intersecting story arcs propel this narrative. The first concerns the dynamics of Peter's American family, unknowingly affected by his misrepresentation of his past and his Jewishness. The second concerns Peter's European family, enfolded in his growing obsession with Frank's diary. The first story arc reaches a climax in Peter's suicide attempt, after he finds himself hovering over his son with a drawn weapon. Alone in the house with the infant, he has been pulled into the past by the sound of the doorbell. Convinced momentarily that "they" have come to round up his family, Peter reflexively moves to silence the baby so as not to give away the family's hiding place. Afterward, fearing he poses a danger to his family's wellbeing, Peter attempts suicide. The second story arc culminates in Peter's attending the trial concerning a lawsuit over rights to the theatrical adaptation of Frank's diary. Disturbed by the proliferation of negative images of his family and suffused with unwanted memories of the war years, Peter writes to Otto Frank, identifying himself as Peter van Pels. Eventually Peter receives a response from Frank's lawyer, threatening legal action should Peter attempt such a hoax again, noting the pain Peter's letter caused Anne's father. At the trial, Peter stands up, identifies himself as Anne's Peter, and rants about the injury done to his parents by her diary and its dramatic adaptation. Once again, his long deferred embrace of his identity is not believed. He is taken for one of the "cranks" who, as Ian Buruma observed in his discussion of the diary, are attracted to fame and "latch onto redeemers."[20] Both story arcs are resolved by Peter's reclaiming his name and his memory—first privately and eventually with his family. In a visit to Amsterdam and what has become the Anne Frank House (but had also been his home), Peter mourns his lost childhood, his murdered parents, and his long silence and denial, which perpetrated "a second murder of my parents."[21] Peter's belated admission to his family allows them to make sense of his behavior patterns and comfort him. By this time, Peter's children are adults starting families of their own; they name his grandchildren after his parents, reconnecting severed generational ties. Reclaiming an abandoned past also reclaims Jewish identity, seen as inseparable from history and memory.

Both Lourie's and Feldman's novels center on their narrators' boyhood memories, repudiated pasts, and confessions. While both narratives posit a relationship between the protagonist and Anne Frank, they comment differently on the relation between the diary and its readers and on Anne Frank as a cultural figure. *Joop* relies on the iconic status of Frank and her diary; the narrator grapples with a sullied conscience only because of her fame. The ethical challenge he poses to the imagined Anne hinges on her later stature. By contrast, the narrative in *The Boy Who Loved Anne Frank* debunks the sacralization of the girl and her diary, critiquing its use as a life-affirming text and symbol of the Holocaust *in toto*. The divergence of Peter's memories from Anne's account makes clear that all first-hand accounts are subjective, that no one account can serve as a master narrative. The narrative introduces the existence of a second, lost diary—kept by Anne's sister, Margot—that did not survive the war's destruction: "hers, we all assume, would be the one to attract attention. Margot is the serious sister."[22] The suggestion of a second diarist points to the subjective and fragmentary nature of memory, and the arbitrariness that governed not only who survived, but also whose words would determine the shape of cultural memory years later.

Like all mediations of Anne Frank's diary, these novels contend with its pervasive presence and the accretion of unavoidable, if multiple, "authoritative" meanings. Joop and Peter live not only with the memory of their personal past, but also with everyone's memory of that past as narrated by Anne Frank, whose word—"seal[ed] by her death," as Dutch novelist Harry Mulisch observed[23]—becomes final and definitive, at least in the popular imagination. Their wartime secrets—and moreover, their postwar secrets—prevent them from entering into a public discourse on the Holocaust, a discourse delineated by the words of a dead girl whose own possibility for revision has been horribly truncated. At the same time, as imagined versions of characters who lived contemporaneously with Anne, they, too, evolve narratives that are equally "authorized," if subjective. The privilege of living both along with and after Anne Frank permits them to contest and revise the diary and its afterlife.

Through the centrality of Frank's diary, both *Joop* and *The Boy Who Loved Anne Frank* are also about reading, the effects of reading upon the reader, as well as the desires, thwarted and fulfilled, that the reader brings to the act of reading. In highlighting the subject position of fictional readers of the diary, these novels point to its actual readers, who come to it with individual sets of aspirations, anxieties, fears, and who are also culturally situated. To read Frank's diary is to negotiate a web of individual and collective anxieties that are reflected in reading practices and responses.

Close Encounters

Implied in Feldman's novel is a critique of Anne Frank's place in the American imagination: her impossible saintliness, her narrative as a "soft," bearable version of the Holocaust. At the same time, Frank and her diary provide the catalyst for perpetuating Jewish identity as inseparable from Holocaust memory. In perhaps the most complex literary treatment of Anne Frank, Philip Roth embeds a biting critique of her

posthumous stature as celebrity eyewitness, the canonization of her diary and its adaptations, and the centrality of the Holocaust to postwar
Jewish American identity. Like Lourie and Feldman, Roth pursues a
"what-if" scenario, playing out not what happened but what might have
happened. In his 1979 novel *The Ghost Writer*, Roth's multi-novel protagonist, Nathan Zuckerman, encounters a woman whom he identifies
as Anne Frank, who—contrary to reports—has survived the war and
reached the United States under a different name. Through wordplay,
the name Roth assigns her—Amy Bellette—pays homage to Frank's
writerliness, punning on its homophone, belles lettres. *The Ghost Writer*
is the first of Roth's novels to feature Zuckerman, commonly understood
as Roth's postmodern alter ego. Zuckerman, who evolves and ages over
time in Roth's novels, is introduced as something of an enfant terrible,
a budding young writer who has earned a measure of notoriety among
Jewish readers discomfited by his sharply satirical and sometimes vul-
garized representation of Jewish American cultural anxieties. Zuckerman first encounters Bellette at the home of an older, established Jewish
writer, whom he regards as both mentor and rival. The accented cadences
of Bellette's voice betray her European origins, and—based on her age
and the historical moment—Zuckerman understands that she must have
a story of survival and escape.

Zuckerman's first meeting with Bellette follows a confrontation with
his father, who castigates the writer for portraying American Jews in a
negative light and publicly exposing their flaws. He sees Zuckerman's
treatment of Jewish characters and community as a mark of an attenu-
ated Jewish identity, a product of Jewish self-hatred, and a repudiation
of Jewish memory. In the father's view, only a Jew who has forgotten the
Holocaust and its implications would expose American Jews to danger
by feeding the fantasies of anti-Semites. Hoping to persuade his son of
the danger of such writing, he consults with the influential Judge Wapter,
who agrees that "the artist has a responsibility to his fellow man, to the
society in which he lives, and to the cause of truth and justice," which
Wapter understands as an obligation to the Jewish people. He sends
Zuckerman a pointed list of questions that criticize the writer's failure
to provide strong role models for Jews and exemplary Jewish characters
to impress non-Jewish readers. Instead, Wapter cautions, Zuckerman's

writing would "warm the hearts of a Julius Streicher or a Josef Goebbels."[24] Wapter suggests that Zuckerman would "benefit" from a radical plunge into the Jewish past, in the form of a theatrical performance of the adaptation of Frank's diary. Thus, by the time Zuckerman meets Bellette, he is already primed: he already has on his mind his parents' disapproval, the Jewish community's disapprobation, the weight of Jewish history, and the redemptive power of Anne Frank.

Zuckerman imagines Bellette as the postwar Anne Frank, who has survived but has resolved to remain "dead" in order to empower her diary. This "Anne," of course, is more seasoned and darker than the girl of the diary; unlike the diarist, Anne/Amy has lived through the atrocity of the concentration camps, witnessing her mother's and sister's murders. Through this vision of an older Anne, Roth deflates the sentimentality and false comfort of the diary's theatrical adaptation. Moreover, he suggests that there is irony in Jewish American continuity linked to a girl who was "only dimly Jewish."[25] Still, Zuckerman fantasizes reconciling with his father through a relationship with Anne Frank, as an icon of Jewish identity: "Oh, how I have misunderstood my son. How mistaken we have all been."[26]

At the same time, Roth also explores the price and the payoff of choices that writers make. As Bellette (along with Roth) astutely understands, the diary's celebrity and sacralization rest as much on its content as on its author's death. Even Amy/Anne is seduced by her own celebrity, needing to feel "loved, mercilessly and endlessly, just the way I'd been debased."[27] The adoration that the diary receives seals her secret: "They wept for me, . . . they pitied me; they prayed for me; they begged my forgiveness. I was the incarnation of the millions of unlived years robbed from the murdered Jews. It was too late to be alive now. I was a saint."[28] The thwarting of Anne's will to go on living enables the fulfillment of her desire for her words to live on. For her writing to have its greatest impact, its readers must align their already crushed hopes alongside hers—their terrible knowing of what she did not yet know. Bellette lives, but—in Zuckerman's fantasy—Anne Frank remains "dead" so that her art can be her afterlife. While in the Annex, Frank understood that writing must be endlessly perfected, so she amends, rewrites, omits. But afterward, the diary must stand as is, with no further revisions by its author. Thus,

Amy/Anne's secret permits Anne Frank's imaginary readers in Roth's novel what its actual readers experience: a definitive diary whose author's death retroactively sacralizes her life and work. While Zuckerman's artistic vision alienates him from his father, Amy/Anne chooses to allow her father to believe she has died, in service of the diary. One way or another, art challenges the connection between the generations, refuting or reinventing traditions and conventions.

Roth's "what-if" scenario of Anne Frank as a secret survivor both elevated and trapped by the success of her diary opens a place in American letters for imagining the diarist grown old in obscurity while the fame of her wartime writing expands. In Geoff Ryman's 1996 experimental digital novel 253, or *Tube Theatre*, a delusional and traumatized elderly Frank plays a minor role as a survivor of a crash on the Bakerville line of the London tube.[29] American writer Shalom Auslander imagines her as a repulsive and manipulative old woman, befouling the series of homes whose attic spaces she inhabits. At the center of his 2012 novel *Hope: A Tragedy*, Frank is one of several grotesque characters who serve to retrace with less subtlety and less ambiguity some of the themes, such as identity and martyrdom, that Roth introduces in his more masterly novel. Auslander's Frank, an artist haunted by the literary success of her diary, preys on the guilt feelings of American Jews and Germans and the cultural sacredness of Holocaust memory, ruthlessly destroying the lives of those who sanctify her.[30]

While Roth's Frank retains the eros of youth, in his 2007 novel *Exit Ghost,* a much older Zuckerman again encounters Amy Bellette, now dying of brain cancer. Although the later novel does not pursue the Anne Frank fantasy, Roth uses Bellette to explore issues of memory, art, and identity, and the relationship between the writer's life and work. Belatedly, Bellette wonders, "Who is the celebrity, what is the price, what is the scandal. What transgression has the writer committed and not against the exigencies of literary aesthetics but against his or her daughter, son, mother, father, spouse, lover, friend, publisher or pet?"[31] In the late 1970s, Roth's *The Ghost Writer* was among the earliest works to push against the Holocaust's centrality in Jewish American self-perception and the concomitant fear of anti-Semitism that governs Jewish American anxieties. Yet the novel insists upon a lucid and difficult grappling with the past and criticizes the softening—one might say, the vulgarization—of American Holocaust memory, as exemplified by the singular place of a romanticized version of a victimized girl's adolescent narrative.

Other American works trace the symbolic place of Frank without imagining her as an actual character. For example, in Nathan Englander's short story, "What We Talk About When We Talk About Anne Frank,"[32] the young girl comes to stand not only for Holocaust memory, but its significance in the ambivalences of contemporary Jewish identity, whether religious or secular, American or Israeli. Here, as two Jewish couples play the "Anne Frank game"—wondering which of their neighbors would hide them in the event of another Holocaust—they move into riskier territory. Were one of the spouses not Jewish, would he rescue or abandon his Jewish family? The title and structure of the story riff on Raymond Carver's well-known "What We Talk About When We Talk About Love,"[33] placing the story squarely in Jewish and in American letters more broadly, meshing the idioms of both cultural threads to explore the nature of relationships, human character, and both personal and collective memory.

As Roth uses Anne Frank to critique Jewish American Holocaust memory, and Englander to explore the entanglement of memory, identity, and intimacy, Israeli writer Judith Katzir uses Frank to negotiate culture wars in Israel and the Holocaust's shifting place in the construction of Israeli identity. The title of Katzir's 2003 novel, *Hinei ani mathilah*, is the first line of Anne Frank's diary in Hebrew translation—literally, "Here I begin." The novel (translated into English in 2008 as *Dearest Anne: A Tale of Impossible Love*) is one of several works, both fiction and nonfiction, that directly address Anne, often in the form of letters qua diary entries. Set in Israel of the 1970s, *Dearest Anne* presents the diary of Rivi Shenhar, a gifted teenage girl in Haifa. Left to her own devices after her parents' divorce, Rivi feels ugly and unloved. The girl falls in love with her teacher, Michaela Berg, who is drawn to Rivi's talent as a writer and poet. The novel begins with the adult Rivi—now a celebrated writer—at Michaela's funeral, and closes with an extended depiction of Rivi in the narrative present. These two scenes, set in the early twenty-first century, bracket the story of Rivi and Michaela's affair and the ensuing scandal, as told through Rivi's teenage diary. The diary spans roughly

two-and-a-half years, from April 4, 1977, to October 27, 1979, with a coda
dated ten months later. It documents in intimate detail the fourteen-
year-old Rivi's sexual awakening, not only with the married Michaela
but also with several much older men, one at Michaela's initiative.

From the beginning, Rivi imagines herself writing to the Holocaust
diarist, opening each entry with the salutation "Dearest Anne." Her first
entry establishes the connection between the two girls, separated by
thirty-five years: "Let me begin. That's how you opened . . . your diary
in the form of letters to Kitty, your imaginary friend who you took into
hiding soon afterwards. . . . Here I am, Anne Frank, beginning to write."[34]
Through the progression of her entries, Rivi identifies with Frank on several levels: they are girls of the same age, writers examining their inner
lives. They have troubled relationships with their mothers and suffer the
sweet pangs of coming of age sexually. Beginning on her diary's first page,
Rivi sees the two as kindred spirits, while acknowledging the poignancy
of Frank's truncated life: "The diary with the red-and-white checked
cloth cover, which you received from your father on your thirteenth
birthday, stretched out in front of you like a morning at the beginning
of summer, bright and full of promise, with the smell of fresh paper and
with endless pages waiting to be filled; here I am, Anne Frank, beginning
to write, here I am beginning the exciting adventure that is my life; and
you couldn't know that your beginning wouldn't have a continuation, and
that it was so close to the end." Most significant, Rivi connects with Frank
as a writer—moreover, one for whom writing provides emotional shelter,
a sense that "nothing can hurt me," and a connection with the sublime:
"the world is speaking to me in hints, the sea is blinking in Morse code,
the wind is whispering secrets to me, nothing is what it seems, everything
is actually a sign of some other, hidden thing. . . . [P]oems . . . are keys
that help to understand these hints, to connect them and decipher them,
in order to reveal something true and important to the soul." Although
Rivi's diary is a one-way address to Anne, she imagines the relationship
as mutual, with herself as Anne's Kitty, "the one for whose eyes and heart
you wrote your diary."[35]

The Anne of Rivi's diary is more than an icon of Holocaust victimization. Rivi reanimates the girl, quoting extensively from Frank's diary,
which she has read four times over the course of a year. At the same

time, Rivi's diary also reveals her sense of the differences between the two of them. While Anne Frank was confined for over two years to a small space with little privacy, Rivi runs free, partly because of parental neglect, partly because of Israeli cultural norms. Despite the smallness of her mother's apartment, Rivi finds private places. While both diaries document their writers' coming into sexual awareness, Rivi explores her sexuality, eventually grows out of adolescence, and becomes a mother, while Anne Frank dies prematurely, still a virgin.

Although Rivi's diary focuses on the angst of her everyday life rather than on the Jewish past, the Holocaust is significant. Central to the novel is a letter Rivi writes to Anne Frank for a class assignment, selected to be read aloud at the school's Holocaust Remembrance Day assembly. The letter—both the inspiration for Rivi's diaristic address to Anne Frank and the initial draw between Rivi and her teacher—captures Anne's personality and aspirations, as well as the tragedy of her death. Much of Rivi's letter articulates a response to Frank's diary that would be standard in Israel of the late 1970s. In language at once eloquent, passionate, and marked by the overly formal phrases characteristic of a thirteen-year-old girl's notion of ceremony, the letter acknowledges the persecution that drove the Franks into hiding, denying Anne the "right to study, to move freely about the streets of your town, to laugh, to breathe the air of the world, to grow up." In Anne's daily encounter with "the shadow of the war and the fear," the "young, brave, sensitive" girl insists on her own humanity, resisting "the dark hearts and minds of those who decided to exterminate you." For Rivi, Frank's diary personalizes the Holocaust, rendering it less abstract and historical for children born in a different time and place. Frank's account restores the humanness of the "nameless and faceless 'six million,'" particularly during an era when, as Rivi asserts, Holocaust survivors in Israel were "not in the habit of speaking" about their experiences. Thanks to Frank's diary, "we know that all the others too had names, faces, voices, memories, loves, hopes, and wishes, and that each of them was a world and the fullness thereof." In large measure, the letter draws a predictable, if appropriate, message from Anne Frank's experience, situating Israel as the antidote to the threat of annihilation—that because Jews "have a flourishing country defended by a strong army," they are "no longer sentenced to extinction." The con-

nection between the European catastrophe and the establishment of the
State of Israel, as well as its crucial role in the future of Jewry, underlies
Israeli Holocaust commemoration not only in the 1970s but also into the
twenty-first century.[36]

Rivi's letter, however, veers from the conventional Holocaust remembrance theme of "never again." Rather than casting Jews as the world's
perpetual scapegoat, so that the only reasonable "lesson" of the Holocaust
is to defend Jewish continuity, Rivi allows that Jews, too, must determine
not to oppress others. "Have we learned the lesson and made it a rule to
respect the other, the weak, the stranger living in our midst? Even between ourselves there is no respect and no peace." For Rivi, to encounter
Anne Frank is to see that "we were all created in the image of God." Rivi
sees Holocaust memory as calling for a commitment to "conscience," to
"not join those who rob others of their humanity, hurt them and deprive
them of their rights."[37]

Rivi's recitation of her letter draws an enthusiastic response from her
contemporaries. The school's principal, however, berates Rivi's teacher
for selecting a reading that suggests that the Jews and the State of Israel are not "an example to the whole world." He deems it "an insult to
Holocaust survivors" and to Israelis generally, "still fighting for our survival surrounded by enemies who want to destroy us." Insisting on the
uniqueness and incomparability of the Holocaust, the principal deems it
"inconceivable to claim that all human beings, Jews and Arabs and Germans and Thais, are the same."[38] Through these different readings of the
implications of Anne Frank, Katzir's novel captures a sea change in the
Israeli relationship to the European Jewish past. Rivi's interpretation of
Jewish memory leads her to articulate an ethical legacy that is both classically Jewish and universal. Her language gestures back to the repeated
biblical injunction that the memory of slavery in a foreign land obligates
one to an ethical stance vis-à-vis others. The principal—old enough for
the Holocaust and the Israeli wars of 1948, 1956, and 1967 to be in living
memory—understands the Jewish past as an unbroken chain of persecution and endangerment. Rivi and her cohort have grown up in an Israel
strengthened and expanded after the 1967 war; they see their country as
powerful, stable, and permanent. For them, the precariousness of Jewish
existence and of the Jewish state is historical, not ever-present.

The transgressive elements of Katzir's novel—the shock of comparing contemporary teenage angst with Holocaust victimization, the
lesbian relationship between teacher and student—underscore the shift
in Israeli cultural memory and the collapse of past certainties. If Rivi's
recitation at the Holocaust commemoration suggests the possibility that
Israelis, like anyone else, could find themselves to be morally wanting,
the novel's larger context suggests a country still reeling from the trauma
of the Holocaust. Like Rivi—a neglected, abused, yet passionate and
gifted adolescent—Israel in the late 1970s was in a sort of national adolescence, burdened by the past but also pulsating with a life force. This is
underscored by the second Holocaust Remembrance Day featured in the
novel, when Rivi's best friend, Racheli, a child of Holocaust survivors,
loses her virginity. Rivi and Racheli see in this an affirmation of life and
an apt commemoration. Thus, the novel suggests, the antidote to trauma
resides in eros and art.

While set in the late 1970s, the novel reflects cultural attitudes prevalent at the time of its composition in the early twenty-first century.
Embedded in Rivi's diary is an extended discussion of the neglect of
women writers by the Israeli cultural establishment. By the late 1980s
and early 1990s, women authors and critics were publishing feminist
critiques of the Israeli literary canon. Beginning with Amalia Kahana-
Carmon's landmark 1989 essay, translated as "The Song of Bats in Flight,"
these critiques noted the absence of women from the literary pantheon
and from what was considered foundational modern Hebrew literature,
central to the shaping and expression of Israeli cultural memory.[39] At the
same time, these writers and critics began to explore the symbolic association of women with other Israeli Others: Arabs, non-Jewish residents,
foreigners. In this light, the great passion at the center of the novel, which
Rivi later understands as both abusing and nurturing, signals the collapse of the Israeli masculinist ethos. Rivi's catalogue of Israeli Others
includes a list of attributes associated with vulnerability and powerless-
ness and specifies categories of people: "a Jew or an Arab, German or
Dutch or Thai."[40] While the references to Dutch and Germans gesture
back to Frank's diary, and the Otherness of Arabs was already in the Israeli literary consciousness by the late 1970s, the reference to Thais seems
more connected to the wave of migrant workers that burgeoned in the

1990s. Thus, through its focus on the late 1970s, when mythic certainties began to fall apart, Katzir also comments upon the present, characterized by a destabilization of the fixed rubric of Israeli cultural memory.

Oblique Encounters

Literary uses of Anne Frank explore issues other than Jewish memory, as meanings radiate out from her wartime account to encompass other contexts. The novels considered so far engage history by rewriting it. Drawn in by both the power and the celebrity of Frank's diary, they imagine paths into and out of its fulsome but truncated narrative. While the diary inspires these fictional scenarios, it also stifles the voices of their characters, defining or exposing them in ways they cannot contain. In other genres, however, writers use Anne Frank to give themselves voice. Two very different examples illustrate how Frank, or her diary, figures as a model for later writers' acts of political or literary resistance. Marjorie Agosín's 1998 collection of poems, *Dear Anne Frank*, draws upon the poet's family history, her own experience of living under Chilean fascism, and her longtime fascination with Anne Frank, in order to probe the nature of suffering and resistance to dehumanizing oppression. Zlata Filipović, a teenage girl in Sarajevo in the early 1990s, credits Frank's inspiration as she documents the details of living through the Bosnian conflict in her diary, published under the title *Zlata's Diary*. From different contexts and in different genres, both Agosín and Filipović read their respective historical moments and their acts of writing as analogous to Frank's writing of her diary. Agosín's poems and the autobiographical essay that accompanies them introduce a complicated and melancholy relationship among the memory of Anne Frank, the traces that remain of her life, and Agosín's own European Jewish heritage and life under Latin American fascism. *Zlata's Diary* is consciously modeled on Frank's, even as Filipović is both seduced and repulsed by identification with Frank. What Ian Buruma identifies as the "curse" of celebrity, which haunts Frank's diary and its afterlives, complicates Zlata's relationship to her writing and her readers' response to it, posing incisive questions about what drives and limits historical analogies.

Dear Anne Frank links Frank's victimization and the persecution of European Jewry during the Holocaust to contemporary oppression in Latin America. In an extended autobiographical introduction to the poems, Agosín situates herself in relation to Frank. She recollects a photograph of Anne Frank poised on a bedside table in her childhood home in Santiago. A gift from her Jewish grandfather José, she recollects, "Anne Frank's presence in that little photograph was always at my side during my childhood nightmares." Her great-grandmother, born in Europe, would kiss the photo each night as an "eccentric, sacred ritual." For the young Marjorie, Frank was not only a reminder of the Jewish past but also an emblem of Agosín's Chile under Pinochet's dictatorship; in Agosín's poems, Anne is a symbol of the "human tragedy of nationalism and the contemptible legacy of racism." As was the case for Holocaust survivors, families of the disappeared victims of Chile and other Latin American dictatorships were allowed no corpse, no grave site, no place to mourn, no possibility of "cathartic ceremony." Agosín recollects a strong and immediate identification with Frank's photograph, which "reminded me of myself." In her imagination, Anne becomes her contemporary, a childhood friend who plays with Marjorie and her sisters, "reading fragments of her diary to us."[41]

Years later, having left Chile for the United States, Agosín reflects upon the ethical challenges prompted by Frank's diary. As in wartime Europe, atrocities were abetted in Pinochet's Chile by the nonintervention of bystanders and onlookers. How, Agosín wonders, might one conceptualize and promote a nation's "moral fabric" in a way that resists genocide and other "forces of demagoguery"? Even as she uses Anne Frank and her diary to explore questions about fascism, perpetrators, atrocity, and moral abrogation and accountability, Agosín resists transmuting Frank into a symbol, disconnected from the actual person who lived, wrote, and then perished in the Nazi genocide. Rather, the poems constitute what Agosín calls "a dialogue with Anne Frank," intended to "revive" the memory of her as a young girl who might have lived, rather than as solely a "martyr."[42] The poems imagine Frank's bodily sensations, emotions, and dreams, asking, "Did you really believe that all men are good?" Agosín follows Anne past the diary into her imagined last days, seeing her as "courageous / when the crew of stupid executioners / ... played games with your newly awakened ovaries / ... they shaved your head for greater amusement / sealed up your empty eyes." Many of the poems build on a layered set of identifications. Anne is elided with female victims of Chilean oppression, as well as with the poet herself: "I, Anne, like you, am more than a Jewish girl." Indeed, like the Frank family who fled Nazi Germany, Agosín's fled Chilean anti-Semitism to live in the United States. Agosín's identification with Anne is so strong that at points the two become interchangeable. "Obsessed" with Anne Frank, in her poems Agosín comes, through her association with the young diarist, to resemble her: a writer committed to truth and compassion under impossible circumstances, who can "change . . . the world with your pen."[43]

Inasmuch as Frank's diary presents the murdered girl's voice to later readers, to read the diary is to listen to Anne, whose words were composed during her lifetime but heard only after her death. Her death, of course, ostensibly ends the possibility for revision, for elaboration, for rethinking, and closes off possibilities for real dialogue. Agosín's poetic address to Anne seeks to restore an impossible engagement with the girl. Having listened to the voice of the diary, the voice of Agosín's poems speaks to Anne, demanding that she clarify her thoughts, challenging her with the knowledge of what happens after the diary falls silent— deportation, humiliation, brutality, and death—not only for Anne but for others, later and elsewhere. Agosín situates Anne as a listener to her poems, but the questions that Agosín poses—about human goodness, moral courage, the rhetoric of resistance—are also reflexive, pointing to the poet in her own time and place. This results in a dual commentary—on both the Holocaust and Latin American fascism. Loquacious in her diary, the Anne of Agosín's poems remains silent; as Agosín knows, the dead cannot speak. The dialogic encounter with Anne, then, cannot go beyond its second act: read the diary, address its author. And so, despite the endurance of her diary, Anne is made to stand also for those victims who disappeared without leaving a trace. The figure of Anne in Agosín's poems, then, shifts back and forth through a set of identifications—with Europe's murdered Jews, vanished Chilean victims, and Agosín herself—becoming a prism through which the poet refracts her own responses to personal and family memory and experience in Europe and later in Chile. As a Jewish, female, Latina writer, Agosín sees the Holocaust as her story, just as Latin American fascism is her story. For Agosín's readers, Anne Frank becomes a bridge, drawing them from one historical horror to another, from a publicly commemorated but also deeply personal outrage to one that is equally personal yet less widely acknowledged.

While Zlata Filipović does not address Anne Frank directly, she addresses her own diary in self-conscious imitation of Frank. As Scott Simon noted in his review of the Holocaust Memorial Museum's Anne Frank exhibition in 2003, the significance of Frank's diary extends beyond its evocation of the Holocaust to a universal symbol of resistance to oppression, particularly for children. She serves, he observed, as "a kind of patron saint for children from Monrovia to Rangoon whose lives are oppressed by fear today."[44] Young adult diarists documenting their lives under politically repressive regimes are often inspired by Anne's diary and, at times, consciously imitate it. These young writers see their own journaling as Frank-esque resistance, perseverance, and affirmation of the forces of good. Filipović began keeping a diary in the 1990s, during a time of relative stability in Sarajevo. As events took a turn for the worse, she documented the violence that overtook her city and the disruption of her everyday life. Her diary spans two years of her life, September 1991 to October 1993, from the ages of eleven to thirteen. At first relatively infrequent, the entries increase in length and frequency as the Bosnian conflict begins to affect her life, documenting shortages of food and other resources, suspension of schooling, and confinement to her family's apartment. That Filipović was aware of Frank's diary is clear from an early entry, in which she decides to address her writing to an imagined reader: "Hey, Diary! You know what I think? Since Anne Frank called her diary Kitty, maybe I could give you a name too."[45] From that point on, her entries begin "Dear Mimmy," in homage to and in mimicry of Anne Frank. Like Frank, Filipović writes with an audience in mind. By October 1992, Filipović began thinking of her writing as publishable, rather than strictly private. At the urging of a teacher, she submitted selected excerpts from her diary to the City Assembly, and in her October 21 entry, she reveals that "Mimmy" will be published.

There is little evidence in her writing that Filipović consciously claimed the mantle of a Bosnian Anne Frank. Early on, however, others construed her as such. During an event in late July 1993, arranged by the International Peace Centre, in which several Sarajevo children read messages about the suffering of war and their hopes for peace, Filipović caught the attention of an international cadre of journalists, who featured her on news broadcasts in several countries. Filipović observes in her diary, "Several people compare me with Anne Frank." The English-language publication of Filipović's diary contains an introduction by Janine di Giovanni, an American journalist who met the girl in the summer of 1993. By that time, di Giovanni recollects, Filipović was already termed the "the Anne Frank of Sarajevo." Although she modeled some aspects of her journaling on Frank's diary, the comparison "frightens" Filipović. Several times she expresses her hope "that I will not suffer the fate of Anne Frank."[46]

Nonetheless, the comparison sticks and becomes central to the book's promotion. The jacket copy of its English-language publication calls the Bosnian diary's voice "innocent and wise, touchingly reminiscent of Anne Frank's." In a review of *Zlata's Diary*, Francine Prose raises several issues that pertain not only to Filipović's diary but also to scores of other diaries and blogs whose authors are termed the "Anne Frank of." In these writings, the association with Anne Frank in publicity, on jacket copy, or self-consciously within the work itself is intended to position the later writing as both authentic and important, claiming for it the attributes commonly ascribed to Anne Frank: courageous, life-affirming, humanistic, universal. Prose's review points to the venality of this tactic, calling the comparison between Filipović and Frank a "most tasteless and gruesome" marketing ploy and the beginnings of "a new form of war profiteering" that exploits young writers, inviting readers to compare the suffering of children. How can one fail to note the "happy ending" for Filipović, Prose warns, and the fact that she saw her diary in publication even as she continued to write it, while Anne Frank's diary, published posthumously, gestures to its author's brutal death in obscurity?[47] The association with Anne Frank's diary also highlights its superior writing, unintentionally detracting from the stature and impact of those written or read under its influence. In an earlier and much harsher review of Filipović's diary published in the same newspaper as Prose's, Christopher Lehmann-Haupt, too, sees the girl as "exploited" and faults the book's tone and style in strong terms for what he deems its "inauthentic, posturing quality," "coy self-consciousness," and lack of "the dramatic shape" and "genius" of Frank's diary.[48] Prose's review, appearing barely a week later, in effect softens some of Lehmann-Haupt's more biting criticism, while sharing his concerns about what one might call the use of Anne Frank as a brand.

In different ways, Agosín and Filipović illustrate the power, complexity, and problems of historical analogy. Agosín's poems seek to both emulate and interrogate the possibilities of literary resistance and its relationship to political resistance. Frank's celebrity allows her to encompass other unknown victims. Zlata's quick rise to fame builds on her own and others' association of her diary with Frank's famous one. The comparison between the two girls and their life and times, when pushed, implodes in discomfiting ways. If Anne Frank represents the voice of history for these writers resisting oppression in their own time and place, she also remains, squarely, a voice *from* history. Thus, in negotiating the terms of an analogy with Frank and her writing, these later writers must keep history intact and in its place. Unlike the novelists discussed above, who open up an imaginative space for other outcomes and perspectives, both Agosín and Filipović remain bound to Frank's life and death. For Agosín, this permits a puncturing of the saintly aura that surrounds Anne in her later cultural mediations, allowing the girl the possibility of anguish, doubt, and despair *in extremis*. For Filipović, Frank's historicity attests to the importance of the Bosnian girl's own writing but also unsettles her with the possibility that events do not always end well; one senses Filipović's fear that, in taking on Anne's celebrity, she tempts fate. Ultimately, the comparison with Frank carries with it the failure attached to all unexamined analogies.

Performed Encounters

In two films produced at the turn of the twenty-first century, reading *The Diary of a Young Girl* plays a strategic role in dramas about the struggles of other young women. Perhaps because Frank's appearance on screen would concretize her presence in a way that is very different from depicting her only through the text of her diary, Anne does not appear in either film as an actual character. Still, her evocation contributes in important ways to the working out of central issues in these films. Francine Zuckerman's 1997 *Punch Me in the Stomach* captures New Zealand performance artist Deb Filler's reenactment of her "whirlwind tour of Eastern European concentration camps" with her father, a Polish Jew who survived several concentration camps before settling in New Zealand.[49] Lisa France's 2003 *Anne B. Real* traces the struggles of Cynthia Gimenez, an Afro-Latina teenager in New York City, to overcome racial oppression and despair. Both films engage with Anne Frank through performance, positing in different ways a relationship with the past and the present that is mediated through the act of reading the diary. Filler's performance is autobiographically based and stays close to the subject of the Holocaust and its aftermath. France's film relates a fictional story and refracts contemporary racism and sexism through the prism of the Holocaust.

Both films negotiate the memory of Anne Frank and the diary's presence not only through drama, but through performance art. In performance art, the artist's body is the vehicle and medium of artistic expression, inseparable from and synonymous with the work of art. The artist does not merely produce art but embodies it. Filler performs an autobiographically based version of herself and others. Cynthia secretly aspires to be a performer, rapping poems to a live audience. While other art forms take on a life of their own away from the artist, with an audience that encounters only the product, performance art is predicated on a relationship not only between the art and the audience, but between the audience and the artist.

Both Filler's persona and Cynthia identify with Anne Frank. Like other works by children of survivors, Filler's performance explores what it was like to grow up with the Holocaust as a familial and foundational story that was both intimate and unapproachable. Her attraction to Anne Frank is both an assertion of the way that her own life has been shaped by the Holocaust—that she, too, is a child of the Holocaust—and an acknowledgement of her distance from it. Her performance engages her audience as voyeurs, positioning them as similarly intimate with and distanced from her life. In *Punch Me in the Stomach,* the relationship with Frank is one point in a much longer performance that probes the effects of Holocaust memory and trauma over time and across generations. In *Anne B. Real,* the relationship with Frank is more elaborately explored and drives the film forward. In different ways than *Punch Me in the Stomach, Anne B. Real* also depicts a relationship with Anne that is both intimate and distanced—intimate in its use of repeated voiceovers reciting passages from the diary; distanced, because Cynthia makes no claims to familial or cultural connections to the events depicted in the diary.

Building up to the visit to Auschwitz, the film's dramatic and emotional center, *Punch Me in the Stomach* explores the effects of the father's wartime experiences on his two children. Filler uses dialect, mime, makeup, and props to perform not only herself at various ages, but also her father, her sister, and other members of the extended family, as well as New Zealand and North American acquaintances. The film negotiates Filler's ownership, as it were, of the European catastrophe, articulating the extent to which it was and was not "my Holocaust, too." Frank's diary stands for Filler's childhood obsession with the Holocaust and the ways in which her family background separates her from her New Zealand cohorts. In one vignette, Filler enacts her difference from other children. She begins by recollecting the contrast between her childhood reading habits and those of her friends, saying to the camera: "While they were all reading *The Cat in the Hat,* I was reading *The Diary of Anne Frank.*" The scene that ensues shows Filler standing in front of a row of library bookcases. In a high-angle shot, the viewer sees "Debbie" gazing up toward the camera (and the viewer), past the surface of the librarian's desk, the perspective conveying her child stature. In a girlish voice and with exaggerated politeness, she requests of the off-camera librarian, "Do you have any good books for the 'thirties setting? [Pause.] Anything more about girls trapped in attics?" The brief scene rests on the ubiquity of Frank's diary and the presumption that the audience will understand the reference. Moreover, it shows Debbie's caginess, not daring to name the Holocaust but couching it in other, more neutral descriptors.

The scene is sandwiched between two other vignettes that reinforce the isolation and sense of separateness that her father's European past imposes upon Debbie's New Zealand present. These scenes highlight young Debbie's difference from her peers as "the little Jewish girl" and—again, without naming it—identifies Jewishness with the Holocaust, gestured to by referring to "obstacles" that Jews have had to overcome. Underlying these scenes is the notion of the Jews' radical Otherness that is a precondition to both anti-Semitism and philo-Semitism and tightly links the two. These scenes exemplify what the sociologist Zygmunt Bauman terms "allosemitism," referring to the pervasive "practice of setting the Jews apart as people radically different from all others, needing separate concepts to describe and comprehend them and special treatment in all or most social intercourse," and what literary scholar Bryan Cheyette terms "semitic discourse," wherein a "protean instability or ambivalence" is the one consistent aspect of the Jew as a cultural signifier.[50] Thus, the position of the library vignette between two pointed performances of Jewish difference in postwar New Zealand expresses an affinity between Filler and Frank based on a shared experience of outsiderness and exclusion, despite their shared secularism and integration into the culture of the countries in which they lived.

This sequence of scenes buttresses Filler's claim to the Holocaust as, in some measure, hers. Frank's diary allows the girl that Filler was to imagine her way into a child's wartime past, transporting herself into the lived experiences of a girl her own age. This imaginary shared past allows her not only to recollect the war through the prism of her father's memories, but also to draw upon childhood memories merged into her own. The identification with Anne opens up for Filler an "as-if" viewpoint on the inside. At the same time, the need to enter the diarized world of another, to seek out books from a librarian, simultaneously reinforces the fact that Filler remains also on the outside, capturing her ambivalent position with respect to her father's Holocaust. In *Punch Me in the Stomach*, the Holocaust is an ambivalent legacy, conferring a special knowledge but also a burden on survivors and their descendants. As in Katzir's novel, trauma is both debilitating and a source of creativity, producing an art that is both an expression of and a counterpoint to traumatized memory. For Filler, Anne Frank functions as an emblem of Holocaust suffering—the girl hidden in the attic. Perhaps because Frank did not survive to respond to her experiences, perhaps because the biting humor of *Punch Me in the Stomach* undercuts sentimentality, the evocation of Frank does not connote a mastery over suffering, a triumph over evil, or a writerly immortality.

By contrast, in *Anne B. Real,* Anne Frank is the emblem of and the inspiration for rising above the pressures that crush the spirit.[51] Cynthia shares a small, rundown apartment with her mother, grandmother, unmarried sister, and her sister's toddler. The family's economic circumstances are dire because Cynthia's father died several years earlier, and because Cynthia's brother, Juan, a drug addict and dealer, drains the family's finances. Although Cynthia is clearly gifted, she has given up on her future. She absorbs a stream of negative messages about herself from family and mentors at school. An arena for the turf battles of drug traffickers and loan sharks, her neighborhood is plagued by violent crimes. As the outside world pressures her inner life, Cynthia creates private space by putting on headphones, reading, and writing.

Anne Frank's diary is represented by repeated shots of Cynthia reading it and by voiceover readings of quotations from it in fragments and then in their entirety. The diary also has an embodied presence in the form of Cynthia's best friend, Kitty. Frank's Kitty is synonymous with her diary. As the silent recipient of Anne's confidences, one might say that Kitty is Anne's first listener. After the war, after Anne's death, Kitty's role changes. Once passively receiving Anne's words, the diary now propels them into the world, speaking in Anne's stead. Kitty thus transforms from Anne's ear to her mouth, broadcasting the dead girl's voice. Similarly, Cynthia's Kitty is her only confidante; she discloses to Kitty aspirations and struggles that she tells no one else. Cynthia is comforted and emboldened by Kitty's receptivity, but Kitty is no passive listener. Cynthia's Kitty has a loquacious and uninhibited personality and repeatedly urges Cynthia to continue writing, make her poems heard, and perform them publicly. France conceptualized Kitty as the "spirit and voice of Anne Frank" and an embodiment of the diary.[52] France directed Kitty's personality as mischievous, loud, and chatty, like Anne.

A shooting scene that is only partially revealed in the opening moments of *Anne B. Real* lays the ground for Kitty's significance in the film and establishes her connection to Anne Frank, the diary, and the possibilities of memory. As first shown, the scene depicts a confusing mix of guns and people: Cynthia, Kitty, Juan, other men. In an armed encounter among the men, a shot is fired. Cynthia's horrified reaction implies that someone has been killed, but the film does not reveal who until later on. The shooting scene constitutes the narrative present of the film, the point from which the story proceeds and also looks backward. The film moves ahead by intercutting earlier and later moments, backtracking to events preceding the shooting as it moves ahead toward the story's conclusion. Eventually viewers learn that Kitty is the accidental victim of the shooting. Thus, the Kitty that viewers see as the film progresses is already dead by the time the narrative time of the film begins. Like Anne Frank, France explains, Kitty is "alive in the story but she's never really there." In learning to mourn her friend and to be guided by her voice even after her death, Cynthia recapitulates her relationship to Anne and the diary. In a sense, Cynthia and Kitty are doubles; both, in different ways, represent Frank—the one triumphing over oppression, the other falling victim.

In Cynthia's claustrophobic and soul-suffocating world, Frank and her diary serve as a talisman, a link with her dead father, a source of inspiration, and a guide. The film deliberately sets up an association between Anne's life and Cynthia's. Before the title rolls, the film opens with a flashback to Cynthia's childhood. The scene is repeated later in the film, first in fragments, then in its entirety. Filmed in black and white, the scene depicts a remembered moment between a younger Cynthia and her father, a teacher in the high school she now attends. Mr. Gimenez reads to his daughter from his copy of *The Diary of a Young Girl*: "All children must look after their own upbringing. . . . The final forming of a person's character lies in their own hands." There is a particular aptness to that quotation; although the film does not reveal it, Mr. Gimenez is quoting advice that Anne attributes to her father. Telling Cynthia the book was written by "a little girl around your age," he gives it to her. The quotation takes on a prescient quality for Cynthia, as though her father anticipated his own death, preparing his daughter to grow up without him. Throughout the film, Cynthia is seen reading from her worn copy of Frank's diary—at home, in class, on the street. *Anne B. Real* sets up Frank's life as the correlative of Cynthia's. The first set of camera shots of her neighborhood lingers on the Amsterdam Avenue street sign, linking Anne Frank's city of refuge and capture with Cynthia's environment. According to the Director's Commentary on the DVD of the film, this link is reinforced by the use of a blue filter on several shots of the locale, giving the vistas of upper Manhattan the feel of European cinema. Like Anne, Cynthia has an older sister with whom she is sometimes at odds; like Anne, she experiences the sweetness and pain of a sexual awakening.

At moments of crisis we hear Cynthia's voiceover reciting passages from Anne Frank's diary entries. Although the film script originally called for Cynthia to paraphrase Anne's reflections, France insisted that the audience hear Anne's actual words. The Anne Frank-Fonds granted the film permission to quote directly from three passages.[53] The audience hears them in fragments, and eventually as lengthier quotations, throughout the film, creating the impression of a more extensive place for Anne's own words. One frequently repeated quotation highlights Cynthia's connection to Frank as a writer. She reads from the diary entry of April 4, 1944: "I want to go on living after my death, and that is why I am so grateful to God for giving me this gift, which I can use to develop myself and express all that is inside of me." Like Rivi in *Dearest Anne*, Cynthia finds in writing a place of shelter. She quotes from Frank's diary, "When I write, I shake off all my cares. My sorrow disappears, my spirit is revived." Cynthia deals with overwhelming feelings of loss, fear, desire, and rage, first by reading from Frank's entries, then by writing poems. Her notebook has a checkered cover, reminiscent of Frank's famous diary. The film shows Cynthia struggling to find the right language, rewriting and revising. Her rap poems function as a rhymed diary of her inner life.

While Frank lived under constant fear of betrayal from the world outside, Cynthia is betrayed by her brother, who grows increasingly desperate and violent. To support his addiction, Juan sells Cynthia's poems, which he calls "rhymes," to Deuce, a swaggering rapper with a strong stage presence but no writing talent. After hearing Deuce's demo CD using her "rhymes," Cynthia competes with him in an open mike standoff at a local rap club. Momentarily cowed by her natural shyness and by self-doubt, Cynthia mentally conjures up images of Kitty urging her on and of her father reading the quotation from Frank's diary that viewers heard at the beginning of the film and repeated later in snatches and fragments. Thus, the director envisioned the first and last word from Anne Frank in the film as encapsulating its most significant theme: responsibility for oneself in the world.[54] As Cynthia raps onstage, her voice overtakes Deuce's, and it becomes apparent that the rhymes are about her life, a young woman's losses, anger, desires, and dreams. She claims her identity as an artist, announcing her rapper name as "Anne B. Real." The crowd begins to shout "Go, Annie," linking Cynthia, her rapper persona, and the diarist from the 1940s.

Following a longstanding trope in American Holocaust representation, the film uses the genocide of European Jews as a prototype for prejudice and oppression in the United States, especially racism. (Indeed, the film's physical landscape recalls the 1965 film *The Pawnbroker*, also set in Spanish Harlem, which similarly invokes the Holocaust to interrogate American racism.) In *Anne B. Real*, the Holocaust—as emblemized by Frank's diary—becomes the correlative of broader suffering, including not only racism, but also sexism, poverty, and loss. While the film takes care to place Frank's experience in a specific context that does not deny the Holocaust's particularity—we hear her June 20, 1942, entry referring to anti-Jewish laws and decrees—its meaning is universalized, so that an Afro-Latina teenage girl can find in Frank's writing personal meaning.

Punch Me in the Stomach and *Anne B. Real* both use performance art to bring viewers to think about the place of reading and writing in relation to Anne Frank and her afterlives. Filler's performance invites her audience to engage her coming of age as an artist as a means to contend with the aftereffect of the Holocaust. Her performance positions viewers as if within her family, living out her experiences with her, and thereby coming to recognize that all who come later are, in a sense, children of the Holocaust. In *Anne B. Real*, too, viewers witness an artist's coming of age. Within the more formal cinematic narrative, Cynthia's story arc culminates in a live performance of her rap "rhymes." Rap is often understood as belonging to the genre of lyric poetry in both its expression of personal emotions and its musical component. Throughout the film, viewers see Cynthia not only writing and revising but also rehearsing, developing oral intonations, rhythms, bodily moves, so that her art is not only the words of her poems but her rap performance in its entirety. As in Frank's diary, in Cynthia's poems the personal and private are simultaneously an expression of collective circumstances. Both films thus enact artistic performance as a means to convey, contain, and triumph over internal and external forces of destruction, both historical and contemporary.

As the popularity of *The Diary of a Young Girl* brings Anne Frank and her writing to an increasingly globalized readership, the story of the girl in the Annex refracts into intersecting sets of cultural meanings. As a literary figure, Anne comes to stand both for herself and for the interpretations, values, and messages imagined onto her. Given the power and circumstances of her writing, it should not be surprising that her narrative fuels other writers, who merge her historical moment with other times and places. The imaginary Anne reiterates and negotiates some of the controversies that her diary's publication initially prompted, as well as some of the complexities that attend celebrity. In one of the earliest and most influential reviews of the English-language publication of Frank's diary, Meyer Levin uncannily anticipates some of the debates that will follow it across genres. He calls the diary a "drama of puberty," a "stirring confession," a record of "astonishing circumstances," a record of "the universalities of human nature," and "the voice of six million vanished Jewish souls." Frank's family's fear in Amsterdam is "every family['s] . . . fear" in the United States.[55] As writers mine her life and writing for inspiration, they build upon, affirm, refute, and elaborate on some of those aspects of her work and on the accretion of meanings that have become attached to her name. It is a mark of the power of her writing, so unexpected in the darkness of war and terror, that Anne Frank continues to inspire writers, who infuse the charge of her diary into their own creations.

9

Suturing In: Anne Frank as Conceptual Model for Visual Art

Daniel Belasco

Looking beyond the iconic smiling girl portrayed in a handful of widely circulated photographs of Anne Frank, contemporary artists have used diverse strategies to clear a path through the dense thicket of cultural construction around Anne Frank for a more personal and direct reconnection to her. Together, the diary and images offer a profound way into the Holocaust for European and American artists who have no personal or familial connections to the horror, but who were deeply affected as adolescents by their encounter with Anne Frank and her diary.[1] Indeed, for some of them, Anne Frank and her diary became indistinguishable from their own hopes, fears, anxieties, and concerns, prompting them to seek formal means to gain distance from Anne Frank and her diary.

While some artists revalue Frank as a creative artist in her own right —as an active authorial voice and compelling subjectivity that could serve as a model and catalyst for their own creativity—or as a human rights icon, others focus on Anne Frank's iconic image and the images with which she surrounded herself. However different the media or motivation for their works, the artists discussed here engage with Anne Frank, her image and her diary, through a path of identification, disengagement, and selective reintegration.

Image: Anne Frank as Celebrity

The sense of personal responsibility for the fate of Anne Frank runs strong in works by European artists born after World War II. German Felix Droese, born 1950, evokes Frank's body through diaphanous installations that suggest the dematerialization of flesh into saintly status. His paper-cut installation *Ich habe Anne Frank umgebracht (I Killed Anne Frank)*, created for Documenta in Kassel, Germany, in 1982, fuses the informal materials and techniques of post-minimalist sculpture with powerful historical content.[2] Through this work, Droese expresses German guilt and perhaps asks for forgiveness by exalting Frank as martyr. Droese trained at the Düsseldorf Art Academy with Joseph Beuys, who taught the working methods of social sculpture, which integrates the political, the personal, and the material in actions, installations, and time-based productions. Perhaps Droese responded to the sense of inerasable complicity of his teacher, a former Luftwaffe pilot who claimed to have undergone a mystical transformation after being shot down over Russia. By birth Droese certainly is not guilty of any crime; but as an artist who must grapple with tradition, he, like many German artists of his generation, such as Anselm Kiefer, sought reconciliation of his own identity with a national one defined by historical crimes. Active public memorialization of the Holocaust, which made awareness of those crimes ever present, had begun to emphasize an abstract vocabulary during the 1980s.

After the war, the victims of Nazi oppression gained moral authority. European artists, living in proximity to the scene of the crime, felt closer to Frank's fate as a victim, yet they also inherited national histories clouded by wartime complicity. Like Droese, Lotte Konow Lund, a Norwegian artist born in 1967, makes both the trauma and the collective guilt personal by identifying with them. Lund, like many postwar Norwegians, identified with Frank, as their country faced wartime depredations during the Nazi occupation. She says, "I grew up in a time and a place, where Anne Frank symbolically represented both the ultimate innocence and sacrifice. Even in Norway, [which,] as you probably know, was occupied during the WW2 [sic], there was a trauma to treat."[3] Her suite of six drawings *Self-Portrait as Five Dictators and a Victim* (2007) explores her unease with the narrative limitations of the conventional portrait. In five grotesque drawings (figure 1), she merges her own face with each dictator in turn: Adolf Hitler, Saddam Hussein, Ayatollah Khomeini, Francisco Franco, and Idi Amin. The hybrids of male and female, aged and youthful, dead and living, disturbingly personalize her relationship to faces commonly identified with evil. Each drawing is small, roughly 6 × 4 in., and the suite is conceived as an installation hung on a pink painted wall, the small scale and soft color an ironic twist on the authority of the official portrait. The act of drawing has a provisional, exploratory feel, as if the series is an experimental thought-piece that develops through intuitive association without a defined ethical position.

About Anne Frank, the one representative victim in her suite, Lund said, "The more dictators I drew, the more heavy she weighed as a victim," no doubt because of Frank's gender and youth, guarantors of her innocence.[4] While there are many well-known totalitarians of the twentieth century, there is a far smaller canon of victims or martyrs that she felt she could portray, and Frank's fame made her one of them. By not exploring Frank's life or work in any depth, by dealing with only the face, and not the deeds, of the historical figures, Lund exploits the familiarity of celebrity to make distinctions between good and evil and between self and other. She achieves a tellingly superficial integration of the stated binary conditions, with herself as the self-aware mediator of the limitations. The artist appears in this formula as a selector and reproducer of a highly personalized form of moral ambiguity more than as an active critic or polemicist.

Americans have a more geographically remote, if intellectually passionate, engagement with Frank's image. Their interest in Frank is filtered through popular culture more than personal and collective history. California-based photographer Rachel Schreiber (born 1965) uses Frank's image as a tool to investigate class and race differences in the United States. In the series *Anne in New York* (2001), Schreiber digitally inserts an image, resembling a spray-paint stencil, of Anne Frank into photographs she had taken of various sites in New York City. In the sardonic and reductive visual language of street art (figures 2 and 3), Anne Frank becomes equivalent to Andre the Giant, whose caricatured face was circulated internationally by artist Shepard Fairey. The series also recalls "Rimbaud in New York" by David Wojnarowicz (1978), a series of photographs of a man wearing a paper mask with the face of poet Arthur Rimbaud. Working in the studio, as opposed to on the street, Schreiber enjoyed greater flexibility to introduce Frank's image to more challenging spaces, such as on the façade of Bergdorf Goodman, the upscale Fifth Avenue department store. There are about twenty images in the series, which the artist typically prints on soft rag paper, allowing the ink to saturate the surface and blur the distinctions between the artist's digital inclusion and the original photograph.

Schreiber has said: "There is a certain irreverence to using Anne Frank's visage in anything other than a sacred context. By doing so, I attempt to wrench the viewer out of the more familiar trappings of Holocaust imagery: barbed wire, flames, black and white images of trains, etc."[5] The visual language of the ersatz spray-paint stencil icon speaks in the ironic aesthetic of the "Heeb" generation of American Jews, born in the 1960s and '70s; they rejected the melodramatic treatment of the Holocaust they grew up with—the theatrical and filmic portrayals of Frank have certainly kept her in the sentimentalist Holocaust canon for decades—and seek a new critical aesthetic, based in humor and irony.[6] By turning Frank's face into street art, graffiti style, Schreiber engages a countercultural discourse associated with hip-hop to burlesque the mechanical reproduction and commercialization of images, Anne Frank's included, associated with branding and advertising.

Frank as street art makes her immediate and accessible to young Americans. The title of the series *Anne in New York* anchors the work in the system of reception of Frank, not her life or art. One can think of many Annes in New York: the Broadway play, the movies, and the publication of Philip Roth's novella *The Ghost Writer* (1979). Schreiber references Roth in conversation, especially how she was moved by Roth's vivid depiction of his alter-ego Nathan Zuckerman's fantasy of Frank alive in postwar America: vivacious and seductive.[7] Zuckerman thinks when first seeing the woman he takes for Frank: "Where had I seen that severe dark beauty before? Where but in a portrait by Velásquez? . . . I saw myself married to the *infanta* and living in a little farmhouse of our own not that far away."[8] I am struck how Roth compares Frank here, and again a few pages later, to Golden Age Spanish painting. An *infanta* of Velásquez recalls his masterpiece *Las Meninas* (1656). That painting investigates the act of looking and the triple identification that occurs in painting among the subject, the artist, and the viewer. The field of vision in *Las Meninas* is negotiated through an insertion of a self-portrait of the artist, as well as a mirror at the rear of the palace room, which brings the viewer into the conceptual space of the painting. The bright little princess, the ostensible subject of Velásquez, is echoed three dimensionally. Schreiber's move to pull the viewer into a self-conscious space of looking at oneself looking at a portrait of a certain kind of royalty—a princess of memory and martyrdom—updates the triangulated perspective of the Velásquez. The figures in the foreground of the two photographs illustrated in this volume are stand-ins for diverse viewers' engagements with Frank today.

American artists ruminate on the proliferation of Anne Frank images by proliferating them. Abshalom Jac Lahav (born 1977), based in Brooklyn, has conducted an experimental painting series, *18 Anne Franks* (2008 to the present), questioning the long afterlife of Frank's portrait. Each painting is a distortion of one iconic photograph of the writer. Like Schreiber, Lahav works in a standardized, modest scale, painting on square 24 × 24 in. canvases. The limited frame is a way to defeat the overdetermined scale of celebrity in the imagination. Lahav has become known for his wide-ranging painting project "48 Jews" (2007–2009), which explores the myths and authentic bases of contemporary Jewish identity in the diaspora. Though Lahav has painted variations of several subjects in the series, including Bob Dylan and Barry Manilow, no single figure has received the sustained attention and array of treatments as has Anne Frank. Lahav explains: "Anne Frank holds a great depth of emotional content. Her image has become synonymous with her work and its message of hope and despair. I saw in her work a union of opposites; the lowest pits of human depravity coupled with the highest level of strength and hope."[9]

One version, titled *Anne Frank* (2007), presents the recognizable silhouette of an image of Frank. Her visage is blurred beyond recognition, however, in a grisaille palette that recalls the gray-scale paintings after photographs by Gerhard Richter (figure 4). Lahav's entire series of Jewish portraits is an expressionist riposte to Richter's controversially uninflected portrait series of modern German writers and historical figures *48 Portraits* (1971), first presented in the German pavilion at the Venice Biennale in 1972. By adopting Richter's emblematic painting style, Lahav interrogates Richter's aloof, conceptual mode, which deflects the content of memory in photography. Lahav says he is exploring "the idea of the photo" through the contrasting tactility of painting "between the background and the foreground: the background is wiped down and painterly, bringing one back to the paint and surface, yet the foreground image is photo finish."[10] Lahav's paintings combine the unknowable quality of Frank's photographic image with an empathetic connection to her materialized in paint.

Lahav's *Anne Frank (Obama Shirt)* (2008), makes explicit the connections that he and many other artists perceive between Frank and other representatives of human rights struggles (figure 5). "Living in Brooklyn after the Obama election, we saw everyone wearing Obama shirts in support. I think if Anne Frank were alive today, she would have probably been wearing an Obama shirt. This replicates the notion of hope," Lahav says.[11] Obama has joined the limited group of international celebrities whose image on t-shirts represents a single idea, as Che Guevara stands for resistance, Marilyn Monroe for sexual desire, and Obama for hope (at least up to the 2008 election). Lahav's painting inverts Anne's presence, imagining her as a twenty-first century teenager stumping for Obama, and putting the president in the position of dematerialized icon. Lahav joins with Schreiber to reclaim Frank, if ironically, from a kitsch celebrity by rendering her image as a kind of urban punk antihero who is an especially dynamic presence in American conversations about race and class.

Text: Anne Frank as Artist

The publication in English of the *Critical Edition* of *The Diary of Anne Frank* in 1989 initiated an important shift in works of visual art that deal in some way with Anne Frank. The exhaustively researched book revealed to many the reality of Frank as a self-conscious, purposeful writer, who revised her diary for publication. Cynthia Ozick, Francine Prose, and others have asserted the desire of many artists to rethink Anne Frank as an artist, not simply as a victim.[12] Joe Lewis III and Ellen Rothenberg explore this representational shift through text and language, rather than image, as a way of connecting Frank and her diary to human rights movements, particularly the fate of blacks and minorities around the world fighting racist discrimination. The diary becomes a text of mental liberation conceived in physical captivity, comparable to Dr. Martin Luther King, Jr.'s letters from the Birmingham jail and Nelson Mandela's imprisonment on Robben Island.

The connection is most explicit in the large mixed-media sculpture *Mandela and Anne Frank Forever: Endless Column* (2000; figure 6), by California-based American installation artist Joe Lewis III (born 1953). The zigzagging structure is inspired by Brancusi's *Endless Column*, a modernist sculpture that was rediscovered by minimalist sculptors in the United States in the late 1950s. Lewis has said in an interview:

> An ongoing personal struggle within my work is how to present challenging issues without agitprop or beating someone over the head. How do you create a space where someone can understand content as a springboard into their own unknown? Minimalism offers an ideal pathway. When you hang something ironic on a Minimalist framework, you provide ample conceptual space and encourage self-exploration.[13]

Minimalist sculpture, through the use of stark geometries and industrial materials, makes powerful claims on the viewer's physical experience of art while providing little in the way of overt or explicit subject matter. Lewis found a way to aestheticize political content by constructing a vertical form with dozens of Manhattan White Pages: the thick books of names symbolize an inventory of the millions of Jews and blacks victimized during the twentieth century. Mirrors mounted facing inward at the top and bottom of the piece give it the illusion of endless recession both upward and downward. Neon signage spells the names of the two heroes: Anne Frank and Nelson Mandela. Lewis was moved to make the work after learning that Mandela read, and was inspired by, the diary during his long prison sentence. This work brings the two histories together in a single monument representing a continuity of human rights discourse running from Frank's diary to South Africa's new constitution.

The most extensive work of contemporary art to critically reevaluate Anne Frank is the three-part exhibition series, the *Anne Frank Project* (1991–1994), by Chicago-based installation and performance artist Ellen Rothenberg (born 1949). Based on a careful exploration of sources, the series encompasses virtually every aspect of Frank, her life, her diary,

Figure 1. Lotte Konow Lund. *Self-Portrait as Five Dictators and a Victim,* 2007. Graphite on paper, six pages, each 6 × 4 in. National Museum of Art, Architecture, and Design, Oslo. *Photographer: Dag A. Ivarsøy*

Figure 2. Rachel Schreiber. *Untitled*, from *Anne in New York*,
2001. Iris print, 20 × 28 in. *Courtesy of the artist*

Figure 3. Rachel Schreiber. *Untitled*, from *Anne in New York*,
2001. Iris print, 20 × 28 in. *Courtesy of the artist*

Figure 4. Abshalom Jac Lahav. *Anne Frank*, 2007. Oil on canvas, 24 × 24 in.
The Jewish Museum, New York / Art Resource, NY. Photographer: Ardon bar Hama

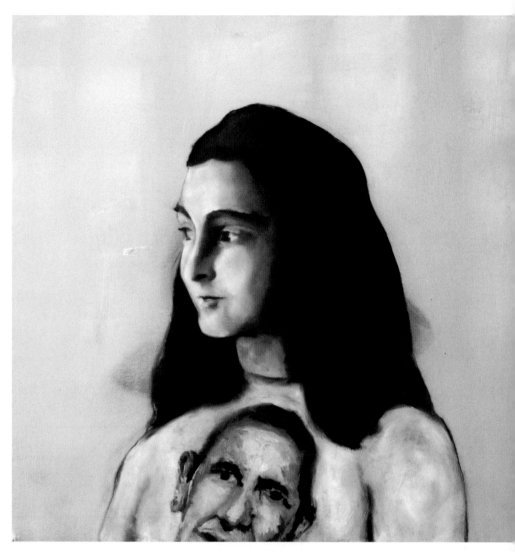

Figure 5. Abshalom Jac Lahav. *Anne Frank (Obama Shirt)*,
2009. Oil on canvas, 24 × 24 in. *Courtesy of the artist*

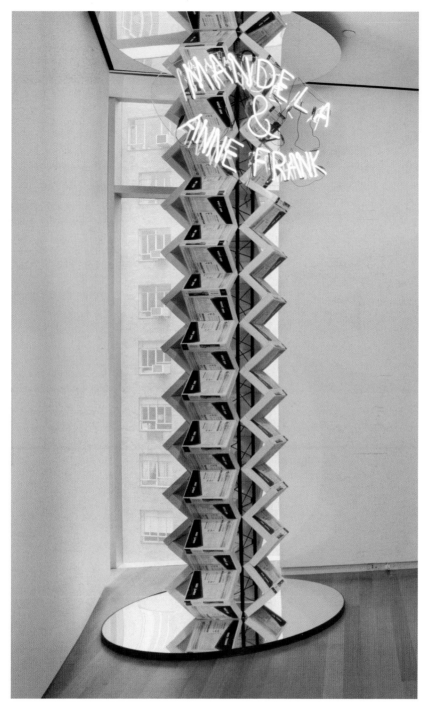

Figure 6. Joe Lewis III. *Mandela and Anne Frank Forever: Endless Column*, 2006.
Neon sign, telephone books, mirrors, wooden/metal column, 20 ft. × 48 in.
Courtesy of the Museum of Arts and Design, New York. Photographer: Ed Watkins

Figure 7. Ellen Rothenberg. Anne Frank Project: "A Probability Bordering on Certainty." *Handwriting Analysis,* 1993. Installation view: University Art Museum, University of California Santa Barbara. Dimensions: 84 × 360 in. *Collection of Charlene Engelhard. Photographer: Sky Bergman*

Figure 8. Ellen Rothenberg. Anne Frank Project: "A Probability Bordering on Certainty." *Business Cards,* 1991–1992. Ten sets of letterpress cards in editions of 100. Dimensions variable. *Courtesy of the artist. Photographer: Bruce T. Martin*

Figure 9. Keith Mayerson. *Anne Frank's Wall*, 2007. Oil on linen, 40 × 60 in. *Courtesy of Zach Feuer Gallery*

Figure 10. Keith Mayerson. *Anne Frank's Room*, 2007. Oil on linen, 26 × 34 in. *Courtesy of Zach Feuer Gallery*

and her legacy. The first part, "Partial Index," presents large blow-ups of documents in an architectural setting that explores Frank's authorial voice and its specific milieu. The second, "A Probability Bordering on Certainty," employs pseudo-artifacts to explore Nazi distortions of Jewish history and identity. The third, "Conditions for Growth," uses quantitative devices and rhetoric to face the impossibility of measuring the loss of life during the Holocaust. In sum, Rothenberg deals with the social context of Jews in occupied Holland, the material culture of the period, floor plans of the Annex, photos from the walls of Frank's room, contemporary tourism, and the complex reception both by those who revere her and by those who claim her diary is a forgery.[14] The artist unifies intensive research with material and spatial construction and image that "questions the social construction of Anne Frank."[15] *Handwriting Analysis* and *A Probability Bordering on Certainty* exemplify Rothenberg's approach to materializing Anne Frank as artist rather than icon.

Large scale blowups of pages of the diary appeared in the first installation of *Handwriting Analysis* (1991; figure 7). Rothenberg had the opportunity to interview at length the graphologist who painstakingly analyzed Frank's handwriting to affirm that she is the sole author of the diary and thereby counter claims of Holocaust deniers and anti-Semites that the diary was a ghost-written hoax. She was also able to compare examples of Frank's known handwriting in the archives at the Anne Frank House and the Netherlands State Institute for War Documentation. The emotive power of the diary meets the cold eye of forensics in a contest for Frank's status as an authentic creative artist.

Aestheticizing the analysis of the characteristics of handwriting as the basis of the authenticity of the diary, Rothenberg depicts the minutia of the politics of moral suasion unfolding in space. Magnified and printed many times their actual size, the letters and the marks of the analysis become abstract swirls and lines, recalling the oversized calligraphic gestures of mid-twentieth-century paintings by Franz Kline and Pierre Soulages. The endless translation and transmutation of her story into dozens of languages, countless plays and theatrical productions, movies, documentaries, music, song, and other creative and documentary expressions shows the fungibility and exchange value of each letter of each word, so powerfully fetishized over the years.

In the second installation, "A Probability Bordering on Certainty," Rothenberg produces ersatz historical artifacts and memorabilia—emblematic of postmodernist art, which conjoins the actual and the possible—forming a trove of objects that exist as counterfactual documents and narratives. *Business Cards* (1992; figure 8) consists of piles of mundane business cards for Anne Frank that Rothenberg had printed. They are in a variety of rectangular shapes and sizes, each with a different typeface and language (English, Dutch, and German) that state: "Anne Frank / author." Through these imaginary documents of Frank's life, had she survived the concentration camps, Rothenberg suggests that Frank aspired to a professional existence as a writer and not an afterlife of iconic martyrdom—perhaps an obvious statement, but one worth making in confrontation with the often overbearing sanctimony that constructs the posthumous image of Frank that Rothenberg seeks to recalibrate. These stacks of professional memorabilia, seen near pink erasers with the word "guilt" printed in gothic script, use humor and irony to take Frank down from the pedestal and bring her into our time.

The desire to connect with the creativity of the "real" Anne Frank runs strong for visual artists. More recently, the cerebral and ironic tactics of Rothenberg and Lewis have been replaced by more sensual strategies. New York-based painter Keith Mayerson (born 1966), known primarily as a portraitist of popular and subcultural celebrities, has created a trio of paintings that project the subjectivity of Frank within the claustrophobic space of the Annex, specifically the visual and architectural elements that embody her creative mindscape. Three colorful, richly painted works from 2007 portray her room as a magical environment, an effect that is heightened and distorted by the artist forcefully removing the room from the world, yet still infusing it with fantasy and cultural representation. Mayerson has said,

> When I first went to the Anne Frank House in the late '80s after college, I was deeply moved by the experience, and in particular, was struck by the way that she had pasted, salon-style, images that gave her optimism, contemplation, and hope in her room. I found an affinity in how she was able to juxtapose art reproductions with pop iconography, and, by being on the same plane and surface, make powerful historical images equitable (and more personable) by bringing them next to charming illustrations and photos from her everyday world.[16]

Anne Frank's Wall (2007; figure 9) presents the diverse images of Holly-wood actresses, magazine clippings, and Leonardo da Vinci reproductions that Frank pasted to her wall to decorate her room. Frank was a passionate consumer of diverse imagery as well as a producer of personal narrative. She received Anton Springer's five-volume survey of art history for her fifteenth birthday and hoped to study art history in London and Paris after the war.[17]

Frank's interest in pop culture, celebrity, and film magazines humanizes her and makes her seem like a typical teenager. It also anticipates her own celebrity, which is another way to interpret her desire to publish her diary, even selecting her author photographs, as the original diary has multiple photographs of Frank pasted into it. The popular culture imagery on Frank's wall—celebrities to whose status she and others might aspire—is as resonant today in Mayerson's gentrified New York as it was then in Frank's wartime Europe. Mayerson's work suggests that the collage-like process of looking, selecting, and arranging is comparable to how a person comes to know herself and, by extension, how we can come to know the person. These little images are the familiar stepping stones across the abyss of time.

Anne Frank's Room (2007; figure 10), evoking the claustrophobia of Van Gogh's apartment, offers a way to understand Frank through her environment. Blending fact and fiction, the artist uses furnishings to connect himself empathetically to his subject. Mayerson describes his method in terms of acting and performance:

> Much like a method actor who would suture his own life into his character in order to both better understand his subject and to breathe life and real emotion into his performance, I try my best to understand the person I'm portraying as I'm painting a portrait, or world of a person or a culture, as to help animate it and make it become alive.[18]

This process-based painting and drawing project allows Mayerson to "suture in" to the reality of Frank beyond her image.[19] Scott McCloud, in *Understanding Comics*, describes the process whereby the reader actively uses imagination to create a complex emotional identification with a schematically rendered cartoon image.[20] Deconstructivists attempted to undo suture in order to reveal the constructedness of images and filmic narratives; they assumed a strong image and a weak viewer. Mayerson, however, reverses the formula; he proposes a strong viewer and weak image, thereby making suture an empowering merger between the self and other, with image as intermediary.[21] Here, the word *suture* characterizes the desire to access histories beyond personal experience, bringing us to Frank's own emotional life in the Annex, where she wrote that she went into "ecstasy" every time she saw a female nude, like the Venuses in her Springer.[22]

* * *

Anne Frank, icon and artist, image and text, continues to inspire contemporary artists by her power to create a new world beyond her limited existence in the Annex. For many visual artists, Anne Frank and her diary represent the inchoate power of art to expand one's consciousness and therefore the world. In many ways, artists' reinterpretations of their experiences reading Frank become the primal scenes of their coming to awareness of their own potential to create new visions from the stuff of their daily lives. Though their personal situations are not comparable to Anne Frank's perilous one, they nevertheless find her an instructive model and authentic voice navigating the personal and the political. The installation and performance artist Fawn Krieger put it most directly in her description of an unrealized project to create a set of short videos about Frank: "I see Anne Frank's historical position as a portal to a time and place where the personal trauma of war can be internalized and processed, and where a deep, enlightened belief in people and positive action revived."[23] Artists, fearing that this portal is continually at risk of oversentimentalization, work to keep Anne Frank and all that she represents fresh.

10

Sounds from the Secret Annex:
Composing a Young Girl's Thoughts

Judah M. Cohen

In her diary entry of December 7, 1942, Anne Frank recounted a rare musical moment in the Annex. "We didn't make much fuss about Chanukah," she wrote. "[W]e just gave each other a few little presents and then we had the candles. Because of the shortage of candles we only had them alight for ten minutes, but it is all right as long as you have the song."[1] Obliquely referenced and made to balance the abbreviated Hanukkah ritual, this moment presented the diary's sole account of communal music making. Aside from a few references to local bell tower chimes and radio music broadcasts, Anne's descriptions more often noted enforced quiet in the Annex.[2]

After the diary appeared in print, those who wished to bring Anne's voice beyond the text used this passage as a source for musical extrapolation, most notably when creating the diary's dramatization. Otto Frank, for his part, recalled the "song" as "Ma'oz Tsur" ("Rock of Ages"), a stately Hanukkah hymn believed to be of Central European origin.[3] Meyer Levin, Anne Frank's first American champion, honored this recollection and used "Ma'oz Tsur" in the Hanukkah scene ending the middle act of his 1952 play based on the diary.[4] The song's Hebrew lyrics, pining for divine intervention against oppressors, complemented Levin's portrayal of Anne as a proud Jewish nationalist.

"Ma'oz Tsur," sung in English translation as "Rock of Ages," also survived several drafts of Frances Goodrich and Albert Hackett's dramatic adaptation, *The Diary of Anne Frank,* which would supersede Levin's effort as the official theatrical version of the diary. Director Garson Kanin, however, found the song too slow, and felt the lyrics and hymn style too parochial. Ultimately, through a recommendation by Jack Gilford (the actor who played Alfred Dussel in the 1955 production), Kanin exercised his creative license and substituted a much lighter song a week before the production opened. The new selection, "Oh Hanukkah, Oh Hanukkah," had a fast melody, emphasized the communal joy of the season, and, in the English translation used for this production, eschewed references to specific Jewish holiday practices in favor of general good cheer.[5] As part of Hackett and Goodrich's adaptation, the upbeat song both reinforced their lithe, apolitical characterization of Anne and created a stronger dramatic tension with the offstage break-in to the Opekta office below the Annex. To Kanin, moreover, this change resolved a concern with pacing and tone at the end of the first act, which prevented it from becoming, in his words, "flat as a latke."[6]

In subsequent stagings of Goodrich and Hackett's play, this musical moment came to characterize broader dramaturgical debates about the portrayal of Anne Frank. European productions restored "Maʻoz Tsur," on the assumption that their audiences would not recognize or relate to "Oh Hanukkah, Oh Hanukkah." Otto Frank himself disapproved of "Oh Hanukkah, Oh Hanukkah" and attempted in vain to reintroduce "Maʻoz Tsur" into the 1959 film version.[7] Not until Wendy Kesselman's authorized reworking of the script for the 1997 Broadway revival were Otto Frank's wishes fulfilled, this time as part of a larger effort to bolster the show's sense of historical authenticity.[8] Since then, local productions of the play have opted for one song or the other.[9] This choice of "Maʻoz Tsur" or "Oh Hanukkah, Oh Hanukkah," like that of the original dramatists, informs each production's understanding of the emotional arc of the scene in question and exemplifies the larger creative considerations involved in telling Anne Frank's story.

The layers of meaning that have accrued around the Hanukkah song since the diary's earliest dramatic adaptations exemplify how music mediates Anne Frank's life, enhancing and reconsidering the source text. The diary's brief Hanukkah episode, with its passing reference to an unidentified song, became a key moment for adaptors to address Jewish identity in the face of existential adversity. Music plays a strategic role in this moment, due in part to its efficiency in addressing these themes outside of verbal communication. At the same time, music adds a cultural literacy of its own to Anne Frank's story by representing certain emotions, social spaces, and historical moments. In this way, one song can alter the significance of the entire narrative.

From this starting point, musicians went on to craft a wide variety of works that express their own relationships to the diary and its author, offering their own ideas about sound's place within Anne's world and within the worlds of those who experience it. These works, viewed over time, reveal shifting understandings of Anne's life and work while commenting on the larger role of music in modes of Holocaust remembrance generally.[10] The examples discussed below do not exhaust the inventory of compositions relating in some fashion to Anne Frank—which numbers more than 125 as of early 2012 and continues to expand—nor do they comprise a single cohesive narrative of musical creativity.[11] Yet in their patterns of diversity, they offer insight into the ways a historical subject can develop unique musical approaches that complement other memorial strategies while attending to its own autonomous modes of expression.

Early Soundings of Anne Frank

When Levin and Hackett and Goodrich attempted to dramatize the diary, they opened up space for musical interpolation not only through the Hanukkah song but also through the conventions of theatrical sound design. In doing so, they created the first opportunities for musical links to the diary. Meyer Levin's adaptation, for example, called for recorded music to open and close the dramatic action: a setting of "Absalom, O Absalom" (King Solomon's lament of his son's death, in II Samuel 19:4) preceded the first act,[12] and a cantorial rendering of the traditional Jewish memorial prayer "El Malei Rahamim" ("God full of compassion") accompanied the final curtain.[13] These somber musical works frame his play within religious tropes of mourning while highlighting the script's preoccupation with religious identity. Goodrich and Hackett, in contrast, opted for a more diegetic sound design at the prompting of director Garson Kanin. Instead of superimposing recorded music upon the scenario, they incorporated into their script a palette of environmental sound cues: passing marching bands, ship's horns, carillon chimes, and

radio programs, all piped through the theater's sound system at prear-
ranged cues. The actors themselves performed the rest of the music—
including "Oh Hanukkah, Oh Hanukkah" and a hummed version of
the Dutch national anthem—in the course of reenacting Annex life.
Each approach enhanced the staged material in a different way: the first
by placing Anne's narrative with a Judeocentric moral framework, and
the second by selectively heightening the realism of the characters' life
in hiding.

As the diary and its dramatization gained international popularity,
the role of music expanded in the creation of new works that explicitly
or implicitly invoked Anne Frank's memory. For example, choreographer Kenneth Macmillan's 1958 dance work "The Burrow"—set to Swiss
composer Frank Martin's "Concerto for Seven Wind Instruments"[14]—
never made explicit reference to Anne Frank. Nonetheless, the combination of music and dance caused the reviewer from the *Times of London*
to remark that "the source of the scenario would seem to be *The Diary
of Ann* [sic] *Frank*," due in part to its portrayal of "acute claustrophobia"
and its inclusion of an "Adolescent Girl" as one of the main characters.[15]
Audiences' willingness to read Anne Frank into relatively abstract expressive forms not only indicates the extent of her presence in public
culture by the late 1950s, but also suggests how this presence had begun
to foster an interest in rendering her story in an array of media, including music.

This expanding interest produced three notable musical works the
following year, in 1959. The most prominent of these was the score composed by Alfred Newman to accompany the 20th Century-Fox film version of Goodrich and Hackett's play.[16] In addition to providing an overture, intermission music, and closing music, Newman's score embraced
what Kathryn Kalinak has described as the "classic" film soundtrack
idiom that dominated major film releases since the 1930s: "selective
use of nondiegetic music; correspondence between that music and the
implied content of the narrative; a high degree of direct synchroniza-
tion between music and narrative action; and the use of the leitmotif
[or musical theme] as a structural framework."[17] Newman's score introduces a handful of musical themes, written in a late romantic style,
that underline the presence of certain characters, objects, or emotions.

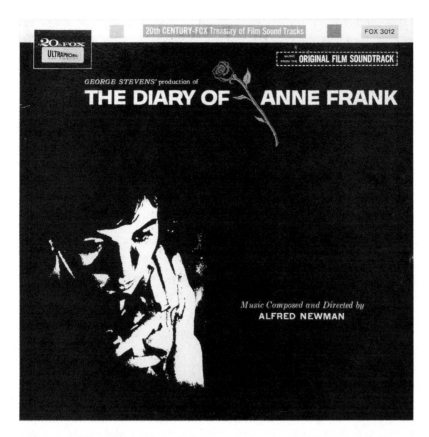

Jacket of the LP recording of Alfred Newman's soundtrack for the
1959 film *The Diary of Anne Frank*. Photographer: Matt Jones

Anne Frank's theme, which is first heard as the film's title appears, is a
lilting, eight-bar violin melody in a major key that uses grace notes and
selected octave leaps to imply innocence and coquettishness. Newman
subsequently uses this theme to underscore important emotional moments that involve or invoke Anne throughout the film, including Anne's
receipt of the notebook in which she kept her diary, her romantic scenes
with Peter, and Otto Frank's postwar return to the Annex—where the
musical theme takes the place of Anne herself. Along with a "tragedy"
theme that underscores moments of tension and a Viennese-style waltz
theme that accompanies episodes of fun and social ease, the Anne Frank
melody connects the diary to conventions of a musical genre—the film

score—for the first time. Newman's effort, which received an Academy Award nomination, also enjoyed a life of its own as a separately issued long-playing record.

That same year, Anne Frank became the subject of a jazz composition by clarinetist Tony Scott. Recorded over two days in late October—a few months after the film's release—"Portrait of Anne Frank" was one of several musical memorials to contemporary figures that Scott captured on tape. His three-minute-and-forty-six-second tribute to Anne Frank offers an abstract portrayal of its subject that lacks any specific connection to words, images, or explanations beyond the title. Scott bases his piece on an eight-note core phrase, which he repeats at various speeds and pitch levels on three overdubbed tracks: on clarinet, on baritone saxophone, and on baritone saxophone in what sounds like a distant echo chamber. Compared with Scott's other musical tributes, the composition is spare and unique in its lack of a rhythm section (piano, guitar, bass, drums) or regular rhythmic pulse. Rather than seeking a literal representation, moreover, Scott's tribute to Anne Frank—comparatively quiet, slow, abstract, solitary, and distant (due to the use of the echo chamber)—paints an impressionistic image of her through the innovations of avant-garde jazz. "Portrait of Anne Frank" was not released on record until the mid-1980s, yet it offers valuable insight into the ways a musician might conceive of Anne Frank in a manner completely separate from the diary's text.

The accompaniment to a dance piece based on the diary provided yet another strategy for mediating Anne Frank's life and work through music in 1959, this time through a familiar "Jewish" musical framework. On April 11, choreographer and dancer Adam Darius presented a modern dance piece variously known as "The Anne Frank Ballet" or "The Story of Anne Frank" with the Audrey Share School of Dance in Long Beach, California.[18] This half-hour-long work provides a narrative of Annex life that seems to be based more on the Hackett and Goodrich stage version than on the diary itself. Like the play, the dance puts the character of Otto Frank in control of the story, while enacting an extensive celebration of Hanukkah in the middle. Darius presents the story without any spoken text, using dance idioms that range across classical, modern, and folk styles. The choreography and costumes offer a rich commentary on the role of Anne Frank within contemporary dance conventions: Anne appears in a white ballet skirt; the action progresses through a series of solos, pas de deux, and group scenes; and the diary itself, as a physical prop, becomes a central object of attention. To accompany the dance, Darius chose a succession of tracks from a recently released album of Jewish folk song arrangements by Swiss composer and conductor Benedict Silberman.[19] Edited to correspond with specific sections of the dance, these familiar tunes accompany clearly delineated scenes where Anne receives her diary, celebrates Hanukkah, and then is captured and taken away with her family.

The "traditional" nature of the music, as characterized in the liner notes to the Silberman album, imparts to Anne Frank's story a particular conceptualization of Jewishness that conforms more to the Yiddish and Zionist sensibilities of American audiences of the 1950s than to a Western European Jewish identity as Anne described it before or during the war. In the Hanukkah scene, for example, the Otto Frank character wears a prop prayer shawl prominently around his neck and organizes the other dancers into a *hora* (a circle dance attributed to Hasidim before becoming a fixture of secular Israeli folk dance). The accompanying instrumental music prominently features an augmented second interval, which is widely understood, by dint of its use in such popular songs as "Hava Nagila," as marking a musical piece as "Jewish." After the Franks are discovered in their hiding place and exit from the stage, the dancer portraying Otto Frank performs a passionate solo to a lushly orchestrated rendition of the Israeli anthem "Hatikvah" (The Hope). In this manner, Darius uses musical materials from the early postwar American Jewish repertoire to place Anne's story as a bridge between Old World nostalgia and Jewish nationalist triumph. The ballet met with intense opprobrium from dance critics such as Louis Horst and Selma Jeanne Cohen, who found the choreography uninventive and overly literal. Nevertheless, "The Anne Frank Ballet" became a centerpiece of Darius's oeuvre. Unlike the critics, audiences acclaimed the work; Darius recounted one 1961 performance in Stockholm that led to at least fifteen curtain calls and precipitated a meeting with Otto Frank.[20]

To the Concert Hall

As the image and cultural capital of Anne Frank became increasingly prominent during the 1960s, composers explored new strategies for adapting her story and character in self-standing concert music works. Several composers presented Anne through musical memorial genres, including the elegy and requiem. These meditative forms, often connected with religious practice, offer traditional expressions of gravitas, and as such were used by a growing number of composers as vehicles for works of Holocaust remembrance. Two of the four large-scale instrumental pieces written about Anne Frank between 1964 and 1981 assumed this tragic memorial character explicitly: Romanian composer Ludovic Feldman's 1966 "In Memoriam (Annei Frank)" and Israeli composer Ari Ben-Shabetai's 1981 "Elegy for Anne Frank." The other two compositions—Uruguayan composer Leon Biriotti's 1964 "Sinfonía Ana Frank" and Spanish composer Jordi Cervelló's 1971 "Ana Frank, un Simból"— were written for string orchestra, an orchestration composers have used to highlight pathos or introspection (most notably in Samuel Barber's 1938 "Adagio for Strings"). These musical choices, coming at first from lesser-known composers, situated the remembrance of Anne Frank within communal discourses of regret, mourning, and loss.

Other composers made more direct verbal reference to Anne Frank in their compositions, by setting recently published texts that mention her in passing. One of the best known of these early texts is Yevgeny Yevtushenko's 1961 poem "Babi Yar," which includes an extended meditation on Anne Frank. Several composers wrote musical interpretations of this work; most famous is the first movement of Dmitri Shostakovich's 1962 Symphony No. 13 (Op. 113). In the United States, Anne Frank had achieved such prominence that even brief references to her in larger works could provoke comment. When, for example, composer and conductor Vladimir Heifetz created his own 1962 cantata based on "Babi Yar," the *New York Times* publicized Otto Frank's request for autograph copies of the parts of the score that mentioned his daughter. The *Times* reporter speculated that the score would become a part of the permanent display at the Anne Frank House in Amsterdam (which had opened to the public in 1960), where the proliferation of multiple forms of Anne Frank remembrance was becoming a phenomenon of interest in its own right.[21]

Other composers incorporated a range of texts into their memorials of Anne Frank, from lines from the diary itself to poetry addressing the Holocaust and thematically related literary works. In 1957, Italian composer Niccolò Castiglioni set a four-line lament by eighteenth-century German poet Novalis to music in a work dedicated to the memory of Anne Frank. Using the title "Elegia," Castiglioni connected his work for voice and ensemble to the classical tragic form by adapting Novalis's meditation on the death of a teenaged beloved, a "sweet spring flower that God transplanted . . . into a better life."[22] Heinz Lau's 1961 *Requiem für eine Verfolgte: In Memoriam Anne Frank,* scored for tenor and string quartet, likewise evokes Anne through texts on persecution by twentieth-century German-language poets Günter Eich and Paul Celan. While Anne Frank remains a somewhat abstract figure in these works, composers' use of increasingly diverse poetic sources in their musical tributes to her reflects her expanding symbolic role as a figurehead for Holocaust remembrance and human suffering more generally.

By the late 1960s, composers' increasingly common use of passages from the diary in their compositions evinced growing interest in representing Anne Frank's own voice, even as these composers drew on a variety of contemporary techniques to express the emotions and concerns of a teenage girl in hiding. While previous works employed both male and female voices, the compositions of this period standardized the practice of using the female voice (sung or spoken, solo or choral) to present Anne's words. Instrumental accompaniment supplemented this voice with layers of psychological subtext, turning passages from the diary into complex and often emotionally charged, large-scale performances.

Consider, for example, "From the Diary of Anne Frank," a 1970 composition by Czech-born, Canadian-naturalized composer Oscar Morawetz. Scored for soprano and orchestra, this seventeen-minute piece sets to music Anne Frank's diary entry of November 27, 1943, in which she offers a nightmarish vision of her friend Lies's fate at the hands of the Nazis. The singer who delivers the text must utilize the entire female classical vocal range, including frequent shifts between speech and song and upper and lower registers, to articulate the text's full emotional scope.

Supporting her, a full orchestra creates a detailed psychological back-drop, which alternates among high foreboding string effects, twisting woodwind lines indicating moments of verbal exchange and emotional transition, and sudden punctuations of brass and percussion denoting revelation or terror. These layers of musical interpretation combine to create a dark journey through Anne Frank's psyche, transforming her written voice into a large-scale representation of inner turmoil and guilt.

While Morawetz's piece relies on a single singer to deliver Anne's words and bases its musical progress on the contours of the diary entry itself, other contemporary musical works inspired by Anne Frank assign her voice to collectives of women within established art music genres. In 1968–1969, French composer Edith Lejet wrote the cantata-like work "Le Journal d'Anne Frank" for the Radio-France women's choir. Over the course of ten short sections, the twenty-seven-minute piece uses passages from Anne's diary that, in the composer's view, follow a path of progressive emotional development: "[A]t first a carefree little girl, she will evolve as she is going through the terrible ordeal and become pre-cociously mature, which will allow her to meet her tragic end of life with exemplary courage and intelligence."[23] In keeping with Anne Frank's general emergence as a role model for girls around the world, these musi-cal works presented young female singers with new opportunities to per-form an increasingly iconic role with both artistry and emotional depth.

On the Musical Theater Stage

In the United States, both the prominence of Hackett and Goodrich's play and the careful regulation of permission to cite the diary under Otto Frank's aegis all but precluded musical adaptations between 1959 and 1970. When such works began to appear in the American context, however, they often took the form of musical theater. Along with other musical theater works, such as *Cabaret* (1966) and *Follies* (1971), that ven-tured into darker, more serious subjects, Peter Nero's *Anne Frank: Diary of a Young Girl* marks an important threshold in presenting Anne's life and work on the American musical stage. First performed in concert in a Great Neck, Long Island, synagogue on September 17, 1970, Nero's version addressed an American Jewish community's commitment to

Poster advertising a 1973 performance of Peter Nero's musical version of
Anne Frank: Diary of a Young Girl, performed in Trenton, New Jersey.

transmitting Anne's story to a new generation. This "Rock-Symphony"
employed the forces of a full orchestra, a jazz combo, a collegiate choir,
and a children's choir to present an overture and fourteen original settings of Anne's own words, spanning "the idioms of jazz, folk, and
rock."[24] Contemporary descriptions of the work characterize it as an
intergenerational dialogue, with each generation represented by char-

acteristic musical genres: classical music for adults, jazz and rock music for young people. Ultimately, Nero combines the musical idioms at the end "to bring [Anne Frank's] message forcefully to both younger and older listeners."[25] This approach transformed Anne Frank into a force of intergenerational mediation. Thus, a review of the premiere in *Billboard* magazine hailed Nero as "America's new peace spokesman, not simply in political terms but in sociological terms as well."[26]

Shortly after Nero's version of Anne Frank's diary premiered, author Enid Futterman and composer Michael Cohen began work on their own musical theater version, eventually titled *Yours, Anne*. Futterman and Cohen originally decided to "musicalize" Goodrich and Hackett's play by adding a series of songs to the existing script. Entrenched ideas about the musical theater's tendency toward light comedy, however, led them to receive intense, sometimes withering scrutiny from Otto Frank when they sought his permission. Only after Futterman and Cohen played some of their songs for Frank and representatives of the Anne Frank-Fonds in a hard-earned 1975 meeting did the project receive approbation. Even then, however, further creative and financial challenges shelved the project for several years. Not until Futterman and Cohen began to rework the piece into a freestanding and original musical theater work, with only a few structural references to the original play, did a performance become possible.

Despite broadly held expectations of conventional musical theater, Futterman and Cohen offer a serious and sustained engagement with the diary in *Yours, Anne*. They use music to communicate Anne's inner thoughts, explore tensions among the Annex's residents, and dramatize the characters' emotional development. The show's opening song (also the first piece Futterman and Cohen created for the project), titled "Dear Kitty," presents a soliloquy for Anne in the form of a melodic diary entry. Its frequent, almost improvisatory shifts in tone and speed every few seconds reflect the active, changing thoughts of a thirteen-year-old girl. In contrast, the Hanukkah/break-in scene that ends the musical's first act—perhaps the most direct vestige of the Hackett and Goodrich play—features a lively counting-style song, "On the First Chanukah Night." Sung by the entire ensemble as they light the menorah, the song begins tentatively, gains increasing momentum through the addition of more complex orchestration and a *klezmer*-style clarinet descant, and then cuts off abruptly as intruders enter the building below. After the danger passes, the ensemble sings a brief reprise of the song before blowing out the Hanukkah candles, ending the act in darkness. These and other songs contributed to a score that for the first time envisioned Anne Frank's voice in musical dialogue with the voices of others in the Annex.

These musical theater works indicated a desire among a new generation of composers to commemorate Anne Frank through their own musical sensibilities, even if they differed from the values of the previous generation. In public discussions, both works faced questions of appropriateness that emerged in reaction to contemporary depictions of the Holocaust in popular genres (most famously, the 1978 *Holocaust* television miniseries); critics expressed particular concern with the repercussions of associating Anne Frank with popular musical styles. Yet to their creators, these new works of music drama hardly seemed inappropriate. On the contrary, they sought to reestablish Anne's relevance among a younger population that had grown up with the published diary and claimed Anne as its own.

Diversifying Anne's Voice

Three events that took place at the end of the 1970s helped spark new interest in musical works based on Anne Frank's life and work. The introduction of Holocaust Remembrance Day in the United States in 1978 paved the way for large-scale public commemorations, which sometimes included performances of new musical compositions. In 1979, the fiftieth anniversary of Anne Frank's birth presented opportunities for artists and scholars to reaffirm her role in Holocaust memory. And Otto Frank's death in August 1980 shifted the prime responsibility for regulating Anne's memory to the Anne Frank-Fonds and other institutions dedicated to her remembrance, thereby enabling new possibilities for representing her life and work. As a consequence, the ensuing decades witnessed a growing number of new musical compositions that approached Anne Frank not only as an icon of Holocaust commemoration but also as a symbol of human rights. The breadth of musical styles and approaches emerging at this time suggests that Anne's voice had become associated with a variety of causes, as people from diverse backgrounds felt inspired to add music to her words and memory.

Two works created in the early 1980s ascribe a saintlike status to Anne Frank by situating her within large-scale religious ritual forms. Greek composer and political activist Mikis Theodorakis placed Anne in the middle of his 1982 "Liturgy No. 2," a multi-movement work for unaccompanied chorus modeled on an all-night Greek Orthodox vigil. Subtitled "For the Young Killed in Wars," this large-scale piece—which addresses war in general, without any specific historical focus—begins with musical settings of devotional Greek poems by Tasos Livaditis, followed by a series of movements highlighting other texts created or selected by the composer. Anne Frank appears as the subject of Theodorakis's own poem, her name summoned using a prayerlike formula (followed by similar appeals to children named Ibrahim and Emiliano).[27] Dutch composer Hans Kox's 1984 "Anne Frank Cantate: A Child of Light" takes the notion of sacralizing Anne Frank further. As the final part of his *War Triptych* (the first two sections are titled "In Those Days," about the Battle of Arnhem, and "Requiem for Europe") the forty-five-minute cantata evokes Anne as a paradigm of wartime innocence, reflecting Kox's philosophy of enacting "memory in sound" through a pastiche of biblical readings (from Exodus, Psalms, Esther, Lamentations, and Job), the writings of Adolf Hitler, and philosophical texts by Martin Buber, Paul Celan, and Augustine.[28] These choices, which include no reference to Anne Frank or the diary, give her a nearly timeless, mythical status. First presented in Amsterdam's Westerkerk, the poster advertising a 2001 performance of the cantata further intimated Anne Frank's status as a sacred subject: showing a pair of hands together in prayer, holding a blurred portrait, which might be of Anne Frank, as if receiving the host during communion.

Anne Frank's viability as a topic of musical theater received its first formal test in 1985, when Futterman and Cohen's *Yours, Anne* finally opened with a short run at New York's Off-Broadway Playhouse 91. Ostensibly presented as a hybrid of musical theater and chamber opera, with a completely new book by Futterman, the work received what would become a familiar critical reaction. Almost all critics questioned

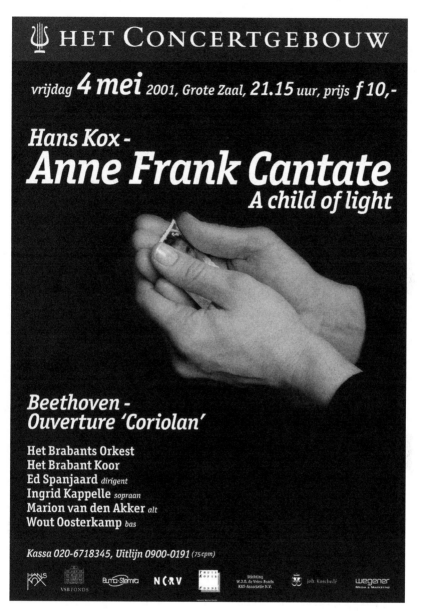

Advertisement for Hans Kox's 1984 *Anne Frank Cantate: A Child of Light*,
performed in 2001 in Amsterdam's Concertgebouw.
Courtesy of Het Concertgebouw. Designer: Werner Studio.
Photographer: Leander Lammertink

the creators' judgment to portray Anne Frank through musical theater, perhaps none more so than the *Village Voice*'s theater critic Michael Feingold. "Of all possible ways to memorialize the suffering of these European Jews, and the bravery of the Gentiles who risked death to hide them and help them," he noted, "a commercial musical entertainment is the least able to express the meaning of their lives." Clive Barnes's more positive review in the *New York Post* seemed to answer the unspoken question of genre appropriateness with the title "Anne Frank Musical: It Works," while Miriam Rubenstone's less supportive *USA Today* review informed readers with the headline, "Anne Frank's Diary is Better Read Than Sung."[29] Taken in aggregate, this reaction continued a trope that has pervaded critical discussions of Holocaust-themed works for decades, criticizing genres or media that were deemed inappropriately popular, commercial, or lowbrow for their challenging subject.

Despite such objections, music works about Anne Frank increasingly began to appear in popular forums. On the heels of extensive public discussion of NBC's 1978 *Holocaust* miniseries, which included Elie Wiesel's critique of the broadcast's use of a composed musical soundtrack,[30] new television productions of Hackett and Goodrich's play aired in East Germany, the Netherlands, England, and the United States in the 1980s. In keeping with the conventions of television drama, seasoned film composers provided each of these broadcasts with original incidental music. Strings and melodic wind instruments often establish mood and mark tonal transitions in these settings, thereby standardizing for mass consumption the musical modes used to articulate the affective significance of Anne's life.

Whereas television and film scores articulate the emotional drama of Anne's life for contemporary audiences, popular songs of the period invoke Anne to reinforce moral commentary on significant social issues. Popular European singer-songwriters Benny Neyman (Dutch) and Louis Chedid (French-Lebanese), for example, recorded songs about Anne Frank that appealed to moral centrism in 1979 and 1985, respectively. Neyman's song, "Chanson Pour Anna," offers a general description of Anne's story with the refrain adapted from the diary itself: "Dear Kitty, tell me, why us? Why are the Jews outlawed? Will the war ever end?" Chedid's "Anne, Ma Sœur Anne" protests the rise of the French far

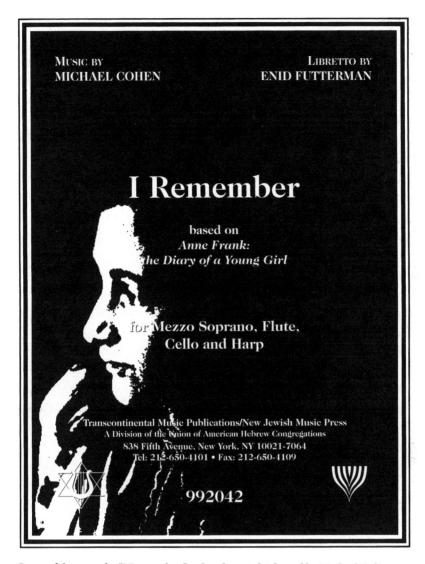

Cover of the score for "I Remember," a chamber work adapted by Michael Cohen and Enid Futterman, from *Yours, Anne,* their 1985 musical based on Anne's diary.

right and its "Nazi-Nostalgie." Using lyrics to connect Anne Frank's story ("Anne, my sister Anne, if I could only tell you what's coming") with that of the sentinel in Charles Perrault's 1697 story "Bluebeard" ("Anne, my sister Anne, don't you see anything coming?"), Chedid calls on the young girl's memory to counter a new threat of nationalism and xenophobia.

By the start of the 1990s, art music compositions about Anne Frank had become fixtures of memorials associated with her life and work. American composer Lukas Foss, for example, composed his 1989 "Elegy for Anne Frank" for a commemoration of the sixtieth anniversary of Anne Frank's birth, sponsored by the American Friends of Anne Frank and the Anti-Defamation League at the Cathedral of St. John the Divine in New York. In 1990, UNICEF commissioned composer/conductor Michael Tilson Thomas to create "From the Diary of Anne Frank," which was performed at one of the United Nations' Concerts for Life that year, held in the UN's General Assembly Hall. The similarities of these works and their performance contexts are telling. Both address larger humanitarian concerns and appeared on programs featuring well-known humanitarian speakers; both compositions include a female reader presenting excerpts of the diary between instrumental sections; and both premieres occurred in spaces with great symbolic significance but notoriously muddy acoustics.[31] These parallels suggest the emergence of tacit standards for including Anne Frank in public musical performances, tying her fate to that of all children in adverse living conditions.

Other new works, especially choral compositions, continued to use texts by other writers to evoke the character and historical significance of Anne Frank. Like Kox's work earlier, British composer Howard Goodall's 1994 piece "In Memoriam Anne Frank," composed for choir and string quartet, employs a variety of literary texts, including poems by Richard Lovelace, Christina Rossetti, and Robert Louis Stevenson.[32] This strategy may have been due, in part, to restrictions on direct citations from Anne's diary. Yet it also takes advantage of the symbolic effect that a simultaneous, multivocal layering of texts can represent. Goodall argued that this approach presented a more nuanced meditation on Anne Frank from a contemporary perspective, noting that "the sentiments were complicated, mixed ones for people living in another society and time."[33] His music achieves this effect in ways that merge contrasting voices, time periods, and sentiments into a musically unified whole, while allowing the setting of passages from an array of literary works to situate Anne Frank implicitly as a writer among major literary figures.

After an absence of more than twenty years, new dance works based on Anne Frank's life began to reappear in the early 1980s. Some of these works used contemporary musical compositions, such as New York–based choreographer Linda Diamond's "Secret Annexe" (1980, with music by Roque Cordero) and a 1981 "Anna Frank" ballet in Verona, Italy, that boasted a new score by Luciano Chailly. Argentinian-born choreographer Mauricio Wainrot's 1984 "The Diary of Anne Frank," a modern dance work performed in bare feet and simple costume, employed a fractured version of Béla Bartók's 1936 "Music for Percussion, Strings, and Celeste" interspersed with sounds of thunderstorms and stomping boots, periods of silence, and a vintage German recording of the popular World War II-era song "Lili Marlene." Creating a sonic montage that followed the emotional development of the piece, Wainrot (and to some extent Diamond as well) experimented with existing music to emphasize a sense of confinement and fear, reflecting an era that had recently emerged from the Argentine "Dirty War" and the social unrest of the American 1970s.[34]

The Sound of the Next Generation

In the mid-1990s, a generation of musicians who had encountered Anne Frank through multiple mediations—works for stage, film, television, and other forms of media, as well as the published diary itself—started their own musical explorations of Anne's life and work. While some works of music theater, such as retellings of Anne's life in hiding staged in Madrid (*El Diario de Anna Frank: Un Canto a la Vida,* 2008) and Paris (*Anne, le Musical: Hommage à Anne Frank,* 2009), continued to approach their subject in a more direct narrative form, others engaged Anne Frank with a wide-ranging sense of inventiveness and play. Recent works of musical theater have paired Anne Frank with the African American abolitionist Harriet Tubman, thereby linking their narratives of entrapment and freedom (*Harriet and Anne,* 1999); imagined a meeting with Anne in Bergen-Belsen (*Saving Anne,* 2003); and critiqued Anne's cult of celebrity (*Margot Frank: The Diary of the Other Young Girl,* 2008).

Artists in the innovative and often introspective indie rock scene have found that Anne's words resonate with their own contemporary concerns and invoke her in their music as both muse and soulmate. Mac McCaughan's 1995 song "In the Manner of Anne Frank" (recorded as part of his Portastatic project) mentions Anne Frank as a diarist whose

Promotional card for Jean-Pierre Hadida's *Anne, le Musical: Hommage à Anne Frank*, performed in Paris in 2009.

writing talent makes him anxious about his own writing abilities. Jeff Mangum, founder of Neutral Milk Hotel, created the group's 1998 album *In the Aeroplane Over the Sea* partly as an extended meditation on Anne after reading her diary. Mangum's account of discovering the diary illustrates how the convergence of self-reflection and emotional intimacy brought Anne from the written page into his musical world:

> I walked into a bookstore, and there was The Diary of Anne Frank. I'd never given it any thought before. Then I spent two days reading it and completely flipped out . . . spent about three days crying . . . it stuck with me for a long, long time. . . . While I was reading the book, she was completely alive to me. I pretty much knew what was going to happen. But that's the thing: you love people because you know their story. You have sympathy for people even when they do stupid things because you know where they're coming from, you understand where they're at in their head. So here I am as deep as you can go in someone's head, in some ways deeper than you can go with someone you know in the flesh. And then at the end, she gets disposed of like a piece of trash. I would go to bed every night and have dreams about having a time machine, having the ability to move through time and space freely, and save Anne Frank. Do you think that's embarrassing?[35]

In a book-length interpretation of *In the Aeroplane Over the Sea,* music critic Kim Cooper characterizes the album's flexible identity as "a surrealistic text loosely based on the life, death, and reincarnation of Anne Frank."[36] Although the group's music and lyrics range widely in their subject matter, Anne's periodic, often cryptic presence throughout the recording seems merged with the musicians' own explorations, transforming her into something akin to a patron saint of creativity in the face of adversity.

Reading Anne Frank's diary as a work of artistic inspiration also figures prominently in two recent films about inner city youth cultivating their own creative talents to overcome disadvantage, with each using music differently to dramatize the relationship between Anne and those she inspires. In Lisa France's 2003 independent hip-hop film *Anne B. Real,* reading the diary motivates the main character—Cynthia, who lives in Spanish Harlem—to write and later perform her own rap lyrics. Cynthia ultimately gathers the strength to confront a male rapper, who has been performing her lyrics as his own, during a hip-hop freestyle contest and proceeds to assert her own skill as a rap artist by performing under the hip-hop name Anne B. Real—an act of homage to Anne Frank. The soundtrack to Richard LaGravenese's 2007 film *Freedom Writers* evokes the lives of its subject: underprivileged students in Long Beach, California.[37] Alongside hip-hop cues by will.i.am, Gang Starr, and Digable Planets, the score's composer, Mark Isham, gives Anne Frank her own musical theme, which consists of a slow succession of string chords—by now an established musical convention for representing Anne Frank, and the Holocaust more generally—accompanied by a repeated descending line on the piano.[38] Anne's theme appears twice: first during a montage about halfway through the film as students begin to read the diary, and then during a school visit by Miep Gies, who had helped protect Anne and her family while in hiding. Noticeably different from most of the other music heard in the film, Anne's theme is skillfully integrated into the rest of the soundtrack through the interpolation of strings into other instrumental sequences, most significantly by featuring hip-hop violinist Miri Ben-Ari. These sonic cues help link the movie characters' personal transformations with their encounters with Anne's life and work.

In contrast to works that present earnest engagement with Anne Frank as a source of moral inspiration, other popular music artists intentionally take a less reverent approach, whether through passing reference—such as funk rap duo OutKast's line, "I love who you are, I love who you ain't / You're so Anne Frank / Let's hit the attic to hide out for 'bout two weeks"[39]—or the name of the short-lived death metal group The Diarrhea of Anne Frank. The glibness of these references speaks to Anne's status as a part of popular culture, and challenges the discourse of propriety that has come to surround her life and work. In 2007, for example, comedian Stephen Lynch used Anne Frank's story to initiate a set of brief "diary entry" songs that describe famous people blissfully unaware of impending disaster. Accompanying himself on folk guitar, he sings in a James Taylor-like lilt:

> Dear Diary, today was a good day
> Papa and I picked wildflowers
> Mama joined and we lay in the sunshine
> Then we sang and danced for hours
> I know tomorrow will be even better
> So the good Lord I thank
> I'll write more later. Love, Anne Frank.[40]

In one live performance video, uploaded to YouTube, Lynch's song receives an immediate (and intended) wave of shocked laughter. Rather than moving on, however, Lynch extends the routine by playing with the acceptability of Anne Frank as a comic foil, crying: "Don't get mad at me, I'm just the messenger! I don't know who this Anne Frank is, but I'm sure she lived a long and"—before being cut off by more audience laughter.[41] Such instances use music to push the boundaries of socially acceptable discussions of Anne Frank targeted toward a population that has largely encountered her as a figure of unquestioned authority. By engaging in musical creations that intentionally play with genre and moral expectations, these populations can consider Anne in ways that lie outside of the glare of institutional propriety—while allowing them to glare back at propriety and claim her for themselves.

These examples show how musicians continue to bring Anne Frank into an expanding array of genres and forms, seeking sounds to express her multiple, shifting places in communal memory and popular culture. Originating with early responses to Anne Frank's brief comment about a Hanukkah song, composers and songwriters imagined their own connections to the young girl by drawing on familiar sounds, forms, and musical traditions. Over time, they literally imbued Anne Frank with a variety of voices, bringing her image and words beyond the enforced quiet of the Annex into sonic realization and public performance. In the process, their music has given us a distinctive mode for exploring Anne Frank's life and work: inspired by her text, yet not bound by it; proficient in nonverbal expressions of cultural literacy; and responsive to broad-ranging aural histories and social conventions. The sound of Anne Frank's voice has been lost to time. Yet in her place, the diary has inspired a vibrant musical landscape all its own.

IV CONTESTING

11

Critical Thinking:
Scholars Reread the Diary

Sally Charnow

The publication of *De Dagboeken van Anne Frank* by the Netherlands State Institute for War Documentation in 1986 marks a threshold in how Anne's diary has been read, taught, and discussed. An English translation, *The Diary of Anne Frank: The Critical Edition* (referred to hereafter as the *Critical Edition*), appeared in 1989, followed by translations into German, French, and Japanese; a revised edition was issued in Dutch and in English in 2003.[1] This new version of the diary initiated a wave of new scholarly scrutiny of the already iconic work long known to American readers as *The Diary of a Young Girl*. Whereas the diary had long received attention from historians as a document of Jewish resistance to Nazi persecution during World War II, more recent scholarship has read and discussed Frank's work as an example of women's or adolescent writing, autobiography, coming-of-age narrative, or Holocaust literature. Cultural historian Berteke Waaldijk, for example, argued in 1993 that "Anne Frank's symbolic value as an innocent victim of fascism should not prevent us from reading her diaries as a literary work. The outrage of her death is in no way diminished by taking her seriously as a writer."[2] More recently, author Francine Prose explains: "Like most of Anne Frank's readers, I had viewed her book as the innocent and spontaneous outpourings of a teenager. But now, reading it as an adult, I quickly became convinced that I was in the presence of a consciously crafted work of literature."[3] Waaldijk, Prose, and other scholars and writers offer, in effect, new mediations of the diary through a distinctive approach to reading the text made possible in large measure by the publication of the *Critical Edition*. These new readings also reflect recent developments both in the academy and in public discussion. In particular, more recent scholarship on Anne's diary draws on historians' interest in diary writing as social practice, on literary scholars' attention to diary writing as a form of women's writing and literature, and on the study of adolescence from a variety of perspectives.[4]

The *Critical Edition* was published with more than one end in mind. Of primary importance was the refutation, once and for all, of allegations that the diary was a forgery, charges that neo-Nazis have made since the late 1950s. To that end, the *Critical Edition* provides an extensive discussion of the forensics conducted to establish the authenticity of the original diaries as being written by Anne Frank during World War II. Of greater significance for the new wave of scholarship on the diary, the *Critical Edition* presents on the same page each entry in three different versions: Anne's original entries (termed "version a"), her own edited version of the text ("version b"), and the posthumously published text, edited primarily by her father, Otto Frank ("version c"). This format enables readers to compare the different versions easily and track the changes from one version to another. Also included in the volume are extensive introductions that detail the Frank family's history and that of the diary. Thus, the *Critical Edition* explicates the literary significance of the diary and affirms its historical value as both highly significant and irrefutable.

Waaldijk contends that the publication of the unabridged texts goes well beyond demonstrating that they are not forgeries, and she links the effort to authenticate the text with its literary worth: "Although the differences [in the handwriting] may be negligible from the point of view of the political and judicial claims of authenticity, they are extremely significant for readers interested in Anne Frank as a woman writer."[5] The publisher of the English version of the *Critical Edition* concurs, explaining on its dust jacket: "In comparing Anne's two versions, the reader sees how her thinking and ability to write developed during her two years in hiding. Her corrections to both versions demonstrate how she worked; rarely has one had such an opportunity to follow the process of writing so closely."[6] Noting the increased academic interest in Anne's artistic process, Prose likewise observes that the "various drafts provide evidence of [Anne's] creative process, of her gifts for revision, of her first and second thoughts about how she wanted to portray herself and those around her."[7] The *Critical Edition* enhances this turn to reading the diary as literature by suggesting that, like paintings by Henri Matisse or poems by Elizabeth Barrett Browning and Allen Ginsberg, it warrants a variorum edition, which offers insight into the stages of the creative process that culminates in a renowned and respected work.[8]

When examined together, the three versions of Anne's diary reveal a complexly written and collaboratively redacted work. The *Critical Edition* enables readers to observe that Anne was writing new entries at the same time that she was rewriting earlier ones and reveals her indebtedness as a writer to literary works, especially Dutch popular fiction for adolescent girls. Readers of the *Critical Edition* also learn about Anne's other literary efforts: in addition to her diaries, she wrote short stories while in hiding, some of which her father incorporated into the first published version of the diary, and she kept a book of quotations that she copied from her reading. Thus, the *Critical Edition* encourages new ways to consider this famous text as a literary work in progress, shaped by a dynamic interplay among literary genres: memoir, spiritual confession, novel, documentary, and reportage.

By the time the *Critical Edition* appeared, Otto Frank's edited version of the diary, first published in translations into major European languages in the early to mid-1950s, had become a widely taught text in secondary schools and even in some college courses.[9] The widespread inclusion of Anne's diary in school curricula also stimulated new academic interest in the work, especially in relation to the expansion of feminist discourse in literary, cultural, and gender studies, as well as in the fields of women's and social history. In particular, Anne Frank's diary became a prized subject for feminist literary critics interested in examining the work within the traditions of women's writing and coming-of-age narratives. According to Waaldijk, feminist literary criticism has developed a critical approach that enables scholars to study women's writing in its own intertextuality. "Instead of claiming an abstract literary value that should grant women a place in the literary canon," she suggests, "feminist research has sought traditions of female writing that can be detected in common stylistic and thematic characteristics and intertextual references. In the case of Anne Frank, this approach seems to offer a particularly useful way of rereading her diaries."[10] Waaldijk's use of the notion of "rereading" implies not only a prior familiarity with the text but also a revised, rather than simply a repeated, reading.

Diary Writing as Social Practice

At the same time that literary scholars began to show new interest in Anne's diary, the text also informed historical scholarship on diary writing as a social practice. Diary writing burgeoned in the late nineteenth and early twentieth centuries, especially among adolescent girls, as adolescence itself emerged as a new subject of attention in European and American public life. According to historian Joan Jacobs Brumberg, diaries reveal "so much about the heart of being a girl. . . . I use them whenever possible to provide entry into the hidden history of female adolescents' experience, especially the experience of the body." Brumberg points to Frank's diary as an early example of a young woman talking openly and honestly about her body.[11] Like literary scholars, much of the work by historians on diary writing concerns issues of gender and sexuality. In many cases, youth diaries, including Anne's, became vehicles for self-actualization of a personal and, sometimes, a public, professional self.

Anne Frank began keeping the diary as a private record of her life when she turned thirteen years old on June 12, 1942, and, unbeknown to her, three weeks before she and her family went into hiding. The last entry in her diary is dated August 1, 1944, three days before the Franks and the other Jews hiding with them were arrested. During the period in which Anne Frank kept her diary, the devastating impact of World War II on her life coincided with the upheavals of her personal coming of age. Despite the extraordinary circumstances of the war, Anne's diary is in many respects typical of those kept by other adolescent girls. Like them, she wrote about movie stars, romance, and sexuality, including discussions of her changing body. Yet Anne's diary is distinguished by discussions of adolescent emotional relationships that were shaped by being in hiding, especially her struggles with her mother; her desire for close relationships with girlfriends and older female role models, which being in hiding made impossible; and her growing attachment to Peter van Pels, the fifteen-year-old son of the family that went into hiding with the Franks.

Central to the rugged terrain of Anne's adolescence was her experience of puberty, a notable subject of discussion in the diary. Brumberg argues that, since the turn of the twentieth century, adolescent girls in the United States and Western Europe have experienced self-consciousness and discomfort with their changing bodies. As a society, she writes, Westerners are certainly more open about many aspects of their sexual lives than they were fifty or even twenty-five years ago. "And yet, despite this national preoccupation with sex and the body, there is still a deeply embedded cultural reluctance, even in supposedly 'enlightened' circles, to talk honestly or openly about certain aspects of the female body." Women still struggle with finding a vocabulary to talk about their bodies that does not rely on "Victorian euphemisms, medical nomenclature, or misogynistic slang."[12] But unlike so many girls at the turn of the twenty-first century, who are concerned with the shape and appearance of their bodies as a primary expression of their individual identity, nineteenth-century girls' concerns about moral character kept a preoccupation with their bodies in check. Victorian diaries never mentioned menstruation or intimacies with young men, but by the 1920s, girls were writing about their changing bodies, their understanding of sexuality, and their intimate relationships with boys, even if they had difficulty finding the right language.[13] Few, however, were as forthright on this subject as Anne Frank.

Anne's diary entries about her changing body reveal an increasing nuance in her understanding of sexuality and especially in her emotional intelligence. In an entry in the first version of her diary dated October 10, 1942, Anne details the physical changes in her body with scientific precision. She notes the enlarging of her sexual organs but also evinces a somewhat vague understanding of female sexuality. In closing, she refers to her remarks to Kitty (the imaginary girlfriend to whom she addressed her diary entries) as a "peculiar conversation," suggesting her lack of ease with the subject. Ten days later, Anne writes that she will begin menstruating soon, because she is noticing changes in her body.

Because of the absence of Anne's original diary entries between December 5, 1942, and December 22, 1943 (one or more notebooks of the original diary were lost or perhaps destroyed), it is not possible to know whether she continued to make similar observations about her sexual development. But in an original diary entry dated January 6, 1944, Anne writes about having read an article in *Libelle,* a women's magazine, that made her blush. The article explained that during puberty a girl becomes quiet within and begins to think about the wonders that are happening to her body. Anne writes: "I experience that too and that is why I get the feeling lately of being embarrassed in front of Margot, Mummy, and Daddy.... I think what is happening to me is so wonderful, and not only what can be seen on my body, but all that is taking place inside." By late January 1944, as she becomes conscious of her feelings for Peter, Anne offers a graphic, scientifically precise description of female anatomy and the mechanics of sexuality.[14]

Anne's use of explicit, scientific language is not surprising. Brumberg explains that in the early years of the twentieth century it was assumed that girls would receive knowledge about their bodies, menstruation, and reproduction through popular health books, written by male doctors, with mothers cast in a supporting role. Like these girls, Anne relied on information about sexuality from similar publications, as well as magazines like *Libelle.* She writes on March 18, 1944: "I learned about maidenhead and quite a few other details from a little book on sex education."[15] The general assumption that popular pamphlets, rather than parents, should provide sex education to adolescent girls did not assuage Anne's anger at her mother, who was perhaps not playing even her supporting role well. Shaped by a very different sensibility of the post-World War I era, Anne was angry with her middle-class family—especially her mother—for their sexual repression and the lack of some sort of sex education at home. Anne characterized this behavior as an abdication of maternal responsibility, writing: "If a mother doesn't tell her children everything, they learn it bit by bit and that must be wrong!" Anne understood grownups' fear that children would no longer look at marriage as something sacred and pure. Nevertheless, she proclaimed: "I don't think it's at all a bad thing for a man to bring a little experience into a marriage; it's got nothing to do with the marriage itself, has it?"[16]

Beyond offering a critique of her parents and their generation, Anne used her diary to develop an independent voice, articulating her own ideas separate from family constraints and cultural norms. Here, too, Anne followed an established precedent in diary writing. Historian Jane Hunter notes that private diaries enabled adolescent girls in the Victorian era to entertain an imaginative freedom and release rebellious impulses while preserving close networks of affiliation and not breaking away from their families.[17] Hunter characterizes diaries as transitional objects, in the psychological sense, for the way that they allowed adolescent girls to separate from their parents. The diary was a place to confess, protect, daydream, and imagine secrets too private for speech. Literary critic Laureen Nussbaum suggests that there is a marked shift toward introspection in Anne's diary writing about ten weeks after having gone into hiding. In an entry dated October 18, 1942, she describes a daydream focused on escape: Anne and her father somehow make it to Switzerland, where they share a room in their relatives' house. He even gives her money to go out and buy a new wardrobe; her diary includes the shopping list. There, Anne attends eighth grade and becomes friends with other girls, including one named Kitty. Anne learns to figure skate with her cousin Bernd; the two of them become very successful ice skating partners and are eventually filmed! "We make a lovely pair and everyone is mad about us," she writes, and also includes a sketch of her skating outfit.[18]

Being in hiding with her family made separation from them physically impossible and unusually challenging psychologically for Anne. While she lived in close quarters with her family and the other Jews hiding with them, Anne's diary allowed her a certain degree of autonomy and contributed to the development of an "enhanced sense of self," as diary keeping had done for her Victorian counterparts.[19] From all accounts, Anne's family and the others in hiding respected her privacy as a diarist. Miep Gies, an employee of Otto Frank, who played a key role in caring for those hiding in the Annex, recalled in an interview that she once unwittingly walked in on Anne while she was writing in her diary: "I felt awkward, not knowing whether to retreat or approach. At that moment she fixed me with an expression that I will never forget. It was not the Anne I knew—the friendly, charming child. She had an expression of pent-up fury." In her memoir, Gies described Anne at that moment as having a look of "dark concentration, as if she had a throbbing headache.

The look pierced me, and I was speechless."[20] Gies then recalled hurrying back down the stairs.

Complementing the diary's role as providing Anne with independence from those with whom she lived was its role as a surrogate for her absent peers. Since the turn of the twentieth century, same-sex cohorts came to be regarded as vital to the maturation of European and American youth.[21] The protective impulse to support the moral character of female adolescents, which had prompted Victorian mothers to avoid discussing intimate subjects with their daughters, also led to the development of a vast organizational complex of single-sex groups, such as the Girl Scouts, the Camp Fire Girls, and the Young Woman's Christian or Hebrew Association, among others, devoted to "keeping girlhood wholesome and chaste." Most of these groups were originally identified with a religious denomination and offered a heavy dose of religious morality, so as "to uphold the Christian standard of honor and morality, and to encourage purity of life, dutifulness to parents, faithfulness to employers, and thrift."[22] Brumberg terms this phenomenon a "protective umbrella," under which girls found camaraderie and cooperation as well as a certain degree of peer pressure. Although the religious overtones of many of these organizations diminished in the 1920s, same-sex social activities that were regarded as morally healthy—such as dramatics, handicrafts, nature study, literature, and music—remained a vital aspect of girls' organizational lives throughout the interwar period.[23] In her diary, Anne describes the girlfriends who comprise her "ping-pong club," and, while in hiding, she mourns the loss of contact with them, especially as a same-sex cohort with whom to discuss her changing body, fantasies, crushes, mood shifts, and the problems she faced with her parents. For example, on January 6, 1944, she writes, "If only I had a girlfriend!"[24]

Indeed, in the first version of the diary Anne invents a cohort of girls to whom she addressed her entries, thereby simulating the socializing with her same-sex peer group that she missed in hiding. Anne wrote diary entries in the form of letters to a range of imaginary correspondents: Conny, Jetty, Emmy, Marianne, as well as Kitty, the name she later chose to address all the entries in her revised version of the diary. Anne took many of these names, including Kitty, from characters in *Joop ter Heul*, a series of young adult novels that she adored. By choosing to address her diary to fictional characters, Anne Frank consciously blurred the boundary between her actual circumstances and her potent imaginative life.

Even as Anne turned to her diary to simulate communing with girlfriends, her writing also demonstrates her ability to, in Hunter's words, "summon a world of high seriousness distant from casual schoolgirl banter."[25] Engaging with ideas of "high seriousness," analyzing and creating adult roles, and developing an active concern for justice are common themes in adolescent thinking, according to psychologist George Scarlett. Although Anne's diary engages all these themes, he argues that her commitment to justice is the most striking feature of the book.[26] Central to Anne's sense of justice was an insistence on her own moral improvement; she was extremely hard on herself. Aware of the absence of satisfactory women role models and a female peer group, Anne wrote, "I must become good through my own efforts without examples and without good advice. . . . I frequently feel weak, and dissatisfied with myself; my shortcomings are too great. I know this, and everyday I try to improve myself, again and again and again."[27] Scarlett argues that this egocentric reflection is pivotal in the process by which adolescents construct adult roles for themselves. He does not find Anne's self-scrutiny beyond the experience of common adolescent behavior. Rather, he suggests that the ability to think about one's thoughts and to analyze one's actions is a distinctly adolescent skill.[28]

Other critics disagree with Scarlett, arguing that Anne's struggle to develop her own moral compass transcended the typical adolescent experience. Poet and literary critic John Berryman considers Frank's diary a unique literary event, produced by a person who becomes more mature than most people ever become. Questioning whether the universal process of adolescence is, in fact, universally interesting, he argues that Anne Frank's experience was unique: "It is not universal, for most people do not grow up, in any degree that will correspond to Anne Frank's growing up. . . . It took, I believe, a special pressure forcing the child-adult conversion, and exceptional self-awareness and exceptional candor and exceptional powers of expression, to bring that strange or normal change into view."[29] Similarly, Jewish studies scholar Rachel Feldhay Brenner argues that Frank's self-scrutiny went beyond what is considered common for adolescent girls.[30] Moreover, she contends that Anne's experience of being forced into hiding, literally disappearing from social life, had the effect of encouraging her process of individuation. According to Brenner, Anne constantly sought separation from those who surrounded her while in hiding, even as she yearned for close relationships.[31]

Brenner's description of Anne's need for both independence and connectedness recalls Hunter's description of how Victorian adolescent girls used their diaries. Like Anne, Victorian adolescent girls recorded their efforts to better themselves, seeking moral uplift and self-improvement as part of their new-found independence.[32] In that sense, Anne's new morality signaled a loss of innocence with regard to her relationship with adults. She recorded her separation both from her father—who, she wrote, could not accept her as "Anne-on-her-own-merits"—and from her mother, who did not offer the intellectual and professional model that she sought.[33] Indeed, Anne seemed to be modeling herself on the image of the New Woman of the interwar period, known for attending college, marrying late (if at all), developing a career, and campaigning for sex education and women's suffrage.[34]

Determining whether Anne's self-criticism was common or extraordinary is less important than is the recognition of this new attention to her diary as an example of a writing practice with literary as well as psychological implications. Of course, the preponderance of scholars' evidence for assessing Anne's development both as a young woman and as a writer comes from the diary. Moreover, the publication of the *Critical Edition* offers scholars the opportunity to read across the various versions of the diary—not only to examine the entries themselves but also to consider what comes and goes between them—as a strategy for considering Anne Frank's psychological development as well as her evolution as a writer. Indeed, without an awareness of the diary's rewriting and redaction, information not familiar to most readers of the diary in its original published version, many of these insights would not be possible.

Redactions

On March 29, 1944, Gerrit Bolkestein, the minister of education, art, and science in the Dutch government-in-exile in London, appealed over Radio Oranje to the Dutch people in the Netherlands "to make a collection of diaries and letters and other personal documents" as evidence of their resistance to Nazi occupation.[35] After hearing the announcement, Anne embarked on a revision of her original diary entries, written not in a notebook but on loose sheets of paper. Anne envisioned her revised text as a publishable book, to be titled *Het Achterhuis,* referring to her hiding place, usually translated into English as the "Secret Annex." Anne revised her original diary during what proved to be the last ten weeks of her life in hiding. At the same time, she continued to write new entries in her diary, which had expanded from the original notebook given to her on her thirteenth birthday to fill additional notebooks. Thus, during the final months of her life in hiding, she was simultaneously writing and rewriting her self.

As a young woman of fifteen, Anne became, in effect, an editor and began refashioning the writings that her younger, more childlike self had composed during the preceding two years. Revising her diary became a subject of interest in itself. Anne discussed the task of editing her original writing in her new diary entries, in which she reveals how she consciously saw herself not simply as a diarist but as an author: "Just imagine how interesting it would be if I were to publish a romance of the 'Secret Annex,' the title alone would be enough to make people believe it was a detective story."[36] Six weeks later, she wrote that her greatest wish was to become a journalist and then a famous writer. The shift from writing to rewriting marked a shift from keeping a private diary to composing a literary work that she imagined would be read by the public. In addition, these shifts straddled her coming of age, which was the subject of much of her writing and, in a different way, of her editing.

Indeed, newly attentive to a potential readership, Anne became her own censor, reining in the fantasies that she had recorded in the first version of her diary and leaving out what she considered inappropriate for public consumption. In particular, she removed much of the explicit material about changes in her body, erotic desire, and sex. At one point in her revising process, Anne was horrified with her own previous candor. While rereading earlier entries, she wrote on January 22, 1944, the following comment on a blank page in her original diary, near her original entry for November 10, 1942: "When I look over my diary today, 1½ years on, I cannot believe that I was ever such an innocent young thing. . . .

I really blush with shame when I read the pages dealing with subjects that I'd much better have left to the imagination. I put it all down so bluntly!" In the same entry she also revealed a profound empathy toward her younger self: "[N]o matter how much I should like to, I can never be like that again. I still understand those moods, those remarks about Margot, Mummy and Daddy so well that I might have written them yesterday."[37] Given her new mission of writing a publishable work about living in hiding under Nazi occupation, she may well have imagined that her readers would not be interested in the intimate details of her body and nascent sexuality. Like some "new women" before her, including the progressive educator Annie Winsor and the suffrage activist Harriet Burton Laidlaw, Anne saw writing as a vehicle through which she would claim a public voice.[38] Serving as her own editor provided Anne with an even more active exercise in fashioning an autonomous self through writing, in part by using the opportunity to imagine herself as an adult pursuing her chosen profession of author.

In her revised diary, Anne orients the reader by offering contextual information that did not appear in the original. For example, in the first version she does not mention the situation of the Jews in the Netherlands before she went into hiding, but in her revision she alerts the reader (in the entry of June 20, 1942) to the deteriorating conditions that Jews then faced. Anne also reorders events in the course of her revisions to suit a larger narrative arc, which a diary, written incrementally in real time, cannot offer. Thus, in the revised entry for July 5, 1942, Anne has her father announce in advance the existence of the hiding place, and on July 9, 1942, she describes the whole building at 263 Prinsengracht, not only the Annex, when she and her family arrive there to go into hiding. The literary critic Philippe Lejeune describes her editorial process as one of "condensation and redistribution." Moreover, as she continued to revise the original diary, Anne the editor became closer in age to Anne the ongoing diarist. As a result, her later diary entries more closely resemble the style of those she had revised. Anne's composition style becomes more assured, or, as Berryman describes her writing, "vivid, witty, candid, astute, dramatic, pathetic, terrible."[39]

Lejeune points out striking differences between the entries in Anne's original and redacted diaries dated June–November, 1942. In addition to suggesting that Anne found the original version "too free and verbose," he notes that Anne revised the diary with the more developed style of a "novelist."[40] Anne's entries became more focused and concise as a result of her editing. Lejeune characterizes the reworked diary as having the "economy of an epistolary novel."[41] Each entry is substantial in length and has a principle, organizing subject, rather than many disconnected ones, which is typical of diary entries generally. Anne also strived to avoid repetitions, which are inevitable in an unedited diary. As critic Henry Pommer explains, "Life in the annex was terribly repetitious, but there is little repetition in the diary itself."[42]

For the most part, Otto Frank's redaction of his daughter's diary for publication, first appearing in Dutch in 1947 as *Het Achterhuis*, followed her own revisions. Lejeune notes that because Anne was not able to complete her revised version of the diary and a large section of the unrevised original diary was missing, her father was obligated to create a single work from the two partial versions that survived the war. Otto created a montage, according to Lejeune, only making changes demanded by the Dutch editors and subsequent translators.[43] Lejeune does not hide his irritation with the postwar editors, who believed they had the right to bowdlerize Anne Frank's style. However, before the publication of the *Critical Edition*, Otto Frank was sometimes criticized for censoring his daughter's diary, expunging the detailed descriptions of her maturing body, discussions of her nascent sexuality, and bursts of anger directed against her mother and the other adults in hiding. But now that the *Critical Edition* makes it easy to compare the different versions of the diary, it becomes clear that Anne was often the one who had edited out those sections. In fact, her father restored to the published version much of the material that Anne had excised in her revisions. Nussbaum suggests that Anne's father may have repeatedly selected the more emotional passages of the original diary out of a need "to preserve the image of his beloved, tempestuous little Anne and didn't quite know what to do with the more mature, objective, and autonomous young writer." Nussbaum was impressed by the amount of self-criticism and literary insight that "the barely-fifteen-year-old Anne brought to bear upon her revision" in order "to create a most interesting and readable text."[44]

The most extensive of Anne's self-censoring efforts concerned her relationship with Peter. She obscured much of what she had first written about their relationship, transforming it from a romance into a friendship, by eliminating much of the original entries from January through March, 1944, which trace the development of their relationship. Lejeune notes that Anne revised these entries in June and July of that year; therefore, it is unclear how she intended to depict her relationship with Peter, as Anne's process of revising the diary was interrupted by her arrest, together with the others in hiding.[45] Lejeune notes that Otto Frank decided to reinsert almost all of the entries about Anne and Peter's evolving relationship that Anne had eliminated. Given the changed context of the postwar years, with Anne and Peter both dead, Anne's father made different editorial choices, seeking to recover the psychological richness of the emotional bond that Anne had experienced from her love for Peter. However, Otto Frank respected his daughter's censoring of the passages that dealt with sexuality. Given that Anne believed her text would be published under her name after the war, Lejeune suggests that it is more surprising—and audacious—to read what she kept in the revised version of the diary, rather than what she deleted.[46]

Otto Frank also omitted from the diary some of Anne's harshest remarks about her mother, who had also died during the war, including one "especially disagreeable [entry] that focused on her parents."[47] Anne's conflicts with her mother seem typical for adolescent girls but were doubtless intensified by the stresses of their life in hiding. Waaldijk notes that Anne's remarks about her mother expressed feelings both of rejection as a daughter and of superiority as a woman.[48] For example, Anne wrote that she had no interest in leading the sort of life lived by her mother, Mrs. van Pels, and "all the women who work and are forgotten. I must have something besides a husband and children, something that I can devote myself to."[49] Waaldijk suggests that Anne's wish to be a writer was deeply linked with her desire to lead a life very different from that of her mother. Thus, in the same passage, Anne writes about her need for meaningful work and her desire to become a journalist: "I know that I can write, a couple of my stories are good. . . . I am the best and sharpest critic of my own work, I know myself what is and what is not well-written."[50]

Reading, Writing, and Self-preservation

For some critics, the key to understanding Anne's writing is its combination of "high" and "low" literary genres. According to Waaldijk, Anne's diary reveals that schoolgirl novels—in particular, Cissij van Marxveldt's *Joop ter Heul* series of four novels, published between 1919 and 1925[51]—were just as important in forming Anne's sense of identity as a writer as were the classical German works by Schiller and Goethe that she read with her father.[52] In October 1942, Anne wrote: "As a matter of fact Cissij van Marxveldt is first class. I shall definitely let my children read her."[53] The *Joop ter Heul* novels influenced Anne's writing in both form and content. Van Marxveldt's series of novels describing the life of Joop, a girl in an upper-middle-class Dutch family in Amsterdam, offered Anne an important model of the diary as an epistolary novel. In the series, Joop starts writing letters to friends, but her father forbids her to continue her correspondences, because he is afraid it will interfere with her studies. Joop then turns to writing in her diary. The diary form of *Joop ter Heul* helped Anne imagine her own diary as a literary work and offered her a heroine, similarly cheerful on the outside but "lonely, insecure, and serious" on the inside, as a literary role model.[54] But unlike Joop, Anne found encouragement in her writing from her father. Indeed, their writing moves in opposite directions: Joop shifts from writing letters to keeping a diary, whereas Anne moves from keeping a personal diary to writing letters to imaginary friends, then to writing fictional stories, and ultimately to preparing a revised diary, conceived as a novelistic memoir. And whereas Joop's writing moves inward with her shift to diary keeping, Anne reaches outward from the oppressive reality of her life in hiding to engage with her envisioned future readership.

As much as Anne Frank employed her identification with fictional young women as a vehicle for self-reflection, there are significant differences between Anne's notions of womanhood and those of van Marxveldt. Anne probed more critically into questions of female identity, struggling to redefine what it meant to be a woman. Indeed, Waaldijk argues that Anne's diary, which was written twenty years after the first four Joop novels appeared in print, offers a glimpse into a nascent feminist consciousness, especially in the diary's original version.[55] Anne envisioned herself as a maturing young woman with professional goals and filled with desire. By contrast, van Marxveldt portrays Joop as unquestioningly entering the world of marriage, motherhood, and charity work, thereby aligning her heroine with the confines of a Victorian sensibility regarding proper middle-class womanhood. Anne also questioned women's historical subordination to men. Why, she asked in the first version of her diary on June 13, 1944, "did so many nations in the past, and often still now, treat women as inferior to men?" In the same entry, which marked her fifteenth birthday, Anne laments that men lack respect for the part women play in society: "It is stupid enough of women to have borne it all in silence for such a long time, since the more centuries this arrangement lasts, the more deeply rooted it becomes. Luckily schooling, work, and progress have opened women's eyes."[56]

As her passion for *Joop ter Heul* demonstrates, reading was a necessity for Anne and the others in hiding with her. On July 11, 1943, Anne writes to Kitty: "Ordinary people simply don't know what books mean to us, shut up here. Reading, learning, and the radio are our amusements." A voracious reader, Anne spent hours discussing and criticizing books in the evenings with Peter and the others; she and her sister kept a card file of titles and authors of the books they read. Books, magazines (especially *Cinema and Theater*), and newspapers were most welcome gifts. According to literary scholar Sylvia Patterson Iskander, Otto Frank encouraged his daughters to read broadly: history, science, music, biographies, mythology, and folklore, including very recent publications in Dutch, French, German, and English. Iskander concludes that this broad and varied reading, along with critical discussion, "perhaps contributed to [Anne's] tolerance for others and her hope for the future in midst of undeniable fear and horror."[57]

As is true for many other young diarists and autobiographers, Anne's reading led directly to writing. A study of autobiographies written by adolescent Eastern European Jews collected by the YIVO Institute for Jewish Research, based in Vilna, Poland, in the 1930s, demonstrates a correlation between "the act of reading and a marked turn toward introspection, a development associated with the discovery of a language with which to depict the inner self."[58] Sociologist Moshe Kligsberg, the first scholar to examine these autobiographies after World War II, noted in the 1950s that there was a direct "connection between the reading and discussing of literature, of whatever genre, and the drawing of individualistic self-awareness through identification with literary heroes." This identification, he suggested, "fostered the capacity to voice aspects of the inner life that, without the mediation of literature, would not and could not have come to light."[59]

Anne's self-awareness as a diarist also entailed writing about herself as a Jew in relation to the complex and frightening world around her. Brenner argues that the context of Nazi-occupied Amsterdam played a key role in shaping Anne as an artist: the "poignancy of Frank's writing ... emerges from her awareness of the terrifying historical reality against which, as a Jew, she writes her life story. . . . This consciousness forges Frank's artistic skills and shapes her ethics."[60] Brenner sees Anne's diary as a story of Jewish solidarity and suggests that she was completely aware of the plight of European Jews under Nazi occupation: "Fully conscious of her fate as a Jew, Frank seeks a rhetoric which would both name and defy the unparalleled reality of horror."[61] Anne astutely observed how her life in hiding was shaped by outside events. She wrote about how every day her living space grew smaller and wondered if she would suffocate or die of hunger before the war was over. At the same time, Anne often expressed a clear sense of a future for herself and other Jews. She wrote that it would seem "quite funny ten years after the war if we Jews were to tell how we lived and what we ate and talked about here."[62] Even as the material conditions of her life in the Annex deteriorated, she continued to hold onto aspirations for the future, expressed in terms of becoming a professional writer.

Indeed, Brenner suggests that writing itself afforded Anne this sense of the future. Following Paul Tillich's notion that the ability to abstract, interpret, and transform through language signals the vitality of being, Brenner suggests that Anne drew strength from her aspiration to become a writer. As an interpretive process, writing offered Anne a counterweight to the despair she experienced in hiding. Her literary creativity was a life-sustaining system.[63] The therapeutic power of writing is evident in some of her diary entries. For example, in April 1944 she wrote: "I can shake off everything if I write; my sorrows disappear, my courage is reborn! . . . I can recapture everything when I write, my thoughts, my ideals and my fantasies."[64] Anne continually reasserts herself as a writer who defeats fear through writing. Furthermore, Brenner argues that Anne's constant preoccupation with her diary and the recording of life in the Annex "infuses the duration of her hiding with an on-going artistic invention. Looking at reality as material for diaristic recording elicits a sense of meaningful continuity." By writing about her daily life, Anne was able to transform an "existence of incapacitating helplessness and despair into a humorous adventure." Writing and revising her own story "defiantly affirms Frank's dignified self-perception as an individual whose story deserves to be recorded."[65]

* * *

Since the first publication of her diary, Anne Frank has grown into an iconic figure for an international audience who, of course, has known her only through various mediations, beginning with reading the diary. By presenting this wide readership with the three versions of Anne's diary in a comparative format, the *Critical Edition* inspired volumes of new scholarly interpretations, even as it underscored the unfinished quality of the work. Anne Frank's life was tragically cut short before she had an opportunity to test her aspirations of becoming a professional writer. The diary is unfinished, as all diaries are; but this one ends abruptly, with no foreshadowing of what happens soon thereafter. There is a great impulse to complete the diary in a narrative sense, and most published editions do just that by including an afterword explaining what happened to Anne and the others after her last entry. As Prose writes, "What makes the diary moving is the shadow cast back over it by the notice of the death at the end."[66]

By revealing the emergent artist's process, the *Critical Edition* encourages literary scholars to contemplate Anne Frank's early achievements and to imagine the writer that she might have become. And yet only her partial diaries, parts of which are lost, remain to suggest possible futures for her; it is hard to admit how little writing there actually is. And this is where the literary project of seeing Anne Frank as a young woman and an artist encounters the unavoidable tragedy of her time and place. The unwritten end of her story, her death, is irreconcilable with the desire to conjure her. Her legacy is fragmented and cannot be made whole.

12

Anne Frank on Crank:
Comic Anxieties

Edward Portnoy

There was a certain actress, a terrible actress, that played Anne
Frank. She was so bad that when the Nazis came on [stage],
the audience yelled out, "She's upstairs in the attic!"

—Fyvush Finkel in *Der Komediant*, 1999

Making a joke about Anne Frank seems to be widely regarded as an act of
bad taste. Why, then, would someone do so? Such jokes may engage some
of the same challenging ideas about Anne's significance in contemporary
culture as do works of avant-garde video, performance, or visual art, but
joking lacks the protective valence of these "high-culture" media. In addition to being provocative, these jokes are lowbrow; they are vulgar in
both senses of the term. Seeking to explain this kind of humor, the psychologist Martin Grotjahn argued that "jokes grow best on the graves of
fresh anxieties."[1] What then, are the anxieties on which Anne Frank jokes
rely, and what makes them fresh, nearly seventy years after her death?

The joke told by veteran Yiddish actor Fyvush Finkel about the
terrible actress who played Anne Frank was not new. Different versions
had been told about various actresses, and one variant was even believed
to be true, making it an "urban legend."[2] However, when told in the
documentary about Yiddish actor Pesachke Burstein, the joke prompted
J. Hoberman, senior film critic for the *Village Voice*, a progressive weekly
newspaper published in New York, to anticipate strong opposition: "Actually, it's a joke about the representation of Anne Frank, but—who
knows?—it might be sufficient to get *The Komediant* denounced by Me-
nachem Rosensaft and picketed by Dov Hikind," both of them Jewish

"I don't like Holocaust jokes…," one of several dozen memes using this portrait of Anne Frank posted on memegenerator.net, 2011.

community activists and children of Holocaust survivors.[3] Indeed, any humorous treatment of Anne Frank provokes anxiety, as does humor associated with the Holocaust more generally. These jokes test the limits of humor's special status as something "not to be taken seriously" and therefore possessing a kind of immunity to ethical judgment. Holocaust humor is a limit case, to the extent that the special status of the Holocaust trumps the special status of humor and denies it immunity to ethical judgment.

But Finkel's joke is more complex. Its humor is predicated on a double violation: performing Anne Frank badly, and then making a "Holocaust joke" about the bad performance. The humor depends on the extreme incommensurability of "crime" (bad performance) and punishment (audience betrays "Anne" to the "Nazis"), in a parody of the historical Anne's tragic fate. The power of the joke—what makes it so funny and offensive at the same time—is how the audience both enters and breaks the theatrical frame: in order to shorten a bad performance, the audience speeds up the disclosure of "Anne's" hiding place by yelling its whereabouts to unknowing characters ("Nazis"), which are performed by knowing actors. It is not easy to dismiss a joke so clever in its construction and caustic in its indictment of an audience who violates the proscenium's fourth wall and implicates itself in the betrayal of "Anne's" whereabouts. By laughing at Finkel's joke, his audience also implicates itself in the betrayal. To refuse to laugh is to refuse to be implicated in the joke's scenario, a refusal to treat the mediation of Anne Frank's diary—in this case, a theatrical mediation—as anything other than her sacrosanct story, a refusal to grant the performance and the joke immunity from ethical judgment.

Concerns that humor about Anne Frank degrades the value of her remembrance are only part of a larger anxiety about the many responses to her life and work. Some scholars, such as the historian Henry Huttenbach, want to wrest the legacy of Anne Frank from "those who would make an icon of her": Anne "is not a saint; she was no martyr; neither idol nor icon, neither symbol nor superheroine. She was 'just' a child-victim of a merciless genocide aimed at Jews."[4] Yet Anne's iconic stature is precisely what makes her such an easy target of deflationary humor. That humor, in turn, offers rich material for exploring the discontent surrounding her singular stature and the limits of humor's "immunity to ethical judgment."

Oblivious to the Obvious

Widespread awareness of Anne Frank's moral significance has engendered humor predicated on its opposite, namely, obliviousness. Consider, for example, author and monologist David Sedaris's short story "Possession," originally published in the *New Yorker* on April 19, 2004. Sedaris recounts his and his partner's search for an apartment in Paris, during which his partner falls in love with an apartment that they purchase, despite Sedaris's misgivings about the place. The two men then travel to Amsterdam, where they happen upon the Anne Frank House. Sedaris, still obsessed with apartment hunting, responds in kind to this landmark building:

> On our first afternoon we took a walk and came across the Anne Frank House, which was a surprise. I'd had the impression she lived in a dump, but it's actually a very beautiful seventeenth-century building right on the canal. Tree-lined street, close to shopping and public transportation: in terms of location, it was perfect. My months of house hunting had caused me to look at things in a certain way, and on seeing the crowd gathered at the front door, I did not think, *Ticket line*, but, *Open house!*[5]

Sedaris then elaborates on this skewed encounter with the Anne Frank House by one so absorbed in the search for an apartment that the building's powerful historical and moral significance is overlooked; the Annex becomes another prospective residential property. The pursuit of real estate trumps everything—even the Holocaust. Sedaris's caricature of obsessive apartment hunting takes on deliberately disturbing resonances: "The first words that come to mind are not 'I still believe all people are really good at heart' but 'Who do I have to knock off in order to get this apartment?'" The writer assumes, of course, that his audience knows the fate of the Annex's last residents, while coyly suggesting that, in his driven state, he has forgotten this. Undaunted by the sentiments of Anne's most famous words and dismissive of the tourists milling about the Annex, Sedaris is finally brought to reason by a quotation from Primo Levi that appears on one of the walls in the Anne Frank House: "A single Anne Frank moves us more than the countless others who suffered just as she did but whose faces have remained in the shadows. Perhaps it is better that way. If we were capable of taking in all the suffering of all those people, we would not be able to live." To this sobering reminder of the importance of Anne Frank as an icon for a tragedy of unimaginable enormity, Sedaris responds, "He did not specify that we would not be able to live in *her house*, but it was definitely implied, and it effectively squashed any fantasy of ownership." Sedaris then mitigates his callous solipsism by noting how "the added tragedy of Anne Frank is that she almost made it"—that is, she nearly escaped detection in hiding and ended up dying in Bergen-Belsen shortly before it was liberated. In a final comic reversal, as Sedaris looks out a window from the Anne Frank House, wondering how someone could inform on Anne and the other Jews who had hidden in the Annex, he sees across the way "the most beautiful apartment."

Sedaris's comedy of ignorance relies on and ultimately acknowledges the moral power invested in Anne Frank, even as his comic narrative appears to flout her well-known symbolic worth. To overlook what is patently obvious to the other tourists in the Annex—and, it is assumed, to his readers—is to epitomize insensitivity. The story's arch self-mockery recalls a similar disquisition on the Anne Frank House by the actress Whoopi Goldberg. In her eponymous one-woman show, per-

Eric Cartman hides his "Kitty" in the attic, *South Park,* 2008.

formed on Broadway in 1985, Goldberg offered a monologue by Fontaine, a highly educated junkie, who visits the Anne Frank House in what at first appears to be an addict's haze of obtuse irreverence and winds up offering an earnest, incisive meditation on the ordeals of a life in hiding and the cruelty of crushing an innocent child's spirit. In both of these comic narratives, their tellers ultimately wake up to the moral force that Anne Frank represents.

Fear that Anne Frank's moral significance might be lost to obliviousness also informs "Major Boobage," a 2008 episode of *South Park* (Comedy Central, 1997–present). *South Park,* an animated television comedy series, is renowned for fearless provocation and bad taste in its biting social satire.[6] Although the episode exploits Anne Frank as grist for its comic mills, it does so obliquely and less offensively than is usually the case with sensitive topics on *South Park.*[7]

In "Major Boobage" the residents of South Park, Colorado, discover that some of their children are getting high on cat urine. The town declares cats illegal, and all cats are confiscated. While most residents accept the ban as a necessary step to prevent abuse, some actively oppose the order. Among them is the usually heartless boy Eric Cartman, who hides his cat in the attic of his house. He tells the cat, "Kitty, you have to live in the attic for now. Write a diary." Allusions to Anne Frank and to the Holocaust continue throughout the episode. After his cat begins meowing, Cartman tells it to be quiet or else he'll get caught, and a clarinet is heard playing a sad, lilting, "Jewish" tune. Later, as Cartman debates whether or not to take in other homeless cats, who look at him with pitiful, wide eyes, the same music plays in the background.

For regular viewers of *South Park*, portraying the heartless Cartman as the savior of cats, who stand in for Jews, has a comic irony of its own. Usually selfish and insensitive, Cartman frequently taunts his friend Kyle with anti-Semitic remarks. In other *South Park* episodes, Cartman dresses up as Hitler on Halloween and appears in a Nazi uniform while presiding over a meeting of the Mel Gibson fan club.[8] In addition to a ready familiarity with the history of Anne Frank and the Holocaust, the "Major Boobage" episode assumes a faithful audience that knows Cartman's "history." Both literacies are key to the episode's comic conclusion.

In keeping with *South Park*'s formula, "Major Boobage" ends with the boys discussing the lesson learned from the events that have transpired, usually skewing the episode's morals for comic effect. Cartman says he has learned that "you cannot deprive a living being of its freedom," a straightforward explanation of the episode's lesson. But upon hearing this, Kyle asks Cartman whether he notices a similarity between the recent occurrences in South Park and anything else in history. Oblivious, Cartman replies, "Hmm—nope, I have no idea what you're talking about, Kyle," delivering the episode's ultimate punch line. The larger historical lesson has presumably not been lost on anyone—except, of course, on Cartman, obtusely unaware that he has been playing a simulation of the Holocaust, in which he is the valiant rescuer of stand-ins for Jews.[9] The seasoned audience member knows that the joke is not on Anne Frank, but on Cartman.

Ignorance of the symbolic value of Anne Frank's life and work was employed to a more pointed comic end on a broadcast of *Robot Chicken*, a popular late-night animation series aired on the Cartoon Network, during the series' debut season in 2005. In one brief sequence, called

An animated Hilary
Duff as Anne Frank in
a 2005 mock film trailer
on *Robot Chicken.*

"Toy Meets Girl," *Robot Chicken* aired a minute-long parody of a movie trailer for a faux dramatic adaptation of *The Diary of Anne Frank* that spoofs the genre of teen films and television shows.[10] The promo opens with established representations of what is assumed to be a familiar story: a snow-covered model of houses along a canal in Amsterdam appears as a voiceover intones, "The amazing true story that touched the hearts of generations is now a motion picture you'll never forget." A hand is shown writing in an open book, "Dear Diary, This is my chronicle of a most unfortunate time," as this text is read aloud by an unseen young woman.

Then the faux promo shifts from faithfully replicating shopworn tropes of dramatizing Anne Frank's story to spoof by introducing incongruous elements. Electronic music is heard on the soundtrack, as the names of the popular teen stars Hilary Duff and Chad Michael Murray appear on the screen. "My name is Anne," the voiceover announces, "Anne Frank—awesome." A blond Barbie doll is shown, sitting at a writing desk, then a figure representing Peter van Pels appears, reading from a Torah scroll, accompanied by a parody of Duff's pop song "Come Clean":

> Let the Nazis come and take my friends,
> I'm going to pray all day, till the Sabbath ends.
> I wanna to punch that Hitler with a [unintelligible].
> Put it all down in my diary—
> Anne Frank's diary.

With this, Anne Frank's story morphs into a teen action film. Dressed in a variety of trendy outfits, Anne is shown running through the streets of Amsterdam, intercut with images of Nazi soldiers marching and Jews cowering. After her father shouts, "The Nazis are here!" Anne thwarts their attacks with slapstick stunts reminiscent of the 1990 comedy *Home Alone*. "You're really something, Anne Frank," says Peter, holding her around the waist as they stand on a canal bridge. Giggling, she responds, "I'm just me!" The piece closes with a mock version of the animated ending of the *Hilary Duff Show*, with the cartoon Hilary saying, "Nazis are so uncool."

What might at first appear to be a comic assault on Anne Frank's life and work is, rather, an attack on works of contemporary mass media targeting a teenage demographic. The moral integrity of Anne Frank is a foil for vacuous American teen culture, which is characterized as ignorant, self-involved, and superficial, obsessed with fashionable trends in clothing and music, and incapable of imagining history without recourse to the clichés of popular film genres. The comedy and its incisive cultural critique rely on an audience fluent in the popular culture that is under attack as well as sufficiently aware of Anne's life and work to recognize the disparity between this icon of morality and their own frivolity. So sanctified is Anne Frank that the actual teenager—who was also mad about boys, movies, and clothes—vanishes, and all that remains is the girl who pondered the epochal events taking place around her. Indeed, the parody relies on the assumption that Anne represents whatever Hilary Duff (or her fans) do not.

Imagining Hiding

Familiarity with the intimate details of Anne Frank's diary prompts readers to imagine themselves in her extraordinary situation. This projection can take a comic turn away from high-minded empathy and toward bathetic anxieties. The daunting circumstances of Anne's life in hiding have attracted the most attention from humorists. Comedian Judy Gold, for example, imagines her family—in particular, her overbearing mother—being forced to hide in the Annex:

A few years ago I had the opportunity to visit the Anne Frank House in Amsterdam. When I got there I was very emotional because I kept imagining my family in that situation. These people had to keep quiet and make no noise the entire day for fear of being caught by the Nazis, which would have been the demise of my entire family, because there's no way my mother would have kept her mouth shut for an entire afternoon.

"Judith, I asked you to wash that dish ten minutes ago."

"Ma, shut up, we're gonna get caught."

"That's right, we're gonna get caught and we're all gonna die, because you couldn't wash a goddamn dish!"[11]

Here, as in Finkel's joke about the bad actress, the comic routine rests on the incommensurability of crime (not washing dishes) and punishment (getting caught and dying), but the situations are framed differently. In Finkel's joke, the audience hastens the plot by "betraying" Anne's hiding place, whereas Judith imagines that, were her own family in hiding, her mother's voluble behavior would "betray" them.

The challenge of keeping quiet—and the fear that the slightest sound will give away the hiding place—inspires an episode of the animated series *Family Guy* (Fox, 1998–present), aired in 2000, in which Peter, the solipsistic head of the family, describes how his voracious appetite has caused him trouble in the past. In a flashback, rendered in black and white, Peter has joined Anne Frank (who is shown clutching her diary) and the other Jews hiding in the Annex. As they remain silent, because the Nazis are downstairs searching for them, a loud crunching noise is heard—it is Peter, blithely eating potato chips—the sound of unbridled appetite magnified by the disciplined silence of everyone else.[12]

A 2009 posting on the website historicaltweets.com brings the anxiety of hiding up to the present. "The Tweets of Anne Frank," a parody of the diary in the form of a 140-character "status update" that subscribers to Twitter send and receive, reads: "forgot to put the iPhone on vibrate, tense few minutes, there."[13] In all three cases, ordinary sounds—loud reprimands, potato chips crunching, cell phone ringing—could be fatal in the extraordinary situation of hiding. The people responsible for the sounds in these imagined scenarios are either unable to control their compulsions or are careless, and those are the ultimate dangers in the situation that readers of Anne's diary may find themselves imagining with no little anxiety.

A mock news report on the media parody website *The Onion* addresses a different anxiety prompted by Anne's diary—namely, the idea that something so private should have become so public:

> Shocked to learn that the diary containing her most intimate thoughts and feelings has been read by millions of people worldwide, the ghost of Anne Frank held a press conference Monday to tell the world to "stop reading my diary, and put it back where you found it right this second." "I am so embarrassed," Frank said. "I cannot believe that for the last 50 years, millions of people I don't even know have been reading my diary, reading about my first kiss, my huge crush on the boy upstairs, my first period—everything." "It's bad enough to have your sister sneak into your room and read your diary. But to have it bought by Doubleday and published in 33 languages? That's just mortifying," Frank said.[14]

This parody plays on two widely shared experiences—reading Anne's diary and keeping a diary of one's own—and the idea that a diary is for one's own eyes only. The parody places readers of Anne's diary in the uncomfortable position of violating her privacy, overlooking the fact that Anne had literary aspirations and rewrote her diary during her final months in hiding in the hope that it might one day be published. Rather, like the jokes about the inability to keep quiet while living in hiding, this humor begins with the widely familiar circumstances of Anne's life and work but ultimately redounds to the joke's audience and its own anxieties.

Taking Liberties with Anne

Unlike the faux-juvenile rancor that shapes the humor of *South Park* and *Robot Chicken*, or the adult chafing at the ordeal of civility that informs Judy Gold's routine and *Family Guy*, the idiom of Ilya Sapiroe's drag comedy *The Diary of Anne Frankenstein*, performed in an Off-Off-Broadway theater in 2009, is camp, marked not only by its use of drag but also by its knowing delight in the ironies of misalliances and inversions. Instead of indirectly validating Anne Frank's iconic value, as do the works discussed above, Sapiroe's script plays subversively with the familiarity of Anne and her work, starting with the work's title. *The Diary of Anne Frankenstein* is but one of many subversive plays on her name: Anne Frank on Crank and The Diarrhea of Anne Frank are rock bands; "Anne

Lavinia Co-op as the Diary in Ilya Sapiroe's *The Diary of Anne Frankenstein*, New York, 2009. *Photographer: Alex Kotlik* © *Alex Kotlik/www.AlexKotlikPhotography.com*

Frankly" and "The Frank Diary of Anne" are online videos.[15] The issue here is not ignorance of Anne Frank's moral value, but rather Anne's overexposure.

The Diary of Anne Frankenstein relies on the humor of mismatch and inversion to challenge Anne Frank as an emblem of goodness. This provocative, if oblique, juxtaposition of make-believe horror with the actual horrors of the Holocaust is already signaled in the title's pun, which conflates Mary Shelley's monster with Anne's life and work. Sapiroe's play burlesques vintage Hollywood horror films, using the disruptive force of drag. It is similar in approach to the 1975 cult film *Rocky Horror Picture Show,* but adds to the mix not only World War II espionage melodrama but also Anne Frank's story. In this mash-up of subjects, genres, and sensibilities, Anne herself becomes a hybrid with yet another reason to hide: as a hermaphrodite, the result of a Nazi doctor's botched medical experiment (reminiscent of the 1998 musical *Hedwig and the Angry Inch*), she is forced into an attic, where her only steady companion is her diary. In what is perhaps an even more disruptive intervention in Anne Frank's iconic stature, the diary becomes a "living book," portrayed by Lavinia Co-op, who incites Anne to commit murder. Instead of being a solace, in this inverted world Anne's diary is a menace. Rather than exploiting anxiety about the ignorance of Anne Frank's moral value, *The Diary of Anne Frankenstein* expresses a different anxiety—that, having become too well known, this icon may have lost its power.

Icon War

As a limit-case phenomenon, Anne Frank humor can serve as a social or cultural proving ground, as do other examples of humor considered offensive, in which a joke is told with the expectation that some people will find it amusing and others will regard it as unacceptable. People on either side of the divide form cultural subgroups, articulated by those who laugh in response to the joke vs. those who respond with "unlaughter"—that is, refusing to laugh when prompted to do so. The folklorist Moira Smith describes "unlaughter" as a foil "used deliberately by both joke instigators and members of joke audiences to highlight the supposed differences between them and so heighten exclusionary social boundaries."[16]

It is in such a deliberately contentious comic context that Anne Frank was pitted against the Prophet Mohammed in an icon war, waged in offensive cartoons. The war began on September 30, 2005, in the Danish newspaper *Jyllands-Posten*, with the publication of cartoons depicting the Prophet Mohammed. Outraged by graphic depictions of Mohammed offensive to Islam, the Iranian newspaper *Hamshahri* announced a competition for the best Holocaust cartoon, a subject of parallel sanctity in the West.[17] The Arab European League, an Islamist, Pan-Arab civil rights organization based in Brussels, also retaliated with cartoons deprecating the Holocaust, which they published on their website in 2006. One of them depicts a postcoital scene of Anne Frank in bed with Adolf Hitler, in which he says, "Write this one in your diary, Anne."

Whereas *Jyllands-Posten* defended their publication of the Mohammed cartoons by citing the Western principle of free speech, including

One of several cartoons assailing the Holocaust posted online in 2006 by the
Arab European League. These cartoons were posted in response to cartoons
depicting Mohammed, which had been published by a Danish newspaper earlier
that year and defended by the paper on the grounds of freedom of expression.
This graphic attack on the Holocaust—and on Anne, one of its most cherished
icons—was intended to be highly affronting as a way of demonstrating
how deeply offensive were the Danish cartoons to Muslims and to point
up a double standard in the West with regard to freedom of expression.

speech that some might find offensive, Muslim critics pointed to laws
in European countries banning speech that denies the Holocaust or
champions Nazism as evidence that the West has, in fact, limits on free
speech according to its own criteria of offensiveness. Dyab Abou Jahjah,
the Arab European League's founder, explained, "Europe has its sacred
cows, even if they're not religious sacred cows."[18]

Sacred cows invite desecration (or, as Abby Hoffman once quipped, they "make the tastiest hamburger"). Westerners have also questioned the sanctions surrounding Holocaust remembrance, including the fascination that Nazism holds for many in the West, even as they repudiate its ideology.[19] Sometimes this critique is realized using the idioms of humor. Israeli artist Nir Avigad confronts the taboo surrounding Hitler as an icon in *The Daily Hitler*, a series of 150 cartoons exhibited at Jerusalem's Bezalel Academy of Arts and Design in 2008.[20] About the use of Hitler in his cartoons, he says: "We are prohibited from investigating it, prohibited from developing, prohibited from touching, prohibited from laughing." Avigad's cartoons mock Hitler's signature mustache or merge his features with dozens of common memes, products, or situations and with an array of cultural icons, including Looney Tunes cartoons, Absolut Vodka, Gene Simmons, Theodor Herzl—and Anne Frank.[21] Though playful and irreverent, these images offer a deadly serious interrogation of iconicity. "Anne Hitler," a spare and geometric portrait of Anne Frank with a Hitler moustache, is disconcerting and ambiguous. Whereas the Arab European League cartoon juxtaposes Anne and Hitler in relation to acts of aggression, both past and present, Avigad merges the two icons as part of a series that reduces Hitler's symbolic power through repeated comic assaults. These images also question the symbolic investments made in the other icons incorporated into this art project, including Anne Frank.

* * *

Jokes about Anne Frank fall within the genre of dark humor, which includes gallows humor and what the folklorist Willie Smyth terms the "humor of disaster."[22] Such jokes appeared even during the Holocaust itself and continue to appear in the wake of such catastrophes as the explosion of the Challenger space shuttle in 1986 and destruction of the World Trade Center in 2001. However, unlike humor that arises during or just after a tragedy, jokes about Anne Frank have appeared decades after her murder. They do not respond to her tragedy, or to the Holocaust itself, but rather to the popularization of Anne Frank through the publication of her diary, performance of her life story on stage and screen, and opening of the Anne Frank House. A generation raised on official presentations of Anne's story and the reverential way in which one is supposed to respond to it pushes back with irreverence. Apparently "immune to ethical judgment," art and humor find their moral center in an irreverence that reenergizes fatigued icons for a new generation.

Epilogue: A Life of Its Own—
The Anne Frank Tree

Barbara Kirshenblatt-Gimblett

If not for Anne Frank's diary, the chestnut tree that stood behind 263 Prinsengracht in Amsterdam would have lived and died unnoticed during the almost 180 years of its life. But once news spread that this tree was ailing, it acquired a life of its own—moreover, a life that seems destined to continue in perpetuity. Alive or dead, the Anne Frank Tree, as it has come to be known, has become the most protean of metaphors. Many people have found meaning and solace in the tree in ways they never seem to have found in the diary, although the diary is always cited as the source text for the tree's singular significance. The tree joined the other two material icons of Anne Frank's story, the original diary notebook and the building at 263 Prinsengracht, well after their stature was secured and is inherently dependent on them for its significance. However, the tree's ontological status as a living organism endows it with an immortality of a different order. And what truly gives the tree its immortality—what makes it more than just another tree—are the creative responses it has generated within a wide public.

The Tree in the Diary

The enduring location of the tree that once stood outside the Annex is in the pages of Anne's diary.[1] A passage from the diary is usually cited as a kind of epigraph—and then epitaph—for the tree, in the form of a very short excerpt, stripped of its context. For example, this reference in the diary entry of May 13, 1944: "Our chestnut tree is in full bloom. It's covered with leaves and is even more beautiful than last year."[2] Considering the importance now accorded the tree, it might come as a surprise that Anne mentions the tree only three times in the diary and only in the last few months in hiding. A closer look at these passages reveals that the tree is but one element in Anne's newfound interest in nature, the others being sky, sun, moon, stars, dew, raindrops, and birds. Minor as that might seem, Otto Frank was surprised, on reading the diary for the first time, at Anne's new interest in nature. During a speech in 1968, he said:

> How could I have known how much it meant to Anne to see a patch of blue sky, to observe the seagulls as they flew, and how important the chestnut tree was for her, when I think that she never showed any interest in nature. Still, she longed for it when she felt like a bird in a cage. Only the thought of the freedom of nature gave her comfort. But she kept all those feelings to herself.[3]

Even Anne was surprised by her newfound interest in nature, writing on June 13, 1944, that, while before going into hiding nature held little interest for her, "That's changed since I've been here. . . . It's not just imagination on my part when I say that to look up at the sky, the clouds, the moon and the stars makes me calm and patient. . . . Mother Nature makes me small and prepared to face every blow bravely!"[4]

Consider now the other two passages in the diary where Anne mentions the tree:

> I look up at the blue sky, the bare chestnut tree, on whose branches the little raindrops shine, and at the seagulls and other birds gliding on the wind and looking like silver. . . . "As long as this exists," I thought, "and I may live to see it, this sunshine, the cloudless skies, while this lasts, I cannot be unhappy." (February 23, 1944)[5]

> We are having a superb spring after our long, lingering winter. April is really glorious, not too hot and not too cold, with little showers now and then. Our chestnut tree is already quite greenish and you can even see little blooms here and there. (April 18, 1944)[6]

Anne interprets her immediate experience of nature, seen from captivity, as a sign that God ordained the world to be beautiful and people happy. In her diary entry of July 15, 1944, she writes that sunshine and cloudless skies, a source of comfort in dark times, will ultimately triumph over the "approaching thunder." This entry includes the lines for which Anne is most famous. Reflecting on the many reasons to despair, she concludes: "[I]n spite of everything I still believe that people are really good at heart" (July 15, 1944).[7] God's will that the world be beautiful and people happy will prevail over the urge in people "to kill, to murder and rage and until all mankind, without exception, undergoes a great change, wars will be waged, and everything that has been built up, cultivated and grown, will be cut down and disfigured, to begin all over again after that!" (May 3, 1944).[8] The way that Anne introduces human agency into the natural world, both positive (cultivation) and negative (destruction), provides a starting point for the redemptive metaphor that the chestnut tree will become.

An even closer look at different versions of the passage of February 23, 1944, reveals that Anne was not alone when looking out the window in the original entry, but in subsequent redactions of her diary her romantic companion, Peter, is made to disappear altogether or to recede. In the first version of the diary, Peter is with Anne in the attic: "[W]hen I sat down on my favorite spot on the floor, he joined me. Both of us looked at the glorious blue of the sky, the bare chestnut tree on whose branches little raindrops shone. . . ."[9] In Anne's redacted version, there is no mention of Peter at first: "I look up at the sky" is a solitary activity.[10] In the first published version of the diary, Peter is mentioned as being in the attic, and the text says, "I look up," a sort of a compromise between the two versions: "From my favorite spot on the floor I look up at the blue sky and the bare chestnut tree. . . . When I looked outside right into the depth of nature and God, then I was happy, really happy."[11] The redacted version purifies the moment of looking at the tree of romance, leaving Anne alone with nature, as do virtually all subsequent quotations from the diary that are brought forward in defense—and in memory—of the chestnut tree.

Why the Chestnut Tree?

Of everything that Anne mentions—sky, sun, moon, stars, birds, dew—only the tree is singular and enduring. Though it may change with the seasons, the tree remains fixed in place. Everything else is pervasive, fleeting, out of reach, impossible to grasp. But the tree is tangible—indeed, so tangible at an estimated weight of thirty tons that it subsequently posed a risk to life and limb should it topple over. Moreover, the tree is tangible in ways that lend it to a whole range of metaphors and memorial practices, whether rooted in the tree's living progeny or in its dead remains.

The tree has become one of three material anchors for Anne's story, but with a critical difference from the original diary notebook and the Annex: the tree can reproduce itself and is doing so all over the world as both living substance and protean metaphor. Also, both the diary and the Anne Frank House are densely coded cultural works, in contrast with the tree, which is a "found object" of the natural world, onto which Anne projected her feelings, hopes, and fears—as do all those who rally round the tree. Indeed, the Anne Frank Tree was codified by the local citizens who came to its defense—it was never the "Anne Frank Tree" in the diary—and who find in their mission to keep the tree alive, even after its death, a more active and redemptive way to express their connection to Anne than reading the diary or visiting the Anne Frank House. Together with various mass media, the tree's champions have had a free hand to determine what it means, unfettered from the tight control exerted over the diary by the Anne Frank-Fonds and over 263 Prinsengracht by the Anne Frank Stichting. The tree "belongs" to the public in a way that the diary and house never can, notwithstanding the many liberties taken with both, as explored in this volume.

The Ailing Tree

It was only when the chestnut tree became vulnerable that it became much more than the subject of a diary entry and much more than a plant. The first threat to the tree came in 1989, when the Anne Frank Stichting proposed to remove a large part of its root system to make way for an extension of its buildings. The root system was spared, thanks to local residents who opposed any action that would hurt the tree. The second threat to the tree came in 1993, when an oil spill threatened the tree's well-being. Custody for its care was placed in the hands of the Amsterdam City Center Borough. The third threat came in 2005, this time as fungus and minor moths took their toll. When the authorities failed to respond to requests to reverse the disease, local citizens took matters into their own hands and waged a garlic offensive: they planted "two thousand garlic cloves around the foot of the chestnut tree."[12] Shortly after the garlic action, Pius Floris, the company employed by the borough to care for the tree, reduced the tree's crown to prevent it from falling over in a windstorm. By 2006, the tree was on a deathwatch: not only were tree doctors regularly checking its vital signs, but also the world could keep vigil every minute of the day and night, via a live webcam, on the Anne Frank House website.

Steady reporting on the dying tree essentially treated it as a person fighting for its life, first in a long battle with disease and then on death row, awaiting execution. The announcement in November 2006 that the tree was to be cut down galvanized local residents, working together with the Dutch Tree Foundation, to oppose the decision of the borough. By December 2007, they had formed the Support Anne Frank Tree Foundation, whose mission was "to prevent the tree from being prematurely and needlessly cut" and "to guarantee proper care for the preserved tree until his [sic] natural death."[13] To do otherwise would be murder, whether euthanasia or execution, of the proxy for Anne herself. The tree became a moral force in its own right (it had given Anne solace and hope) and its struggle to survive a *cause célèbre* for those who would do for the tree what they could not do for Anne.

Was the tree a symbol of hope for "the girl who embodied courage in the face of barbarism" or a "diseased horse chestnut" that should be put "out of its misery with an axe and chainsaw"?[14] Scientists argued that the tree had lived a very long life, its time had come, it could not be saved, it was rotten to its core, and it posed a grave risk to life, limb, and property should it topple. "It's not that we want to kill it. It's already dying," commented Henk Werner, a tree expert who had closely followed its deterioration.[15]

The emotional force of the tree's symbolism finally won out over unsentimental scientific reasoning. The matter was taken to court. In November 2007 the judge issued "a stay of execution" at the eleventh hour, thereby stopping the chainsaws, lumberjacks, and tower cranes from felling the tree at dawn, and instructed the warring factions to find a compromise. In the end, the tree was propped up with a metal frame and monitored periodically by international and Dutch experts. The tree was expected to live another five to ten years and to die a natural death but not topple, thereby posing a serious risk to thousands of tourists and to the Anne Frank House itself. Before this decision was made, steps had been taken to allow the tree to live on by reproducing itself naturally through saplings taken from its trunk or sprouted from its chestnuts. Even earlier, in 2006, the Anne Frank House website had both installed a webcam, so the world could see the tree while it was still alive, and launched its "virtual chestnut tree." Inviting visitors to the site to post their names, locations, and brief messages on images of chestnut leaves, the website explained: "Now, the more than 150 year old tree is diseased, but online it will live on. Leave your leaf in the virtual chestnut tree, forward it and keep Anne Frank's ideals alive."[16]

A Hero in Its Own Story

The fateful day arrived. On August 23, 2010, the tree crashed to the ground, the victim of a violent storm. "This was a terrible and unexpected event," reported the Support Anne Frank Tree Foundation.[17] Eulogies followed, along with forensic investigations into the failure of the tree's support frame. Who was responsible for the collapse of the metal support structure, and who should pay for removing all the debris, repairing property damage, and storing the remains? What was to be done with the estimated thirty tons of wood? Complex legal questions arose, including over the tree's ownership. The Anne Frank Tree, which seems to belong to the world, is actually private property: it stood not on the grounds of the Anne Frank House but in a neighbor's garden.

The dead tree continues to be at the center of very live disputes. Raising the stakes in the feud's latest volley are unfortunate metaphors comparing the current conflict over the tree to the Holocaust itself. A board member of the Support Anne Frank Tree Foundation accused the man contracted to build the metal support structure of knowing that its collapse was his own fault and rushing to clear away the evidence. According to the *New York Times*, the dispute intensified when the contractor accused the board member of making comparisons between those who "killed" the tree and those who killed the Jews, specifically mentioning Auschwitz. The board member apparently sent a fax that accused the contractor of being "like many who, in the footsteps of the destruction

Inspecting the chestnut tree behind the Anne Frank House, Amsterdam, shortly after the tree collapsed during a storm on August, 23, 2010. *United Photos. Photographer: Robin von Lonkhujsen*

of millions of Jews, took their possessions," and likened the letter from the contractor's lawyer "to Nazi commands."[18] The contractor has filed a libel suit.

With the fusing of two narratives—those who "killed" the tree and the Nazi murderers of Jews—the tree became the star in the story of its rescue not only in life, but also on stage and screen. The documentary film *Rescuing the Anne Frank Tree*—which features the "exciting building of the safety construction, hoisting construction vehicles and machines over the rooftops of the surrounding buildings," and interviews with those behind the effort—is another volley in the current court battle over who is responsible for the collapse of the metal support. The premiere of *Annes Baum,* a play by Olga Eigenbrood with Käthe Sluijter, was also the subject of a documentary film, while Anneloes Groet's film, *Annes Boom,* also tells the story of "the dramatic effort to save the Chestnut."[19] Noting that Anne would be in her eighties today, one blogger asked: "What would Anne do?" and concluded that the "Treegate" soap opera would appall her.[20]

Front-Page Story

The day the tree fell over, reporters rushed to the scene. Pragmatists treated the tree's demise as the end of the story. Arnold Heertje, a member of the Support Anne Frank Tree Foundation, expressed resignation: "You have to bow your head to the facts. The tree has fallen and will be cut into pieces and disappear." As he explained, "The intention was not to keep this tree alive forever. It has lived for 150 years and now it's over and we're not going to extend it."[21] Others concurred: "The tree is gone, time to move on," commented a reader on the news.[22] But neither the media nor the public moved on. In response to the question of "how and why a tree falling down can become such front-page news," Hans Westra, executive director of the Anne Frank House, explained to the reporter that "[i]t's a tree with a long history," most importantly in relation to Anne Frank: "All her longing for freedom came to be tied up with that tree." This statement prompted the reporter to invite further reflection: "Do we need tangible aids to help us comprehend and remember the Holocaust? When Anne Frank's chestnut tree falls, as has just happened, or, even more to the point, as the survivors pass away, is it then harder for new generations to connect with and understand the Holocaust?" To these questions, Westra responded, "We are doing everything we can to keep this story alive."[23] The tree—alive, dead, and reborn—has become a powerful tool in the Anne Frank Stichting's repertoire for keeping her story, and the story of the Holocaust, alive.

Online readers of the press provided their own explanations for why the tree should be a front-page story. The tree, "an incredible piece of living history," joins the diary: "Long after her life was over, Anne's story and her tree remain symbols of her struggle, and her continuing belief in the good of mankind." Miraculously, "when arborists inspected the fallen tree, they discovered something amazing: In a poignant reflection of Anne's own story, a small shoot was growing from the tree's splintered trunk, continuing life in the face of destruction."[24] Earlier, a fallen branch occasioned a "tree-mendous" news story: "Tree surgeons were stunned when they found the image of a tiny tree imprinted" on the cross section of the fallen branch, the result of rot.[25]

Readers who were incredulous that anyone could insist "it's just a tree" struggled to express just why the tree meant so much to them. For Grumpella Jeanne, the tree trumped the diary: "Sic transit, alas. One more reminder gone . . . [F]or those who are squawking about a TREE making the news, this news story drove home to me the poignancy of Anne's story like her diary never did."[26] For Amazed-746808, "it is like another small piece of Anne Frank is gone, as well. . . . I wish I had been able to see this tree. To gaze upon this tree that Anne Frank also gazed upon."[27] A young reader, beanicus, worried that the loss of the tree was a sign of things to come: "It may only be a tree, but everyday I'm seeing and reading about more and more historic items, places and people passing away, destroyed, damaged, etc. It makes me wonder if it will all be gone by the time I become an adult."[28] In the absence of the most tangible Anne—or her body or grave—the tree is the next best thing.

An Answer to Holocaust Denial

Reasoning recursively, Crafty Archivist admonished the naysayers: the tree "might not be Anne Frank's grave but that tree was much more than just a tree. . . . [W]e need tangible things like that to stand in the face of those who would say that the Holocaust didn't happen. That tree was viewed by someone who was a victim of the [H]olocaust. She mentions it in a diary that talks about her experiences during the Holocaust. Ergo, the [H]olocaust existed. Find some sensitivity please!"[29]

But as the tree fell, Holocaust denial also rose. Responding to a 2007 report in *Haaretz* that the tree would not be axed, Jonathan S commented, "In Amsterdam people are preoccupied with the chestnut tree of Anne Frank, in the town of Pretzien near Magdeburg in central Germany, her diary was burnt publicly and people shouted that it was full of lies and deception. The mayor who attended together with about 100 righteous citizens remained silent. One year after the event, the perpetrators are still free and a majority of citizens favours to put things to rest. These are like two different worlds!"[30] Roxana from Iran responded: "A holy tree, perhaps as holy as the wailing wall.... I suggest to make papers from the wood of this tree, and keep the papers for another false herion [sic] like Anne, to write her diary."[31] The intense media coverage of the felled tree provoked anti-Semitic reactions: Lavard commented, "Soon the Jews will sell the splinters from the Anne Frank Holocaust tree."[32]

Remains

In fact, upon its collapse, opportunists exploited the occasion to sell fragments of the tree, its chestnuts, and saplings sprouted from them through online auctions (marktplaats.nl and eBay), with bids rising as high as $8,000. By 2011, the tree had joined the list of "10 Most Bizarre Celebrity Items Ever Sold on eBay."[33] The owner of the tree decided to donate its remains "to Jewish museums in Berlin, New York, Tel Aviv and Amsterdam. The Anne Frank House will be given a section of the trunk, which will be displayed in the museum in the future."[34] Museums, however, have been turning down the offer. The Support Anne Frank Tree Foundation, which opposed the sale of any part of the tree, considered the possibility of having someone create a work of art or souvenir from the wood.[35] The wood remains in storage awaiting a final decision on its disposition.

While institutions demur, the public's imagination is running wild with ideas for what might be done with it. The very idea of shredding the wood lent urgency to the public search for alternatives. Several online readers commenting on the news of the tree's demise also noted the disturbing irony of the remains ending up as firewood. At the very least, people suggested, parts of the tree could be donated to museums or parts (or things made with the parts) auctioned to raise money for Holocaust awareness. There was enthusiasm for Steve from Texas's proposal: "Take and preserve a cross section of [the tree] and use the annual rings in the cross section as a timeline. Highlight the annual rings that correspond to the time that Anne lived and wrote her diary," and display hundreds of such rings around the world.[36] Proposals to carve a bust or statue of Anne materialized metaphors that had already merged Anne and the tree, while the idea of making copies of the diary out of the tree—using the wood to make paper for a special edition of the diary, or making wood covers for the diary—effectively materialized the metaphor that identified the diary with the tree. The tree could even become an instrument for writing a diary: "What better way to memorialize Anne's writings than to make pens out of the wood from the tree she saw?"[37] Others focused on the place where the tree once stood: carve a wooden bench from the dead wood, as a kind of monument, or replace the dead tree with a metal sculpture of the tree. Most recently, a Tennessee sculptor has started to make a documentary about a project to create a sculpture from the tree because, he asserts, the tree's important symbolism lives on in the wood. He is especially interested in the limbs, "because that's what Anne Frank saw."[38]

The Progeny

While nothing has yet been done with the dead wood, the tree's progeny are literally taking root across the globe and adapting to local ecologies both natural and cultural. Saplings have been designated for Yad Vashem in Jerusalem and the White House in Washington, D.C., among other sites selected for their special connection to Anne Frank, Holocaust memorialization, tolerance education, or the defense of human rights. In Corsica, where the local population hid Jews from the Germans, a seedling, accompanied by a certificate of authenticity, is being planted in a mountain forest of protected chestnut trees that are 500–600 years old.[39]

These tree-planting projects follow on considerable precedent. For more than half a century it sufficed simply to plant a tree, whether an individual tree or an entire grove, in memory of Anne Frank and all that she represents. Memorial groves and parks in Anne Frank's name can now be found in the United Kingdom, the United States, Israel, France, and Argentina, among other places. This practice is in keeping with a tradition of planting trees in memory or commemoration of someone or something; the creation of Arbor Day in the nineteenth century encouraged the practice, as did campaigns to plant trees in Israel to "make the desert bloom." But once the Anne Frank Tree was ailing, and especially after it fell over, it was no longer enough to plant a tree—any tree, but presumably one appropriate to the local soil and climate—in

Anne Frank's memory. Now, each Anne Frank Tree, no matter what its provenance, was a symbolic "replacement" for the singular one that had given her hope while in hiding.

The transformation of a somewhat generic practice for commemorating Anne Frank into one that memorialized the Anne Frank Tree itself has implications for what both Anne Frank and the Anne Frank Tree have come to represent. This can be seen in the evolution of a tree-planting project introduced by the Anne Frank Trust UK in 1998; Buddy Elias, a first cousin of Anne and the only one of her blood relatives still alive, attended the first planting. After the chestnut tree behind 263 Prinsengracht fell, the Trust updated its Anne Frank Tree Planting Pack, created in 2009 to commemorate her eightieth birthday. The original pack contained precise instructions for an appropriate dedication ceremony, complete with invitation, plaque, Anne Frank Tree Poem, readings from Anne's diary, lessons to be learned from it, and the Anne Frank Declaration: the planting of an Anne Frank Tree was to memorialize "all children killed through wars and persecution."[40] The next pack added the following appeal: "This programme has been running since 1998, but has become more pertinent because of the sad news that on 23 August 2010 strong winds caused the iconic chestnut tree behind Anne Frank's hiding place in Amsterdam to topple. We are therefore asking you to keep Anne's hopes and dreams alive by planting a tree to symbolically replace this special tree that has now been lost to the world."[41] By this time, the pack reported, more than five hundred places had answered the call and planted a tree. In a word, the planting of "replacement trees" addressed a memorialization crisis precipitated by the loss of an irreducibly material piece of the past.

The arrival of saplings from the Anne Frank Tree raised the symbolic stakes and offered the most protean—and literal—of metaphors in the Anne Frank Tree's symbolic repertoire. Dead as matter, the tree was never so alive with meaning. A cascade of metaphors took root, so to speak, in the tree's reproductive powers. Unlike the dead tree, the saplings are not inert matter that will deteriorate over time but embody eternally renewable vitality. And unlike the diary, the saplings have the ability to reproduce "naturally," rather than mechanically. In this spirit, the Anne Frank Tree has prompted a plethora of vitalist metaphors.

"The tree is ill and failing but its descendents [sic] will live on," reported *Offbeat Travel.*[42] Thanks to its saplings, the tree is "reborn," forms a "living connection" with Anne, offers a "living reminder" of the Holocaust, marks "a life lost, but memories that live on," and keeps "hope alive" today as the tree did for Anne then.

The tree had done what Anne could not: it had defeated death itself. "Reborn as a sapling" and living on "through its young offspring," the tree's immortality offered consolation to those who mourned its death as well as inspiration for new memorial practices and meanings.[43] "With every ending comes a new beginning," declared Sonoma State University in a press release announcing the arrival of the eighteen-inch sapling to be planted in the school's Holocaust and Genocide Memorial Grove. (The sapling must remain in quarantine for three years because of a disease attacking horse chestnuts in Europe.) Thanks to such saplings, the press release could declare that "Hope Springs Eternal for the Anne Frank Tree" and, by extension, for Anne Frank herself.[44]

Anne herself had created the scenario for these generative metaphors when she wrote on February 23, 1944, that, as long as the natural world she glimpsed from the Annex attic window continued to exist, "I know there will always be comfort for every sorrow, whatever the circumstances."[45] These words have become a mantra: "Hope for a harvest of tolerance from Anne Frank's tree" is how the Anne Frank Center in Manhattan characterizes its efforts to distribute saplings from the Anne Frank Tree—and raise its own public profile.[46] A sapling now in quarantine is earmarked for the 9/11 Memorial Plaza, just steps away from the Anne Frank Center's new home next to the World Trade Center site. The sapling will join a "9/11 survivor tree," a Callery pear, the sole tree to survive the attack on the Twin Towers and itself a "symbol of renewal … just like the city's recovery from the attacks."[47]

Even before the Anne Frank Tree fell, as early as 2005, the Anne Frank House had been sprouting chestnuts removed from the tree and nurturing its seedlings. In 2009, the organization designated 150 saplings for the Amsterdamse Bos woodland park and distributed others to parks and schools named for Anne Frank. Since then, schools have participated in competitions for a sapling. Painsley Catholic College's winning project consisted of "spreading Anne's message across the school community: by hiding sixty-five tags, one for each year since Anne's death, around the premises of their school. The inspirational messages on the tags range from quotes of Anne's diary to the hopes and aspirations of the student who has penned the tag themselves [sic], with the idea that it may inspire and spark the curiosity of those who find it."[48]

The tree—and especially the saplings—set a new standard for the completeness of Anne Frank memorialization, as can be seen in the evolution of the Anne Frank Memorial Park, which was added to the Martyrs' Forest in the hills around Jerusalem in 1960; Otto Frank was accorded the honor of planting the park's first tree. The Jewish National Fund had created the Martyrs' Forest in the Jerusalem hills in 1951 to memorialize victims of the Holocaust, with the idea that six million trees would stand as six million living, green memorials, one for each victim. On Israel's Holocaust Remembrance Day in 2011, a new memorial element was added to the Anne Frank Memorial Park. Long pathways are lined with plaques bearing passages from Anne's diary in Hebrew and English translation, especially those mentioning the tree, and supplemented with quotations from other texts, including one from Primo Levi about Anne, which can also be found on a wall at the Anne Frank House. The paths lead to an installation intended to convey the constriction of Anne's hiding place as she looked out to the freedom of nature; incorporated into an abstracted room and bench made of rusty steel is a stylized version of the famous chestnut tree. Visitors sitting on the bench can see through the outlines of its "leaves" to the surrounding forest.[49] The addition of a sapling from the Anne Frank Tree will transform an otherwise generic memorial tradition—there are many kinds of trees in the Martyrs' Forest and their individuation rests on memorial plaques—into a gesture uniquely and tangibly tied to Anne Frank, while the sculpture materializes the *mise-en-scène* described in the diary.

Boise, Idaho, which suffers from its image as a haven for rightwing extremists, is one of the eleven places in the United States to which the Anne Frank Stichting has given a sapling of the Anne Frank Tree. In 2001, after six years of planning, the Anne Frank Human Rights Memorial in Boise made headlines with the announcement that it was being built on the site of the former compound of the white supremacist group

The Anne Frank Memorial, designed by Piet Cohen, erected in 2011 in the Martyrs' Forest, Jerusalem. *Photographer: Avishai Teicher*

Aryan Nation on Hayden Lake.[50] The Boise memorial made news again in 2011, when it announced that it would receive the sapling, thereby completing the site's suite of touchstones—invoking the diary, the Annex, and Anne herself—for materializing Anne Frank's story.[51] At this and dozens of other sites, each sapling will become a living representative of Anne Frank, not for a day and not for a year, but, ostensibly, forever. The two stories—Anne's and the tree's—fuse, becoming a naturalized fixture of memorial landscapes around the world.

NOTES

Citations from and references to English-language editions of Anne Frank's diary are indicated in the endnotes as follows:

CE = Critical Edition, i.e., The Diary of Anne Frank: The Critical Edition, Prepared by the Netherlands State Institute for War Documentation; Introduced by Harry Paape, Gerrold van der Stroom, and David Barnouw; With a summary of the report by the State Forensic Science Laboratory of the Ministry of Justice, compiled by H. J. J. Hardy; Edited by David Barnouw and Gerrold van der Stroom; Translated by Arnold J. Pomerans and B. M. Mooyaart-Doubleday (New York: Doubleday, 1989).

DE = Definitive Edition, i.e., The Diary of a Young Girl: The Definitive Edition, edited by Otto H. Frank and Mirjam Pressler, translated by Susan Massotty (New York: Doubleday, 1995).

RCE = Revised Critical Edition, i.e., The Diary of Anne Frank: The Revised Critical Edition, Prepared by the Netherlands State Institute for War Documentation; Introduced by Harry Paape, Gerrold van der Stroom, and David Barnouw; With a summary of the report by the Netherlands Forensic Institute, compiled by H. J. J. Hardy; Edited by David Barnouw and Gerrold van der Stroom; Translated by Arnold J. Pomerans and B. M. Mooyaart-Doubleday (New York: Doubleday, 2003).

When citations from the CE or RCE refer to one of the three versions of the diary on a given page, it is indicated by the letter a, b, or c, as they are identified in the CE and RCE (e.g., RCE, 352a = Revised Critical Edition, page 352, version a).

INTRODUCTION

1. Tim Cole, Selling the Holocaust: From Auschwitz to Schindler, How History is Bought, Packaged and Sold (New York: Routledge, 1999), 23.

2. DE, Bantam edition, 1997, back cover; RCE, back cover.

3. Asteroid: "Astronomy Picture of the Day," November 13, 2002, http://apod .nasa.gov/apod/apo21113.html; Facebook: http://www.facebook.com/pages/ Anne-Frank/10959048299; UNESCO: "Memory of the World: Registered Heri-

tage," http://portal.unesco.org/ci/en/ev.php-URL_ID=26874&URL_DO=DO_
TOPIC&URL_SECTION=201.html (sites accessed May 6, 2011).

4. Shalom Auslander, *Hope: A Tragedy* (New York: Riverhead, 2012); Nathan
Englander, *What We Talk About When We Talk About Anne Frank* (New York:
Knopf, 2012).

5. See, e.g., "Was Anne Frank Baptized by Mormons?" http://www.usatoday
.com/news/religion/story/2012-02-23/anne-frank-mormon-baptism/53226808/1;
"Claims surface of Anne Frank baptism by Mormon church, week after officials
issue apology," http://www.washingtonpost.com/national/on-faith/claims-
surface-of-anne-frank-baptism-by-mormon-church-week-after-officials-issue-
apology/2012/02/23/gIQA115PWR_story.html (accessed February 26, 2012).

6. Carol Ann Lee, *The Hidden Life of Otto Frank* (New York: Viking, 2002);
Cara Wilson, *Love, Otto: The Legacy of Anne Frank* (Kansas City: Andrews McMeel,
1995); *Anne Frank and Family: Photographs by Otto Frank* (Amsterdam: Anne Frank
House, 2004); François Uzan, dir., *Anne and the Reverend* (France, 2007).

7. Ellen Feldman, *The Boy Who Loved Anne Frank: A Novel* (New York: Norton,
2005); Sharon Dogar, *Annexed* (New York: Houghton Mifflin, 2010); Nanda van
der Zee, *The Roommate of Anne Frank* (Soesterberg: Aspekt, 2003); Miep Gies with
Alison Leslie Gold, *Anne Frank Remembered: The Story of the Woman Who Helped to
Hide the Frank Family* (New York: Simon and Schuster, 1987); John Erman, dir., *The
Attic: The Hiding of Anne Frank* (U.S., 1988); Rick Kardonne and Victor Kugler: *The
Man Who Hid Anne Frank* (Jerusalem: Gefen, 2008).

8. Hanneli Goslar and Alison Leslie Gold, *Hanneli Goslar Remembers: A Child-
hood Friend of Anne Frank* (London: Bloomsbury Publishing, 1999); Berthe Meijer,
Leven na Anne Frank (Amsterdam: De Bezige Bij, 2010); Jacqueline Van Maarsen,
Inheriting Anne Frank (London: Arcadia Books, 2009), among other titles; Ed Silber-
berg: see James Still, *And Then They Came for Me: Remembering the World of Anne
Frank* (Woodstock, Ill.: Dramatic Publishing, 1999); Juanita and Betty Wagner: see
Susan Goldman Rubin, *Searching for Anne Frank: Letters from Amsterdam to Iowa*
(New York: Harry N. Abrams, 2003); Bernd Elias: see Mirjam Pressler, *Treasures
from the Attic: The Extraordinary Story of Anne Frank's Family* (New York: Doubleday,
2011); Eva Schloss, *Eva's Story* (London: W. H. Allen, 1988).

9. Gordon F. Sander, *The Frank Family That Survived* (Ithaca: Cornell University Press, 2008).

10. Mary Berg, *Warsaw Ghetto: A Diary* (New York: L. B. Fischer, 1945); Sara
Nebig Veffer, *Hidden for a Thousand Days*, "as told to Ray Sonin" (Toronto: Ryerson,
1960).

11. These sentences originally appear in Anne's diary in her entry of March 25,
1944 (*RCE*, 591a); they appear in the first published version of the diary at the end of
the entry of April 4, 1944 (*RCE*, 609c). In the revised published version of the diary,
these sentences appear in the entry of April 5, 1944 (*DE*, 245).

12. Alvin H. Rosenfeld, "Anne Frank—and Us: Finding the Right Words," *Re-
construction* 2, no. 2 (1993): 92.

13. Lawrence L. Langer, "The Uses—and Misuses—of a Young Girl's Diary: 'If Anne Frank Could Return from among the Murdered, She Would Be Appalled,'" *Forward* (English-language edition), March 17, 1995: 1, 5. Reprinted in Hyman A. Enzer and Sandra Solotaroff-Enzer, eds., *Anne Frank: Reflections on Her Life and Legacy* (Urbana: University of Illinois Press, 2000), 203–205.

14. Cole, *Selling the Holocaust*, 42, 45.

15. Cynthia Ozick, "Who Owns Anne Frank?" *The New Yorker*, October 6, 1997, 87.

16. See "Urban Dictionary: Anne Frank," http://www.urbandictionary.com/define.php?term=anne%20frank (accessed June 29, 2010).

17. Zlata Filipović, *Zlata's Diary: A Child's Life in Sarajevo*, trans. Christina Pibichevich-Zorić (New York: Viking, 1994); Đặng Thùy Trâm, *Last Night I Dreamed of Peace: The Diary of Đặng Thùy Trâm*, trans. Andrew X. Pham (New York: Harmony Books, 2007); Hélène Berr, *The Journal of Hélène Berr*, trans. David Bellos (New York: Weinstein Books, 2008); Elizabeth Becker, *Bophana: Love in the Time of the Khmer Rouge* (Phnom Penh: Cambodia Daily Press, 2010); Hadiya, *IraqiGirl, Diary of a Teenage Girl in Iraq* (Chicago: Haymarket Books, 2009); Nina Lugovskaya, *I Want to Live: The Diary of a Young Girl in Stalin's Russia*, trans. Andrew Bromfield (New York: Houghton Mifflin, 2006).

18. Diane L. Wolf, *Beyond Anne Frank: Hidden Children and Postwar Families in Holland* (Berkeley: University of California Press, 2007).

19. Ernst Schnabel, *Anne Frank: Spur eines Kindes: ein Bericht* (Frankfurt a.M.: Fischer Bücherei, 1958).

20. On East German responses to Anne Frank, see Sylke Kirschnick, *Anne Frank und die DDR: Politische Deutungen und persönliche Lesarten des berühmten Tagebuchs* (Berlin: Ch. Links Verlag, 2009).

21. See Shirli Gilbert, "Anne Frank in South Africa: Remembering the Holocaust during and after Apartheid," *Holocaust and Genocide Studies* 26, no. 2 (Fall 2012).

22. Diary entry of October 10, 1942 (*RCE*, 302a).

23. James E. Young, "The Anne Frank House: Holland's Memorial 'Shrine of the Book,'" in *The Art of Memory: Holocaust Memorials in History*, ed. James E. Young (New York: Jewish Museum with Prestel-Verlag, 1994), 131–137.

1. FROM DIARY TO BOOK

1. *Ana Franks togbukh: 12 yuni 1942–1 oygust 1944*, trans. Sh. Rubinger (Bucharest: Melukhe-farlag far literatur un kunst, [1958]); *Dos togbukh fun Ana Frank*, trans. Ester Halpern (Buenos Aires: Argentiner opteyl fun alvetlekhn yidishn kultur-kongres, 1958); Ana Frank, *Togbukh fun a meydl: 12 yuni 1942–1 oygust 1944*, trans. Yeshaye Shiluni (Shleyen) (Tel Aviv: Farlag menoyre, 1958). This spate of translations may have been inspired by the first performances of the diary's dramatization in Yiddish translation in 1958.

2. Aladdin Online Library, "The Diary of Anne Frank," www.aladdinlibrary.org/node/32 (accessed September 27, 2010).

3. Documentation Center of Cambodia, http://www.dccam.org/Publication %20and%20research/Anne_Frank.htm (accessed September 27, 2010).

4. "Anne Frank Center USA: Frequently Asked Questions," http://www.anne frank.com/who-is-anne-frank/faqs/ (accessed February 6, 2011).

5. Anne Frank, *Journal de Anne Frank* (Paris, Tournon, 1959); Anne Frank, *Diary of a Young Girl: Het Achterhuis* (West Hatfield, Mass.: Pennyroyal Press and Jewish Heritage Publishing, 1985).

6. Claire Bloom: Caedmon, 1977; Julie Harris: Audio Partners, 1992; Winona Ryder: Listening Library, 1995.

7. L. De Jong, "The Origin of the Diary," *A Tribute to Anne Frank*, ed. Anna G. Steenmeijer (Garden City, New York: Doubleday, 1971), 18–19.

8. Miep Gies with Alison Leslie Gold, *Anne Frank Remembered: The Story of the Woman Who Helped to Hide the Frank Family* (New York: Simon and Schuster, 1987), 246.

9. For an overview of the different versions of the diary that were recovered after Anne's arrest, see *RCE*, 59–61, 727.

10. See *RCE*, 728–729.

11. Ibid., 634.

12. Ibid., 204b.

13. Ibid., 197a.

14. Ibid., 201b, 201–202c.

15. See, e.g., *RCE*, 303a.

16. Ibid., 600a.

17. For a discussion of how various scholars analyze the diary's posthumous redaction, see the essay by Sally Charnow in this volume.

18. The list, drawn up on an undated separate sheet of paper, is reproduced in *RCE*, 60.

19. "Five Fragments from the Diary of Anne Frank" [Dutch], *De Nieuwe Stem* (June 1946), 432–442.

20. See *RCE*, 72.

21. On the first, unsuccessful attempts to publish the diary, see *RCE*, 66–67. For translation of Romein, see *RCE*, 67–68.

22. De Jong, "The Origin of the Diary," 19.

23. *Diario de Ana Frank* (Buenos Aires: Hemisferio, 1959); *Anne Frank naplója* (Budapest: Európa Könyvkiadó, 1959); *Denník Anny Frankovej* (Bratislava: Mladé Letá, 1960).

24. Anne Frank, *The Diary of a Young Girl* (London: Pan Books, 1954), front cover.

25. Anne Frank, *Journal de Anne Frank* (Paris: Calmann-Lévy, 1952), back cover.

26. Anne Frank, *The Diary of a Young Girl* (New York: Pocket Books, 1953), front cover.

27. *Das Tagebuch der Anne Frank* (Frankfurt a.M.: Fischer, 1956), front cover.

28. See essays in this volume by Daniel Belasco, Sara Horowitz, and Leshu Torchin.

29. Francine Prose, *Anne Frank: The Book, The Life, The Afterlife* (New York: HarperCollins, 2009), 84, who reports that Otto Frank selected the photo for the cover of this edition.

30. Translation in "Prefaces to the Diary," *A Tribute to Anne Frank*, 34.

31. Marie Baum, "Einführung," *Das Tagebuch der Anne Frank*, trans. Anneliese Schütz (Heidelberg: Verlag Lambert Schneider, 1950), vii, v; my translation. In 1955, the German translation of the diary was issued by a different publisher, Fischer Verlag, with a different introduction, written by German writer and Protestant theologian Albrecht Goes.

32. Eleanor Roosevelt, "Introduction," Anne Frank, *The Diary of a Young Girl*, trans. B. M. Mooyaart-Doubleday (Garden City, N.Y.: Doubleday, 1952), unpaginated.

33. Prose, *Anne Frank*, 85–87.

34. See Ilya Ehrenburg and Vasily Grossman, eds., *The Black Book: The Ruthless Murder of Jews by German-Fascist Invaders throughout the Temporarily Occupied Regions of the Soviet Union and in the Death Camps of Poland during the War of 1941–1945*, trans. John Glad and James S. Levine (New York: Holocaust Publications/ Schocken Books, 1981).

35. Il'ia Erenburg, "Predislovie" [Foreword], *Dnevnik Anny Frank* [Diary of Anne Frank], trans. R. Rait-Kovalev (Moscow: Izdatel'stvo inostrannoi literatury, 1960), 5, 10; my translation.

36. Anne Frank, *The Diary of a Young Girl* (New York: Pocket Books, 1953), unpaginated.

37. Meyer Levin, "The Child Behind the Secret Door," *New York Times Book Review*, July 15, 1952, 1.

38. E.g., the dust jacket of the Modern Library edition of *The Diary of a Young Girl*, published in 1952, describes the book as "one of the classics of our time." The front cover of the 1953 paperback edition issued by Pocket Books describes the book as having "become a classic of our time."

39. This supplement, inserted between pages 116 and 117 of the diary, was prepared "under the supervision of an editorial committee directed by Harry Shefter, Professor of English, M.S.Ed.," [i].

40. *RCE*, 302a.

41. *CE*, rear dust jacket.

42. *RCE*, 186.

43. According to an interview with Otto Frank in the television documentary *The Eternal Light: The Legacy of Anne Frank*, 1967 (National Jewish Archive of Broadcasting: T72).

44. *DE*, ix.

45. Ralph Blumenthal, "Five Precious Pages Renew Wrangling Over Anne Frank," *New York Times*, September 10, 1998, A1.

46. These five pages were included in the *Revised Critical Edition* of the diary; see *RCE*, 172–185. See also Lior Kodner, "Anne Frank's Secret Annex," *Ha'aretz Magazine*, May 18, 2001, 14–18.

47. *RCE*, 64.

48. *DE*, 335.

49. Bożena Shallcross, *The Holocaust Object in Polish and Polish-Jewish Culture* (Bloomington: Indiana University Press, 2011), 6–7.

50. *Anne Frank: Mooie-zinnenboek* (Amsterdam: Uitgeverij Bert Bakker, 2004).

51. *Dos togbukh fun Ana Frank* (Buenos Aires, 1958). A photograph of the cover of the original first diary notebook appears on p. 11.

52. See Torchin's essay in this volume, pp. 113–115.

53. Frances Goodrich and Albert Hackett, *The Diary of Anne Frank* (New York: Random House, 1956), 6, 25. In the "Acting Edition" of *The Diary of Anne Frank* (New York: Dramatists Play Service, 1958), the stage directions refer to the diary as "a worn, velour-covered book" (9); the properties list specifies an "old diary," for the opening and closing scenes, and a "new diary" (108, 109).

54. Frances Goodrich and Albert Hackett, *The Diary of Anne Frank*, rev. ed., "newly adapted by Wendy Kesselman" (New York: Dramatists Play Service, 2001), 70, 69.

55. See Deborah Lipstadt, *Denying the Holocaust: The Growing Assault on Truth and Memory* (New York: Free Press, 1993), 229–235.

56. "Anne Frank's Handwriting," *A Tribute to Anne Frank*, 23.

57. Ibid., 22.

58. *CE*, 103.

59. "Hollow Book Secret Safe (Diary of Anne Frank)," www.etsy.com/listing/31311183/hollow-book-secret-safe-diary-of-anne (accessed September 26, 2010).

60. Susan Stewart, *On Longing: Narratives of the Miniature, the Gigantic, the Souvenir, the Collection* (Durham: Duke University Press, 1993), 44, 90.

61. Jaap Tanja, "Anne Frank's Diaries in Facsimile," trans. Lorraine T. Miller, November 2002. www.annefrank.org/upload/downloads/auniqueset.doc

62. *RCE*, 197.

63. Marjorie Agosín, *Dear Anne Frank: Poems* (Hanover, N.H.: Brandeis University Press, 1998), vi.

64. Caryl Phillips, "On 'The Nature of Blood' and the Ghost of Anne Frank," *Common Quest* 3, no. 2 (summer 1998): 7.

65. Malkah Fleisher, "'Photograph' Marks Anne Frank's 80th Birthday," *Israel National News*, June 8, 2009; www.israelnationalnews.com/news/news.aspx/131761 (accessed September 26, 2010).

66. "Forensic Art: Age Progression and Regression," http://phojoe.com/forensic_compositing.html (accessed September 26, 2010).

67. Anne Frank, *Het Achterhuis: Dagboekbrieven van 12 Juni 1942–1 Augustus 1944* (Amsterdam: Contact, 1947), 7; my translation.

68. Anne Frank Stichting, *Anne Frank House: A Museum with a Story* ('s Gravenhage: Sdu Uitgeverij Koninnginegracht, 1992), 78.

69. See James E. Young, "The Anne Frank House: Holland's Memorial 'Shrine of the Book,'" in *The Art of Memory: Holocaust Memorials in History*, ed. James E. Young (New York: Jewish Museum with Prestel-Verlag, 1994), 131–137.

70. Anne Frank Foundation, *The Restoration of the Anne Frank House: "A House with a Story"* [brochure] (Amsterdam: Anne Frank House, [1990]), [5].

71. Henri van Praag, "The Anne Frank Foundation and the International Youth Center," *A Tribute to Anne Frank,* 114.

72. "Free2choose: Les limites de la liberté" [pamphlet] (Amsterdam: Anne Frank Stichting, 2006), 3; my translation.

73. Young, "The Anne Frank House," 136.

74. *Anne Frank House: A House with a Story* [CD-ROM] (Summit, N.J.: Cinegram Media, Inc., 2000).

75. Much of the content of the CD-ROM, including its virtual tour of the building, has since been made available on the Anne Frank House website: http://www .annefrank.org/en/Subsites/Home/ (accessed February 14, 2011).

2. FROM PAGE TO STAGE

1. See Peter Brooks, *The Melodramatic Imagination: Balzac, Henry James, Melodrama and the Mode of Excess* (New York: Columbia University Press, 1985); John G. Cawelti, *Adventure, Mystery, and Romance: Formula Stories as Art and Pop Culture* (Chicago: Chicago University Press, 1976).

2. An earlier stage work that dealt with this subject is Ben Hecht's *A Flag is Born,* which included a direct evocation of death pits and crematoria in Europe. This propaganda play, produced by the American League for a Free Palestine, ran on Broadway for 120 performances (September 5, 1946, to December 14, 1946) before going on a national tour. See Edna Nahshon, "From Geopathology to Redemption: *A Flag Is Born* on the Broadway Stage," *Kurt Weill Newsletter* 20, no.1 (spring 2002): 5–8. In 1952, George Tabori's *Flight Into Egypt,* a drama highlighting the plight of Jewish refugees trying to gain entry to the United States, was produced on Broadway. Directed by Elia Kazan and starring Zero Mostel, the production proved unsuccessful.

3. Henry F. Pommer, "The Problem of the Last Line," *Allegheny College Bulletin,* September 1962, 10.

4. The play's increased popularity may have been the result of the international success of the 1959 film version of the play, directed by George Stevens. The film played in more than fourteen thousand theaters in the United States and Canada and was dubbed in French, German, Italian and Spanish; subtitled versions were screened in other countries, including Japan. See Pommer, "The Problem of the Last Line," 10.

5. Miep Gies with Alison Leslie Gold, *Anne Frank Remembered: The Story of the Woman Who Helped to Hide the Frank Family* (New York: Simon and Schuster, 1988), 11.

6. See, e.g., the online document created by the Park Square Theatre in St. Paul, Minnesota, in conjunction with its 2007 production of the play: http://www .sainthelena.us/school/classrooms/middle/language/images/Annefrank_theatre _guide.pdf

7. For example, in 1961 then teenager Liza Minnelli appeared as Anne in her Scarsdale High School production of the play. See Scott Schechter, *The Liza Minnelli Scrapbook* (New York: Citadel Press, 2004), 51.

8. Theodore J. Shank, "Play Selection in American Colleges and Universities, 1958–1959," *Theatre Journal* 12, no. 2 (May 1960): 140.

9. In the 2008–2009 season Dramatists Play Service licensed 87 productions of the original script by Goodrich and Hackett and 92 for the version adapted by Wendy Kesselman. Email message from Craig Popisil, Director of Nonprofessional Licensing at Dramatists Play Service, August 14, 2009.

10. Meyer Levin, *The Obsession* (New York: Simon and Schuster, 1973), 36.

11. Joseph Schildkraut, *My Father and I* (New York: Viking Press, 1959), 228.

12. A rare example of another dramatized diary is George Bartenieff and Karen Malpede's *I Will Bear Witness*, based on the diaries of Victor Klemperer. This play, unlike *The Diary of Anne Frank*, is a solo piece. When it opened in 2001 in New York at the Classic Stage, an Off-Off-Broadway theater, the *New York Times* reviewer noted that the show "is so reverent toward and reliant on the text that it seems almost willfully untheatrical." See Bruce Weber, "Year by Year, a Witness to the Nazis' Affronts," *New York Times,* March 13, 2001.

13. Ben Brantley, "This Time, Another Anne Confronts Life in the Attic," *New York Times,* December 1, 1997, E1.

14. The first of several break-ins is described in the diary on March 25, 1943; see *RCE*, 367.

15. Frances Goodrich and Albert Hackett, *The Diary of Anne Frank* (New York: Random House, 1956), 107–108.

16. *RCE*, 622c.

17. Goodrich and Hackett, *The Diary of Anne Frank*, 168.

18. Goodrich and Hackett, *The Diary of Anne Frank*, 168, repeated on 174.

19. Lawrence Graver, *An Obsession with Anne Frank* (Berkeley: University of California Press, 1995), 85.

20. Letter from Frances Goodrich and Albert Hackett to Rabbi Max Nussbaum, August 8, 1959, Goodrich/Hackett file, Wisconsin Center for Film and Theater Research. Cited in Judith E. Doneson, "The American History of Anne Frank's Diary," *Holocaust and Genocide Studies* 2, no.1 (1987): 155.

21. Barbara Hogenson, *Reminiscences of Albert and Frances Hackett* (New York: Columbia University Oral History Research Office, 1983), 29. Cited in David L. Goodrich, *The Real Nick and Nora: Frances Goodrich and Albert Hackett, Writers of Stage and Screen Classics* (Carbondale and Edwardsville: Southern Illinois University Press, 2004), 206–207.

22. Goodrich, *The Real Nick and Nora*, 208.

23. Cited in Goodrich, *The Real Nick and Nora*, 209.

24. William Hawkins, "Diary of Anne Frank," *New York World-Telegram*, n.d., n.p.; Performing Arts Research Library, New York, Billy Rose Theatre Collection, Clippings, "The Diary of Anne Frank," File MWEZ + n.c. 17, 522.

25. Carol Ann Lee, *The Hidden Life of Otto Frank* (New York: Harper Perennial, 2003), 264.

26. "Kermit Bloomgarden, Producer of Many Outstanding Plays, Dead," *New York Times*, September 21, 1976, 40.

27. The sixty general partners also included Frances Goodrich and leading figures from the performing arts (Joshua Logan and his wife, Howard Dietz, Lillian Hellman, Doris Vidor, Abe Lastfogel, and Ruth Gordon, Garson Kanin's wife). The production recouped its production costs on February 25, 1956. A press release issued on March 14, 1956, by Proctor-Debussey notes that the production opened on October 5, 1955, with an advance of $20,000 and was now enjoying an advance of over $100,000. Performing Arts Research Library, New York, Billy Rose Theatre Collection, Clippings, "The Diary of Anne Frank," File MWEZ + n.c. 17, 522.

28. Frances and Albert Hackett, "Diary of 'The Diary of Anne Frank,'" *New York Times*, September 30, 1956, X3.

29. Schildkraut, *My Father and I*, 228–229.

30. Quoted in Goodrich, *The Real Nick and Nora*, 213.

31. Quoted in Goodrich, *The Real Nick and Nora*, 226.

32. Walter K. Kerr, "Theater: Anne Frank and Family," *New York Herald Tribune*, October 23, 1955.

33. Bernard Kalb, "Diary Footnotes," *New York Times*, October 2, 1955, X3.

34. Goodrich, *The Real Nick and Nora*, 212.

35. Garson Kanin, "Dialogue from Boris Aronson in Conversation with Garson Kanin" [videotape], March 20, 1975. Theatre Collection, New York Public Library at Lincoln Center. Quoted in Frank Rich and Lisa Aronson, *The Theatre Art of Boris Aronson* (New York: Knopf, 1987), 127.

36. See Rich and Aronson, *The Theatre Art of Boris Aronson*, 127.

37. See Anne's detailed description of the layout of the Annex in the diary entry of July 9, 1942, *RCE*, 230–234.

38. Brooks Atkinson, "Theatre: 'The Diary of Anne Frank,'" *New York Times*, October 6, 1955, 24.

39. Unidentified clipping; Performing Arts Research Library, New York, Billy Rose Theatre Collection, Clippings, "The Diary of Anne Frank," File MWEZ + n.c. 17, 522.

40. Schildkraut, *My Father and I*, 237.

41. Quoted in Heinz-Dietrich Fischer, *The Pulitzer Prize Archive 12: pt. D, Belles lettres. Drama, comedy awards 1917–1996* (Munich: Saur, 1998), liii.

42. Arthur Miller, "The Shadow of the Gods," *Harper's*, August 1958, 41.

43. Bruce McConachie, *American Theater in the Culture of the Cold War* (Iowa City: University of Iowa Press, 2003), 139.

44. Elaine Tyler May, *Homeward Bound: American Families in the Cold War Era* (New York: Basic Books, 2008). Goodrich and Hackett's portrait of Otto Frank brings to mind the father figures in situation comedies on American television of the period, epitomized by *Father Knows Best*.

45. Readings of Anne's diary as emblematic of others' suffering extended beyond the United States. At the time that *The Diary of Anne Frank* was enjoying success on stages in Europe, the diary was widely read by anti-apartheid activists in South African prisons, so much so that its subversive use was recognized by the white prison authorities. "Its circumstances," wrote political activist Govan Mbeki of Anne Frank's diary, "were very similar to those in apartheid South Africa" (quoted in *History after Apartheid: Public Memory in a Democratic South Africa* [Durham: Duke University Press, 2003], 86).

46. Meyer Levin, *The Fanatic* (New York: Simon and Schuster, 1964); Meyer Levin, *The Obsession* (New York: Simon and Schuster, 1973); Tereska Torrès, *Les maisons hantées de Meyer Levin* [The haunted houses of Meyer Levin] (Paris: Editions Phebus, 1974).

47. Ralph Melnick, *The Stolen Legacy of Anne Frank: Meyer Levin, Lillian Hellman and the Staging of the Diary* (New Haven: Yale University Press, 1997); Graver, *An Obsession with Anne Frank*. On *Compulsion*, see, e.g., Donald Brown, "Compelled to Suffer," *Forward*, February 19, 2010.

48. Meyer Levin, *Anne Frank*, arranged by Batya Lancet and Peter Frye for the Israel Soldiers Theatre as directed by Peter Frye, "Published by the Author for Literary Discussion" (n.p., 1970), 75.

49. Algene Ballif, "Metamorphosis into American Adolescence," *Commentary*, November 1955, 464–465.

50. Lawrence L. Langer, "The Americanization of the Holocaust on Stage and Screen," in *From Hester Street to Hollywood: The Jewish-American Stage and Screen*, ed. Sarah Blacher Cohen (Bloomington: Indiana University Press, 1983), 213–231.

51. See, e.g., Tim Cole, *Selling the Holocaust: From Auschwitz to Schindler, How History is Bought, Packaged and Sold* (New York: Routledge, 1999), 30.

52. See, e.g., Judith Goldstein, "Anne Frank: The Redemptive Myth," *Partisan Review* 70, no. 1 (winter 2003): 16–23; Francine Prose, *Anne Frank: The Book, The Life, The Afterlife* (New York: HarperCollins, 2009), 177–223.

53. Hasia R. Diner, *We Remember with Reverence and Love: American Jews and the Myth of Silence after the Holocaust, 1945–1962* (New York: New York University Press, 2009).

54. See, e.g., the discussion of Holocaust dramas aired on American radio and television in the 1940s and '50s in Jeffrey Shandler, *Jews, God, and Videotape: Religion and Media in America* (New York: New York University Press, 2009), 98–103.

55. Unidentified clipping; Performing Arts Research Library, New York, Billy Rose Theatre Collection, Clippings, "The Diary of Anne Frank," File MWEZ + n.c. 17, 522.

56. Brooks Atkinson, "Affairs of State," *New York Times*, June 17, 1956, 97.

57. "Jews in Moscow Hail Anne Frank," *New York Times*, April 12, 1963, 28.

58. Quoted in Walter Waggoner, "'Diary' Affects Dutch Audience," *New York Times*, November 29, 1956, 4.

59. Walter Waggoner, "'The Diary' in Amsterdam," Unidentified clipping; Performing Arts Research Library, New York, Billy Rose Theatre Collection, Clippings, "The Diary of Anne Frank," File MWEZ + n.c. 17, 522.

60. Waggoner, "'The Diary' in Amsterdam."

61. Waggoner, "'Diary' Affects Dutch Audience."

62. Hanno Loewy, "Saving the Child: The 'Universalisation' of Anne Frank," *Marginal Voices, Marginal Forms: Diaries in European Literature and History*, eds. Rachael Langford and Russell West (Amsterdam: Rodopi, 1999), 167.

63. Quoted in Brooks Atkinson, "Seasonal Blues," *New York Times*, October 14, 1956, X1.

64. "Berlin Audience Didn't Even Breathe...," *New York Post*, October 4, 1956.

65. Kenneth Tynan, "At the Theatre: Berlin Postscript," *The Observer*, October 7, 1956, 13.

66. Arthur J. Olsen, "Anne Frank Speaks to the Germans," *New York Times*, February 17, 1957, SM18. Olsen identifies Remarque's play as *Last Days of Berlin*.

67. "Ana Frank 'al ha-bama ha-polanit" [Anne Frank on the Polish Stage], *Kol Ha-'am*, April 21, 1957, n.p.

68. The first play on this subject staged in Israel was a 1950 production of Chaim Sloves's *The Time of Song*, in a Hebrew translation of the original Yiddish script, presented by the Ohel Theatre in Tel Aviv. The production was unsuccessful and largely ignored by the press; after a very brief run, the play was all but forgotten.

69. Ben-Ami Feingold, *Ha-shoa ba-drama ha-'ivrit* [The Holocaust in Hebrew Drama] (Tel Aviv: Hakibutz Hameuchad, 1989), 23.

70. Shimon Finkel, *Bama u-kla'im* [On Stage and Backstage] (Tel Aviv: Am Oved, 1968), 261.

71. *The Diary of Anne Frank* file, Israeli Documentation Center for the Performing Arts, Tel Aviv University.

72. "Ben-Zvi at 'Diary' Official Premiere," *Jerusalem Post*, February 1, 1957.

73. Clipping, *The Diary of Anne Frank* file, Israeli Documentation Center for the Performing Arts, Tel Aviv University.

74. Baruch Karu, "'Yomana shel Ana Frank' be-Habimah" ["The Diary of Anne Frank" at Habima], *Ha-boker*, January 25, 1957.

75. Ch[aim] G[amzu], "Emesh ba-teatron: Ana Frank be-Habimah" [Last Night at the Theatre: Anne Frank at Habima], *Ha-arets*, January 23, 1957. Two days later, Gamzu published a detailed review of the production.

76. Nachman Ben-Ami, "Reshimot teatroniyot: kol na'ara ba-shoah" [Theatrical Notes: A Girl's Voice in the Holocaust], '*Al Ha-mishmar*, February 1, 1957; "Ha-teatron shuv me'orer vikuah" [Again the Theater Triggers Debate], clipping, *The Diary of Anne Frank* file, Israeli Documentation Center for the Performing Arts, Tel Aviv University.

77. A[sher] Nahor, "Yomanah shel Ana Frank" [Anne Frank's Diary], *Herut*, February 1, 1957.

78. R. Khava, "Hadashot ba-sifrut uva-omanut" [Literary and Cultural News], *Davar,* February 7, 1958, 6.

79. "Safra ve-sayfa: 'Ashrey ha-gafrur'" [Book and Rapier: "Blessed be the Match"], *Ma'ariv,* February 14, 1958, 15.

80. Brantley, "This Time, Another Anne Confronts Life in the Attic," E1, E16.

81. http://www.mjhnyc.org/safrahall/visit_safra_24.htm.

82. James Still, *And Then They Came For Me: Remembering the World of Anne Frank* (Woodstock, Ill.: Dramatic Publishing, 2000); Cherie Bennett, *Anne Frank and Me* (Woodstock, Ill.: Dramatic Publishing, 1997); on *Anne and Emmett* (2006), see http://anneandemmett.com; Bernard Kops, *Dreams of Anne Frank* (London: Samuel French, 1993); on Box's *Anne Frank: Within and Without* (2005), see http://www.puppet.org/perform/anne.shtml; on *The Diary of Anne Frankenstein* (2009), see http://www.thediaryofannefrankenstein.com; *Margot Frank: The Diary of the Other Young Girl* debuted in 2008 at William Paterson University in Wayne, New Jersey.

3. MOVING IMAGES

1. Chris Rojek, "Indexing, Dragging, and the Production of Tourist Sights," in *Touring Cultures: Transformations of Travel and Theory,* ed. Chris Rojek and John Urry (London and New York: Routledge Press, 1997), 52–74.

2. John Durham Peters, "Witnessing," in *Media Witnessing: Testimony in the Age of Mass Communication,* ed. Paul Frosh and Amit Pinchevski (New York: Palgrave Macmillan, 2009), 23.

3. Ben Child, "David Mamet to Tackle Anne Frank," *The Guardian,* August 12, 2009.

4. For example, David Rees of the True/Slant blog provided the joking exclusive, "David Mamet's 'Anne Frank' Script LEAKED," in which Anne, writing in her diary, voiceovers, "Slow day. Nothing doing. Fuckin' Nazis." http://trueslant.com/davidrees/2009/08/14/trueslant-exclusive-david-mamets-anne-frank-script-leaked/ (accessed October 27, 2010).

5. Morton Wishengrad, *Anne Frank: The Diary of a Young Girl* [teleplay], Jewish Theological Seminary Archives, RG IIC, box 32, folder 36, mimeograph, p.1.

6. Ibid., 3.

7. Ibid., 9.

8. Ibid., 19.

9. Ibid., 24.

10. Ibid., 25.

11. Jeffrey Shandler, *While American Watches: Televising the Holocaust* (New York: Oxford University Press, 1999), 62.

12. Wishengrad, *Anne Frank,* 33.

13. Cathy Caruth, *Unclaimed Experience: Trauma, Narrative, and History* (Baltimore: Johns Hopkins University Press, 1996), 1–24.

14. "Kraler" merges the real-life Opekta and Pectacon employees Johannes Kleiman and Victor Kugler, who had helped protect the Jews hiding in the Annex

during the war. In the redacted diary, Kraler was the pseudonym Anne assigned to Kugler, while Kleiman became "Koophuis."

15. Francine Prose, *Anne Frank: The Book, The Life, The Afterlife* (New York: HarperCollins, 2009), 228–229.

16. Cited in Tim Cole, *Selling the Holocaust: From Auschwitz to Schindler, How History Is Bought, Packaged, and Sold* (New York: Routledge, 1999), 32.

17. See Cole, *Selling the Holocaust,* 32–39, and Judith E. Doneson, *The Holocaust in American Film,* 2nd ed. (Syracuse: Syracuse University Press, 2002), 57–84.

18. "How 'Cheerful' is 'Anne Frank'?" *Variety,* April 1, 1959, 2.

19. Cole, *Selling the Holocaust,* 34.

20. Melissa Müller, *Anne Frank: The Biography* (New York: Metropolitan Books, 1998).

21. Cynthia Ozick, "Who Owns Anne Frank?" *The New Yorker,* October 6, 1997, 78.

22. Thomas K. Grose and Margaret Shrout, "A Frank Portrait of Anne," *U.S. News and World Report,* May 21, 2001, 70; Marc Peyser, "Out of the Attic at Last," *Newsweek,* May 21, 2001, 57; Bernard Weinraub, "TV Film Rekindles Dispute Over Anne Frank Legacy," *New York Times,* April 10, 2001, E1.

23. An earlier animated film, titled *Anne no Nikki: Anne Frank Monogatari* [*Anne's Diary: The Story of Anne Frank*], was made for Japanese television in 1979.

24. *DE,* 1.

25. Fuyuki Kurasawa, "A Message in a Bottle: Bearing Witness as a Mode of Ethico-Political Practice," *Theory, Culture and Society* 26 (2009): 95–114.

26. My translation from the French.

27. Cited in Richard Brooks, "BBC unveils Anne Frank the sexual teenager," *The Sunday Times* (UK), January 4, 2009, http://entertainment.timesonline.co.uk/tol/arts_and_entertainment/tv_and_radio/article5439489.ece (accessed December 12, 2009).

28. Cited in Brooks, "BBC unveils Anne Frank the sexual teenager."

29. *RCE,* 307a. This entry appears as a postscript to the diary entry of November 2, 1942, in DE, 59.

30. *RCE,* 251 b.

31. Ibid., 715a.

32. Cited in Brooks, "BBC unveils Anne Frank the sexual teenager."

33. Cited in Simon Wroe, "A typical teenager in extraordinary times," *Camden New Journal,* December 30, 2008, www.thecnj.co.uk/review/2008/123108/feature123008_02.html (accessed December 12, 2009).

34. Paul Frosh, "Telling Presences: Witnessing, Mass Media, and the Imagined Lives of Strangers," in *Media Witnessing,* ed. Paul Frosh and Amit Pinchevski, 49.

35. The film's reworking of the dentist's family situation follows that of the diary's history of revision. Anne's diary entry of November 10, 1942, in her own revised version, mentions that Pfeffer "lives with a younger, nice Christian woman, to whom he is probably not married, but that doesn't matter." In his postwar redaction of the di-

ary, Otto changes the entry to read that the dentist's "wife was fortunate enough to be out of the country when war broke out." *RCE,* 323.

36. The Anne Frank House has since made this short film available on their YouTube channel (www.youtube.com/watch?v=4hvtXuO5GzU), thereby extending encounters with Anne beyond the diary and the museum and situating this encounter on a platform that is simultaneously public and private. The footage is also found on the page of YouTube user Aerobe Blue (www.youtube.com/watch?v=kEXuviihrrs), and user 101marine3 reposts the same footage, drawn from *Anne Frank Remembered* (http://www.youtube.com/watch?v=VZmykeBLi9U). Sites accessed July 29, 2010.

37. The choice of a projected backdrop as the seaside background grants a decidedly artificial look, when compared to the use of actual locations used in other scenes. This use of distinctly different registers of vision suggests the sense of a photograph that has been tucked into a diary.

38. *Mr. Show,* season 3, episode 8: "It's a No Brainer," HBO, airdate November 14, 1997.

39. Harry Thompson and Shaun Pye, *Monkey Dust,* season 1, episode 1, BBC, airdate February 9, 2003.

40. Jay Bolter and Richard Grusin, *Remediation: Understanding New Media* (Cambridge: MIT Press, 1999).

41. Logan Hill, "The Vidder: Luminosity upgrades fan video," *New York Magazine,* November 12, 2007.

42. Malin Wahlberg, "YouTube Commemoration: Private Grief and Communal Consolation," in *The YouTube Reader,* ed. Pelle Snickars and Patrick Vonderau (Stockholm: National Library of Sweden, 2009), 218–235.

43. For instance, in FantasyisKey, "Anne Frank—What Did I Do to Deserve This?" www.youtube.com/watch?v=72Mbbf6JpxI&feature=related (accessed October 30, 2010).

44. Ubuntubird, "Anne Frank 'Speaks' + Holocaust Documentary," www.youtube.com/watch?v=xVkc-ocI910 (accessed October 30, 2010).

45. These were published in *Anne Frank's Tales from the Secret Annex,* ed. Susan Massotty and G. van der Stroom (New York: Bantam USA, 2003).

46. Mariliacorrea, "Anne Frank Tribute," www.youtube.com/watch?v=PrqzfGnUGSo (accessed October 30, 2010).

47. HallonFjun92, "Mad World—Anne," www.youtube.com/watch?v=DxFCnHCjMwI (accessed October 30, 2010).

48. HallonFjun92, "My Heart Will Go On—Anne," www.youtube.com/watch?v=YLfJlKNjyGc (accessed October 30, 2010).

49. Margot1626 and MargotFrankFan are avid posters, declaring her underrated and suffering from the lack of fame granted to Anne. MargotFrankFan has even begun a diary of Margot Frank. For example, see: www.youtube.com/watch?v=ucZ66M8s5RA (accessed December 12, 2009).

50. HallonFjun92, "Anne ♥ Peter: Kiss The Girl" (www.youtube.com/ watch?v=QtSb-GgXRXs&feature=related (accessed October 30, 2010).

51. Maine12's "Anne and Peter: One in a Million" (www.youtube.com/watch?v =ga3DmbNTDrk&feature=related) and AnnalieseMarieFrank's "02 May Angels Lead You In" (www.youtube.com/watch?v=L_901woyb_U) both highlight this image (videos accessed October 30, 2010). Meanwhile, other romantic tribute videos include Vicketytoria, "Anne Frank/Peter Van Pels: At The Beginning," www.youtube.com/watch?v=ucZ66M8s5RA (accessed July 29, 2010). More of Vicketytoria's videos can be found at: www.youtube.com/user/vicketytoria. SarBear4Ryan uses the Stevens version for her Peter/Anne romantic videos, such as "The Diary of Anne Frank's (1959) Anne & Peter: So Contagious" (www.youtube .com/watch?v=UkXzMwOB8YA) and "The Diary of Anne Frank's (1959) Anne & Peter: Love . . ." (www.youtube.com/watch?v=KmYlvRiPq8I). (Videos accessed July 29 2010.)

52. Henry Jenkins, *Textual Poachers: Television Fans and Participatory Culture* (New York: Routledge, 1992).

53. AnnalieseMarieFrank, "01. What hurts the most" (www.youtube.com/ watch?v=Ye1VA8NvMC0). Last accessed October 30, 2010. Notably, in the description the vidder refers to the video as containing "the ship Anne/Pfeffer." "Ship" refers to a type of fan fiction that explores relationships that are not part of the source material, with the combination expressed in the names divided by a "slash."

54. HallonFjun92, "Somebody Help Me: Anne" (www.youtube.com/watch?v= _W6K9PMGYVk). Last accessed October 30, 2010.

55. Aviva Weintraub, "Anne Frank: Moving Images" [conference presentation], Mediating Anne Frank: A Colloquium, presented by the Working Group for Jews, Media, and Religion, the Center for Religion and Media, New York University, Tuesday, May 10, 2005.

4. HAUNTINGS AND SITINGS IN GERMANY

1. In this essay, *Germany* generally refers to West Germany, i.e., the Federal Republic of Germany, before the reunification of Germany in 1990. The political and historical culture of East Germany, i.e., the German Democratic Republic, remained completely separate until reunification. On East Germany's response to the Holocaust, see Angelika Timm, "Ideology and Realpolicy: East German Attitudes towards Zionism and Israel," in *Anti-Semitism and Anti-Zionism in Historical Perspective: Convergence and Divergence* (London: Jeffrey Herf, 2007), 186–205; Martin Sabrow, "Erinnerungskultur und Geschichtswissenschaft in der DDR" [Memory Culture and the Study of History in the German Democratic Republic], in *Diktatur—Krieg—Vertreibung: Erinnerungskulturen in Tschechien, der Slowakei und Deutschland seit 1945* [Dictatorship—War—Expulsion: The Cultures of Memory in the Czech Republic, Slovakia, and Germany since 1945] (Essen: Christoph Cornelißen, 2005), 83–101.

2. See Willy Lindwer, *The Last Seven Months of Anne Frank* (New York: Anchor Books, 1992).

3. Fritz Bauer, "Die Humanität der Rechtsordnung" [The Humanity of Justice], in Fritz Bauer, *Ausgewählte Schriften* [Selected Writings], ed. Joachim Perels and Irmtraut Wojak (Frankfurt a.M.: Campus Verlag, 1998).

4. Werner Bergmann, "Die Reaktion auf den Holocaust in Westdeutschland von 1945 bis 1989" [The Reaction to the Holocaust in West Germany from 1945 to 1989], in *Geschichte in Wissenschaft und Unterricht* [History in Research and Instruction] 43 (Stuttgart, 1992): 327.

5. See Norbert Mühlen, "Jugendbewegung um Anne Frank" [Youth Movements on Anne Frank], in *Die Weltwoche* (Zürich), March 29, 1957.

6. On the history of the memorial site, see Joachim Wolschke-Bulmann, "The Landscape Design of the Bergen-Belsen Concentration Camp Memorial," in *Places of Commemoration: Search for Identity and Landscape Design,* ed. Joachim Wolschke-Bulmahn, Dumbarton Oaks Colloquium on the History of Landscape Architecture, vol. 19 (Washington, D.C.: Dumbarton Oaks Research Library and Collection, 1999), 269–300; Wilfried Wiedemann, "Bergen-Belsen: Von der Zerstörung und der Wiedergewinnung des Gedächtnisses" [Bergen-Belsen: From the Destruction and the Regaining of Remembering], in *Auschwitz in der deutschen Geschichte* [Auschwitz in German History], ed. Joachim Perels (Hannover: Offizin-Verlag, 2010), 205–217.

7. Mühlen, "Jugendbewegung um Anne Frank."

8. Hans Gressmann, "Anne Frank rief die Jugend" [Anne Frank Calls to Youth], *Die Zeit,* March 21, 1957.

9. K.R.G., "Wallfahrt deutscher Jugend nach Bergen-Belsen" [Pilgrimage of German Youth to Bergen-Belsen], *Aufbau* (New York), March 29, 1957, 1, 7.

10. *Rundbrief der Gesellschaft für christlich jüdische Zusammenarbeit* [Newsletter of the Society for Christian-Jewish Cooperation], no. 6, December 30, 1952.

11. Rudolf Küstermeier, "Wie wir in Belsen lebten" [How we lived in Belsen], in Derrick Sington, *Die Tore öffnen sich* [The Gates Open] (Hamburg: Hamburger Kulturverlag, 1948), 87–124.

12. Hamburg Youth Circle, announcement of a trip to Bergen-Belsen on May 29, 1959, issued May 5, 1959. Forschungsstelle für Zeitgeschichte (Research Center for Contemporary History), Hamburg, Collection: "Hamburger Jugendring," file 42.

13. Marion Siems, *Anne Frank: Tagebuch—Erläuterungen und Dokumente* [Anne Frank: Diary—Commentary and Documents] (Stuttgart: Reclam Verlag, 2003), 110.

14. "Die Ketten sind weg: Bergen-Belsen bekam jetzt einen neuen Obelisk" [The Chains Are Off: Bergen-Belsen Now Has a New Obelisk], *Welt der Arbeit,* August 22, 1958.

15. Eberhard Kolb, *Bergen-Belsen: Geschichte des "Aufenthaltslagers" 1943–1945* [Bergen-Belsen: A History of the "Detention Camp" 1943–1945] (Hannover: Verlag für Literatur und Zeitgeschehen, 1962).

16. On the historical context of the response to Nazi crimes in Germany, see Norbert Frei, *1945 und wir, Darin: Deutsche Lernprozesse, NS-Vergangenheit und Generationenfolge seit 1945* [1945 and Us, in the Middle of It: German Learning Processes, the Nazi Past, and Generational Change since 1945] (Munich: Verlag C. H. Beck, 2005).

17. On the Bitburg controversy, see Geoffrey Hartman, ed., *Bitburg in Moral and Political Perspective* (Bloomington: Indiana University Press, 1986).

18. For an analysis of this period in German history, see Henri Lustiger Thaler, "Remembering Forgetfully," in *Re-situating Identities: The Politics of Race, Ethnicity and Culture,* ed. Vered Amit Talai and Caroline Knowles (Toronto: Broadview Press, 1996), 190–217.

19. Ronald Reagan, "Remarks at a Commemorative Ceremony at Bergen-Belsen Concentration Camp in the Federal Republic of Germany," May 5, 1985. Ronald Reagan Library, Simi Valley, California.

20. Ronald Reagan, "Remarks at a Joint German-American Military Ceremony at Bitburg Air Base in the Federal Republic of Germany," May 5, 1985. Ronald Reagan Library, Simi Valley, California.

21. Motion of the SPD Group, Council of the City of Bergen, May 8, 1985. Hohls Collection, Anne Frank School, Bergen.

22. Motion of Rudolf Ernst, Council of the City of Bergen, June 27, 1985. Hohls Collection, Anne Frank School, Bergen.

23. Letter to the editor, *Stadt-Anzeiger* (Bergen), July 3, 1985, 4.

24. Letter from Günter Grabow, mayor of Bergen, to Klaus Rathert, president of the Celle region, September 24, 1985. Hohls Collection, Anne Frank School, Bergen.

25. A comprehensive record of the activities and history of the school can be found in The Elke-von-Meding Collection, Anne Frank School, Bergen.

26. From the founding document of the CVJM After-School and Educational Institution, Oldau, undated. Archive of the CVJM, Oldau.

27. Avishai Margalit, *The Ethics of Memory* (Cambridge: Harvard University Press, 2002), 182.

28. Objects left by visitors at the Vietnam War Memorial in Washington, D.C., are similarly collected and archived; see Thomas B. Allen, *Offerings at the Wall: Artifacts from the Vietnam Veterans Memorial Collection* (Atlanta: Turner Publishing, 1995).

29. The Tuol Sleng Genocide Museum was established in 1975, five years after the Khmer Rouge Reign of Terror.

30. The philosopher Emmanuel Levinas argued in this sense that justice must be commensurate with a cultural recognition of the crime committed against the other and is a powerful counterpoint to justice as a sanctioning force, although the former cannot do so without application of the rule of law. This process unfolds at the intersection of memory and justice. On Levinas's work in relation to Holocaust remembrance, see Henri Lustiger Thaler, "Holocaust Lists and the Memorial Museum," *Museum and Society* 6, no. 3 (November 2008): 196–211; Henri Lustiger Thaler, "When Empty is Full," *Memory* (Guggenheim Publications), November 2009, 1–3.

31. Anne Frank's death anticipates what Jacques Derrida has called the need for a "justice of time," when the crimes afflicted upon the other, and their reverberating resonance through the generations, are acknowledged. See Jacques Derrida, *Specters of Marx* (New York: Routledge, 1994), 7.

5. TEACHING ANNE FRANK IN THE UNITED STATES

1. The generous input of educators has been an invaluable source of information in researching this article. I would like to thank especially Christina Chavarria of the U.S. Holocaust Memorial Museum (USHMM) and the following, all USHMM Museum Teacher Fellows: Dr. Bill Younglove, Elaine Culbertson, Ellen Bisping, Karen Ferris-Fearnside, and Pamela Blevins.

2. Francine Prose, *Anne Frank: The Book, The Life, The Afterlife* (New York: HarperCollins, 2009).

3. Henri van Praag, "The Diary in American Schools," in *A Tribute to Anne Frank,* ed. Anna G. Steenmeijer (Garden City, N.Y.: Doubleday, 1971), 105.

4. Personal communication, Julie York Coppens, Associate Editor, Educational Theatre Association and the International Thespian Society, March 29, 2011.

5. "Anne Frank-Fonds: Purpose," http://www.annefrank.ch/purpose.

6. Henri van Praag, "The Anne Frank Foundation and the International Youth Center," in *A Tribute to Anne Frank,* 114.

7. Maureen McNeil, "Practicing Freedom: An Enduring Model in Anne Frank," *On The Issues,* spring 2010, http://www.ontheissuesmagazine.com/2010spring/2010spring_McNeil.php.

8. "The Exhibition: Anne Frank—The History for Today," http://www.zydziw polsce.edu.pl/frank/aindex_frank1.html.

9. Anne Frank Center USA, "Anne Frank: A History for Today," http://www.annefrank.com/exhibitions/traveling-exhibits/anne-frank-a-history-for-today/.

10. Utah Education Network, "Anne Frank in the World, 1929–1945: Teacher Workbook," http://www.uen.org/annefrank/.

11. McNeil, "Practicing Freedom."

12. Thomas D. Fallace, *The Emergence of Holocaust Education in American Schools* (New York: Palgrave Macmillan, 2008).

13. Referred to in Fallace, *The Emergence of Holocaust Education in American Schools,* 89.

14. Hyman Enzer and Sandra Soltaroff-Enzer, eds., *Anne Frank: Reflections on Her Life and Legacy* (Urbana: University of Illinois Press, 2000), 11.

15. Email from Dr. William Younglove, USHMM Teacher Fellow, master teacher, January 18, 2011.

16. Email from Pamela Blevins, Oklahoma City educator, USHMM Museum Fellow and Regional Educator, November 24, 2008.

17. Elaine Culbertson, "The Diary of Anne Frank: Why I Don't Teach It," in Samuel Totten, ed., *Teaching Holocaust Literature* (Needham Heights, Mass.: Allyn and Bacon, 2001), 64.

18. USHMM, "Anne Frank, the Writer: An Unfinished Story," http://www
.ushmm.org/museum/exhibit/online/af/htmlsite/; National Endowment for the
Humanities, "Anne Frank: Writer," http://edsitement.neh.gov/lesson-plan/anne-
frank-writer; Prose, *Anne Frank*.

19. *RCE*, 433b.

20. Understanding by Design, "Unit 4: Tragedies & Triumphs," http://rela.wico
mico.wikispaces.net/file/view/Grade+8+-+Unit+4.pdf.

21. Prose, *Anne Frank*, 262.

22. Email from Ellen Bisping, February 8, 2011.

23. Scott Christian, *Exchanging Lives: Middle School Writers Online* (Urbana:
National Council of Teachers of English, 1997), 3.

24. Karen Spector and Stephanie Jones, "Constructing Anne Frank: Critical Literacy and the Holocaust in Eighth-Grade English," *Journal of Adolescent and Adult
Literacy* 5, no. 1 (September 2007): 36–48.

25. Frances Goodrich and Albert Hackett, *The Diary of Anne Frank* (New York:
Dramatists Play Service, 1956), 101.

26. Culbertson, "The Diary of Anne Frank: Why I Don't Teach It," 64; personal
communication, January 14, 2011.

27. Quoted in Fallace, *The Emergence of Holocaust Education in American Schools*,
121.

28. Susan Llewelyn Leach, "Role-playing Helps Kids Learn Moral Complexity,"
Christian Science Monitor, July 6, 2005, http://www.csmonitor.com/2005/0706/
p15s02-legn.html.

29. Samuel Totten, "Diminishing the Complexity and Horror of the Holocaust:
Using Simulations in an Attempt to Convey Historical Experiences," in Samuel
Totten, ed., *Teaching Holocaust Literature*, 244–245.

30. ThinkQuest, "The Diary of Anne Frank," http://library.thinkquest.org/
TQ0312521/webquest.html.

31. Orlee Miamon, "Florida Students Live Like Anne Frank," *Tablet*, October 14,
2009, http://www.tabletmag.com/scroll/18306florida-students-live-like-anne
-frank/.

32. North Carolina State University Middle School Education, "The Diary of
Anne Frank: Unit Daily Lesson Plans," http://www.ncsu.edu/project/middletech/
spotlight/laurieint/franklesson/lessonplans.html.

33. Teaching Tolerance, "Classroom Simulations: Proceed With Caution," http://
www.tolerance.org/magazine/number-33-spring-2008/classroom-simulations-
proceed-caution.

34. Prime Stage Theatre, resource guide for *The Diary of Anne Frank*, http://
www.primestage.com/resource_guide_anne_frank.pdf.

35. Teaching Tolerance, "Classroom Simulations."

36. Prime Stage Theatre, resource guide for *The Diary of Anne Frank*.

37. Simone Schweber, "Simulating Survival," *Curriculum Inquiry* 33 (Spring
2003): 183.

38. See, e.g., Ann Abramson, *Who Was Anne Frank?* (New York: Penguin, 2007); Ruth Ashby, *Childhoods of World Figures: Anne Frank* (New York: Simon and Schuster, 2005); Jonathan A. Brown, *People We Should Know: Anne Frank* (New York: Gareth Stevens, 2004); Ann Kramer, *Anne Frank: The Young Writer Who Told the World Her Story, World History Biography Series* (Washington, D.C.: National Geographic Society, 2007); Anne E. Schraff, *Anne Frank: Biographies of the 20th Century* (Costa Mesa, Calif.: Saddleback Educational, 2008); Jim Whiting, *What's So Great About . . . ?: Anne Frank* (Hockessin, Del.: Mitchell Lane, 2007).

39. http://www.annefrank.org/en/Worldwide/news/2010/September/The-life-of-Anne-Frank-the-graphic-biography/.

40. Utah Education Network, "Anne Frank: Nutrition—Anne Frank and Me," http://www.uen.org/Lessonplan/preview.cgi?LPid=1016.

41. Utah Education Network, "Anne Frank: Movement—Isometric Exercises," http://www.uen.org/Lessonplan/preview.cgi?LPid=1017.

42. Utah Education Network, "Anne Frank: Movement—Isometric Exercises."

43. Education World, "Showcasing Jim DeLong and the 'Anne Frank Wall,'" October 4, 2004, http://www.educationworld.com/a_curr/teacher_feature/teacher_feature047.shtml.

44. Anne Frank Wall, http://www.annefrankwall.org/index.html.

45. See Culbertson, "The Diary of Anne Frank: Why I Don't Teach It," 63–69.

46. See Jacob Boas, *We Are Witnesses: Five Diaries of Teenagers Who Died in the Holocaust* (New York: Scholastic, 1996); Michael Leapman, *Witnesses to War, Eight True-Life Stories of Nazi Persecution* (New York: Scholastic, 1998); Wiktoria Sliwowska and Julian Bussgang, eds., *The Last Eyewitnesses: Children of the Holocaust Speak* (Evanston: Northwestern University Press, 1998); Alexandra Zapruder, *Salvaged Pages: Young Writers' Diaries of the Holocaust* (New Haven: Yale University Press, 2002).

47. Robert P. Doyle, *Banned Books 1994 Resource Guide* (Chicago: American Library Association, 1994), 31.

48. Rhonda Simmons, "Head of Schools Defends Pulling Version of Anne Frank's Memoir," *Star Exponent* (Culpeper, Virginia), January 29, 2010, http://www2.starexponent.com/cse/news/local/education/article/head_of_schools_defends_pulling_version_of_anne_franks_memoir/51306/.

49. Michael Alison Chandler, "Anne Frank's Diary Is Back on Culpeper Schools' Reading List," *Washington Post,* February 2, 2010, http://www.washingtonpost.com/wp-dyn/content/article/2010/02/01/AR2010020102427.html.

50. Rebecca Leung, "If Anne Frank Only Knew... Diary Used to Teach U.S. Fear and Hate in North Korea," *CBS News,* February 26, 2004, http://www.cbsnews.com/stories/2004/02/26/60minutes/main602415.shtml

51. Sam Wineburg, *Historical Thinking and Other Unnatural Acts: Charting the Future of Teaching the Past* (Philadelphia: Temple University Press, 2001), 3.

6. ANNE FRANK AS ICON

1. "Anne Frank Ranks as Time Hero but Is Hitler 'Most Influential'?" *Jweekly* *.com,* June 11, 1999, http://www.jweekly.com/article/full/11017/anne-frank-ranks-as-time-hero-but-is-hitler-most-influential/ (accessed April 10, 2011).

2. Tony Kushner, "'I Want To Go On Living after My Death': The Memory of Anne Frank," in *War and Memory in the Twentieth Century,* ed. Martin Evans and Ken Lunn (New York: Oxford University Press, 1997), 16.

3. "About the memorial," http://idaho-humanrights.org/content/article .cfm?article_id=25 (accessed December 8, 2010).

4. "Idaho Drafts Anne Frank to Fight Neo-Nazi Image," *Reuters,* April 11, 2000.

5. James E. Young, "The Anne Frank House, Holland's Memorial 'Shrine of the Book,'" in *The Art of Memory: Holocaust Memorials in History,* ed. James E. Young (New York: Prestel, 1994), 134.

6. *Exploring the Idaho Anne Frank Human Rights Memorial* (undated leaflet).

7. "About the memorial," http://idaho-humanrights.org/content/article.cfm ?article_id=25 (accessed December 8, 2010).

8. For details about the relationship between James Ingo Freed's design of the USHMM and the content of the exhibit, see http://www.ushmm.org/museum/ a_and_a/ (accessed January 16, 2011). To learn more about Daniel Libeskind's architecture of the Jewish Museum in Berlin, see http://www.jmberlin.de/main/ EN/04-About-The-Museum/01-Architecture/01-libeskind-Building.php (accessed January 16, 2011).

9. "Advocacy," http://idaho-humanrights.org/content/article.cfm?article_ id=30 (accessed December 8, 2010).

10. *RCE,* 716c.

11. Alison Landsberg, *Prosthetic Memory: The Transformation of American Remembrance in the Age of Mass Culture* (New York: Columbia University Press, 2004), 135.

12. Amy Shuman, *Other People's Stories: Entitlement Claims and the Critique of Empathy* (Chicago: University of Illinois Press, 2005), 162.

13. Judith Doneson, "The American History of Anne Frank's Diary," *Holocaust and Genocide Studies* 2, no. 1 (1987): 156.

14. Alan E. Steinweis, "Reflections on the Holocaust from Nebraska," in *The Americanization of the Holocaust,* ed. Hilene Flanzbaum (Baltimore: Johns Hopkins University Press, 1999), 173.

15. Quoted in "Rewards Offered for Info about Memorial Vandalism," *KTVB* *.com,* May 22, 2007.

16. Doneson, "The American History of Anne Frank's Diary," 156.

17. Jeffrey Shandler, *Jews, God, and Videotape: Religion and Media in America* (New York: New York University Press, 2009), 141.

18. Deborah Lipstadt, *Denying the Holocaust: The Growing Assault on Truth and Memory* (New York: Penguin, 1993), 230.

19. See Lipstadt, *Denying the Holocaust,* 232–235.

20. See Robert Faurisson, "The Secular Religion of the 'Holocaust,' a Tainted Product of Consumer Society," August 7, 2008, http://robertfaurisson.blogspot.com/2009/03/secular-religion-of-holocaust-tainted.html (accessed January 18, 2011).

21. Robert Faurisson, "Is *The Diary of Anne Frank* Genuine?" *Journal for Historical Review* 3, no. 2 (spring 1982), http://www.ihr.org/jhr/v03/v03p147_Faurisson.html (accessed July 7, 2009).

22. Robert Faurisson, "The Diary of Anne Frank: Is it Genuine?" *Journal of Historical Review,* 19, no. 6 (November-December 2000), translated from the French, http://www.ihr.org/jhr/v19/v19n6p-2_Faurisson.html (accessed July 7, 2009).

23. Faurisson, "The Diary of Anne Frank: Is it Genuine?"

24. On this forensic examination of the diary, see *RCE,* 109–171.

25. Full trial transcript can be found at http://www.hdot.org/en/trial/transcripts (accessed January 19, 2011).

26. "Coffee with Bradley Smith: The Anne Frank House," http://profj.c.topica.com/maanIoEabVEvJaRJwvlbaeQHr5/ (accessed April 11, 2011) and "Coffee with Bradley Smith: Anne Frank Diaries?" http://profj.c.topica.com/maanJxNabVJVEaRJwvlbaeQHr5/ (accessed April 11, 2011).

27. Holocaust deniers use scare quotes to question the veracity of the Holocaust, Anne Frank, six million Jewish victims, etc. They also deride those who accept Jewish claims as "believers," or "brainwashed cult-members." See, e.g., the white supremacist website http://www.stormfront.org/forum/t735874/ (accessed January 19, 2011).

28. Kenneth Stern, *Holocaust Denial* (New York: American Jewish Committee, 1993), 79.

29. Shuman, *Other People's Stories,* 5.

7. A GUEST AT THE SEDER

1. Passover remains one of the most popular holidays for American Jews. In the last nationwide survey of Jews in the United States, 79 percent of Jews said they attended or held a Passover seder. The number jumps to 96 percent when the question is limited to Jews who affiliate within a Jewish denomination. See www.jewishdatabank.org/Archive/NJPS2000_American_Jewish_Religious_Denominations.pdf (accessed May 13, 2010). Data from earlier national and local studies are also archived at the National Jewish Data Bank. For a summary of earlier studies, see the introduction to Liora Gubkin, *You Shall Tell Your Children: Holocaust Memory in American Passover Ritual* (New Brunswick, N.J.: Rutgers University Press, 2007). On the popularity of the haggadah in the United States, see Joel Gereboff, "With Liberty and Haggadahs for All," in *Key Texts in American Jewish Culture,* ed. Jack Kugelmass (New Brunswick, N.J.: Rutgers University Press, 2003), 275–292.

2. The earliest extant versions of the haggadah date to the ninth and tenth centuries CE, when instructions for a Passover seder were included in the daily prayer

book. The earliest free-standing haggadahs are illustrated manuscripts from the thirteenth century, and printed haggadahs date back to the late fifteenth century. Abraham Yaari's authoritative *Bibliography of the Passover Haggadah* (Jerusalem: Bamberger and Wahrman, 1960) lists 2,713 printed editions; a 1965 addendum brings the total to 3,404.

3. See Robert Wuthnow, *After Heaven: Spirituality in America since the 1950s* (Berkeley: University of California Press, 1998). See also Wade Clark Roof, *A Generation of Seekers: The Spiritual Journeys of the Baby Boom Generation* (San Francisco: HarperSanFrancisco, 1993). For Jewish instantiations of this phenomenon, see Steven M. Cohen and Arnold M. Eisen, *The Jew Within: Self, Family, and Community in America* (Bloomington: Indiana University Press, 2000).

4. For examples of DP seders, see the film *Passover: Traditions of Freedom* (1994, Randy Goldman, dir.) and Yosef Dov Sheinson and Saul Touster, *A Survivors' Haggadah* (Philadelphia: Jewish Publication Society, 2000).

5. David and Tamar Sola Pool, *The Haggadah of Passover for Members of the Armed Forces of the United States* (New York: National Jewish Welfare Board, 1943).

6. For a history of early commemoration of the Warsaw Ghetto Uprising, including Passover rituals, see Hasia R. Diner, *We Remember with Reverence and Love: American Jews and the Myth of Silence after the Holocaust, 1945–1962* (New York: New York University Press, 2009), 67–77. For analysis of later additions of the Uprising into haggadahs, see Gubkin, *You Shall Tell Your Children*, 124–154.

7. For a reproduction of the Seder Ritual of Remembrance and discussion of its early history, see Diner, *We Remember with Reverence and Love*, 18–20.

8. Beatrice S. Weinreich, "The Americanization of Passover," in *Studies in Biblical and Jewish Folklore*, ed. Raphael Patai, Frances Utley, and Dov Noy (Bloomington: Indiana University Press, 1960), 354. Weinreich also noted that Orthodox haggadahs tended not to include the Holocaust, which is still true today. "Changes are rarely made in the traditional Orthodox Haggada, but it seems that this addition may become a permanent feature of the Haggada in the future" (355). For an early and important exception to this observation, see Menahem Kasher, *Israel Passover Haggadah* (New York: American Biblical Encyclopedia Society, 1956).

9. The high commitment of American Jews to observing Passover in relation to their commitment to Holocaust remembrance fits with Jews' self-reporting of their values and priorities in a 1997 survey, in which 85 percent of Jews marked the Holocaust as "very important" or "extremely important." Sociologist Lyn Rapaport comments on this statistic that it "exceeded all other items in the survey, including God, the Jewish family, the Jewish people, and American anti-Semitism. Elsewhere in the survey, 65% agreed that 'my feelings about the Holocaust have deeply influenced my feelings about being Jewish.'" See Lynn Rapaport, "The Holocaust in American Jewish Life," in *The Cambridge Companion to American Judaism*, ed. Dana Evan Kaplan (Cambridge: Cambridge University Press, 2005), 202.

10. *RCE*, 716c.

11. Beginning in the late 1960s, the Central Conference of American Rabbis revised its official liturgies, including prayer books for the Sabbath and the High Holy Days (Rosh Hashanah and Yom Kippur), as well as its Passover haggadah, *The Union Haggadah,* first published in 1923.

12. A. Stanley Dreyfus, "The Gates Liturgies: Reform Judaism Reforms its Worship," in *The Changing Face of Jewish and Christian Worship in North America,* ed. Paul Bradshaw and Lawrence Hoffman (Notre Dame: University of Notre Dame Press, 1991), 146.

13. Herbert Bronstein, ed., *A Passover Haggadah: The New Union Haggadah Prepared by the Central Conference of American Rabbis,* rev. ed. (New York: CCAR, 1975), 6. On connections between the Holocaust and Israel in American haggadahs, see Carole B. Balin, "The Modern Transformation of the Ancient Passover Haggadah," in *Passover and Easter: Origin and History to Modern Times,* ed. Paul Bradshaw and Lawrence Hoffman (Notre Dame: University of Notre Dame Press, 1999).

14. Bronstein, ed., *A Passover Haggadah,* 45–46.

15. The instructions in the Talmud that are often replicated and elaborated in haggadahs are *mathil be-genut u-mesayem be-shevah.* According to the Talmudic rabbis, when a father tells the story of the Exodus to his son, he should "begin in shame [or degradation]; end in glory [or praise]." BT, Pesahim 116b.

16. Bronstein, ed., *A Passover Haggadah,* 46.

17. Each of the four cups of wine evokes one of the four verbs God uses in the Torah in the account of God's liberations of the Israelites: "I will free you [*ve-hotseiti*] from the burden of the Egyptians and deliver you [*ve-hitsalti*] from their bondage. I will redeem you [*ve-gaalti*] with an outstretched arm and through extraordinary chastisements. And I will take you [*ve-lakahti*] to be My people, and I will be your God" (Exodus 6:6–6:7).

18. Bronstein, ed., *A Passover Haggadah,* 46. For a history of pairing Israel with the Holocaust in American remembrance, see Diner, *We Remember with Reverence and Love,* 311–316. For a critique of this practice, see Jacob Neusner, *Stranger at Home: "The Holocaust," Zionism, and American Judaism* (Chicago: University of Chicago Press, 1981).

19. Bronstein, ed., *A Passover Haggadah,* 48.

20. Ibid.

21. Elaine Moise and Rebecca Schwartz, eds., *The Dancing with Miriam Haggadah: A Jewish Women's Celebration of Passover,* 3rd ed. (Palo Alto: Rikudei Miriam, 1999), vi. The citation from Anne Frank's diary appears in all three editions of this haggadah.

22. Moise and Schwartz, eds., *The Dancing with Miriam Haggadah,* 10.

23. Ibid., 11.

24. Ibid.

25. Noam Zion and David Dishon, eds., *A Different Night: The Family Participation Haggadah* (Jerusalem: Shalom Hartman Institute, 1997), 180.

26. Ibid., 3.

27. Diner, *We Remember with Reverence and Love,* 375.

28. Ibid., 79–82.

29. Zion and Dishon, ed., *A Different Night,* 138.

30. Ibid., 139.

31. Ibid.

32. *RCE,* 451.

33. Dara Silverman and Micah Bazant, eds., *Love and Justice in Times of War Haggadah* (2003) 1, 2, http://colours.mahost.org/events/haggadah.html (accessed February 10 2007).

34. Ibid., 2.

35. Ibid., 56.

36. Eleanor Roosevelt, "Introduction" in Anne Frank, *Anne Frank: The Diary of a Young Girl* (New York, Pocket Books, 1972), vii.

37. *RCE,* 621.

38. Ibid., 622.

8. LITERARY AFTERLIVES

Research for this article was conducted under the aegis of a Research Fellowship at the Center for Advanced Holocaust Research at the U.S. Holocaust Memorial Museum, Washington, D.C. I wish to thank the museum for access to archival material pertaining to the 2003 Anne Frank exhibition, with particular gratitude for the generous help offered by museum staff, especially Michlean Amir, Ron Coleman, Vincent Slatt, and Brian Burden, the support of Paul Shapiro, Suzanne Brown-Flemming, and Traci Rucker, and the stimulation of my fellow fellows. My thanks to Mia Spiro and Jonathan Richler for their comments on a draft of this article, and to Barbara Kirshenblatt-Gimblett and Jeffrey Shandler for their close reading and suggestions.

1. U.S. Holocaust Memorial Museum, Anne Frank Attendance Figures, n.d.

2. U.S. Holocaust Memorial Museum, Institutional Archives, 2005.138, Box 2.

3. Lawrence L. Langer, "Anne Frank Revisited," *Using and Abusing the Holocaust* (Bloomington: University of Indiana Press, 2006), 21.

4. Francine Prose, *Anne Frank: The Book, The Life, The Afterlife* (New York: HarperCollins, 2009).

5. Elena Lappin, "Wartime Lies" [review of *A Hatred for Tulips*], *New York Times Book Review,* August 12, 2007, 23.

6. Richard Lourie, *Joop: A Novel of Anne Frank* (New York: St. Martin's Press, 2008; previously published as *A Hatred for Tulips*), 144.

7. Lourie, *Joop,* 148, 149.

8. Ibid., 15, 16, 95.

9. Ibid., 8.

10. Ibid., 100, 101.

11. Ibid., 143.

12. Ibid., 8.

13. Ibid., 164, 159, 160

14. Ibid., 169.

15. Sarah Kofman, *Smothered Words*, trans. Madeleine Dobie (Evanston: Northwestern University Press, 1988; originally published as *Paroles suffoquées*, Paris: Galilée, 1987), 14.

16. Lourie, *Joop*, n.p.

17. Rachel Feldhay Brenner, *Writing as Resistance: Four Women Confronting the Holocaust* (University Park: Penn State Press, 1997), 5.

18. Ellen Feldman, *The Boy Who Loved Anne Frank: A Novel* (New York: Norton, 2005), 115, 121.

19. Ibid., 130.

20. Ian Buruma, "The Afterlife of Anne Frank," *New York Review of Books*, February 19, 1998, 4.

21. Feldman, The Boy Who Loved Anne Frank, 253.

22. Ibid., 80.

23. Harry Mulisch, "Death and the Maiden," *Anne Frank: Reflections on her Life and Legacy*, ed. Hyman A. Enzer and Sandra Solotaroff-Enzer (Urbana: University of Illinois Press, 2000), 95.

24. Philip Roth, *The Ghost Writer* (New York: Vintage, 1979), 101, 104.

25. Ibid., 144.

26. Ibid., 196.

27. Ibid., 153.

28. Ibid., 150.

29. Geoff Ryman, 253, or *Tube Theatre* (1996, available at http://www.ryman-novel .com; in print as *253: The Print Remix*, New York: St. Martin's Griffin, 1998).

30. Shalom Auslander, *Hope: A Tragedy* (New York: Riverhead, 2012).

31. Philip Roth, *Exit Ghost* (Boston: Houghton Mifflin Harcourt, 2007), 185.

32. Nathan Englander, "What We Talk About When We Talk About Anne Frank," *What We Talk About When We Talk About Anne Frank* (New York: Knopf, 2012).

33. Raymond Carver, What We Talk About When We Talk About Love: Stories (New York: Knopf, 1981).

34. Judith Katzir, *Dearest Anne: A Tale of Impossible Love*, trans. Dalya Bilu (New York: Feminist Press, 2008), 17.

35. Ibid., 17, 18, 18, 19–20.

36. Ibid., 64, 64, 65, 65, 65, 66.

37. Ibid., 66, 66, 6.

38. Ibid., 69, 69, 69.

39. Amalia Kahana-Carmon, "Shirat ha-'atalfim be-ma'ufam," *Moznayim* (1989): 3–7. Translated as "The Song of Bats in Flight," in *Gender and Text in Modern Hebrew and Yiddish Literature*, ed. Naomi Sokoloff et al. (New York: Jewish Theological Seminary, 1992), 23–45.

40. Katzir, *Dearest Anne*, 66.

41. Marjorie Agosín, *Dear Anne Frank: Poems*, trans. Richard Schaff (Hanover, N.H.: Brandeis University Press, 1998), vi, vi, ix, ix, vi, vi.

42. Ibid., viii, vi, vii.

43. Ibid., 105, 107, 119, 121.

44. Scott Simon, "Anne Frank Exhibit," Weekend Edition Saturday, National Public Radio, July 19, 2003, http://www.npr.org/templates/story/story.php?storyId =1342383.

45. Zlata Filipović, *Zlata's Diary: A Child's Life in Sarajevo*, trans. Christina Pribichevich-Zorić (New York: Viking, 1994), 29.

46. Ibid., 171, iv, 171, 193.

47. Francine Prose, "A Little Girl's War" [review of *Zlata's Diary* by Zlata Filipović], *New York Times*, March 6, 1994, 7.

48. Christopher Lehmann-Haupt, "Another Diary of a Young Girl" [review of *Zlata's Diary* by Zlata Filipović], *New York Times*, February 28, 1994, C15.

49. All citations are from Francine Zuckerman, dir., *Punch Me in the Stomach*, based on the stage play by Deb Filler and Allison Summers [DVD], National Center for Jewish Film, 1997.

50. Zygmunt Bauman, "Allosemitism: Premodern, Modern, Postmodern," in *Modernity, Culture and the Jew*, ed. Bryan Cheyette and Laura Marcus (Stanford: Stanford University Press, 1998), 143; Bryan Cheyette, "Neither Excuse nor Accuse: T. S. Eliot's Semitic Discourse," *Modernism/Modernity* 10 (September, 2003) 3: 433.

51. All citations are from Lisa France, dir., *Anne B. Real* [DVD], Screen Media Films, 2003.

52. Lisa France, phone interview, March 20, 2011.

53. Ibid.

54. Ibid.

55. Meyer Levin, "The Child Behind the Secret Door: An Adolescent Girl's Own Story of How She Hid for Two Years During the Nazi Terror" [review of *The Diary of a Young Girl* by Anne Frank], *New York Times Book Review*, June 15, 1952, 1.

9. SUTURING IN

1. Most, but not all, of the interpretations in this essay have emerged from conversation with the artists and from looking at the works of many other artists, not discussed here, that deal with Frank and her legacy. An incomplete list of other visual artists with notable works on Anne Frank created since 1990 includes Deborah Grant, Jason Lazarus, Greg Tricker, Lena Liv, David Altmejd, Doug and Mike Starn, Shimon Attie, Melissa Gould, Miriam Schapiro, Nathania Rubin, and Harmony Korine. Thanks to Barbara Kirshenblatt-Gimblett and Aviva Weintraub for informing me about some of these projects.

2. Michael Schwarz, *Felix Droese, Ich habe Anne Frank umgebracht: Ein Aufstand der Zeichen* (Frankfurt am Main: Fischer Taschenbuch Verlag, 1988).

3. Lotte Konow Lund, email to author, August 25, 2009.

4. Ibid.

5. Rachel Schreiber, statement, http://www.rachelschreiber.com/anne/anne
.html, undated. Also telephone interview with author, September 16, 2009.

6. Steven M. Cohen and Ari Y. Kelman, *Cultural Events and Jewish Identities:
Young Adult Jews in New York* (New York: National Foundation for Jewish Culture,
2005), 75, http://huc.edu/faculty/faculty/pubs/StevenCohen/CulturalEvents06
.pdf (accessed January 20, 2011).

7. The relationship with Roth is discussed in L. J. Nicoletti, "No Child Left Behind," in *Visualizing the Holocaust: Documents, Aesthetics, Memory,* ed. David Bath-
rick, Brad Prager, and Michael David Richardson (London: Camden House, 2008),
95–100. See also Nicholas Mirzoeff, "Ghost Writing: Working Out Visual Culture,"
in *Art History, Aesthetics, Visual Studies,* Michael Ann Holly and Keith Moxey, ed.
(New Haven: Yale University Press, 2002).

8. Philip Roth, "The Ghost Writer," in *Zuckerman Bound* (New York: Farrar,
Straus, and Giroux, 1985), 17.

9. Abshalom Jac Lahav, email to author, September 3, 2009.

10. Ibid.

11. Ibid.

12. Cynthia Ozick, "Who Owns Anne Frank?" *The New Yorker,* October 6, 1997.
See also Francine Prose, *Anne Frank: The Book, The Life, The Afterlife* (New York:
HarperCollins, 2009).

13. Walter Robinson, "Joe Lewis: Clairvoyance," *ArtNet.com,* August 16, 2007.

14. Ellen Rothenberg, *The Anne Frank Project* (Santa Barbara: University Art
Museum, University of California, 1993).

15. "Anne Frank Project," http://www.ellenrothenberg.com/anne-frank-project-
about.html (accessed January 24, 2011).

16. Keith Mayerson, email to author, August 26, 2009.

17. *RCE,* 658 (May 8, 1944), 694 (June 13, 1944).

18. Keith Mayerson, email to author, August 26, 2009.

19. Keith Mayerson, interview with author, August 2007.

20. Scott McCloud, *Understanding Comics: The Invisible Art* (New York: Harper,
1994).

21. This emphasis on the imagination filling the space between self and visual
images is a very different concept of "suture" than the psychoanalytic definition of
Lacan, which has been adapted by Kaja Silverman and others within film studies
to describe how emotion is used to manipulate audiences. For related discussion
of "suture" in film in connection to the Holocaust, see Margaret Olin, "Graven
Images on Video?: The Second Commandment and Jewish Identity," in *Complex
Identities: Jewish Consciousness and Modern Art,* Matthew Baigell and Milly Heyd
eds. (New Brunswick, N.J.: Rutgers University Press, 2001), 37.

22. *RCE,* 463 (January 6, 1944 [version a], January 5, 1944 [version c]).

23. Fawn Krieger, proposal, 2006. Artist files, Six Points Fellowship, Foundation
for Jewish Culture, New York. Access to these files generously provided by Rebecca
Guber, director of the Six Points Fellowship.

10. SOUNDS FROM THE SECRET ANNEX

1. *RCE*, 341.

2. Ibid., 333, 423, 507, 612, 633 (radio); 236, 368–369, 523 (bell chimes). Initially unpublished material recounts two additional musical references: Anne's friends singing "Happy Birthday to You" at her thirteenth birthday party (199), and rules about singing in the annex (333: "only softly, after 6 o'clock in the evening").

3. Bathja Bayer, "Ma'oz Ẓur," *Encyclopaedia Judaica*, ed. Michael Berenbaum and Fred Skolnik, 2nd ed. (Detroit: Macmillan Reference USA, 2007), vol. 13, 496–497.

4. Levin concluded the Hanukkah scene with Otto Frank humming the melody of "Ma'oz Tsur," Mrs. Frank adding the lyrics, and the rest of the cast joining in as the lights faded to black (Meyer Levin, "Anne Frank" [n.p. (self-published), 1966/67]).

5. The lyric to "Oh Hanukkah, Oh Hanukkah" used for the 1955 show differs significantly from other commonly known Yiddish, Hebrew, and English versions, which include descriptions of dreidel playing and latke eating and sometimes mention the Hanukkah story as a divine act. Hackett and Goodrich printed the song's vocal line in their 1954 script, but attributed the song to a "folk" source (even though Mordkhe Rivesman is widely credited as the author of the song's original lyrics). Such actions suggest that the lyrics included in *The Diary of Anne Frank* were adapted especially for this production.

6. Frances Goodrich and Albert Hackett, *The Diary of Anne Frank* (New York: Dramatists Play Service, Inc., 1954), 59, 63–64; Ralph Melnick, *The Stolen Legacy of Anne Frank: Meyer Levin, Lillian Hellman, and the Staging of the Diary* (New Haven: Yale University Press, 1997), 147–148.

7. Melnick, *Stolen Legacy*, 148.

8. Frances Goodrich and Albert Hackett, *The Diary of Anne Frank*, adapted by Wendy Kesselman (New York: Dramatists Play Service, Inc., 2001), 41, 43; Charlie Rose, interview with James Lapine, Linda Lavin, and Wendy Kesselman. *The Charlie Rose Show*, WNET, aired January 2, 1998, www.charlierose.com/guests/wendy-kesselman (accessed September 1, 2008).

9. See, *inter alia*, Park Square Theatre, "The Diary of Anne Frank by Frances Goodrich and Albert Hackett: An Educational Study Guide" (St. Paul, Minn.: Park Square Theatre, 2007), 8–9.

10. For an overview, see Ben Arnold, "Art Music and the Holocaust," in *Holocaust and Church Struggle: Religion, Power and the Politics of Resistance*, ed. Hubert G. Locke and Marcia Sachs Littell (New York: University Press of America, 1996), 99–115.

11. See Judah M. Cohen, "Musicography," in this volume.

12. It is unclear which composer's setting Levin intended here, though it is tempting to consider David Diamond's 1946 vocal composition "David Mourns for Absalom" as a possibility.

13. Levin, "Anne Frank."

14. "Music of the 20th Century," *Times of London*, April 8, 1959, 14.

15. "The Royal Ballet: The Burrow," *Times* (London), January 3, 1958, 3. Speculation about the role of Anne Frank's diary as inspiration for "The Burrow" continued well into the twenty-first century; see Clement Crisp, "Into the Labyrinth: Kenneth MacMillan and His Ballets," *Dance Research* 25, no. 2 (2007): 189.

16. Alfred Newman, *Music From the Original Film Soundtrack of George Stevens' Production of The Diary of Anne Frank* [long-playing record], FOX 3015 [1959].

17. Kathryn Kalinak, *Settling the Score: Music and the Classic Hollywood Film* (Madison: University of Wisconsin Press, 1992), 113.

18. Darius apparently changed the title of his dance work numerous times: even newspaper accounts of the premiere call it both "The Anne Frank Ballet" and "The Story of Anne Frank." See "Two Ballets on Program," *Independent-Press-Telegram*, Long Beach, Calif., March 29, 1959, W6; Rachel Morton, "Ballet Superb in Preview," *Independent-Press-Telegram*, Long Beach, Calif., April 8, 1959, B6; "In Charity Dance," *Independent-Press-Telegram*, Long Beach, Calif., April 9, 1959, n.p. In later performances, the work was called the "Ballet of Anne Frank" (see "'Diary' Actor Plans Talk Here," *Independent-Press-Telegram*, May 3, 1959, A10); "The Attic," when it was performed at New York's 92nd St. Y on December 13, 1959 (see Selma Jeanne Cohen, review of Adam Darius, "An Evening of Choreography," *Dance Magazine* 34, no. 2 [February 1960]: 72; Louis Horst, "Adam Darius and Company," *Dance Observer* 27, no. 1 [January 1960]: 9); and "In Memoriam" (see "Anne Frank Ballet," *Dance Magazine* 35, no. 12 [December 1961]: 38). A 1986 video version of the piece, which I have used for my description, employs the title "The Anne Frank Ballet": Adam Darius, *The Anne Frank Ballet* [videorecording] (Long Branch, N.J.: Kino Films, 1986).

19. Benedict Silberman, *Jewish Music: Melodies Beloved the World Over* [long-playing record], Capitol Records T-10064 [1957]; Adam Darius, *Dance Naked in the Sun* (London: Latonia Publishers, 1973), 171–172.

20. Cohen, review of Adam Darius; Horst, "Adam Darius and Company"; Darius, *Dance Naked*, 176–179, 257–258.

21. "Amsterdam Getting Anne Frank Cantata," *New York Times*, May 24, 1964, 9.

22. Castiglioni provided neither a vocal designation nor even a clef in the published score. In one early review of a performance of the piece, however, the "voice" was identified as a soprano; see David Kraehenbuehl, review of Niccolò Castiglioni, "Elegia per 19 Instrumenti e una Voce," *Notes* 2nd Series, 17, no. 3 (June 1960): 485.

23. "Le Journal d'Anne Frank," http://www.edith-lejet.com/english/journal-va .php (accessed March 22, 2010). The work has also received recent performances in 2001 (March, Douai), 2008 (March 7–8, Lyon), and 2010 (March 9, La Côte Saint-André). It is not entirely clear why all these performances took place in early March, though it is worth speculating that they may commemorate Anne Frank's death in early March 1945.

24. Program for Peter Nero, "Anne Frank: The Diary of a Young Girl," Trenton, N.J., War Memorial Auditorium, November 17, 1973. Kermit Bloomgarden Papers, Wisconsin Historical Society, US Mss 8AN, Box 44, Folder 8.

25. Jane Garb Kaplan, "Program Notes," in program for Nero, "Anne Frank."

26. Donald Janson, "A Tribute to Anne Frank," *New York Times,* November 11, 1973, 114; Robert Sobel, "Nero Offers Engaging Work for All Ages." *Billboard Magazine,* October 10, 1970, 30.

27. See http://en.mikis-theodorakis.net/index.php/article/articleview/211/1/46/, (accessed September 14, 2008).

28. Bas van Putten, CD Pamphlet Notes (tr. Jonathan Reeder), *Hans Kox, War Triptych* (Donemus, 2002).

29. Michael Feingold, review of *Yours, Anne, Village Voice,* October 22, 1985, 111; Clive Barnes, "Anne Frank Musical: It Works," *New York Post,* October 14, 1985, 55; Miriam Rubenstone, "Anne Frank's Diary is Better Read than Sung," *USA Today,* October 15, 1985.

30. See Jeffrey Shandler, *While America Watches: Televising the Holocaust* (New York: Oxford University Press, 1999), 155–178; Elie Wiesel, "Trivializing the Holocaust: Semi-Fact and Semi-Fiction," *New York Times,* April 16, 1978.

31. John Rockwell, "New Work by Lukas Foss for Anne Frank," *New York Times,* June 14, 1989; James R. Oestreich, "Audrey Hepburn in Debut of Work on Anne Frank," *New York Times,* March 29, 1990.

32. Howard Goodall, "In Memoriam Anne Frank" [musical score] (London: Faber Music, 1999).

33. Howard Goodall, liner notes to *Howard Goodall: Choral Works* [compact disc], CD DCA 1028 (ASV Digital, 1998).

34. Mark Hemeter, "The City Ballet Premieres a Ballet Based on Anne Frank," *Times-Picayune* (New Orleans), May 18, 1989, 18G.

35. Mike McGonigal, "Dropping in at the Neutral Milk Hotel," *Puncture* 41 (Spring 1998). Reproduced at http://neutralmilkhotel.net/puncture3.html (accessed September 18, 2008).

36. Kim Cooper, *Neutral Milk Hotel's "In the Aeroplane Over the Sea"* (London: Continuum, 2005), 2. See also pp. 3, 35–36, 48, 71–78, 102.

37. The Freedom Writers with Erin Gruwell, *The Freedom Writers Diary* (New York: Doubleday, 1999). The film version condenses the Freedom Writers' story significantly, eliminating the pivotal role that Zlata Filipović (known as the "Anne Frank of Sarajevo") played in their experiences. Filipović's visit to the class preceded that of Miep Gies, and Filipović later wrote the introduction to *The Freedom Writers Diary.* The film adaptation, however, centers on the students' reading of Anne Frank's diary.

38. This theme is, in fact, titled "Anne Frank" on the recorded soundtrack: *Freedom Writers: Music from the Motion Picture* (Burbank, Calif.: Hollywood Records, 2006), track 15.

39. OutKast, "So Fresh, So Clean," *Stankonia* (New York: La Face/Arista, 2000), track 4.

40. Stephen Lynch, "Dear Diary 1," *3 Balloons* (Boulder: What Are Records? 2009), track 3. Used with the permission of Stephen Lynch.

41. See www.youtube.com/watch?v=KJJeHgq5KVo (accessed November 2, 2010).

11. CRITICAL THINKING

1. *The Revised Critical Edition* (*RCE*) includes five previously unknown pages of Anne's diary as well as a few other pages that had been previously omitted at the request of the Frank family. Expanded chapters in the book's front matter authenticate this added material. A new chapter briefly discusses scholarly debates over the diary's authenticity and the 1959 film adaptation. The *RCE* also includes Anne Frank's fiction, previously published separately in English translation as *Tales from the Secret Annex* (New York: Washington Square, 1984).

2. Berteke Waaldijk, "Reading Anne Frank as a Woman," *Women's Studies International Forum* 16, no. 4 (1993): 328.

3. Francine Prose, *Anne Frank: The Book, The Life, The Afterlife* (New York: HarperCollins, 2009), 5.

4. For the most part, scholars, especially literary critics, writing after 1986 cite either the *Critical Edition* (*CE*) or *Revised Critical Edition* (*RCE*) in their work. In a few cases, the 1991 *Definitive Edition* (*DE*) is cited. Published after Otto Frank's death, this edition is an amalgam of what the *CE* and *RCE* term versions "a" and "b," offering more diary material than the earlier *Diary of a Young Girl* (1952) but not divided into original/redacted/published versions like the *CE* and *RCE*. The *DE* is also the edition now most often used in the classroom and read by students.

5. Waaldijk, "Reading Anne Frank as a Woman," 329.

6. *CE*, dust jacket.

7. Prose, *Anne Frank*, 18–19.

8. *Matisse: Radical Invention, 1913–1917* [exhibition], Museum of Modern Art, New York, July 8–October 11, 2010. Elizabeth Barrett Browning, *A Variorum Edition of Elizabeth Barrett Browning's Sonnets from the Portuguese*, ed. Miroslava Wein Dow (Troy, N.Y.: Whitston, 1980); Allen Ginsburg, *Howl: Original Draft Facsimile, Transcript, and Variant Versions...*, ed. Barry Miles (New York: Harper Perennial, 1995).

9. For some experiences of reading and teaching the diary as part of an American educational curriculum, see "Reading the Diary," *Lilith* (Fall 2003): 32–37. The primacy of English as the language in which the diary is discussed is noteworthy. Waaldijk, a scholar of women's studies at the University of Utrecht, wrote and published in English, cited the English version of the *Critical Edition*, and recognized support from Dutch and American women's studies scholars.

10. Waaldijk, "Reading Anne Frank as a Woman," 328.

11. See Joan Jacobs Brumberg, *The Body Project: An Intimate History of American Girls* (New York: Vintage Books, 1997), xxix.

12. Ibid., xxxi.

13. Ibid., xvii–xxx.

14. *RCE*, 296, 307, 462, 589. Also see 484–487 for a discussion between Anne and Peter about female and male sexual organs.

15. Ibid., 567.

16. Ibid.

17. Jane Hunter, "Inscribing the Self in the Heart of the Family: Diaries and Girlhood in Late-Victorian America," *American Quarterly* 44, no. 1 (March 1992): 58.

18. *RCE*, 303. For a discussion of Anne's use of her diary to record fantasies and daydreams, see Laureen Nussbaum, "Anne Frank," in *Anne Frank: Reflections on Her Life and Legacy,* ed. Hyman A. Enzer and Sandra Solotaroff-Enzer (Urbana: University of Illinois Press, 2000), 26.

19. Hunter, "Inscribing the Self in the Heart of the Family," 51, 53.

20. *Dear Kitty: Remembering Anne Frank* [documentary film], dir. Wouter Van Der Suis, 1999; Miep Gies with Alison Leslie Gold, *Anne Frank Remembered* (New York: Simon and Schuster, 1987), 186.

21. Brumberg, *The Body Project,* 16–25.

22. From the Friendly Society Constitution (ca. 1890), quoted in Linda Larach, "Organizing American Girls: 1870–1950" [seminar paper], Cornell University, 1992; cited in Blumberg, *The Body Project,* 17.

23. Brumberg, *The Body Project,* 17–18.

24. *RCE*, 463.

25. Hunter, "Inscribing the Self in the Heart of the Family," 65–67.

26. George Scarlett, "Adolescent Thinking and the Diary of Anne Frank," *The Psychoanalytic Review* 58, no. 2 (1971): 265.

27. *RCE*, 316–317.

28. Scarlett, "Adolescent Thinking and the Diary of Anne Frank," 266.

29. John Berryman, "The Development of Anne Frank," in *Anne Frank: Reflections on Her Life and Legacy,* ed. Enzer and Solotaroff-Enzer, 78.

30. Rachel Feldhay Brenner, "Writing Herself Against History: Anne Frank's Self-Portrait as a Young Artist," *Modern Judaism* 16, no. 2 (1996): 106–107.

31. Ibid., 125.

32. Hunter, "Inscribing the Self in the Heart of the Family," 65.

33. Brenner, "Writing Herself Against History," 126.

34. Hunter, "Inscribing the Self in the Heart of the Family," 73.

35. *RCE*, 600.

36. Ibid.

37. Ibid., 324.

38. Hunter, "Inscribing the Self in the Heart of the Family," 74–75.

39. Berryman, "The Development of Anne Frank," 77.

40. Philippe Lejeune, "L'histoire vraie du journal d'Anne Frank" [The Real History of Anne Frank's Diary], *La Revue des Livres Pour Enfants* 153 (Fall 1993): 52–53.

41. Ibid., 55.

42. Henry F. Pommer, "The Legend and Art of Anne Frank," in *Anne Frank: Reflections on Her Life and Legacy,* eds. Enzer and Solotaroff-Enzer, 75.

43. Lejeune, "L'histoire vraie du journal d'Anne Frank," 52. Waaldijk, in agreement with Lejeune, argues that we see the censoring of male editors when we compare version b with version c.

44. Nussbaum, "Anne Frank," 30.

45. Lejeune, "L'histoire vraie du journal d'Anne Frank," 56.

46. Ibid., 57.

47. Ibid.

48. Waaldijk, "Reading Anne Frank as a Woman," 331.

49. *RCE,* 609.

50. Ibid., 608.

51. Cissij van Marxveldt (pen name of Setske de Haan) wrote five volumes of fiction taking the form of diary entries and letters following Joop and her friends from girlhood through marriage. The first four books—*The High School Years of Joop ter Heul* (1919), *Joop ter Heul's Problems* (1921), *Joop ter Heul Gets Married* (1923), and *Joop and Her Boys* (1925)—were published by Kok Omniboek, Amsterdam, in the years following the end of World War I; the fifth book appeared immediately after World War II: *Joop ter Heul's Daughter* (1946).

52. For a discussion of the range of reading materials mentioned in the diary, see Sylvia Patterson Iskander, "Anne Frank's Reading," *Children's Literature Association Quarterly* 13, no. 3 (1988): 137–141.

53. *RCE,* 297.

54. Waaldijk, "Reading Anne Frank as a Woman," 333–334.

55. Ibid., 330.

56. *RCE,* 700.

57. Quoted in Iskander, "Anne Frank's Reading," 138, 140. Iskander also includes an appendix of all of the books mentioned in *Diary of a Young Girl.* Although she refers to the publication of the *Critical Edition,* it was not yet available when she wrote this article.

58. "Introduction," *Awakening Lives: Autobiographies of Jewish Youth in Poland before the Holocaust,* ed. Jeffrey Shandler (New Haven: Yale University Press, 2002), xxix.

59. Moshe Kligsberg, "The Jewish Youth Movement in Inter-War Poland: A Sociological Study" [Yiddish], in *Studies of Polish Jewry, 1919–1939,* ed. Joshua A. Fishman (New York: YIVO, 1974), 174.

60. Brenner, "Writing Herself Against History," 108.

61. Ibid., 112.

62. *RCE,* 600.

63. See Brenner, "Writing Herself Against History," 118, 116.

64. *RCE*, 700.

65. Brenner, "Writing Herself Against History," 117, 120, 121, 125.

66. Prose, *Anne Frank*, 8.

12. ANNE FRANK ON CRANK

1. Martin Grotjahn, *Beyond Laughter: Humor and the Subconscious* (New York: McGraw-Hill, 1954), 115.

2. "She's in the Attic!" http://www.snopes.com/movies/actors/zadora.asp.

3. J. Hoberman, "Houses of Mirth," *Village Voice* (New York), April 2, 2002, 111.

4. Henry R. Huttenbach, "The Cult of Anne Frank: Returning to Basics," in *Anne Frank in the World: Essays and Reflections,* ed. Carol Rittner (Armonk, N.Y.: M. E. Sharpe, 1998), 79, 82. See also G. Jan Colijn," Toward a Proper Legacy," in Rittner, ed., *Anne Frank in the World,* 99.

5. All citations are from "Possession" in David Sedaris, *Dress Your Family in Corduroy and Denim* (New York: Little Brown, 2004), 180–187.

6. Ethan Thompson, "Good Demo, Bad Taste: South Park as Carnivalesque Satire," in *Satire TV: Politics and Comedy in the Post-network Era,* ed. Jonathan Gray, Jeffrey P. Jones, and Ethan Thompson (New York: New York University Press, 2009), 213.

7. *South Park,* season 12, episode 3, originally broadcast on March 26, 2008.

8. See, for example, *South Park* episodes "Pinkeye" (season 1, episode 7), original airdate October 29, 1997, and "The Passion of the Jew" (season 8, episode 4), original airdate March 31, 2004.

9. *South Park* interrogated the notion of learning lessons from the Holocaust, a subject of concern to both historians and educators, in another episode, "Deathcamp of Tolerance" (season 6, episode 14), original air date November 20, 2002.

10. "Toy Meets Girl," *Robot Chicken,* season 1, original airdate May 1, 2005.

11. Judy Gold, personal communication, October 28, 2010.

12. *Family Guy,* "If I'm Dyin', I'm Lyin','" episode 209, original airdate April 4, 2000.

13. See "Historical Tweets: The Tweets of Anne Frank," http://historicaltweets.com/2009/07/03/the-tweets-of-anne-frank/.

14. "Ghost Of Anne Frank: 'Quit Reading My Diary,'" *The Onion,* February 11, 1998, http://www.theonion.com/search/?q=anne+frank+quit+reading+my+diary&x=0&y=0. See also Scott Dikkers and Mike Loew, *Our Dumb Century: The Onion Presents 100 Years of Headlines from America's Finest News Source* (New York: Three Rivers Press, 1999).

15. Anne Frank on Crank was the name of a Denver-based punk rock band. In choosing this name, band members explain that they intended it to mean "disenfranchised, yet somehow empowered," and also considered it somewhat humorous. See http://annefrankoncrank.com/name.html. On The Diarrhea of Anne Frank, see http://www.amiright.com/names/cool/d_2.shtml. On "Anne Frankly," see http://www.jamieleecomedy.com/video/52/Episode_1_Anne_Frankly_2010_

Created_by_Jamie_Lee__Shawn_Pearlman. On "The Frank Diary of Anne," see http://www.youtube.com/watch?v=UmwadcnX2gc.

16. Moira Smith, "Humor, Unlaughter, and Boundary Maintenance," *Journal of American Folklore* 122 (2009): 151. Though the term "unlaughter" was not coined by Smith, she expands on its definition in significant ways.

17. For more on these controversies, see, among others, Jytte Klausen, *The Cartoons That Shook the World* (New Haven: Yale University Press, 2009), and Robert Tait, "Iran cartoon Show Mocks Holocaust," *The Guardian* (London, online edition), August 20, 2006, http://www.guardian.co.uk/world/2006/aug/20/iran.israel.

18. See "Muslim European Group Posts Anti-Semitic Cartoons," *European Jewish Press*, February 6, 2006, http://www.ejpress.org/article/news/5663.

19. See Norman L. Kleeblatt, ed., *Mirroring Evil: Nazi Imagery/Recent Art* [catalogue] (New Brunswick, N.J.: Rutgers University Press, 2002).

20. Zvi Zinger, "Bezalel Presents: Finding Humor in Hitler," July 21, 2008, *ynet news.com*, http://www.ynetnews.com/articles/0,7340,L-3570709,00.html.

21. "The Daily Hitler," http://www.thedailyhitler.com/.

22. Willie Smyth, "Challenger Jokes and the Humor of Disaster," *Western Folklore* 45, no. 4 (October 1986): 245.

EPILOGUE

1. See Eric Katz, "Anne Frank's Tree: Thoughts on Domination and the Paradox of Progress," *Ethics, Place and Environment* 13, no. 3 (2010): 283–293, whose close reading of these passages notes the context of each mention of the tree and its relatively minor place in the diary.

2. RCE, 670c.

3. Anne Frank House, "Anne Frank Tree: Quotation from Otto Frank," http://www.annefrank.org/en/Worldwide/Anne-Frank-Tree/.

4. RCE, 698–699a.

5. Ibid., 519–520b.

6. Ibid., 636a.

7. Ibid., 716a.

8. Ibid., 650a.

9. Ibid., 519a.

10. Ibid., 519b.

11. Ibid., 519–521c.

12. "Support Anne Frank Tree: History," http://www.support-annefranktree.nl/history.

13. Ibid.

14. Ian Traynor, "Proud, Tall—and Rotting: Anne Frank's Tree Wins a Reprieve," *The Guardian*, November 22, 2007, http://www.guardian.co.uk/world/2007/nov/22/books.secondworldwar?INTCMP=SRCH.

15. Ibid.

16. "Anne Frank House: Anne Frank Tree," http://www.annefrank.org/en/Inspiring/Anne-Frank-Tree/.

17. "Support Anne Frank Tree: History."

18. Sally McGrane, "A Fight Over Anne Frank's Fallen Tree," *New York Times,* June 8, 2011, http://www.nytimes.com/2011/06/09/world/europe/09tree.html?pagewanted=all.

19. "Support Anne Frank Tree: Film Documentaries," http://www.support-annefranktree.nl/node/156.

20. Cyclingrama, "What Would Anne Frank Do?" June 9, 2011, https://cyclingrandma.wordpress.com/2011/06/09/what-would-anne-frank-do/.

21. "Giant Chestnut Tree That Gave Comfort to Anne Frank as She Hid from the Nazis Is Toppled in Storm," *Mail Online,* August 24, 2010, http://www.dailymail.co.uk/news/worldnews/article-1305641/Tree-comforted-Anne-Frank-hid-Nazis-toppled-storm.html.

22. Comment #145, "Anne Frank Tree Falls Over in Wind, Heavy Rain," MSNBC, August 23, 2010, http://www.msnbc.msn.com/id/38814121/.

23. Danna Harman, "Why Anne Frank's Tree Stood for So Much," *Christian Science Monitor,* August 24, 2010, http://www.csmonitor.com/World/Global-News/2010/0824/Why-Anne-Frank-s-tree-stood-for-so-much.

24. "Anne Frank Tree Falls," *American Forests,* Autumn 2010, http://findarticles.com/p/articles/mi_m1016/is_3_116/ai_n56435910/.

25. "Tree-mendous: Disease Leaves Its Mark Inside Horse Chestnut," *Mail Online,* September 10, 2007, http://www.dailymail.co.uk/news/article-481059/Tree-mendous-Disease-leaves-mark-inside-horse-chestnut.html.

26. Comment #180, "Anne Frank Tree Falls Over in Wind, Heavy Rain," MSNBC, August 23, 2010.

27. Comment #81, "Anne Frank Tree Falls Over in Wind, Heavy Rain," MSNBC, August 23, 2010.

28. Comment #276, "Anne Frank Tree Falls Over in Wind, Heavy Rain," MSNBC, August 24, 2011.

29. Comment #73, "Anne Frank Tree Falls Over in Wind, Heavy Rain," MSNBC, August 23, 2010.

30. Comment #1, "Anne Frank's Chestnut Tree Will Not Be Felled This Year Despite Disease," *Haaretz,* April 10, 2007, http://www.haaretz.com/news/anne-frank-s-chestnut-tree-will-not-be-felled-this-year-despite-disease-1.230497; "Burning Books: The Pretzien 'Bücherverbrennung,'" *Indymedia Ireland,* February 27, 2007, http://www.indymedia.ie/article/81226. See also "In Germany, Men Who Burned Anne Frank's Diary Face Trial," *Deutsche Welle,* February 26, 2007, http://www.dw-world.de/dw/article/0,2144,2365002,00.html.

31. Comment #78, "Anne Frank's Chestnut Tree Will Not Be Felled This Year Despite Disease," *Haaretz,* August 24, 2010.

32. Comment #278, "Anne Frank Tree Falls Over in Wind, Heavy Rain," MSNBC, August 23, 2010.

33. "10 Most Bizarre Celebrity Items Ever Sold on eBay," *Theazon,* July 16, 2011, http://theazon.com/2011/07/10-most-bizarre-celebrity-items-ever-sold-on-ebay/.

34. "Anne Frank House: Anne Frank Tree," http://www.annefrank.org/en/Worldwide/Anne-Frank-Boom/.

35. "Opruimen Anne Frankboom begonnen," *NOS News,* August 26, 2010, http://nos.nl/artikel/180736-opruimen-anne-frankboom-begonnen.html.

36. Steve from Texas-2246664, Comment #34, "Anne Frank Tree Falls Over in Wind, Heavy Rain," *Newsvine.com,* August 23, 2010, http://stevefromtexas2246664.newsvine.com/.

37. Comment #34, "Anne Frank Tree Falls Over in Wind, Heavy Rain," *MSNBC,* August 23, 2010.

38. Jon Kalish, "The Arty Semite: Tennessee Sculptor Makes Bid for Anne Frank Tree," *The Forward,* July 13, 2011, http://blogs.forward.com/the-arty-semite/139807/#ixzz1VetE5C1F.

39. "Support Anne Frank Tree: Planted," http://www.support-annefranktree.nl/planted.

40. "Anne Frank Tree Planting Pack," 1, http://www.annefrank.org.uk/files/aftpp.pdf.

41. Ibid.

42. "Anne Frank's Chestnut Tree to Bloom Again Across the USA," *Offbeat Travel,* 2009, http://www.offbeattravel.com/tji-anne-frank-diary-tree-usa.html

43. "Anne Frank Tree Reborn as a Sapling," *Mirror,* August 20, 2010, http://www.mirror.co.uk/news/top-stories/2010/08/28/anne-frank-tree-reborn-as-a-sapling-115875-22519827/.

44. "Hope Springs Eternal for the Anne Frank Tree," http://www.sonoma.edu/newscenter/2010/08/anne-frank-tree.html.

45. *RCE,* 520b

46. David Dunlap, "Hope for a Harvest of Tolerance From Anne Frank's Tree," *New York Times,* April 17, 2009, http://www.nytimes.com/2009/04/17/nyregion/17frank.html.

47. Julie, Shapiro, "9/11 'Survivor Tree' Spreads Its Branches Over the World Trade Center Once Again, *DNAInfo.com,* December 22, 2010, http://www.dnainfo.com/20101222/downtown/911-survivor-tree-spreads-its-branches-over-world-trade-center-once-again.

48. "Painsley Catholic College Win the Anne Frank Tree Competition," Anne Frank Trust UK, December 13, 2010, http://www.annefrank.org.uk/node/250.

49. Joshua Hamerman, "Memorializing Anne Frank's Love for Nature," *Jerusalem Post,* April 29, 2011, http://www.jpost.com/JewishWorld/JewishNews/Article.aspx?id=218362.

50. For details about the Boise monument, see the essay in this volume by Brigitte Sion, 178–187.

51. "Idaho Anne Frank Human Rights Memorial," CityofBoise.org, http://www.cityofboise.org/Departments/Parks/ParksAndFacilities/Parks/page15921.aspx.

Musicography

Judah M. Cohen

The following music and dance works all reference Anne Frank in some form, ranging from the sole subject of a large-scale composition to a quick reference in a title or lyric. They have been arranged chronologically within rough genre designations, with premiere, publication, and recording information included where available. This musicography only includes works that have been documented in some form. (It also excludes full settings of Yevgeny Yevtushenko's poem "Babi Yar," which references Anne Frank.) I am grateful to Caitlin Goldbaum for her assistance in the final stages of compiling this list.

A. MUSIC
1. Cantatas and Choral Works

[c. 1960s]
"Anna Frank"
Music: Joseph Schogrin; text: Moishe Teyf
Cantata for speaker, soloists, choir, and piano
Published by the Jewish Music Alliance. Mentioned in Ann Basart, "Music and the Holocaust: A Selective Bibliography" (*Cum notis variorum* 101 [1986], 28); no additional information available.

1968–1970
"Le Journal d'Anne Frank"
Music: Edith Lejet
For female choir, lute, harpsichord, harp, electric guitar, viola, bass, and two percussionists
Commissioned by Radio-France. Premiere on Radio-France in 1970; performed live in Douai in March 2001, in Lyon on March 7–8, 2008, and in La Côte Saint-André on March 9, 2010. Published by Gérard Billaudot, Éditeur.

1970
"Who Has Allowed Us to Suffer?"
Music: Oskar Morawetz
For SATB choir

Commissioned by the Canadian Jewish Congress. Dedicated to Otto Frank. Music premiered February 20, 1972, in Toronto, with Ben Steinberg and the Temple Sinai Congregation choir. Published by Canadian Music Centre.
Recordings: Canadian Music Centre (CMC), 1981; *Anthology of Canadian Music,* vol. 17, side 6B (1983); Canadian Music Centre, 1999.

1972

"Piano de Matin 'Écoute pour Anne Franck'"
Music: Mihaï Mitrea-Celarianu
For five instruments, five voices, electro-acoustical devices, and projectors
Premiered October in Champigny, France, by Ensemble 2e2m.

1981–1982

Part 8: "Anna Frank–Ibrahim–Emiliano" in *2e Litourgia: Den Kindern getötet in Kriegen/Liturgy No.2: "For the Young Killed in Wars"*
Music and text: Mikis Theodorakis
For SATB choir
Commissioned and premiered (May 21, 1983) by the Dresdner Kreuzchor, under the direction of Martin Flämig, Dresden, Germany.
Recording: Edel, 1984/5 (reissued by Berlin Classics, 1995; currently available online at the NAXOS Music Library).

1985

"Anne Frank Cantate: A Child of Light," Part III of *War Tryptich*
Music: Hans Kox
"Symphonic cantata" for soprano, contralto, bass, choir, and orchestra
Premiered May 4 at Westerkerk, Amsterdam. Published 1985 by Donemus and 1987 by Composers' Voice Special.
Recording: Composers' Voice Special, 1987 (recording of world premiere).

1986

"VI. Chaya and Anna," from the cantata *And Her Children Rise Up and Call Her Blessed*
Music: Herman Berlinski
Commissioned by the Baltimore Hebrew Congregation; first draft completed 1967. Manuscript at the Jewish Theological Seminary, New York.

1992

"Yevreyskiy Rekviem / Jewish Requiem"
Music: Mikhail Borisovich Bronner; texts: Anne Frank, Chaim Nachman Bialik, Jewish liturgy, and the Bible
For four soloists, children's choir, mixed choir, and orchestra
Premiered 1994 in Germany.

1994

"The Scent of Jasmine in the Wilderness"
Music: J. David Moore; texts: Anne Frank, Etty Hillesum, and W. H. Auden

For double men's choir and soli, viola, cello, bass, harp, piano, and percussion
Commissioned by Twin Cities Gay Men's Chorus. Premiered April 17 at Ted
Mann Concert Hall, University of Minnesota, Minneapolis.

1994
"In Memoriam Anne Frank"
Music: Howard Goodall; texts: Christina Rossetti, R. L. Stevenson, and Richard
Lovelace
For chorus, children's chorus, strings, and organ
Commissioned by the Voices Foundation. Premiered Feb. 13 in St. John's, Smith
Square, London. Published by Faber Music (1995).
Recording: on *Choral Works by Howard Goodall*, performed by the Choir of
Christ Church Cathedral, Oxford, on Sanctuary Classics ASV Records (CD
DCA 1028).

1999
"Anna Frank: Cantata Scenica"
Music: Leopoldo Gamberini
For soprano, choir, church bells, electronics, and orchestra
Recording: *Anne Frank: Cantata Scenica* (Sarx, 1999).

2004
"Anne Frank: A Living Voice"
Music: Linda Tutas Hagen
For girls choir and string quartet
Commissioned and premiered by the San Francisco Girls Chorus, in celebration
of their twenty-fifth anniversary. Published by Ephraim Bay Publishing.
Recording: podcast of third movement: http://www.youtube.com/watch?v=
hwTp_Tq9E2M&feature=related

2004
"Tehillim for Anne"
Music: Robert Steadman; text: Hebrew psalms
For choir and strings
Premiered November 27 by the Southwell Choral Society, Southwell, England.
Commemorated Anne Frank's seventy-fifth birthday.

2004-2005
"Annelies: From the Diary of Anne Frank"
Music: James Whitbourn; text: Melanie Challenger
For soprano soloist, choir, and orchestra
Commissioned by the Mostar Foundation and the Jewish Music Institute to mark
the liberation of Bergen-Belsen. Composed 2004, premiered April 5, 2005, at the
Cadogan Hall, London, with Leonard Slatkin conducting the Royal Philharmonic
Orchestra, Choir of Clare College Cambridge, and soprano Louise Kateck. Pub-
lished by Chester Music Ltd. Chamber version premiered in Netherlands, 2009.

2011
"Anthem: Peace, Triumphant Peace"
Music: Karl Jenkins; texts: Carol Barratt, Anne Frank, and St. Seraphim of Sarov
For chorus and orchestra
Final (17th) movement of the hour-long work *The Peacemakers*.
Premiered at Carnegie Hall, New York, January 16, 2012 (Martin Luther King, Jr. Day).
Recording: on *The Peacemakers* (EMI Classics, 2012).

2. Instrumental

1964
"Sinfonía Ana Frank"
Music: Leon Biriotti
For string orchestra
Premiered May 10, 1965, as part of a celebration of the twentieth anniversary of the end of World War II at the Teatro Solís, Montevideo. Awarded best premiere of 1965 by the Critics Circle of Uruguay.

1966
"In Memoriam Annei Frank"
Music: Ludovic Feldman
For orchestra
Recording: Electrecord, ST-ECE 01864, featuring Orchestra de Studio a Radio-televiziunii Romane (Romanian TV and Radio Studio Orchestra).

1971
"Anna Frank, un simbol"
Music: Jordi Cervelló
For string orchestra
Premiered 1972 at the International Music Festival, Barcelona, performed by the Young Israel Strings, directed by Shalom Ronli-Rikliss. Published 1973, Madrid.

1981
"Elegy for Anna Frank"
Music: Ari Ben-Shabetai
For orchestra and a "metalphone" (an instrument of eleven gongs meant to "evoke the sound of a railway")
Premiered in Israel.

2002
"Piano Trio for Anne Frank, '*Het Achterhuis*'"
Music: Colin Decio
For piano, cello, and violin
"Inspired by the Diary of Anne Frank and the artwork of Greg Tricker." Premiered June 12 (Anne Frank Day), Pitville Pump Room, Cheltenham, England.
Recording: Live recording sold on Decio's website (http://www.colindecio.com).

3. Solo Voice and Piano or Ensemble

1957
"Elegia"
Music: Niccolò Castiglioni; text: Novalis
For voice and nineteen instruments
Dedicated to the memory of Anne Frank. Published by Edizioni Suvini Zerboni.

1960
"The Diary of Anne Frank"
Music: Michael White
For soprano and orchestra

1961
"Requiem für eine Verfolgte: In Memoriam Anne Frank"
Music: Hainz Lau; texts: Günter Eich and Paul Celan
For tenor and string quartet

1963
"Trije Dnevi Ane Frank" / "Three Days in the Life of Anne Frank"
Music: Darijan Bozic
For reciter, six instruments, and tape

1965
"In Memoriam Anne Frank"
Music: Godfrey Ridout; text: Bruce Attridge
For soprano and orchestra
Commissioned by the Canadian Broadcasting Corporation. Premiere featured
soprano Mary Morrison.

1966
"Anne Frank"
Music: Aleksandr Vustin; text: Moishe Teyf
For baritone and piano
Published in *Three Poems by Moisei Taif* (Moscow: Composer, 2000).

1970
"From the Diary of Anne Frank"
Music: Oskar Morawetz
For soprano and orchestra
Premiered May 26 in Toronto, with Lawrence Leonard conducting the Toronto
Symphony and soprano Lois Marshall, soloist; performed in Carnegie Hall,
April 16, 1972. Score published by the author in 1973.
Recording: *Anthology of Canadian Music* v. 17, Side 6A (1983).

1989
"Elegy for Anne Frank"
Music: Lukas Foss
For speaker and small ensemble

Premiered June 12 at memorial concert, "Remembering Anne Frank," Cathedral of St. John the Divine, New York. Also a non-narrated version, as a movement of Symphony no. 3 (1991), and a piano/cello arrangement (2000). Narrated version published in 1989 by Pembroke Music Co.

Recordings: Harmonia Mundi HMU 907243 (2001; both versions); Naxos 8.559438 (2005; narrated version).

1990
"From the Diary of Anne Frank"
Music: Michael Tilson Thomas
For narrator and orchestra
Commissioned by UNICEF. Premiered at the Academy of Music, Philadelphia, with Audrey Hepburn and the New World Symphony. Published by Kongcha.

1995[?]
[Title unknown]
Music: Allen Johnson
For soprano and string quartet
Composed for a Holocaust conference at the University of Tennessee. Performed by soprano Elizabeth King Dubberly.

1996
"I Remember"
Music: Michael Cohen; text: Enid Futterman
For mezzo-soprano, harp, flute, and cello
Adaptation of material from the musical *Yours, Anne* for Trio Serenata. Published 2009 by Lauren Keister Music Publishing.
Recording: *Michael Cohen: I Remember* (Newport Classic 1999).

1997
"Mémoire des ombres," third movement of *The Shadows of Time*
Music: Henri Dutilleux
For orchestra and three children's voices
Movement is dedicated "to Anne Frank and all the children, innocents of the world." Soloists sing a paraphrase of excerpts from the diary. Premiered October 15, New York.
Recordings: on *Dutilleux: Complete Orchestral Music* (Chandos, 2000); *Dutilleux: Concertos, Orchestral Works* (EMI 2008).

1999
Cantata: "Iz Dnevnika Anny Frank"
Music: Boris I. Tobis
For soprano, narrator, and instrumental ensemble

2001
"Oh, What Is the Use of War?" Second section of Part II ("The Tired Sunset Glow") of *The Mystic Flame: A Choral Symphony*

Music: Michael Horvit; text: Anne Frank
For soprano, choir, and orchestra
Commissioned by Congregation Emanu El, Houston, Texas.
Recording: Albany Records TROY533 (2002).

2003
"Anne Frank Canata"
Music: Roland Polastro
For soprano and choir
Premiered June 18, Cape Town, South Africa.

4. Soundtracks

1958
Ein Tagebuch für Anne Frank
Music: Wolfgang Hohensee
East German documentary.

1959
The Diary of Anne Frank
Music: Alfred Newman
Film version of the play by Frances Goodrich and Albert Hackett, produced by
20th Century-Fox.
Recording: 20th Century-Fox Treasury of Film Sound Tracks (FOX 3012).

1959
Dnevnik Ane Frank
Music: [unknown]
Televised translation of the play by Goodrich and Hackett, produced by Radio-
televizija Beograd, Yugoslavia.

1967
The Diary of Anne Frank
Music: Emanuel Vardi
Televised presentation of the play by Goodrich and Hackett, aired November 26
on ABC.

1967
"The Legacy of Anne Frank," episode of *The Eternal Light*
Music: Larry Wilcox
Aired December 24 on NBC.

1980
The Diary of Anne Frank
Music: Billy Goldenberg
Televised presentation of the play by Goodrich and Hackett, aired November 17
on NBC.

1982
Das Tagebuch der Anne Frank
Music: Conrad Aust
Televised presentation of the play by Goodrich and Hackett, aired April 3 on DDR-FS (East Germany).

1985
Het Dagboek van Anne Frank
Music: [unknown]
Televised presentation of the play by Goodrich and Hackett, produced by Televisie Radio Omroep Stichting, aired on May 9 in the Netherlands.

1987
The Diary of Anne Frank
Music: Dudley Simpson
Television miniseries, aired January 4 on BBC.

1988
The Attic: The Hiding of Anne Frank
Music: Richard Rodney Bennett
Television movie, produced by Telecom Entertainment Inc. and Yorkshire Television, aired April 17 in the United States.

1995
Anne Frank Remembered
Music: Carl Davis
The soundtrack for this documentary film later appeared in a five-minute version for orchestra and a twelve-and-a-half-minute "Anne Frank Remembered Suite" in three movements.
Recordings: orchestral version on *Carl Davis: The World at War, Pride and Prejudice, and Other Great Themes* (Tring, 1996); suite on *Carl's War* (Threefold Records, 2010).

1995
Anne No Nikki
Music: Michael Nyman
Nyman wrote the songs "If" and "Why" for this Japanese animated film.

1998
The Diary of Anne Frank Part II (A Film in Three Parts)
Music: Harmony Korine
Film/video installation first shown at the Patrick Painter Gallery in Santa Monica, California. The installation focuses on poor, small-town life in the American Midwest, with a soundtrack assembled from existing music and sounds.

1999
Le Journal d'Anne Frank

Music: Carine H. D. Gutlerner
French version of the 1995 Japanese animated film *Anne No Nikki*.

2001
Anne Frank: The Whole Story
Music: Graeme Revell
Television miniseries, aired May 20–21 on ABC.

2002
Het kotte leven van Anne Frank / The Short Life of Anne Frank
Music: Vincent van Rooijen
Documentary issued by Anne Frank Stichting, Amsterdam.

2003
Anne B. Real
Music: Luis Moro & Verse; text: Dean Parker.
Songs for feature film about the rise of a teenage female rap artist in the Bronx, New York, who is inspired by Anne Frank's diary.

[2006]
Dear Anne: The Gift of Hope
Music: Carlo Siliotto
Animated film slated for 2006 release but ceased production at the end of 2007.

2009
The Diary of Anne Frank
Music: Charlie Mole
Television miniseries, aired January 5–9 on BBC One and in the United States on PBS in 2010.

5. Songs/Jazz/New Age

1959
"Portrait of Anne Frank" [instrumental]
Music: Tony Scott
Recording: on *Sung Heroes* (Sunnyside Records, 1986).
Free jazz.

1967
"Anne Frank" [Dutch]
Music: Gaby Dirne
Lyrics: Peter Koelewijn
Performer: Laura [Bordes] & Yvonne [de Nijs]
Recording: on 45-rpm single with "Hello Mr. Echo" (Omega 35.778)
This song generated significant negative response and effectively destroyed the career of Laura Bordes, according to the recent film "Laura Bordes: De Kwestie Anne Frank" (Art Republic Media, 2011).

1968
"Il Diario Di Anna Frank"
Music and lyrics: Cameleonti
Recording: on *Io Por Lei* (CBS).

1974
"Chanson Pour Anna"
Music and lyrics: Pascal Danel
Performer: Daniel Guichard
Recording: on *Mon Vieux* (Barclay, 1974); also released as a single.

1979
"Anne Frank"
Original music and lyrics: Pascal Danel
Performer: Benny Neyman
Recording: on *Gouden Regen* (CNR).
Dutch cover of "Chanson Pour Anna" (1974).

1980
"Anne Frank Story"
Music: Human Sexual Response
Recording: on *Fig. 14* (Passport Records), later reissued as *Fig. 15*
Alternative/Power Pop.

1980
"I Still Believe"
Music: Cantor Stephen Freedman; lyrics: selection from Anne Frank's diary
Recording: on *Childhood Memories: A Choral Dramatization of the Holocaust.*
(Vogt Quality Recordings).

1981
Für Anne Frank
Performers: Lin Jaldati, Jalda Rebling, Eberhard Rebling
Recording: Litera
Recording of a 1980 event honoring Anne Frank, alternating readings from the
diary with Yiddish folk and art songs.

1985
"Anne, Ma Sœur Anne"
Music: Louis Chedid
Recording: on *Anne, Ma Sœur Anne* (Virgin France S.A.).

1985
"Song to Anne Frank (the Annex Blues)"
Music: Mark Dann
On recording issued with *Fast Folk Musical Magazine,* vol. 2, no. 3; reissued in
2004 by Smithsonian Folkways.

1986
"Ikh bin Ana Frank" [Yiddish]
Music: Maurice Rauch; text: Yevgeni Yevtushenko
Setting of a stanza from Yevtushenko's poem "Babi Yar," translated into Yiddish.
Recording: on *My Song is Yiddish*.

1987
"Ana Frank" [Spanish]
Music: Comité Cisne
Recordings: *Ana Frank* (seven-inch promo disc); also released in remix form on
the group's 1987 album *El Final del Mar* (Intermitente).

1989
"I Still Believe"
Music: Marshall Portnoy and Susan Callen; text adapted from *The Diary of
Anne Frank*
Published in *Maginot II* (URJ Press, 2004).
Recording: on *I Still Believe: Songs of Faith By Marshall Portnoy* (Renewal Records,
2010).

1990
"Anna Frank" [Swedish]
Music: Brainbombs
Recording: on EP *Anne Frank 7"* (Big Brothel Communications).

1990–1991
"Letter to Anne Frank"
Music: Lady Isadora
Lady Isadora relates Anne Frank's Jewish identity to her own identity as a pagan
priestess.
Recording: on *Priestess of the Pentacle* (Dance of Life Productions).

1994
"Song for Anne Frank"
Music: Harvey Andrews
Folk song performed with an acoustic guitar lead.
Recording: on *Spring Again* (Hypertension/Ariola).

1995
"In the Manner of Anne Frank"
Music: Portastatic
Recording: on *Slow Note From a Sinking Ship* (Merge).

1995
"Anne Frank"
Music: Phillip Greenlief and Scott Amendola Duo
Free improv jazz.
Recording: on *Collect My Thoughts* (SAZI).

1996
"Shut Up"
Music: The Watchmen
Recording: on *Brand New Day* (MCA).

1997
"Diario de Anna Frank" [Italian]
Music: Mino Reitano
Recording: on *Story, Vol. 1* (Duck Records).

1997
"Did Anne Frank Find Jesus?"
Music: Ani DiFranco
Recording: Hidden track on CD 2 of album *Living In Clip* (Righteous Babe, 1998).
Spoken track on a concert album.

1998
"Holland, 1945" (and other titles)
Music: Neutral Milk Hotel
Recording: on *In the Aeroplane Over the Sea* (Merge). Rumored to be concept
album based on Anne Frank.

1998
"Where's Annie"
Music: Dan Nash
Recording: on *Dan Nash* (BOA Records).

2000
"So Fresh, So Clean"
Music: OutKast
Recording: on *Stankonia* (La Face).

2001
"Dear Anne"
Music: Ryan Adams
Recording: on unreleased album *The Swedish Sessions*. Recorded October 2001 in
Nord Studio AB in Stockholm. Available in several unofficial versions; see http://
www.youtube.com/watch?v=uHqVCortGS8.

2002
"Ballad of Anne Frank"
Music: Johnny McEvoy
Irish Ballad-style.
Recording: on *Celebration* (The Dolphin Group).

2002
"The Diary of Anne Frank"
Music: Creator Kids

A musical introduction to the diary for young readers.
Recording: on *Startup Literature* (Creator Kids LLC).

2003
"Song for Anne"
Music: D'vora (Dorothy Gittelson)
Recording: on *Comfortable Company* (Honeybee Records). Also issued as a CD single and sold by the Anne Frank Center, USA.

2004
"Elegy for Anne Frank"
Music: Cosmosamatics
Recording: on *Cosmosamatics Three* (Boxholder Records).

2004
"Good Friday @ Anne Frank's," second movement of suite "Looking for the Light"
Music: Jerry Fjerkenstad
Recording: on *Looking for the Light* (Jerry Fjerkenstad).

2004
"Annie, Hannah"
Music: Massimo Bubola
Recording: on *Il Cavaliere Elettrico: Live,* vol. 4 (Eccher Music).

2005
Untitled theme song, from mock trailer for fictional film version of the *Diary of Anne Frank*, which parodies Hilary Duff's 2003 song "Come Clean."
Recording: on Season 1, Episode 11 of *Robot Chicken* ("Toy Meets Girl"); aired May 1.

2005
"Anne Frank's Eyes"
Music: Craig Sonnenfeld
Recording: on *Storm Clouds Rising* (New Roots Records).

2006
"Anne Frank" [instrumental]
Music: Mark Isham
Recording: on *Freedom Writers: Music From the Motion Picture* (Hollywood Records).

2006
"Diary of Anne Frank"
Music: Russ McDaniel
Country bluegrass.
Recording: on *Tribute to World Hero's Friends Places* (Folk Art Records).

2006
"Anne Frank's Ghost"
Music: Rabbinical School Dropouts
Jazz instrumental.
Recording: on *Vehicles Behind Comets* (Ethnic Warrior Productions).

2006
"Anne Frank" [elsewhere called "Achterhouse"] [Dutch]
Music: De Vliegende Panters
Dutch comedy troupe.
Recording: on *Sex, Live* (CNR Entertainment).

2007
"The Chronicles of Diarrhea—Chapter VII—The Diarrhea of Anne Frank"
Music: Aborted Jesus
Death metal group.
Recording: on *Carnival of Gonorrhea* (Christ Puncher Records).

2007
Songs for Anne Frank
Music: Bauer and Bentle
Recording: Self-published inspirational album: http://www.youtube.com/watch
?v=MwMww8vz4No.

2007
"June 12, 1943"
Music: Secret Annexe
Recording: on *Seven Headed Monster* (Ocelot Records).
Date references Anne Frank's fourteenth birthday.

2007
Lost Pages of the Diary
Music: Anne Frank [group name]
Recording: demo album
Las Vegas-based punk group.

2007
"Dear Diary, Anne Frank Version"
Music: Stephen Lynch
One of a series of short "diary" songs of characters facing impending doom,
introduced by performer on tour.
Recording: on 3 *Balloons* (What Are Records?, 2009) as "Dear Diary 1"; unofficial
concert version at http://www.youtube.com/watch?v=VE29_2BvLD8.

2007
"Ana Frank" [Spanish]
Music: Equilibrio Perfecto
Pop-rock group based in Valencia, Spain.

Recording: on *Equilibrio Perfecto* (Contraseña Records), reissued on . . . *A Algún Lugar* (2008).

2008
"Anne Frank Wasn't a Blonde" [instrumental]
Music: Gilad Benamram
Incidental music linked to a line of dialogue in the 2005 film.
Recording: on *Pretty Persuasion: Original Motion Picture Soundtrack* (EverBliss Music).

2008
"Through My Eyes (in Memory of Anne Frank)"
Music: Chris Foster
Christian contemporary singer.
Recording: on *Peace Expressing* (Chris Foster).

2008
"Anne Frank Song"
Music: ThoseDudesRock08
Recording: amateur YouTube video http://www.youtube.com/watch?v=alYZoM7BaOs.

2008
"Anne Frank's Blind Date: Who the Fuck is Helen Keller?"
Music: Snake Eater
Recording: on EP *The Rock & Roll Apocalypse*.

2009
"Anna Frank" [Hungarian]
Music: Spions
Recordings: on *Menekülj Végre* (1G Records); http://www.youtube.com/watch?v=C49zgYXZAsM.

2009
"Anne Frank Bash 2009"
Music: Rucka Rucka Ali
Parody of Flo Rida song "Sugar."
Recording: Serchlite Music/Pinegrove; http://www.youtube.com/watch?v=H3NnAQVn-Dk.

2009
"The Diarrhea of Anne Frankenstein"
Music: Chupaskabra
Recording: on *Run While You Can*
Ska band from Gainesville, Florida.

2009
"Love Is . . ."
Music: Bo Burnham

Comedian, references Anne Frank in lyrics.
Recording: on *Bo Burnham* (Comedy Central Records).

2010
"Dear Anne"
Music: White Rhino
Recording: on *In Common Places* (self-published).

2010
"The Diary of Anne Frank"
Music: East of Eden
Recording: http://www.purevolume.com/EastOfEden39610
New Zealand–based "Hardcore/Progressive/Christian" band.

2010
"Anne Frank" [French]
Music: La Grange
Recording: on *Un Doigt dans la Crise* (self-published).

2011
"Anne Frank"
Music: René Breton
Recording: on *Asleep in Green* (Fifth Ace).

2011
"Anne Frank"
Music: noego
Recording: on *Sacred Female* (noegomusic.com).

6. Opera and Musical Theater

1969
Dnevnik Anny Frank
Music: Grigori Frid; text: Anne Frank
Mono-opera
Premiered 1972 (piano), 1977 (orchestra) in USSR; United States premiere at
Syracuse University, 1978.

1970
Anne Frank: Diary of a Young Girl
Music: Peter Nero; text: Anne Frank
"Rock-Symphony" for orchestra, jazz combo, adult choir, and children's choir
Premiered (in concert) September 17 at Temple Beth-El, Great Neck, New York.

1985
Yours, Anne
Music: Michael Cohen; book and lyrics: Enid Futterman
Musical theater

Premiered October 13 at Playhouse 91, New York.
Recordings: That's Entertainment Records (LP, 1987); reissued on Jay Records (CD, 2005).

1992
Dreams of Anne Frank
Book and lyrics: Bernard Kops
Play for children; script includes lyrics to be set to music as each production sees fit.
Premiered at Polka Theater, London.

1994
Prince Canal
Music: Lou Rodgers
Opera/musical theater piece
Premiered December 8 in New York through Golden Fleece, Ltd.
Based on visit to the Anne Frank House.

1995
The Secret Annex
Music: William Charles Baton; book and lyrics: Robert K. Carr
Musical theater
Premiered September 8 at Playhouse 91, New York.

1996
I Am Anne Frank
Music: Michael Cohen; book and lyrics: Enid Futterman
One-woman song cycle
Written for Andrea Marcovicci. Premiered October 28, Alice Tully Hall, New York.
Recording: Anne Frank Center (1996).

1997
Anne Frank: A Voice Heard
Music: E. A. Alexander; book and lyrics: Lezley Steele
Musical theater for children's production, touring production by American Theater Arts for Youth.

1999
Harriet and Anne
Music: Deborah Pittman and Laurie Friedman-Adler
"Theater piece with music"
About Anne Frank and Harriet Tubman.
Workshopped at Sacramento State University; workshop performance September 25 at Producer's Club Theater, New York.

2002
Saving Anne
Music: Jay Gaither; book and lyrics: Owen Robertson

Musical theater
Premiered in May at the Greenwich Theatre's Musical Futures Festival, London.
Time travel theme.

2006
Anne Frank: Within & Without
Music: Chip Epstein
Puppet theater piece. Created at the Center for Puppetry Arts, Atlanta.

2007
The Voice of Anne Frank
Music: Petr Bohac; text: Mirenka Cechova
Multimedia one-woman piece
Performed by Mirenka Cechova. Developed and possibly premiered in Prague;
subsequent performances used improvised cello.

2008
Anne Frank: A Song to Life / El Diario de Ana Frank: Un Canto A La Vida
Music: Jose Luis Tierno, Oscar Gomez, and Arturo Díez Boscovich; book and
lyrics: Bonnie Morin and Jaime Azpilicueta
Musical theater
Premiered in Madrid at Teatro Häagen-Dazs-Calderón.

2008
Margot Frank: The Diary of the Other Young Girl
Music: Cooper Cerulo and Michael Sangiovanni; book and lyrics: Diana Rissetto
and Lori Mooney
Musical theater
Premiered April 9 at Shea Center of the Performing Arts, William Paterson
College, Wayne, New Jersey. Winner, Fourth Annual New Jersey Playwright
Contest competition.

2008
Dear Anne: A Tribute to Anne Frank
Music: Mahinder Toelaram, Pan Blasky, and Jeroen Joustra; text: Mahinder
Toelaram
"Theatrical concert" for tenor, soprano, rock band and orchestra.
Premiered May 4 in Theater Tuschinski, Amsterdam.

2009
Anne, le Musical: Hommage à Anne Frank
Music and text: Jean-Pierre Hadida
Musical theater
Premiered March 19 at Théâtre Espace Rachi, Paris.

2009
Anne Frankenstein: The Musical
Book and lyrics by David Holstein.

Musical theater
Premiered July 17 at the Ringwald Theater, Ferndale, Michigan.
Anne Frank reimagines the Frankenstein story in the Secret Annex. Script includes lyrics to be set to music by the actors, plus a reference to "A Whole New World" (Menken/Rice) and a parody of "Anything You Can Do" (I. Berlin).

2012
Souvenir d'Anne Frank
Music: Colin Decio; text: Elizabeth Mansfield with Richard Alwyn (visual artist)
Premiered January 27 at Zion Arts Centre, Manchester, England.
Multimedia piece, based on the story of the "Souvenir d'Anne Frank" rose that Otto Frank sent to Japan.

B. DANCE

1959
"The Anne Frank Ballet"
Choreography: Adam Darius
Music: Selections from the album *Benedict Silberman—Jewish Music* (Capitol T-10064, c. 1957).

1981
"Anna Frank"
Choreography: [unknown]
Music: Luciano Chailly
Ballet premiered in Verona, Italy.

1984
"The Diary of Anne Frank"
Choreography: Mauricio Wainrot
Music: Bela Bartok, "Music for Strings, Percussion, and Celeste"
Performed by the Grupo de Danza Contemporaneo. Awarded APES (Journalist Prize) as "best production" in Santiago, Chile, in 1991.

1985
"Secret Annexe"
Choreography: Linda Diamond
Music: Roque Cordero, "Permutaciones 7" (later music possibly changed to George Crumb).
Premiered December 3 by the Linda Diamond Dance Company in New York.

1993
"The Attic"
Choreography: Frances Smith Cohen
Music: [unknown]
Mixed media piece performed by Center Dance Ensemble, Phoenix, Arizona. Incorporated newsreel footage compiled by the Simon Weisenthal Center and a recording of a voice reading selections from Anne Frank's diary.

1996
"Soul of a Young Girl: Dances of Anne Frank"
Choreography: Gina Angelique and Eveoke Dance Company
Music: George Crumb, "Black Angels," recorded by the Kronos Quartet
Premiere unknown. Restaged in 2000 in collaboration with the San Diego Repertory Theatre for the Seventh Annual Jewish Arts Festival.

1999
"Naked (Ber)"
Choreography: Ekka Dance Theatre Company
Music: Frank Pay; texts: Anne Frank, Ingunn Valgerour Hendriksen, Jacques Prévert, and Sigfús Daoason
Premiered in Tjarnargata Reykjavik, Iceland.

2001
"About Anne: A Diary in Dance"
Choreography: Helios Dance Theater
Music: Rob Cairns
Premiered excerpt in 2000, full work in April 2001, Los Angeles.

2001
"Girl in the Window"
Choreography: Beth Braun
Music: Arthur Miscione
For three dancers and reader. Premiered at the Tucson Jewish Community Center.

2005
"From the Pages of a Young Girl's Life"
Choreography: Johanne Jakhelln
Music: Selections from works by Mozart and six Jewish composers
Created at the request of the Jewish Federation of the Quad Cities. Premiered May 24 by Ballet Quad Cities, Davenport, Iowa.

2007
"Lest We Forget: Anne Frank and Other Stories"
Choreography: Frances Smith Cohen
Music: Sergei Prokofiev
Premiered October 18 by Center Dance Ensemble in Phoenix, Arizona.

2008
"Shadows in the Attic"
Choreography: Graham Lustig
Sound design: Karin Greybash
Premiered March 5 by American Repertory Ballet in Princeton, New Jersey. Sound design incorporated street sounds, German composers, popular music, and radio broadcast.

Videography

Aviva Weintraub

Following are lists of films and television broadcasts that deal with the life and work of Anne Frank. They are ordered chronologically within the following generic categories: (1) documentary films and telecasts, (2) film and television dramas, and (3) various films and broadcasts in which a reference, sometimes fleeting, is made to Anne Frank. A brief annotation follows information on each work's creators and country of origin. Thanks to Leshu Torchin for her assistance in compiling this videography.

1. DOCUMENTARIES

1958
Ein Tagebuch für Anne Frank
Director: Joachim Hellwig
Producer: DEFA-Studio für Wochenschau und Dokumentarfilme
German Democratic Republic
Beginning with the story of a young girl picked to play the role of Anne Frank in the Deutsches Theater in Berlin, the film proceeds to the history of Bergen-Belsen and an indictment of West Germany's failure to prosecute Nazi war criminals.

1964
Episode: "Who Killed Anne Frank?"
Series: *The Twentieth Century*
Director: Arthur Holch
Network: CBS
United States
News documentary narrated by Walter Cronkite on Nazi war criminals.

1967
Episode: "The Legacy of Anne Frank"
Series: *The Eternal Light*
Executive Producer: Milton Krents
Network: NBC
United States

Features an interview with Anne Frank's father, Otto Frank, and others who knew Anne as a child. The program visits the school Anne attended and the building where the family hid.

1972
Episode: "The Heritage of Anne Frank"
Series: *Directions*
Producer: Sid Darion
Network: ABC
United States
ABC News London Bureau Chief George Watson travels to the home where Anne Frank and her family were hidden during World War II.

1975
Anne
Director: Jan Wiegel
Network: NOS-TV Amsterdam
The Netherlands
A tribute to Anne Frank with footage of the Anne Frank House in Amsterdam, an interview with Otto Frank, and dramatizations of diary excerpts.

1981
Episode: "The Holland of Rembrandt and Anne Frank"
Series: *Eternal Light*
Network: NBC
United States
Holland as seen through the eyes of Rembrandt and the words of Anne Frank.

1988
The Last Seven Months of Anne Frank
Director: Willy Lindwer
The Netherlands (aired in United States on PBS in 1989)
Features interviews with women who recall Anne Frank's final months in concentration camps. Winner of International Emmy Award.

1988
The Man Who Hid Anne Frank
Network: A&E
United States
A documentary on the Frank family's experiences while in hiding, which includes interviews with the people who hid them.

1989
Episode: "Anne Frank Remembered"
Series: *Bill Moyers*
PBS

United States

Moyers talks with four students at the Bronx High School of Science, who are taking an elective course in Holocaust studies.

1995

Anne Frank Remembered

Director: Jon Blair

Producer: Jon Blair Film Company in cooperation with the Anne Frank House, Amsterdam, and in association with the BBC and the Disney Channel.

England / United States

A feature-length overview of the life and legacy of Anne Frank, with interviews with the Franks' friends and family. Narrated by Kenneth Branagh, with extracts from Anne's diary read by Glenn Close. 1996 Academy Award Winner for Best Documentary.

1998

Episode: "Anne Frank: The Missing Pages"

Series: *Investigative Reports*

Network: A&E

United States

Documentary report on the discovery of five pages from Anne's diary that her father had removed, because of their harsh portrayal of his relationship with Anne's mother.

1999

Dear Kitty: Remembering Anne Frank

Director: Wouter van de Sluis

Producer: Anne Frank House, Amsterdam, in partnership with Jon Blair Film Company

The Netherlands

Miep Gies recalls Anne, her family, and the other Jews whom she helped to hide in the Annex.

2002

The Short Life of Anne Frank

Producer: Anne Frank House, Amsterdam

The Netherlands

A short documentary for young viewers, narrated by Jeremy Irons.

2007

Anne and the Reverend

Director: Francois Uzan

France

Tells the story of Makoto Otsuka, a reverend from Hiroshima, who met Anne Frank's father thirty years ago and, since then, has undertaken a mission to teach Anne's story to Japanese children.

2008
Classmates of Anne Frank
Director: Eyal Boers
Israel
An Israeli inventor of games returns to his childhood neighborhood in the Netherlands to reunite with five of his and Anne Frank's former classmates, only to discover a confusing truth about the village where he was hidden during World War II.

2008
Dear Anne Frank
Director, Producer: Ahmad El-Sanhouri
United Kingdom
Aisha, a thirteen-year-old Muslim girl, gets the part of Anne Frank in a school play, which leads to a conflict with her mother.

2008
From Anne Frank's Window
Director: Ornit Barkai
United States
Readings from Anne Frank's diary accompanied by scenes of a visit to the Anne Frank House in Amsterdam.

2010
Otto Frank, Father of Anne
Director: David De Jongh
The Netherlands
Documentary on Otto Frank's life before, during, and after World War II, especially his seminal role in overseeing the remembrance of his daughter's life and writing.

2. DRAMAS

1952
Episode: "Anne Frank: The Diary of a Young Girl"
Series: *Frontiers of Faith*
Script: Morton Wishengrad
Network: NBC
United States
The first American dramatic adaptation of Anne Frank's diary.

1959
The Diary of Anne Frank
Director, Producer: George Stevens
20th Century-Fox
United States

Screenplay by Frances Goodrich and Albert Hackett, based on their authorized stage adaptation of the diary. Cast includes Millie Perkins as Anne, Joseph Schildkraut as Otto Frank, and Shelley Winters as Mrs. Van Daan. Winner of three Academy Awards.

1959
Dnevnik Ane Frank
Director: Marjana Samardzic
Producer: Radiotelevizija Beograd
Yugoslavia
Production of Goodrich and Hackett's stage play for Yugoslavian television.

1967
Episode: "The Diary of Anne Frank"
Series: *Sunday Night at the Theatre*
Network: ABC
United States
The first U.S. television production of the stage play by Goodrich and Hackett, featuring Diane Davila as Anne.

1980
The Diary of Anne Frank
Director Boris Sagal
Producer: 20th Century-Fox Television
United States
Televised production of the stage play by Goodrich and Hackett, featuring Melissa Gilbert as Anne, Maximilian Schell as Otto Frank, and Joan Plowright as Edith Frank.

1982
Das Tagebuch der Anne Frank
German Democratic Republic
Televised presentation of the play by Goodrich and Hackett.

1984
Episode: "The Ghost Writer"
Series: *American Playhouse*
Director: Tristram Powell
Network: PBS
United States
A dramatization of Philip Roth's novella about a mysterious young woman who at first appears to be Anne Frank, featuring Claire Bloom and Mark Linn-Baker.

1985
Het Dagboek van Anne Frank
Director: Hank Onrust
Producer: Televisie Radio Omroep Stichting

The Netherlands
A Dutch telecast of the stage play by Goodrich and Hackett.

1986
The Anne Frank Ballet
Choreographer: Adam Darius
Producer: Piers Hartley Pictures
[United Kingdom]
Film of a ballet of the life of Anne Frank and her family, originally created in 1959 by Adam Darius, an American-born dancer, choreographer, mime artist, and writer.

1987
The Diary of Anne Frank
Director: Gareth Davies
Producer: BBC
United Kingdom
This miniseries, written by Elaine Morgan, stars Katharine Schlesinger as Anne Frank.

1988
The Attic: The Hiding of Anne Frank
Director: John Erman
Producer: Telecom Entertainment
Network: CBS
United States / United Kingdom
Drama based on Miep Gies's memoir, *Anne Frank Remembered,* featuring Mary Steenburgen as Gies.

1995
Anne No Nikki
Director: Akinori Nagoaka
Japan
Animé version of Anne's life and work. Also released in French as *Le Journal d'Anne Frank.*

2001
Anne Frank: The Whole Story
Director: Robert Dornhelm
Network: ABC
United States
Miniseries based on Melissa Müller's unauthorized 1998 biography of Anne Frank.

2003
Anne B. Real
Director: Lisa France
Producer: Luis Moro

United States
A coming-of-age story of a young female rapper in New York City inspired by
reading Anne Frank's diary.

2009
The Diary of Anne Frank
Director: Jon Jones
Network: BBC
United Kingdom (aired in the United States on PBS in 2010)
Authorized miniseries, based on Anne's complete diary.

2010
Mi ricordo Anna Frank
Director: Alberto Negrin
Producers: IIF-Italian International Film / RAI Fiction
Italy
Freely based on the memoir *Hanneli Goslar Remembers: A Childhood Friend of
Anne Frank.*

3. REFERENCES TO ANNE FRANK

1959
. . . Als wär's ein Stück von dir!
Director: Peter Schier-Gribowsky
Producer: Norddeutscher Rundfunk, Hamburg
Federal Republic of Germany
Documentary about Bergen-Belsen; mentions Anne Frank's death there.

1959
The People of Israel Live / Am Yisrael Chai
Director: Hazel Greenwald
Producer: Hadassah, the Women's International Zionist Organization of America
United States
This short fundraising documentary mentions the Anne Frank Haven, among
other institutions in Israel.

1965
We Remember
Director: Lasar Dunner
Producer: Lasar Dunner, for the Jewish National Fund
Israel / United States
This short fundraising documentary mentions the Anne Frank Memorial Forest,
among other sites in Israel.

1985
Whoopi Goldberg: Direct from Broadway
Director: Thomas Schlamme

United States
Includes a segment in which Whoopi appears as Fontaine, a highly educated drug
addict, who visits the Anne Frank House in Amsterdam.

1994
Diamonds in the Snow
Director: Mira Reym Binford
United States
At the beginning of this documentary film, Ada, a hidden child during the
Holocaust, says, "Anne Frank, she had a beautiful war."

1994
Episode: Pilot
Series: *My So-Called Life*
Director: Scott Winant
Network: ABC
United States
In the opening scene of the series, Angela's high-school class is reading Anne
Frank's diary. Angela says Anne was "lucky," because she spent two years in an
attic with a boy she liked.

1997
Punch Me in the Stomach
Director: Francine Zuckerman
Canada
In this film version of a stage play by Deb Filler and Allison Summers, young
Debbie, a child of Holocaust survivors growing up in New Zealand, explains
that while her friends were reading *The Cat in the Hat,* she was reading Anne
Frank's diary.

1997
Episode: "It's a No Brainer"
Series: *Mr. Show*
Network: HBO
United States
A sketch on this comedy show, satirizing the MTV reality TV show *Road Rules,*
is set in the Anne Frank House. There, two vacuous, self-absorbed young men
on a scavenger hunt discuss both Anne Frank and where to get good hash in
Amsterdam.

1998
Episode: April 4, 1998
Series: *Saturday Night Live*
Network: NBC
United States
In an animated segment, Anne Frank (voiced by Molly Ringwald) appears as a
passenger on the Titanic.

2000
Episode: "If I'm Dyin', I'm Lyin'"
Series: *Family Guy*
Network: Fox
United States
Peter, the protagonist of this animated series, recalls hiding in an attic with (a presumed) Anne Frank and others, but betrays them by compulsively eating crunchy potato chips.

2003
Heroes of Jewish Comedy
Directors: Lisa Charles and Tina Jenkins
Network: Comedy Central
United States
A stand-up performance by Judy Gold includes a segment about Anne Frank.

2003
Episode: "The Story of Anne Frank and Skeevy"
Series: *8 Simple Rules for Dating My Teenage Daughter*
Director: James Widdoes
Network: ABC
United States
Bridget lands the lead in the high-school production of the story of Anne Frank but, after reading Anne's diary, doubts her ability to play the role.

2003
Episode: Season 1, Episode 1
Series: *Monkey Dust*
United Kingdom
The episode includes a mock trailer for a Hollywood adaptation of *The Diary of Anne Frank.*

2004
Paper Clips
Directors: Elliot Berlin and Joe Fab
United States
Documentary film about a Holocaust memorial in rural Tennessee includes a brief reference to Anne Frank.

2004
Episode: February 26, 2004
Series: *Sixty Minutes*
Network: CBS
United States
Report that North Korea is using Anne's diary not to teach how she suffered at the hands of the Nazis but to warn students how they could suffer at the hands of "American Nazis."

2004
Episode: "Tag Sale: You're It!"
Series: *Venture Brothers*
Network: Cartoon Network
United States
The Monarch's henchmen are carrying on a spirited debate, the exact nature of which is not clear, until the Monarch shouts, "Hey, guess what? Nobody cares who would win in a crazy fantasy fist-fight between Anne Frank and Lizzie Borden."

2005
Episode: "Toy Meets Girl"
Series: *Robot Chicken*
Director: Matthew Senreich
Network: Cartoon Network
United States
A sketch on this animated comedy series offers a mock trailer for an adaptation of Anne Frank's diary, starring teen idol Hilary Duff.

2006
Fatherland
Director: Manfred Becker
Canada
When his school is studying Anne Frank, a high-school student of German descent is called a Nazi by his classmates.

2007
Episode: "Not Without My Daughter"
Series: *The Sarah Silverman Program*
Director: Rob Schrab
Network: Comedy Central
United States
Sarah recites a passage from Anne Frank's diary at a beauty pageant audition.

2007
Freedom Writers
Director: Richard LaGravenese
United States
Based on the actual story of high school teacher Erin Gruwell, this feature film places Anne's diary at the center of the creative and moral transformation of a class of Los Angeles high school students. They keep and eventually publish diaries of their own and arrange to meet with Miep Gies.

2008
Entre les Murs (English title: *The Class*)
Director: Laurent Cantet

France
Students in a tough Parisian junior high school read and discuss Anne Frank's diary.

2008
Episode: "Major Boobage"
Series: *South Park*
Network: Comedy Central
United States
Eric Cartman, a central character on this animated series, defies his town's ban on keeping cats and hides his "Kitty" in an attic, telling her to keep a diary.

2010
Voices Unbound: The Story of the Freedom Writers
Director: Daniel Anker
United States
Documentary about Los Angeles high school teacher Erin Gruwell, who used Anne's diary to inspire students to keep and eventually publish diaries of their own.

Contributors

ILANA ABRAMOVITCH was Manager of Curriculum at New York's Museum of Jewish Heritage—A Living Memorial to the Holocaust. She is co-editor of *Jews of Brooklyn* and has been a New York Council for the Humanities Speaker on Rescuers during the Holocaust. Abramovitch teaches in the Department of Judaic Studies at Brooklyn College.

DANIEL BELASCO is a curator and art historian specializing in modern and contemporary art and design. As Henry J. Leir Associate Curator at The Jewish Museum, New York, he organized the exhibitions Reinventing Ritual and Shifting the Gaze: Painting and Feminism, while managing the museum's contemporary Judaica program of acquisitions and commissions. In 2010, Belasco co-curated The Dissolve, SITE Santa Fe's Eighth International Biennial.

SALLY CHARNOW is Associate Professor in the Department of History at Hofstra University. She is the author of *Theatre, Politics, and Markets in Fin-de-siècle Paris*. Her articles and review essays have appeared in *Historical Reflections/Reflexions Historiques, Radical History Review,* and *H-France.*

JUDAH M. COHEN is the Lou and Sybil Mervis Professor of Jewish Culture and Associate Professor of Folklore and Ethnomusicology at Indiana University. He is author of *Through the Sands of Time: A History of the Jewish Community of St. Thomas, U.S. Virgin Islands; The Making of a Reform Jewish Cantor: Musical Authority, Cultural Investment;* and *Sounding Jewish Tradition: The Music of Central Synagogue* and is co-editor of *The Culture of AIDS in Africa.*

LIORA GUBKIN is Associate Professor of Religious Studies at California State University, Bakersfield. She serves as co-chair for the Religion, Holocaust, and Genocide group of the American Academy of Religion. She is the author of *You Shall Tell Your Children: Holocaust Memory in American Passover Ritual.* Gubkin has held fellowships at the U.S. Holocaust Memorial Museum in Washington, D.C., and the USC Shoah Foundation Institute for Visual History and Education.

SARA R. HOROWITZ is Professor of Humanities and Director of the Israel and Golda Koschitzky Centre for Jewish Studies at York University in Toronto. She is the author of *Voicing the Void: Muteness and Memory in Holocaust Fiction,* which received the *Choice* Award for Outstanding Academic Book. Horowitz was the senior editor of the Azrieli Series of Holocaust Memoirs—Canada and editor of *Bits and Pieces,* a memoir by Henia Reinhartz. She was a senior research fellow at the U.S. Holocaust Memorial Museum in Washington, D.C., and sits on its Academic Advisory Committee. Horowitz is founding co-editor of the journal *KEREM: A Journal of Creative Explorations in Judaism* and is co-editor of *Encounter with Aharon Appelfeld* and *Jewish American Women Writers: A Bio-Bibliographical and Critical Sourcebook.*

BARBARA KIRSHENBLATT-GIMBLETT is University Professor, Professor of Performance Studies, and Affiliated Professor of Hebrew and Judaic Studies at New York University. Her books include *Image Before My Eyes: A Photographic History of Jewish Life in Poland Before the Holocaust; Destination Culture: Tourism, Museums, and Heritage; The Israel Experience: Studies in Youth Travel and Jewish Identity; Writing a Modern Jewish History: Essays in Honor of Salo W. Baron; They Called Me Mayer July: Painted Memories of a Jewish Childhood in Poland Before the Holocaust* (co-authored with her father, Mayer Kirshenblatt), and *The Art of Being Jewish in Modern Times,* among other titles. She is currently Program Director for the Core Exhibition for the Museum of the History of Polish Jews, now being built on the site of the former Warsaw Ghetto.

EDNA NAHSHON is Professor of Hebrew and Theater at the Jewish Theological Seminary and senior associate at Oxford University's Centre for Hebrew and Jewish Studies. She has written extensively on the intersection of Jews, theater, and performance. Her books include *Yiddish*

Proletarian Theatre: The Art and Politics of the Artef 1925–1940; From the Ghetto to the Melting Pot: Israel Zangwill's Jewish Plays; Jews and Shoes; Stars, Strikes, and the Yiddish Stage: The Story of the Hebrew Actors' Union 1899–2005; Jewish Theatre: A Global View; and *Jews and Theater in an Intercultural Context.* Forthcoming publications include a co-edited volume, *Countering Shylock: Jewish Responses to "The Merchant of Venice."* Currently, Nahshon is working on a study of Maurice Schwartz and the Yiddish Art Theatre.

EDWARD PORTNOY received his Ph.D. from the Jewish Theological Seminary, writing his dissertation on cartoons of the Yiddish press. His articles on Jewish popular culture phenomena have appeared in *The Drama Review, Polin,* and *The International Journal of Comic Art.* He currently teaches Jewish literature and Yiddish language at Rutgers University.

JEFFREY SHANDLER is Professor of Jewish Studies at Rutgers University. His books include *While America Watches: Televising the Holocaust; Adventures in Yiddishland: Postvernacular Language and Culture;* and *Jews, God, and Videotape: Religion and Media in America.* Among other titles, he is the editor of *Awakening Lives: Autobiographies of Jewish Youth in Poland before the Holocaust,* co-author/co-editor of *Entertaining America: Jews, Movies, and Broadcasting,* and translator of *Emil and Karl,* a Holocaust novel for young readers by Yankev Glatshteyn.

BRIGITTE SION received a Ph.D. in Performance Studies from New York University and specializes in the study of memorial sites and commemorative practices in Germany, Argentina, Cambodia, and France. She is a fellow at the Center for International Research in the Humanities and Social Sciences, a joint initiative of the French CNRS and New York University. Sion is the author of *Absent Bodies, Uncertain Memorials: Performing Memory in Berlin and Buenos Aires* (forthcoming), and the editor of *Staging Violent Death: The Performance of Dark Tourism.* Prior to her academic work, Sion was the director of an organization fighting Holocaust denial and other forms of anti-Semitism in Switzerland, and as a journalist she has written numerous articles on this issue.

HENRI LUSTIGER THALER is Associate Researcher at the Ecole des hautes études en sciences sociales in Paris and Professor of Cultural Sociology at Ramapo College. He is the author and editor of six books

and many scholarly articles on issues ranging from cultural globaliza-
tion and human rights to the Holocaust. His most recent article, entitled
"Memory," appears on Sociopedia.isa. Lustiger Thaler is the executive
producer of the documentary film *Memory After Belsen* and is currently
writing a book titled *Lost Memories: The Holocaust and the Orthodox.*

LESHU TORCHIN is Lecturer (Assistant Professor) in Film Studies at
the University of St. Andrews. She is the author of *Creating the Witness:
Documenting Genocide in Film, Video, and the Internet.* Torchin's essays on
film and activism have appeared in *American Anthropologist, Third Text,*
and *Moving People, Moving Images: Cinema and Trafficking in the New
Europe,* which she co-authored with William Brown and Dina Iordanova.

AVIVA WEINTRAUB is Associate Curator at The Jewish Museum, New
York, and Director of the New York Jewish Film Festival, a collaborative
project of The Jewish Museum and The Film Society of Lincoln Center.
She has published and spoken widely on Yiddish and Jewish culture, film,
photography, and performance. Her most recent exhibition projects at
The Jewish Museum include Isaac Bashevis Singer and the Lower East
Side: Photographs by Bruce Davidson; They Called Me Mayer July:
Painted Memories of a Jewish Childhood in Poland Before the Holo-
caust; and Maya Zack: Living Room. Weintraub has served on the jury
for the Adi Prize for Jewish Expression in Art and Design in Jerusalem.

WILFRIED WIEDEMANN served as Managing Director of the Gedenkstätte Bergen-Belsen and Chair of the Advisory Board of the Gedenk-
und Bildungsstätte Haus der Wannseekonferenz Berlin until his retire-
ment in 2007. His recent publications include essays on the history of
Bergen-Belsen as a memorial site in *Bergen-Belsen: Kriegsgefangenenlager
1940–1945, Konzentrationslager 1943–1945, Displaced Persons Camp 1945–
1950,* and *Auschwitz in der Deutschen Geschichte.* Wiedemann is a member
of the Centre of Garden Art and Landscape Architecture at Leibniz University and serves on the Editorial Advisory Board of *The Holocaust in
History and Memory.*

Index

Note: "AF" is the abbreviation for Anne Frank; "AFD" is the abbreviation for Anne Frank's diary. Page numbers in italics refer to illustrations.